European Legal Method –

Paradoxes and Revitalisation

Ulla Neergaard, Ruth Nielsen
and Lynn Roseberry (eds.)

European Legal Method –

Paradoxes and Revitalisation

DJØF Publishing Copenhagen
2011

Ulla Neergaard, Ruth Nielsen and Lynn Roseberry
European Legal Method –
Paradoxes and Revitalisation

DJØF Publishing is a company of the
Association of Danish Lawyers and Economists

Cover: Bo Helsted
Print: Narayana Press, Gylling
Binding: Damm's Forlagsbogbinderi, Randers

Printed in Denmark 2011
ISBN 978-87-574-2377-8

Sold and distributed in Scandinavia by:
DJØF Publishing
Copenhagen, Denmark
Email: forlag@djoef.dk
www.djoef-forlag.dk

Sold and distributed in North America by:
International Specialized Book Services (ISBS)
Portland, OR 97213, USA
Email: orders@isbs.com
www.isbs.com

Sold in all other countries by:
The Oxford Publicity Partnership Ltd
Towcester, NN12 6BT, UK
Email: djof@oppuk.co.uk
www.oppuk.co.uk

Distributed in all other countries by:
Marston Book Services
Abingdon, Oxon, OX14 4YN, UK
Email: trade.orders@marston.co.uk
www.marston.co.uk

Contents

Introduction

Ulla Neergaard, Ruth Nielsen and Lynn Roseberry

This book brings together essays by leading legal scholars from a number of European countries on European legal method(s). We use this concept in a broad and open sense as it is subject to development. Both in Europe and in North America there is, and has for some years been, a seemingly renewed debate on methodology in legal research. In the first years of its existence, EU law was generally perceived as rather superficial, immature and fragmentary with many gaps and inconsistencies. Now, EU law is ripening and the mutual embeddedness of EU law and the national law of its Member States is becoming more intense. It is therefore both more possible and more necessary to identify and explain the legal method that is applied by European legal actors, in particular legal scholars and courts, when analysing EU law and the law of EU Member States within the scope of application of EU law.

The essays in this book are based on papers presented at a research conference held at the Copenhagen Business School in cooperation with the University of Copenhagen, on 19 November 2010.[1] The conference, as well as this book, is part of a research project: 'Towards a European Legal Method: Synthesis or Fragmentation?' funded by the Danish Social Science Research Council for the years 2010-2012.[2] The project examines the extent to which it is possible to identify a coherent legal method (doctrine of the sources of law and their interpretation) that may be applied when analysing EU law and the law of EU Member States within the scope of application of EU law. It looks at what characterises the sources of law and the interpretative methods that are actually used by European legal actors, especially judges and researchers, today, i.e. in the early 21st century when analysing what is valid law. It studies the changes in the relative importance of various sources of law and inter-

1. See www.cbs.dk/elm1.
2. The research group behind the project consists of: professor Ulla Neergaard (Faculty of Law, University of Copenhagen), professor Ruth Nielsen (Law Department, Copenhagen Business School), and associate professor and head of department Lynn Roseberry (Law Department, Copenhagen Business School).

pretative methods that occur in connection with the mutual integration of EU law and national law. The basic thoughts in the prevailing legal theories in Europe (legal positivism, natural law theories, the institutional theory of law, etc.) date back to the time before the EU's creation and were conceived with a view to either national law in various European countries or public international law. In the early days of the EU's existence, most legal scholars therefore approached EU law with theoretical and methodological tools developed in a non-EU context. The project – 'Towards a European Legal Method' – examines to what extent these pre-EU theories and methods can explain and facilitate the functioning of those characteristics of EU law that differ from national law and public international law, in particular the pluralistic and flexible approach in EU law to sources of law and their interpretation, the combination of an 'internal' (relatively narrow legal dogmatic) and a broader 'external' (economic, sociological, etc.) perspective on law, and the relationship between law and politics including the judiciary's role in majority democracies (UK and the Nordic countries) and constitutional democracies (the rest of Europe and probably the EU). If the answer to the above question is that the 'old' theories and methods are insufficient to grasp EU developments, it is part of the project to contribute to presenting and formulating alternative theoretical and methodological approaches. The contributions in the present book, which is the first book from the 'Towards a European Legal Method'-project, mainly deal with analysing existing approaches either at a general level or from specific national perspectives.

The authors of the essays in this book are all legal scholars. They have their main professional activity within different legal disciplines and represent different legal cultures and research styles partly related to different geographical backgrounds. There are contributions both from scholars with common law and civil law backgrounds, from Eastern and Western Europe and from the Northern and Southern part of Europe. In editing the book we have endeavoured not to interfere with the diversity of the authors and have abstained from 'harmonising' the different contributions.

The book contains nine contributions (written by altogether twelve authors), each of which addresses different dimensions of the general theme. The five contributions in Part One consist of more general perspectives and are written by: Rob van Gestel and Hans-W. Micklitz, Wulf-Henning Roth; Ulla Neergaard and Ruth Nielsen, Martijn Hesselink; and Dennis Patterson. Part Two takes up a more comparative approach to the general theme in the sense that the perception of European Legal Method(s) viewed from a Member State perspective is examined. This part includes contributions from: Jane

Reichel; Kristina Koldinska; Sophie Robin-Olivier; and Tamara Hervey and Natalie Sheldon.

The first essay in Part One by *van Gestel and Micklitz* is entitled: 'Revitalising Doctrinal Legal Research in Europe: What About Methodology?' The authors have observed that both in the USA and in Europe there is an apparently increasing debate on methodology in legal research, and that doctrinalists and multidisciplinarians appear to be in different camps fighting over the 'true nature' of legal scholarship. With a point of departure taken in observations such as these, they put forward a hypothesis that an increased instrumentalisation of European law and legal research has decreased the attention for methodology, for legal theory, and for keeping enough professional distance to one's object of research, and that this has, among others, resulted in a lack of scholarly criticism towards European integration. They suggest that doctrinal legal research should be revitalised so that it is up for the challenges that European law is facing, such as increased multi-level governance, plurality of legal sources, and mixtures between different modes of government and governance. Also, they argue that as far as some of the most important developments with respect to European integration are concerned, many legal scholars are not asking the right questions simply because they focus too much on EU lawmakers who see European integration as an ongoing process with no horizon and few constitutional limits. The authors believe that raising methodological awareness can be an important improvement in the study of European law and may encourage legal researchers not to limit themselves to recycling what the European Court of Justice (hereinafter the CJEU) or other EU institutions have to say about European law. They also point out that a methodology debate in Europe should not start with what separates legal scholars from practitioners, as it seems more fruitful to start with a debate about what may be the added value of a scholarly legal approach focussing on the development of positive EU law, compared to what EU institutions and legal practitioners think of it. They also claim that the instrumentalisation of European law has stimulated 'herd behaviour' for legal research. This implies that researchers choose to follow 'hot topics' and trends, often initiated by policymakers instead of developing their own agendas.

In their analysis, van Gestel and Micklitz, among others things, focus on three stages of development. They distinguish between: 1) integration through law (the first stage from 1968 until approximately 2002); 2) integration without law (since 2002); and 3) integration beyond law (spurred by the 2005 French and Dutch no against a European Constitution). They view all three stages as united in a particular instrumental understanding of law, of legal scholarship and of legal methodology.

Van Gestel and Micklitz conclude their essay by setting up an agenda for revitalisation of European doctrinal research through increased emphasis on methodology and theory. They regard the following as important elements in such an agenda: 1) It should start with a disclosure of ideological preconceptions; 2) It should be freed from the role model and research methods of the judge as its sole point of reference and look for answers to the question: what could be the added value of a legal scholarship that goes beyond being a service for legal practice; 3) It should start asking critical questions; 4) If consensus can be reached about the importance of a 'law in context' approach, it needs to ensure that it is reflected in legal education in order to ascertain that lawyers and legal researchers are cognisant of the most important parameters of political science, law & economics, comparative law and empirical legal research methods; 5) It should ensure that these other 'non-legal' research methodologies do not replace the training in doctrinal research but come on top of that training and be taught in combination with doctrinal methods; 6) It should be aware of what methodology actually entails and why it is particularly important for those scholars who focus on European law in their research; 7) It should give more attention to the advantages of a solid research design, with special attention for the formulation of a good research question/hypothesis; and 8) It should not be too strict on separation between methods of legal scholarship and methods of law and policymaking.

The second essay in Part One, 'The Importance of the Instruments Provided for in the Treaties for Developing a European Legal Method', by *Roth* begins by considering whether the public international law of treaties can provide a benchmark against which the existence of a specific European legal method can be identified. He notes that there are two basic features of the EU Treaties that distinguish them from traditional international treaties: 1) The notion of the EU as a 'union based on the rule of law', and 2) The enforcement mechanisms established at both the Union/Community and national levels. He suggests that these two features provide the impetus for the development of a European legal method.

Roth points out that the EEC Treaty itself laid the foundations for the notion of a Community based on the rule of law through its creation of institutions with competences the use of which would necessarily lead to 'constitutional' conflicts. The Treaty provided the framework for resolving those conflicts and thus fueled the development of Community law for the last 40 or 50 years.

Further, Roth notes that by establishing Community institutions with legislative and policy competences on the one hand and a court to supervise the use of these competences on the other, the EC Treaty (now the Treaty on the

Functioning of the European Union, TFEU) has gone beyond a mere international treaty. The proceedings of annulment, infringement, and actions for damages put the CJEU in a position to supply a uniform and consistent application of the Treaties. The jurisdiction of the Community courts in these areas provide one basis for developing a specific European legal method.

Roth asserts that the preliminary ruling procedure is probably the most important instrument whereby the CJEU creates and applies a European legal method because it is meant to ensure that European primary and secondary law has the same effect – as far as possible – within all the Member States. Roth points to the Societas Europaea (SE) as an example of the interest in uniform interpretation. The SE would simply not be accepted by the business community as a viable instrument if the provisions of the SE-regulation were interpreted differently by national courts. The meaning and impact of particular provisions would vary from Member State to Member State. Accordingly, Article 267 TFEU provides opportunities for development of a European legal method through the effort to provide a uniform interpretation of EU law.

Finally, the role of the individual in enforcing EU law is also identified as an important instrument supporting the development of a European legal method. Roth points out that individual enforcement proceedings in the national courts were made possible by the CJEU's development of the principle of supremacy, the concept of direct effect, and the obligation to interpret national law in conformity with EU law. Roth sees these developments as essential elements in the creation of a powerful instrument to engage national courts in the enforcement of EU law. This combined with the preliminary reference procedure ensure the CJEU a central position in interpretation and development of European law, and thus for development of a specific European legal method.

The essay by *Neergaard and Nielsen* is entitled: 'Where Did the Spirit and Its Friends Go? On the European Legal Method(s) and the Interpretational Style of the Court of Justice of the European Union'. The essay takes its point of departure in the observation that in the first ten to fifteen years or thereabouts the CJEU was rather explicit with what was characteristic of its interpretational style, so that its legal method seemed more transparent than in later years. Accordingly, the authors focus on detecting and analysing – at least some of – the changes which might have occurred. More precisely, the primary research question of the essay is whether the legal methods so far identified by especially legal scholarship, and which have become to be regarded as 'truths', may be considered as 'real truths', and whether they still can be considered as 'truths' today (2011). Four classic legal science 'truths' about the CJEU's judicial method and their later development have been chosen by the authors for examination, namely: 1) The application of the teleological method as justification for the CJEU's interpretations of EU law; 2) Reference to uniformity in EU law as the goal of interpretations under Article 267 TFEU; 3) The application of Article 4 TEU as a justification for the CJEU's interpretations of EU law; and 4) The application of general principles and fundamental rights as justifications for the CJEU's interpretations of EU law.

In the essay the expression 'legal method' is used as referring to the doctrine of the sources of law and their interpretation. The analysis is based on a sample of preliminary judgments from the CJEU (altogether 200) as well as a number of other judgments (both preliminary rulings and other types of judgments). Also, a limited selection of literature is included.

In the essay, it is observed that in the early period, the CJEU generally interpreted the Treaty of Rome as a framework Treaty that as stated in its preamble was intended to facilitate an on-going development towards an ever closer union among the peoples of Europe and ever more integration, in particular with regard to the economic aspects of society. Thus, the Treaty of Rome was seen as basically different from (other) international trade treaties. In this early period, the CJEU produced a limited number of judgments, which are now considered as classics, where it exercised a creative, dynamic style of interpretation building on an overall vision of the grand design of the EU construction.

These classic judgments built on the classic 'truths' which have been examined in the essay. However, the authors emphasise that in fact the classic cases were a-typical in the sense that from a quantitative point of view, even in the first period, the CJEU in most other cases interpreted EU law in a manner not very different from that national courts – at least in the civil law part of Europe. Also, the authors conclude that in later cases the CJEU tends to express itself in a more limited way and abstain from putting forward grand visions of the way the EU is developing or should develop and focus more on interpreting particular elements of EU law.

In addition, Neergaard and Nielsen conclude that in the early period, the CJEU generally took a rather hierarchical approach – for example in establishing the doctrines of direct effect and supremacy – to the relationship between elements of the European legal order originating from the EU level and elements originating from the national level. The authors note that in later cases the CJEU seems to be turning towards a more interactive, horizontal approach to the relationship between layers originating from EU actors and layers originating from national actors. They stress that it is not clear whether the judges of the CJEU collectively see the EU legal order as one big system comprising elements of both national and EU origin, or as a distinct legal system in addition to the national legal systems.

As regards the four 'truths', the essay concludes firstly that it is still true to say that the CJEU applies a teleological method of interpretation taking account of the objective of the particular provisions under interpretation, however with certain modifications. Secondly, it is concluded that the CJEU often strives to give a uniform interpretation to particular words or concepts, but it has also developed principles and concepts, for example the principle of proportionality and the concept of indirect discrimination, in a way that allows for considerable diversity from country to country. Thirdly, it is concluded that the CJEU still relies on Article 4(3) TEU but tends not to refer explicitly to it in support of interpretations which have been established in settled case law from the CJEU. Finally, it is concluded that general principles, in particular fundamental rights as part of the general principles of the EU, are increasingly being referred to in case law. Thus, with reference to the title of the essay, Neergaard and Nielsen find that the spirit and its friends are still there, however in a changed setting.

In the fourth essay, *Hesselink* explores what it will mean for courts if an instrument on European contract law (ECL instrument) becomes a toolbox for the European legislator, either formally or informally.[3] Hesselink takes his point of departure in the Green Paper on policy options for progress towards a European Contract Law for consumers and business launched by the European Commission in July 2010. He explains that if the parties to a contract opt into an optional instrument as provided for in an EU regulation, then judges will have to apply the instrument as the applicable law between the parties. However, what he is interested in is what will happen outside such cases of formal applicability, as he thinks that a court might wish to take the ECL instrument as a source of inspiration, or even as a source of law. He asserts that judges are bound to apply the law, and that although they are allowed to further develop the law, they are constrained by the existing sources or legal materials, and by recognised methods. Therefore he finds it relevant to raise the question of how the text of the instrument, in cases where it has not been positively opted into by the contracting parties, can ever become a source of inspiration that a court is allowed or even obliged to take into account. More precisely, the central question in the essay is whether there is a legitimate place for an ECL instrument within the developing European legal method. Therefore, among other things, he discusses three main types of le-

3. COM(2010) 348 final, 1.7.2010.

gitimation: new European legal methods (sincere cooperation and Europe-friendly interpretation, soft harmonious interpretation and general principles of EU law), classical methods of interpretation (grammatical, historical, systematic, teleological and comparative), and political legitimation (in terms of political support, substantive quality, authorship, good governance, or political philosophy).

In the process of answering the main question, Hesselink also reflects further on the concept 'European legal method'. He explains that in his opinion there are at least three different ways of looking at European private law and European legal method, *i.e.* a nationalist, a dualist, and a Europeanist way.

Hesselink concludes that which mode of legitimation will prove to be more convincing will often depend on the circumstances of the case at hand and the characteristics of the particular model rule or definition that is being borrowed. To this he adds that legitimation in terms of the general principles of civil law that the CJEU has recently been developing seems a particularly promising strategy. Also, he finds that it seems unlikely that European courts could even come under a duty, following from the principle of sincere cooperation, to use the instrument as a toolbox.

Patterson's essay examines the question of whether there is a European legal method from a perspective informed by Richard Rorty's analysis of the demarcation between natural science and other disciplines, Wittgenstein's account of the distinction between understanding and interpretation, and H.L.A. Hart's Rule of Recognition.

Patterson begins with Richard Rorty's essay 'Texts and Lumps', in which Rorty disputes the assertion that the distinction between natural and human sciences lies in their objects of research, e.g. rocks versus literature. Instead, he sees the difference between science and non-science located primarily in the extent to which there is agreement on the methodology to be applied to obtain answers to the questions posed within each field. That we perceive natural science as being objective and determinate is due primarily to the fact that natural scientists have managed to achieve deep consensus about method, whereas scholars in other disciplines have not.

However, Patterson urges that disagreement about the correct interpretation of a text or legal rule is not a symptom of complete lack of agreement on method. Here he turns to Wittgenstein's account of the distinction between understanding and interpretation, which asserts that interpretation is only possible against the background of a shared understanding. Further, that understanding is grounded in repeated practice-based iterations. It is through the process of forming judgments in accordance with shared criteria that 'understanding is engendered and the stage is set for interpretation.'

Patterson then links Wittgenstein's theory of interpretation to H.L.A. Hart's argument that legal judgment is made possible by the existence of intersubjective agreement on criteria for legal sources and on how the sources are to be construed when judging compliance and divergence. Patterson notes, though, that the Rule of Recognition is itself neither valid nor invalid, as it is simply a social, customary practice. Further, while the Rule of Recognition includes agreement on the customary ways of applying sources of law to cases and arriving at decisions, Patterson acknowledges that it lacks the necessary agreement at the final stage of making a judgment that is found in natural sciences and is what imparts to it its aura of undisputable objectivity.

Nevertheless, Patterson asserts that even without deep consensus on methodology, law is largely determinate as evidenced by the fact that there is convergence (i.e. agreement in judgment) about a wide range of legal materials and their significance. Most legal rules and their application are common knowledge and non-contentious. If they were not, many social and economic relationships that we take for granted would simply not function. Contentious cases in law are thus exceptions to the rule and can be understood as theoretical disagreements that arise against the background of shared practice.

Patterson applies the foregoing analysis to the debate about whether it is possible to speak of a European legal method. In Patterson's view, this debate is primarily a conflict between legalist and pragmatist positions. The legalist position is that a case is correctly decided when a particular decisional path (method) is followed. However, Patterson reminds us that following this method is simply an affirmation of the sociology of the legal order. The pragmatist position, on the other hand, notes that methodology is less important in contentious cases because the intersubjective consensus that is otherwise present in the majority of legal matters is absent. Consequently, pragmatists would argue that a lack of intersubjective consensus on elements of European legal method does not mean there is no European legal method.

The five essays in Part One deliver altogether many interesting inputs to an understanding of European legal method(s) as well as the challenges we are all facing in trying to understand, define, develop and critisise it. One particular element should be emphasised as being of particular importance, which is also emphasised by among others van Gestel and Micklitz. That is, there is no longer one pyramid-like organised national legal system in which judges and legal scholars function as 'gatekeepers' who are supposed to guard and maintain the consistency of the system. Instead we are facing a plurality of legal systems, in which hierarchy plays a less important role. Another important element seems to be that comparative law methods are gaining in importance. A third element worth stressing is that the interpretative methods applied by the CJEU seem to have changed over the years. Altogether, the impression gained is that it still constitutes a rather fragmented area.

The essays in Part Two address European legal methods in a comparative perspective seen from different national perspectives. *Reichel*'s essay is entitled 'European Legal Method from a Swedish Perspective – Rights, Compensation and the Role of the Courts.' The Swedish legal landscape has undergone significant changes in the past decades. From being largely self-reliant in the production of legal norms applicable within its borders, Swedish jurists today deal with internationally enacted norms from the EU, the Council of Europe and many other international organisations. Reichel addresses the question of how this development has affected the traditional perception of the law, legal sources and their legal value within Swedish law. The object of her study is thus the Europeanisation of Swedish legal method seen from the perspective of Swedish legal actors. She asks how European sources of law are dealt with by the Swedish courts and other legal actors, and whether and how the way they handle European sources of law differs from the 'traditional' Swedish solutions. Specific focus is placed on the perception of individual rights, rights to compensation and how the Europeanised view of these matters has affected the role of the courts in Sweden. The essay is structured in the following way: The first part describes and analyses some basic features of the traditional Swedish view on law and legal sources, including Scandinavian legal realism, the doctrine of parliamentary sovereignty and the issue of judicial review. The effects of Europeanisation, in particular the emphasis on individual rights, the juridification of politics and the importance attributed to the possibility of receiving compensation from the state when rights are not duly upheld are addressed in part two. The effects of pluralisation are discussed in part three, regarding both the content of the legal sources and their hierarchies. An assessment of the effects of Europeanisation on Swedish legal method is made in part four. Some conclusive remarks are given in the final Part Five.

Even if the Swedish tradition in the period prior to EU membership (as of 1 January 1995) has shown an open attitude to accepting different legal sources, Swedish lawyers and courts have traditionally been loyal to the Swedish legislature. In line with the majoritarian democratic model, Swedish courts in general have been reluctant to review acts of law, insofar as it has entailed setting aside legislation, in order to uphold general principles of constitutional law or human rights. On this last point, Swedish law has undergone important changes during recent decades. Swedish courts have not hesitated to set aside acts of law on the basis of their being contrary to European legal sources on human rights, as well as broad principle-oriented provisions with strong economic and political connotations, as the Treaty-based EU rules on free movement. The importance of general principles of law, court-based legal instruments, has increased, whereas legislative preparatory works, emanating from the legislator, have undergone a decrease in importance. Reichel finds that European legal sources are not avoided by Swedish courts and other legal actors, but that they are still treated, at least to some extent, as foreign objects in Swedish law. Swedish courts in general have not been reluctant to assume the task of protecting EU law in Sweden. Quite often, the methodological choices are, however, not made explicit, with the legal handiwork performed in a more cautious and subtle manner. There seems to be an indirect adjustment of Swedish law to EU law, in that the Swedish courts choose to apply Swedish sources in accordance with European sources, without actually mentioning EU law.

The title of *Koldinská*'s essay is 'EU Compatible Interpretation of the National Law with Some Constitutional Reservations – Case of the Czech Republic.' The main focus of her essay is an analysis of national case law, i.e. above all the case law of the Czech Constitutional Court and Supreme Administrative Court, and primarily in relation to EU law. She discusses how EU law and the jurisprudence of the CJEU are reflected in the decision-making of these two national courts. Particular attention is devoted to questions of the relationship of national laws to EU law, concerning which the Czech national courts have already expressed themselves several times. Through an analysis of some selected rulings she demonstrates how Czech law works with EU law, as well as with the case law of the CJEU. The fact that the Czech Republic, through its President, was the last Member State to approve the Lisbon Treaty, is also discussed in this essay, especially in light of two findings of the Constitutional Court relating directly to the Lisbon Treaty. Finally she discusses some preliminary questions that the Czech courts have submitted to the CJEU.

Koldinská's essay starts with a brief account of the historical background. More than 20 years have passed now since the collapse of communism in Central and Eastern Europe. Throughout the Communist era, no judicial authority was empowered to review complaints of violations of the fundamental rights guaranteed by the Constitution. The situation after 1989 and a fundamental change in the cases arbitrated by the justice system brought about radical change in Central Europe. The Czech Constitutional Court and the Supreme Administrative Court were both established after 1989. The fundamental change in the cases decided by the law epitomises not only the transition to democracy in the early 1990s, but also the subsequent entry of the

Czech Republic into the European Union, which brought about the need for decisions to be taken in the light of EU law, or more precisely, in accordance with it. The essay sheds light on this requirement and how Czech case law is reacting to EU law. The essay concentrates primarily on the jurisprudence of Czech courts, as the EU legal method is not the subject of much analysis or discussion in the Czech legal scholarship. In conclusion, the author argues that, based on the existing case law of national courts in the Czech Republic, as well as on the literature reflecting current discussions among Czech legal scholars, it can be concluded that, in its consistent attitude towards the duty to adhere to the CJEU's interpretation of EU law, as well as in its critical study of some aspects of EU law or CJEU case law, Czech legal theory and judicial practice may be contributing significantly to the consolidation of a European Legal Method.

The essay by *Robin-Olivier* examines four cases decided by three different European courts – the CJEU, the European Court of Human Rights (ECtHR) and the French Cour de Cassation – in which each court cites legal sources from different legal orders, which are not necessarily binding in the case at hand, as providing the legal basis for the judgment. Robin-Olivier argues that these cases are evidence of a trend among the European courts, especially noticeable in cases concerning labour and social rights, to combine domestic, European and international sources, not all of which are binding, to arrive at their conclusions without applying any specific method to the combination of sources. Robin-Olivier first identifies in each case the different sources cited by the courts and points out that some of the sources cited were not even binding on the parties. None of the courts commented on how to assess the legal value of external legal sources and interpretations of them in other fora. They all seem to offer combinations of binding and non-binding norms from different legal orders as evidence of convergence toward a new norm – in these cases a new fundamental right – that is then treated as a binding norm and applied to the cases before them. Robin-Olivier observes that although the combination of binding and non-binding sources from different legal orders is unusual in all of the judicial systems considered, the ECtHR is the only court that explicitly recognised that its use of such a wide variety of sources in order to interpret the ECHR was unconventional technique and offered an explanation for doing so.

Robin-Olivier notes that while common law courts may be better able to deal with differences in legal sources because they are accustomed to handling both binding and 'merely' persuasive legal sources, and have developed a method for doing so, civil law courts and the CJEU, which has been under the influence of the civil law tradition, do not have the same habits. It is accordingly not surprising that civil law courts like the French – or courts like the CJEU that have been under the influence of the civil law tradition – neglect questions concerning such distinctions between the authorities they refer to. Nevertheless, Robin-Olivier argues that the trend among the European courts undermines the persuasiveness of their judgments and calls for the development of a European method for combining legal sources that can provide the basis for more persuasive argumentation for the resulting legal developments.

The essay by *Hervey and Sheldon* bears the title 'Judicial Method of English Courts and Tribunals in EU Law Cases: A case study in employment law.' To focus their study on the judicial method of interpretation of EU law in English courts and tribunals, the authors have chosen to select one substantive area of law for closer analysis, namely employment law. This selection followed after a review of English textbooks on EU law, to determine which English cases were referred to as important examples of the ways EU law has been received in English law from the 1970s to the present day. The authors noted that many of the English cases concerning the most contentious doctrines of EU law – supremacy, direct effect, indirect effect – are in the field of employment law. Employment law is also an appropriate case study because there is a significant body of national law in the field that pre-dates the UK's membership of the European Union. In this respect, employment law, like consumer law, can be contrasted with an area such as 'commercial agency law', which was effectively 'created' in English law by a Directive in 1986. The authors also note that the selection of EU employment law as a case study limits the analysis and their conclusions to areas of EU law where the ordinary legislative procedure (see now Article 294 TFEU) is used. To focus their analysis further, the authors drew up a list of employment law cases, mainly those cited in English langugage textbooks, involving points of EU law. The list formed the broad context for their analysis. From the list, they selected some 10 cases for in-depth analysis. In order to consider the question what changes have happened over in judicial approaches to EU law, they selected two-three key cases from each of the decades, 1970s, 1980s, 1990s and 2000s. Selection was on the basis of considering how the national judges reasoned in the case; what was their approach; and what, if any, difference the relevant EU law made to the judge's approach. Discussion of a few cases allowed for depth of analysis in terms of the courts' reasoning in their approaches to EU law. Many of these key cases were appealed, so that the authors were able to include analysis of courts at different levels in the appellate hierarchy.

The authors state that in English literature discussing cases from the last five centuries of English law, emphasis is placed on four main 'rules' that assist judges in decision making. These 'classical' rules of interpretation or 'canons of construction' are said to be as follows:

- The Literal Rule: The court looks to the exact meaning of the words. The correct interpretation is the plain, literal reading of the words that Parliament chose to employ.
- The Golden Rule: The court looks at the whole of the statute, placing the word or section in its context, and gives the words their ordinary meaning, unless this produces absurdity.
- The Purposive Rule: The court focuses on what Parliament may have intended by the words. This is done through examining the general purpose of the section and then looking at it in context. Courts may also look at the record of Parliamentary debate.
- The Mischief Rule: The court examines previous common law and the history of the statute, to find what legal deficiency or 'mischief' Parliament sought to remedy when it enacted the statute.

The key findings in the essay are that the approaches and reasoning of English judges have changed significantly over time; that the current position (the 'EU compliance mischief rule') departs significantly from traditional English rules of statutory interpretation, applicable to ordinary domestic cases; that the current position involves a re-conceptualisation of the relationship between courts and Parliament in the context of interpretation of national law within the scope of EU law; and that English judges conceive of EU and English law as essentially separate systems.

The four essays in Part Two analyse the changes brought about by EU membership in one Nordic country (Sweden), one Eastern European country (the Czech Republic), the UK and include a case study of four cases decided by the CJEU, the ECtHR and the French Cour de Cassation. They throw light on different approaches to EU law in jurisdictions with common law background and civil law background and on a number of approaches to sources of law and interpretative methods used in different parts of Europe.

Most of the essays in this book deal with several different aspects of European legal method(s) in an evolutionary perspective. There is considerable debate on methodological and theoretical issues in many parts of Europe and on how legal research should be conducted. The essays in this book do not offer comprehensive or final answers to such questions but provide a number of useful partial and provisional answers.

As mentioned in the beginning this book is part of the research project: 'Towards a European Legal Method: Synthesis or Fragmentation?' conducted at the Copenhagen Business School and the University of Copenhagen from 2010-2012 and thus represents work in progress.

The next international research conference within the Copenhagen European Legal method project will take place on 18 November 2011. The title of the conference will be: 'European Legal Method(s) in a Multilayered Legal Order v. Multi-Level Governance – Different theoretical and methodological approaches to the study of EU law'. The focus of the conference is on the changes in the legal methods and relative importance of various sources of law that occur in connection with the on-going development of EU law as an interactive, multi-layered legal order and on contrasting traditional legal research methods with broader social and humanistic science approaches, including political science perspectives on EU law as a multi-level governance system.

PART I

General Perspectives

Revitalising Doctrinal Legal Research in Europe: What About Methodology?

Rob van Gestel and Hans-W. Micklitz[1]

I. Setting the scene

1. Is doctrinal legal research dead?

On June 10th 2008, the newly established Research Group for Methodology of Lawmaking and Legal Research of Tilburg University's law faculty organized a kick-off conference about the importance of methodological awareness in lawmaking and legal research. Two of the keynote speakers, Professor Dame Hazel Genn (Socio-legal studies: University College London) and Professor Eric Posner (Law & economics: Chicago Law School) held a passionate plea for more emphasis on multidisciplinary legal research, which was welcomed by the audience. Eric Posner, however, went a lot further than just arguing for an enrichment of traditional legal scholarship with empirical methods or economic insights. In his lecture, he claimed that 'doctrinal legal research is dead'.

Posner's statement, first and foremost, referred to the situation in the U.S. but judging from his response to questions from the audience, he seemed quite convinced that law schools in Europe will sooner or later follow America's footsteps in burying 'black letter law'.[2] Doctrinal legal research might

1. This paper is the outcome of an intensive debate over the last year. Whilst we closely co-operated and interfered into the mutual parts, we would nevertheless underline that the prime responsibility of parts I and III lies with Rob van Gestel, whereas Hans-W. Micklitz is primarily responsible for part II. This paper is part of a more encompassing project on methodology of law and legal research between Tilburg University and the EUI, which is supposed to result in a casebook on methodology of legal research for educational purposes and a book on the meaning of methodology and legal theory for European legal scholarship.
2. In theory it is possible that the current credit crunch led to modesty in the Chicago School of Law & Economics about the scientific possibilities to predict the effects of regulatory interventions to 'fix' malfunctioning financial markets. At first sight, how-

still be useful for legal practice but it has little to do with science, appeared to be the message. In this contribution we will argue that if Posner actually meant what he said, he is wrong, not only for the situation in the Netherlands but for Europe more in general. It is more likely that on this side of the Atlantic, doctrinal and non-doctrinal approaches towards law and legal research are becoming more intertwined.

Interesting with respect to the claim that doctrinal research is dead, or at least close to death, is that Richard Posner, another prominent member of the Chicago School of Law & economics, and judge in the Court of Appeals for the Seventh Circuit, recently defended quite a different position than his son did in Tilburg.[3] In a sparkling debate with the former dean of Colorado Law School, Professor Pierre Schlag, Posner senior claims that 'The law schools *need* legal analysts, not merely as teachers but also as scholars. Doctrinal analysis cannot be left to judges.' As Schlag puts it, 'Courts have dockets. Legal academics have time.' Given this asymmetry, the academics could always outdo the courts in the intricacy of their analyses. In one of his latest books, he adds to this that sound doctrinal research is intellectually demanding, requiring vast knowledge and the ability to synthesize fragmentary materials.[4] According to Posner senior, this type of research is important for the vitality of the legal system and of greater social value than much esoteric interdisciplinary legal scholarship. We fully agree with Richard Posner that doctrinal research cannot be left to judges and other legal practitioners. At the same time, we also believe that the negative image concerning legal doctrine that Eric Posner apparently shares with so many others has much to do with the formalism and the strong divide between the law as it is and the law as it ought to be, which are all too often associated with a dogmatic approach towards academic legal research. Especially interdisciplinarians often perceive doctrinalists to be intellectually rigid, inflexible, formalistic, and inward-looking.[5] Other accusations include that doctrinalists show an unhealthy pre-

ever, this seems unlikely looking at the recommendations to restore the market for mortgages at the lowest possible costs. See <http://www.thebigmoney.com/articles/mothers-milk/2009/03/03/better-cheaper-mortgage-fix>. After all, was the search for lowest costs 'solutions' not one of the major drivers behind the collapse of the financial sector in general and the mortgage market in particular?

3. Richard A. Posner, The State of Legal Scholarship Today: A Comment on Schlag, The Georgetown Law Journal, Vol. 97, pp. 845-855 (2009).
4. Richard Posner, How Judges Think, Harvard University Press, Harvard 2008 p. 211.
5. Douglas Vick, Interdisciplinarity and the Discipline of Law, Journal of Law and Society, Vol. 31, nr. 2, p. 164 (2004).

occupation with technicalities,[6] often focus on unimportant topics, repeat existing knowledge, and fail to connect law to life by assessing the real world consequences of doctrinal frameworks. Proceeding otherwise would, according to Deborah Rhode, require significant time, money, and non-legal expertise, which she believes most authors of doctrinal work are more than happy to avoid.[7] As a consequence, many doctrinal works are 'glutted with theory and starved for facts', according to Rhode.[8] Pierre Schlag goes even further. He feels that much of the doctrinal research in the U.S. can be labelled as 'case law journalism'.[9] Many scholarly legal publications offer little more than comments on recent court rulings.

2. Problem definition

As we have just shown, in the U.S. a debate on legal scholarship and methodology is going on between, at least, two camps: 'doctrinalists' and 'multidisciplinarians'. Especially the elite law schools seem to move away from doctrinal research, whereas in education legal doctrine is still leading. In Europe, on the other hand, doctrinal legal research does not appear to be under attack (yet). Nevertheless, a debate on the scientific nature of legal research in general is emerging.[10]

The Netherlands is probably one of the first European countries where methodology of law and legal research became an issue (again) with many

6. R. Cotterell, Subverting Orthodoxy, Making Law Central: A View of Sociolegal Studies, Journal of Law and Society, Vol. 29, p. 633 (2002).
7. Deborah Rhode, Legal Scholarship, Harvard Law Review 115, pp. 1327-1361 (p. 1340) 2002.
8. Id Rhode at p. 1340.
9. Pierre Schlag, Spam Jurisprudence, Air Law, and the Rank Anxiety of Nothing Happening (A Report on the State of the Art), 97 GEO. L. J. 803 (2009), pp. 821-823.
10. For the UK, P. Hillyard, Law's empire: Socio-legal empirical research in the Twenty-first century, Journal of Law and Society 2007, Vol. 34, no. 2, pp. 269-277, H. Genn, M. Partington and S. Wheeler, Law in the real world: Improving our understanding of how the law works, The Nuffield inquiry on empirical legal research, Nuffield Foundation, London 2006: http://www.ucl.ac.uk/laws/socio-legal/empirical/docs/inquiry_report.pdf. Roger Brownsword, An introduction to legal research, www.wellcome.ac.uk/assets/wtx 030897.pdf. For Germany Hans-Eberhard Heyke, Ist 'Rechtswissenschaft' eine Wissenschaft? Rechtstheorie, 2003, 229-244; R.M. Kiesow, Rechtswissenschaft – was ist das? JZ 2010, 585 and for Belgium S. Gutwirth, Evaluatie rechtswetenschappelijk onderzoek: VLIR-model voor integrale kwaliteitsevaluatie van het onderzoek in de rechtswetenschappen, Nieuw Juridisch Weekblad 2007/6, pp. 674-678. For France Eva Steiner, French Legal method, Oxford: Oxford University Press 2002.

references to the situation in the U.S.[11] An interesting conclusion of the latest Dutch research assessment exercise is that law is a 'discipline in transition'. According to the evaluation committee, it is moving from a national to a more European and international discipline, from a teaching monopoly towards competition for students, from service-oriented towards legal practice to a purpose in itself, from overhead financing towards competitive financing and contract research, from single- to multi- and interdisciplinarity, and last but not least from implicit traditions to more focus on methodology.[12]

We wonder where this renewed attention for legal scholarship and methodology is coming from and what is behind it. The trend is obvious and can be observed in many countries.[13] However, it seems as if the Dutch debate is perhaps special in the sense that there is a debate running through various disciplines: public, private, national, international law, etc. There are dozens of articles now, and the debate has, as we already mentioned, even drawn the attention of the national research assessment exercise.[14] It seems likely that sooner or later this debate will spread to the rest of Europe and to European law as such. The first signs of this are already there. Recently Hesselink has, for example, argued that the Europeanization of private law is gradually blurring the dividing line between internal and external perspectives towards legal research, with their respective methods.[15] According to him, this increases the need for a new European legal methodology. But the question is of course: what does that entail: a European legal methodology? Should European legal scholars follow their colleagues in the U.S. and abandon doctrinal legal research altogether at a moment where prominent legal scholars in the U.S. are already making a U-turn in order to try to restore the doctrinal tradition? If the answer is no, does this imply that there is nothing wrong with European legal scholarship?

11. C.J.J. Stolker, Legal Journals in Pursuit of a More Scientific Approach, EJLE 2005, No. 2, pp. 77-94 and Gerrit A. de Geest, Hoe maken we van de rechtswetenschap een volwaardige wetenschap? NJB 2004, pp. 58-66.
12. Evaluatiecommissie Rechtswetenschappelijk onderzoek 2009, Kwaliteit en diversiteit, VU 2009, with an English summary p. 6. (see: http://www.vu.nl/nl/Images/Evaluatie%20onderzoek%20Rechten_tcm9-169244.pdf).
13. K. Riesenhuber (Hrsg.) Europaische Methodenlehre: Grundfragen der Methoden des Europäischen Privatrechts, De Gruyter Recht: Berlin 2004, p. 3, 2nd edition Europäische Methodenlehre, Handbuch für Ausbildung und Praxis, 2010. The second edition also contains reports on the current debate in various Member States.
14. Http://www.vu.nl/nl/Images/Evaluatie%20onderzoek%20Rechten_tcm9-169244.pdf.
15. M. Hesselink, A European Legal Method? On European Private Law and Scientific Method, European Law Journal 15(1), pp. 20-45 (44-45), 2008.

We believe the latter is not the case. There probably is something wrong with European legal scholarship and the study of European law. Our hypothesis is that an increased instrumentalization of law and legal research has decreased the attention for methodology, for legal theory (theory-building), and for keeping enough professional distance to ones object of research, which on its turn has resulted in a lack of scholarly criticism towards European integration. We will argue that the answer to this problem is not to put doctrinal legal research out with the garbage. Instead we suggest it should be revitalized it so that it is up for the challenges that European legal scholarship is facing, such as, increased multilevel governance, plurality of legal sources, and mixtures between different modes of government and governance.

3. Is the debate about the scientific nature of legal doctrine new?

The debate about the scientific nature of legal doctrine is actually a rather old one. It has strong predecessors dating back to at least the 19th century, when legal formalism (Begriffsjurisprudenz) clashed with naturalism. Famous is, for instance, the speech that Julius von Kirchmann, a German Judge, gave in Berlin in 1847 before a society of German legal scholars in which he argued:

> 'Die Juristen sind 'Würmer', die nur vom faulen Holz leben; von dem gesunden sich abwendend, ist es nur das Kranke, in dem sie nisten und weben. Indem die Wissenschaft das Zufällige zu ihrem Gegenstand macht, wird sie selbst zur Zufälligkeit; drei berichtigende Worte des Gesetzgebers, und ganze Bibliotheken werden zu Makulatur.'[16]

Von Kirchmann criticized the arbitrariness in law and argued that doctrinal legal research was not expressing the true spirit of natural law as felt and experienced by the people ('Volksgeist'). He felt that doctrinal work (Jurisprudenz) was merely a reproduction of what legislators and courts had to say. After Von Kirchmann, other former members of the 'Historical school', such as Rudolf von Jhering, followed in his footsteps by taking a distance from the formalism and emphasis on systematization.[17]

In Germany the debate on the scientific nature of legal doctrine reached a new culmination point after the adoption of the new Civil Code, which in the eyes of the member of the Freirechtsschule was using legal doctrine as a

16. J. Von Kirchmann, Die Wertlosigkeit der Jurisprudenz als Wissenschaft, Julius Springer Verlag, Berlin 1848, p. 29.
17. R. Von. Jehring, Im Juristischen Begriffshimmel. Ein Phantasiebild, in: Schertz und Ernst in der Jurisprudenz, Leipzig 1909.

shield against the legal protection of the working class.[18] The Freirechtsschule paved the way for the development of legal sociology as well as for other attempts to integrate social science into the legal system. However, the debate went beyond the German particularities and also led to the search for an appropriate legal methodology, one which reaches beyond a mere textual interpretation of cases and statutes and paves the way for the integration of social facts in theories and methods of law and legal interpretation.[19]

Later more or less similar debates emerged elsewhere. First in the Northern European countries, where Anders Vilhelm Lundstedt, for example, argued that doctrinal research was drenched with superstition instead of based on facts. To redress this he urged legal scholars to take a more empirical perspective on law.[20] In line with Lundstedt, another prominent member of Scandinavian legal realism, Alf Ross, defended that the principle of verification must also apply to legal doctrine.[21] Accordingly, doctrinal propositions should be verified against the outcomes of judicial practice. After Scandinavian legal realism came the French May 1968 revolution, in which legal scholars stressed the socio-economic embeddedness of the legal system and the importance of legal research to redress situations of social injustice.[22] Later on in the paper we will be more elaborate on the impact that the 1968 events had on legal thinking not only from the 'left', in order to transform society via law, but also from the 'right' 'to maintain' and or 'to re-establish' the formalist character of the law.

Critics might argue that instrumentalization of the law was going on long before that? Roscoe Pound was, for example, talking about law as a way of 'social engineering' already in 1910, and we also mentioned Scandinavian legal realism. Our point is not that there has not been a similar debate on the instrumental use of law in legal and political history. We have chosen 1968, as this constitutes a benchmark for societal change in a number of European

18. A. Menger, Das Bürgerliche Recht und die besitzlosen Volksklassen. Eine Kritik des Entwurfs eines Bürgerlichen Gesetzbuches für das Deutsche Reich, 1890.
19. Dugiut, Salleilles and Gény, Méthode d'Interprétation et Sources en Droit Privé Positif, 1899/2nd edition 1919.
20. A.V. Lundstedt, Die Unwissenschaftlichkeit der Rechtswissenschaft, Berlin: Verlag für Staatswissenschaften und Geschichte 1932.
21. Alf Ross, On Law and Justice, London: Stevens & Sons 1958, p. 40.
22. M. Miaille, Introduction critique au Droit, Maspero, Paris, 1976.

countries. It triggered a political debate and it initiated an intellectual wave that challenged the preconceptions of so-called formal a-political law.[23]

Just like in Europe, the American debate about the virtues and drawbacks of legal dogmatics has had its predecessors. In the U.S. the attack on legal formalism dates back to Oliver Wendell Holmes jr., who wrote that the black letter lawyer does not consider law to be a means to an end and therefore does not care about the social conditions in which the law has to function in the real world. According to Holmes, this is a serious mistake and in 'The Path of Law' (1897) he argues in favour of an approach in which law is more than mere logic and includes facts and experience.[24] Holmes heavily criticized the clinical 'law as a science' approach from Christopher Columbus Langdell, the inventor of the so-called case-method, who believed that legal research was first of all a matter of induction and formal logic. Langdell argued that law

> 'consists of certain principles or doctrines. To have such a mastery of these is to be able to apply them with constant facility and certainty to the ever-tangled skein of human affairs, is what constitutes a true lawyer; and hence to acquire that mastery should be the business of every earnest student of law.'[25]

Holmes, however, did not accept Langdell's idea that all the relevant 'empirical' materials of legal science are contained in printed books and that the library is to legal scholars what laboratories are to chemists and physicist.[26] In a review of Langdell's second edition of his famous casebook, he acknowledged the advantages of a more scientific approach to law and legal research but only for as long as it does not result in clinical syllogistic reasoning:

> 'As a branch of anthropology, law is an object of science; the theory of legislation is a scientific study, but (...) to reduce the concrete details of an existing system to the merely logical consequence of simple postulates is

23. There is an abundant literature on the effects of the 1968 revolution/revolt on the society in a number of Member States, analysing the pros and cons of the then initiated transformation processes.
24. O.W. Holmes, The Path of Law, Harvard Law Review 1897, 457 (469).
25. C.C. Langdell, A Selection of Cases on the Law of Contracts, 2d. ed. (Boston: Little, Brown, 1879), vii.
26. C.C. Langdell, 'Harvard Celebration Speeches', Law Quartely Review (1887), p. 124.

always in danger of becoming unscientific, and of leading to a misapprehension of the nature of the problem and the data.'[27]

According to Holmes, the 'bad man' serving as a role model for the judiciary does not care for one moment about axioms and deduction but is only interested in what the courts will do in fact. Inspired by Holmes but also by the German Interessenjurisprudenz and Freirechtsschule, Roscoe Pound developed his 'sociological jurisprudence' in the beginning of the 20th century underlining the importance of the societal effects of law and lawmaking, and taking into account the gap that often exists between the law in 'the books and the law in action'.[28]

Pound's instrumentalistic view on law and lawmaking was the starting point for what is now known as American legal realism.[29] Basically, one can say that American legal realists tried to link the indeterminacy of especially judicial lawmaking with the need to draw on extra-legal considerations to resolve disputes. That of course requires multidisciplinary approaches to the study of law in order to be able to build legal decisions on sound knowledge about the sociological, anthropological, economic etc. foundations of society.

All this is just to show that the current debate is certainly not new. It is an old if not an endless debate on the role and function of doctrinal research and how it should be conceived. Moreover, the debate seems to revolve in cycles with periods in which formalism is dominant alternating with periods of attention for the societal and economic relevance of law. Therefore, if doctrinal legal research has ever been dead, it has until today always succeeded in rising from the grave.

4. Today: An Anglo-American or again also a European debate?

Where some have argued in the past that interdisicplinarians often produce such abstract knowledge that it has little relevance for legal practice, those who criticize doctrinal research normally do not claim that this research has no value for legal practice. In fact much of the criticism towards doctrinal legal research appears to be either outdated or lacking a clear focus.

As far as the first point is concerned; almost no doctrinalist still sees legal research as a matter of discovering the divine law that is somewhere out there

27. O.W. Holmes jr., 'Review Langdell casebook', 14 AM. U. L. Rev. 1880, pp. 233-235 (234).
28. Roscoe Pound, Law in Books and Law in Action, 44 AM. L. REV. 12, 15 (1910).
29. V. Nourse and G. Shaffer, Varieties of New Legal Realism: Can A New World Order Prompt a New Legal Theory?, Cornell Law Review, Vol. 95: 61, p. 71 (2009).

waiting to be found in order to provide the one and only right answer to a legal problem.[30] Doctrinal scholarship has definitely moved beyond this.

Regarding the second point, it seems typical that in an overview of the disadvantages of a doctrinal approach in writing a law dissertation by Michael Salter and Julie Mason, the authors count no less than 42 'main objections'.[31] These objections vary from being too close to legal practice, helping to disguise judicial discretion and political manipulation in the law-making process, to becoming out of touch with that same legal practice. The latter, because of not paying enough attention to new developments, such as the major challenges that European integration are posing for law and legal research.

At this point a comparison between legal scholarship in the U.S. and the EU seems in place. In the U.S., judge Harry Edwards started a debate in the early 1990s because he felt that legal scholarship and legal practice were moving in opposite directions.[32] Edwards claimed: 'While the schools are moving toward pure theory, the [law] firms are moving toward pure commerce, and the middle ground – ethical practice – has been deserted by both.'[33] Edwards' provocative article has not remained unchallenged though.[34] In an interesting and equally provocative book with the catchy title

30. In the same sense Michael Pendeleton, Non-empirical Discovery in Legal Scholarship – Choosing, Researching and Writing a Tradtional Scholarly Article, in: Mike McConville and Wing Hong Chui, Research Methods for Law, Edinburgh: Edinburgh University Press 2007, p. 162.
31. Michael Salter and Julie Mason, Writing Law Dissertations, Harlow: Pearson Education Limited 2007, pp. 112-118.
32. H.T. Edwards, The growing disjunction between legal education and the legal profession, Mich. L. Rev. 34 1992-1993, pp. 34-70.
33. Ibid, p. 34.
34. P.D. Reingold, Harry Edwards' Nostalgia, Michigan Law Review, Vol. 91, No. 8 (Aug., 1993), pp. 1998-2009; Richard A. Posner, The Deprofessionalization of Legal Teaching and Scholarship, 91 MICH. L. REV. 1921 (1993) Jack M. Balkin & Sanford Levinson, Legal Historicism and Legal Academics: The Roles of Law Professors in the Wake of Bush v. Gore, 90 GEO. L.J. 173, 176-77 (2001). For Judge Edwards' surrebuttal, see Harry T. Edwards, Another 'Postscript' to 'The Growing Disjunction Between Legal Education and the Legal Profession,' 69 WASH. L. REV. 561, 567 (1994). Later on the debate shifted to the use of empirical methods in assessing judicial decision-making. See Harry T. Edwards, Collegiality and Decision Making on the D.C. Circuit, 84 Va. L. Rev. 1335 (1998) v. Richard L. Revez, Ideology, Collegiality, and the D. C. Circuit: A Reply to Chief Judge Harry T. Edwards, Virginia Law Review Vol. 85, No. 5 (Aug., 1999), pp. 805-851; K.M. Clermont & T. Eisenberg, Judge Harry Edwards: A case In Point, Washington University Law Quarterly, Vol 80: 2002: pp. 1275-1289 responding to Harry T. Edwards & Linda Elliott, Beware of Numbers (and Unsupported Claims of Judicial Bias, 80 WASH. U. L.Q. 723 (2002);

'Saving the constitution from lawyers', Robert J. Spitzer criticizes the fact that most American law students, including the ones who become legal scholars, are still trained as practicing lawyers instead of as academics. Whereas academics examine a problem by collecting information, investigating alternative explanations and testing their assumptions, law students are in the eyes of Spitzer, trained to gather arguments and evidence that support a certain position or focus on a certain desired outcome; they specialize in what he calls the 'art of persuasion'. In the eyes of Spitzer, this 'advocacy scholarship' is not scholarship at all because it lacks the necessary intellectual openness and is not directed towards advancing the body of knowledge. It is about winning a debate.[35]

As we mentioned before, there also appears to be an emerging debate in Europe about the 'true nature' of law as a science and about the consequences for legal scholarship.[36] Until today, however, doctrinal legal research has managed to keep its dominant position both at the national and the European level. We believe this is not necessarily a bad thing as long as it implies that legal scholars in Europe are not cut-off from important developments in legal practice. Nonetheless, in this paper we will argue that as far as some of the most important developments with respect to European integration are concerned, many legal scholars are not asking the right questions simply because they focus too much on EU lawmakers who see European integration as an ongoing process with no horizon and few constitutional limits.

We believe that raising methodological awareness can be an important antidote in the study of European law. It may encourage legal researchers not to limit themselves to recycling what the ECJ or other EU institutions have to say about European law and hence avoid 'Verzwergung der Rechtswissenschaft zur Rechtsprechungskunde'.[37] What is needed in Europe is not a schism between legal practice and legal scholarship or a wig between legal

Harry T. Edwards & Michael A. Livermore, Pitfalls of Empirical Studies that Attempt to Understand the Factors Affecting Appellate Decisionmaking, 58 DUKE L.J. 1895 (2009).

35. Robert. J. Spitzer, Saving the Constitution from Lawyers: How Legal Training and Law Reviews Distort Constitutional Meaning, Cambridge University Press 2008, pp. 29-30.
36. See for example M. Hesselink, A European Legal Method? On European Private Law and Scientific Method, European Law Journal, Vol.15, No. 1, January 2009, pp. 20-45.
37. K. Riesenhuber (Hrsg.) Europaische Methodenlehre: Grundfragen der Methoden des Europaischen Privatrechts, De Gruyter Recht: Berlin 2004, p. 3, 2nd edition Handbuch für Ausbildung und Praxis, 2010.

research and education as, for instance, Martin Scordato claims is taking place in the U.S.:

> 'Thus one can come to appreciate that the shift from a generally accepted formalist paradigm to the current post-realist instrumentalist paradigm has created a subtle but profound separation between the law professor's role as a legal scholar and her role as a law school instructor and service provider to the bar. In the former role, the scholar seeks to understand the nature of law and legal processes and to state what is true as she sees it. In the latter two roles, she is often obliged to abandon the more cynical or radical aspects of her understanding in an effort to help students and practitioners to work effectively within the existing faiths and conventional understandings of the current system.'[38]

II. Coping with the problem

1. Is there something wrong with European legal scholarship?

Taking into account the lessons from the U.S., a methodology debate in Europe should not start with what separates legal scholars from practitioners. It seems more fruitful to start with a debate about what may be the added value of a scholarly legal approach focussing on the development of positive EU law, compared to what EU institutions and legal practitioners think of it. What sort of new ideas, perspectives, theories and methods can legal scholars generate if they do not just follow law and policy makers but think about why EU law is developing as it does?[39]

Interesting questions emerge in that case. What exactly is the relationship between law, legal research and European integration? Why is European legal research so overwhelmingly policy driven? Why are there so many implicit assumptions in scholarly legal publications, such as: harmonization of laws is good and legal diversity is bad, human rights are a blessing for EU law but economic rights are a curse, consulting stakeholders over new EU laws and policies is right but listening to lobbyists is wrong, transparency in

38. Martin Roger Scordato, Reflections on the Nature of Legal Scholarship in the Post-Realist Era, Santa Clara Law Review, Vol. 48 (2008), pp. 353-440 (p. 380).
39. This comes close to the definition of science by the German Constitutional Court that defines science as: 'serious and systematic attempt to gain new insights, 'capable of' external review and criticism, 'and guided by the 'regulative ideal of truth. See BVerfG 35, 79/113 (2004) and BVerfG 90, 1 (13/14).

decision-making is good, secrecy bad, and so on. Is it not an important academic responsibility for legal scholars studying EU law to test these implicit assumptions instead of taking them for granted?

Moreover, where has all the academic tradition gone that led scholarly research and legal scholarship to discuss and reveal the relationship between 'Vorverständnis und Methodenwahl' (preconception and choice of legal methods), as developed by Josef Esser, whose work on this subject has unfortunately never been translated into English or any other language.[40] We think Josef Esser has being paradigmatic for a particular 'Zeitgeist'[41] that questioned the 'apolitical' character of law. He stands for a series of academics worldwide in the late 1960s and early 1970s who highlighted that law and legal systems cannot be disconnected from all sorts of implicit preconceptions that determine ones perspective, including e.g. the prevalence of Western democracy over any other political system, the need to guarantee private property, to secure freedom of contract and maintain personal responsibility. These theorists did not advocate for a particular role that law and the legal function should meet. They left us with a strong message that the 'poet of the tramps' William Henry Davies[42] enshrined in the following:

> 'What is this life if, full of care, We have no time to *stand and stare*, A poor life this, if full of care, We have no time to *stand and stare*' *(emphasis added, RvG/H.-W. M).*

Stand and stare requires self-reflection and self-control of our own premises from where we start our research activities. Methodology can assist in getting a hold of one's own preconceptions, by challenging us to make our implicit (assumptions) explicit, by raising awareness so that we not only look for confirmation of what we (unconsciously) expect to be the outcome of the research, and by warning us to keep an open eye for alternative explanations and counter-evidence.

40. J. Esser, Vorverständnis und Methodenwahl in der Rechtsfindung, 1972.
41. G.W.F. Hegel, Vorlesungen über die Philosophie der Geschichte, Band 18, Frankfurt am Main, 1979.
42. 1871-1940; We borrowed this wonderful metaphor from our colleague Roger Brownsword, who used the poem as a paradigm for what he misses in the current debate on the theoretical foundations of European private law; see R. Browsword/H.-W. Micklitz/L. Niglia/St. Weatherill (eds.) The Foundations of European Private Law, Hart Publishing Oxford, 2011 forthcoming.

2. Herd behaviour and the instrumental use of law

Our hypothesis is that the answer to the suggested theoretical and methodological deficit that unites so much of today's legal scholarship are somehow related to the aforementioned developments that occurred in and around 1968, the year of what the French call a 'revolution', the Germans remember as a Studentenrevolte, and the Dutch associate with the 'opstand van arbeiders en studenten'. The events of May 1968, we think, initiated a change in the way the law was perceived not only in states where a political turmoil led to visible changes, but for Europe and the European Union as a whole. What happened is that legal scholarship, in the slipstream of law- and policymakers, gradually drifted away from a critical 'stand and stare approach' of Esser and others and slowly became more engaged with the idea that law is a political project and a vehicle for social change. For legislatures all over Europe, the latter resulted in a shift from *codification* (capturing in laws what grew bottom up from society) towards *modification* of human and corporate behaviour (legislation as a policy instrument).[43] It soon became clear, though, that it is impossible to steer a highly complex society with a rational central rule approach and detailed instructions.[44] As a consequence, legislatures started to leave the judiciary with more and more discretion by reverting to open texture, legal principles and delegation of lawmaking powers to the executive. Some have even argued that Montesquieu's concept of the *Trias Politica* transformed into a *Duas Politica* in which the executive and the judiciary took over much of the power of the legislature resulting is a more partial and policy-oriented way of lawmaking.[45]

Much has been written about all this, but what has not been researched thoroughly is what the effects of these fundamental changes in lawmaking have been on doctrinal legal scholarship. Since legal research in Europe has always remained close to legal practice, is it not likely that at least some of this policy-orientedness rubbed off on doctrinal legal research? We think this

43. T. Koopmans, De rol van de wetgever, in: Honderd jaar rechtsleven, Nederlandse Juristen-Vereniging, 1870-1970, Zwolle: Tjeenk Willink, 1970, pp. 211-235.
44. H.R. van Gunsteren, The Quest for Control: A Critique of the Rational-Central-Rule Approach in Public Affairs. By Herman R. van Gunsteren, New York: John Wiley & Sons, 1976.
45. M.G. Rood, Heeft de rechter een taak in zogeheten politieke zaken?, Zwolle: Tjeenk Willink 1975, p. 32, A.F.M. Brenninkmeijer, 'De plaats van de rechter in onze constitutionele rechtsorde', in: J.M. Polak e.a., De rechter als dictator? Dynamiek in de trias. Verschuivingen in de verhouding regelgeving, bestuur en rechtspraak, Lochem: Van den Brink & Co 1987, pp. 51-70, T. Koopmans, Courts and Political Institutions, Cambridge University Press 2003, p. 247.

is the case and believe that in particular those scholars studying European law were affected by it because European law had and still has no strong doctrinal roots that could have functioned as a barrier against the ongoing instrumentalization of European integration.

In our analysis we will focus on three stages of this development. We would like to distinguish *integration through law* – the first stage from 1968 until approximately 2002, *integration without law*, since 2002 and *integration beyond law*, spurred by the 2005 French and Dutch 'no' against a European Constitution, which indirectly underlined the role and function of the charter of fundamental rights. All three stages are united in a particular instrumental understanding of law, of legal scholarship and of legal methodology. We will argue that the instrumental perspective dominates all other possible perspectives on the role of EU law.

We have the feeling that the instrumentalization of European law has had important consequences for legal scholarship as well. It stimulated *'herd behaviour'*. This is a well-known phenomenon in behavioural economics.[46] It describes a behaviour, which has first been identified in the Tulipmania in the 17th century.[47] Herd behaviour means in essence that B follows A, although B has information that A might be wrong. C, D, E then follow B, as they mistakenly believe that A and B's decision is based on better or more convincing information than they posses themselves.[48] Herd behaviour also reminds us of the famous parable of the 'Tragedy of the commons' in which Garret Hardin describes the situation in which a pasture is open to all herdsmen of a village. In such a situation what may happen is that herdsmen keep adding cattle to the herd beyond the point of overgrazing. Most of the herdsmen will probably not (want to) notice that point has passed, simply because it still seems profitable to add extra animals, while the growing shortage of food is shared with the rest of the herd.[49] As a result the herdsmen follow each other until finally tragedy takes place.

46. See for example A. Banerjee, 'A Simple Model of Herd Behavior', Quarterly Journal of Economics 107 (3): pp. 797-817 (1992).
47. A. Maurits van der Veen, The Dutch Tulip Mania: The Social Politics of a Financial Bubble, March 2009.
48. Garret Hardin's, Tragedy of the Commons, Science 1968, pp. 1243-1248.
49. Hardin calls this a double P double C game: A privatizing of profits and communizing of costs. See G. Hardin, Filters against Folly. How to survive despite economists, ecologists, and the merely eloquent, Harissonburg/Virginia: Penguin 1985, chapter 10.

For legal scholarship herd behaviour implies that researchers choose to follow 'hot topics' and trends, often initiated by policymakers (e.g. the European Commission) instead of developing their own agendas. What is worse is that they often do it without questioning the preconceptions on which these choices rest and also without realizing the importance of taking an autonomous approach that calls for: justification of the topic choice and for the development of a research design expressing what is new about the research and which methods will be applied. There is an endless list of dissertations, books, articles, etc., which simply follow mainstream ideas and ideologies, often developed by policymakers or judges, without questioning these. In many cases the authors do not even bother to explain on whose shoulders they stand, where they deviate from fellow researchers or from mainstream beliefs in practice or, more in general, to what extent they add something to the body of knowledge. Think of e.g. the current conflict around the scope of anti-discrimination rules. The European Union heavily contributed to making anti-discrimination one of its – perhaps even *the* – 'guiding' principle in which a genuine European dimension comes clear that reaches beyond its application in the Member States.[50] A conservative reading of the anti-discrimination principle tends to reduce its scope of application in order to keep the private legal order free from a concept, which is said to be alien to the idea that contracting partners can freely choose the contracting partner, whatever the motives and reasons behind the choice might be.[51]

What many scholars tend to forget is that in this example one can also follow the opposite reform-oriented approach in order to defend that the boundaries of the anti-discrimination principle should be stretched to submit private law issues to its application. Otherwise the protection against, for example unequal treatment on the basis of sex by insurance companies, which was recently at stake in case C-236/09 of the ECJ, would come to depend solely on the accidental private or public status of in this case the insurer.[52] One may cast doubts whether this is still justifiable in a context of increasing liberalization of markets and privatization of former public services. Unfortunately, these sorts of questions are usually not brought to the foreground.

50. D. Kennedy, Three Globalisations, where he demonstrates that the nation states exempted family law from the scope of application of the anti-discrimination principle. It was for the European Union to enlarge the principle and to penetrate via citizen rights into national family law regimes.
51. See e.g. J. Basedow, Grundsatz der Nichtdiskriminierung ZEuP 2008, 230; F.-J. Säcker, Vertragsfreiheit und Schutz vor Diskriminierung, ZEuP 2006, 1.
52. AG Kokott, 30.9.2010, ECJ, Case C-236/09 – Test Achats, nyr.

An important lesson for legal scholarship in this case is that one may sympathize with either position depending on our preconceptions and political preferences. What Josef Esser had in mind, however, even reaches beyond this. He was concerned with the question behind the question. Is discrimination really always bad? Do we not also need discrimination, for example, in order to stimulate competition?[53] What exactly constitutes discrimination (is age for example a relevant criterion since we are all aging?), and can law really impose anti-discrimination on deeply rooted social behaviour or can it only deal with some of the symptoms of unequal treatment that appear at the surface of the legal system?

The identification of herd behaviour does not entail that all researchers are constantly running in the same direction. There are, and always have been, exceptional researchers that do not follow the herd. We have already argued that the need for (further) harmonization of national laws and policies is often an implicit assumption in the work of those writing about European law ('harmonization is good, diversity is bad'). There are nevertheless scholars that explicitly stood back in order to stare at why so many others believe in harmonization so strongly and on what evidence they base their ideas that harmonization is in the general interest.

Katherina Sideri[54] and James Scott[55] stand for a methodological approach toward lawmaking that, if taken seriously, raises serious questions with respect to legislative policies that call for full harmonization in certain fields of EU law. Sideri's argument is that instead of top down harmonization in the EU we often need to start more bottom up and try to link EU policy to local practice. The same argument has been made earlier by sociologist James Scott. He has shown that most legal systems working with blue print plans and unification models, such as the former USSR, have dramatically failed in the end because they neglect the importance of 'Metis'. This is a type of knowledge that cannot be reduced to formulaic instructions. The word contrasts with the Greek word 'techne', which describes that knowledge and practice that 'may be logically derived from initial assumptions.'

53. In sports, for example, we do discriminate on the basis of sex on many occasions in order to make sure that men and women have their own competition in order not to discourage the members of the different groups. We even discriminate on many occasions in terms of payment between male and female athletes.
54. Law's Practical Wisdom, the Theory of Law Making in the New Governance Structures of the European Union, Ashgate Farnham, 2007.
55. Seeing it Like a State: How Certain Schemes to Improve the Human Condition Have Failed, New Haven, Yale University Press, 1998.

We are not afraid that legal scholars following their own intuitions and interests are on the verge of becoming extinct. What worries us more is that there is a risk that those who do not want to follow a herd will nevertheless focus on policy-driven research because they feel pressured (by research foundations, faculty managers, publishers, and so on) to justify and explain why they are not ready to accept the overwhelming wisdom that law and hence legal research should have societal relevance. We refer to the current emphasis on 'valorization', on research programming, on matched funding of contract research, and more in general by the strong emphasis on the transfer of knowledge from one party (scholars) to another (business or government) for economic purposes (e.g. the direct link in the Seventh framework programme of the EC with the Lisbon agenda of becoming the most competitive economy in the world).[56]

We do not want to argue that herd behaviour is necessarily and automatically wrong. There might be good and valid reasons why the instrumental use of law is justified in many situations. However, the inherent preconceptions and the reasons lying behind such an assumption have to be disclosed. After all, the history of science shows that 'opting out', 'swimming against the tide', and 'picking the fruits of serendipity' have often resulted in a much deeper knowledge than much of the pre-programmed research that we can see today everywhere around us.

3. Integration through law

We would like to repeat here that there probably is an ideological link between the French revolution and the German student revolt in 1968 and the adoption of the Single European Act in 1986.

1968 constitutes the break-even point in the European post war society, the year that became the start of a new era, a post war society, driven by a new generation that expected from the nation state more than securing a flourishing economy. It demanded from the state the establishment of a just society.[57] The May revolution also triggered a debate on the role and function of law and legal scholarship. In retrospect it seems as if the clock was turned backwards. Once again, the formalist character of (doctrinal) legal scholarship was attacked. And again Julius von Kirchmann,[58] Rudolf von Jhering,[59]

56. See: http://cordis.europa.eu/fp7/understand_en.html.
57. At least this is what could be regarded as a common denominator for France and Germany.
58. Ibid.

Max Weber[60] and the Freirechtsschule[61] served as witnesses for considering the societal role and function of law afresh.

Law, was the overall message, should serve to redistribute wealth, to domesticize economic power and to secure liberty and justice for the weakest in society. Interestingly enough, this message united critical legal thought in Europe and the U.S.[62] Legal scholarship was expected to take a political stance, legal scholarship should stand up for using the legal system for the transformation of the society. 1968 nourished the welfare state and F. Scharpf coined the term of the social-democratization of Member States, whatever their political regime looked like.[63] There is a strong ideological link in the instrumental use of law to transform the Member States' legal order in the aftermath of 1968 and the 1986 EU project to establish the Internal Market.[64] What is sometimes forgotten nowadays is that the establishment of this market was also a gigantic regulatory project. Around 300 directives and regulations should be and were adopted in about five years with the aim to create a market without frontiers. The focus laid on rules meant to guarantee access to the European market. Distributive justice was certainly not the main concern of the inventors of the single market, but completion of this market opened the door for the EU to formulate minimum standards for social protection.[65] Part of the ideological link between 1968 and 1986 lies in the fact that never before in the history of the EU has the law been so systematically used for a particular instrumental purpose; as a means to an end. In other words, there was no market without EU law and, at the same time, the most visible representation of this European market was a set of laws.

Based on the ground prepared by the ECJ in transforming an international treaty into a constitutional charter – integration should be achieved through

59. Der Kampf ums Recht, in alluding to Darwin; see Wieacker, Privatrechtsgeschichte der Neuzeit, 2. neubearbeitete Auflage, 1967, p. 566.
60. Wirtschaft und Gesellschaft. Grundriß der verstehenden Soziologie, 1922.
61. Herrmann Kantorowicz, Der Kampf um die Rechtswissenschaft (unter dem Pseudonym Gnaeus Flavius), 1906
62. Ch. Joerges/D. Trubek (eds.), Critical Legal Thought, 1988. In the U.S. it led to the birth of the Critical legal studies movement. See about CLS: Mark Tushnet, 'Critical Legal Studies: A Political History', Yale Law Journal 100 (1991): pp. 1515-244.
63. F.W. Scharpf, Crisis and Social Democracy in Europe, translated by R. Crowley and F. Thompsen, Ithaca, Cornell University Press, 1991.
64. COM (1985) 310 final.
65. H. Micklitz argued elsewhere that the EU strives for a model of access justice – Zugangsgerechtigkeit, which differs from social distributive justice; see Social Justice and Access Justice in Private Law, EUI Working Paper 2011, forthcoming.

legal means.[66] After 1986 legal scholars turned into co-drafters of the new Internal Market law. In the 1980s and 1990s the European Commission has benefited tremendously from the leeway in the academic research agenda. A close community, an alliance even, between the European Commission and Euro-friendly academics was constituted, and back then the tendering of research projects seldom took place. The envisaged social outlook of the, until then, very much market-based European legal policy facilitated close cooperation. It made EU legal research attractive for 'soixante-huitard' scholars with social reform ambitions from all over Europe.

Meanwhile, the European Commission became one the most important sponsors of policy-driven research as we can witness today in the large European research programmes, such as ESF and KP7. The Member States themselves facilitated this by delegating not only lawmaking competences but also a lot of legal research to the EU. The foundation of the EUI in Florence, with which we as authors of this paper both have close ties, is perhaps the most visible proof of the transfer of research(ers) from the Member States to the EU. Each year around 50 young law students from the Member States start their career there as a PhD or LLM. After completing their projects they spread all over Europe again often ending up in leading positions in business and academia in which European law plays an important role.

An important by-product of 1986 was the increase in status of European law and legal research. Using *Sen*[67] we can speak of a certain hegemony of law over other sciences. Lawyers were omnipresent in the European Commission, law making was high on the agenda, and European legal scholarship was on its peak. Unfortunately though, a price had to be paid for all this. What we have witnessed is a shift from fundamental to applied research, from fully independent research to more hybrid forms of contract research where contractors set the agenda, and from sponsoring of research on the basis of trust and confidence towards tendering and competition. Moreover, research projects were not given to European academia by policymakers in order to learn that their targets could not be reached. The research question was 'how', not 'if'. Whatever the sub-categories might have been, all forces were directed to one major goal – completion of the Internal Market. We do not want to suggest some sort of conspiracy here. The intentions may have been

66. See the research project undertaken at the EUI in Florence, 'Integration Through Law', M. Cappelletti, M. Seccombe & J. Weiler (eds), Berlin-New York: Walter de Gruyter, 1986.
67. Amartya Sen, The Idea of Justice, Cambridge, Mass.: Belknap Press/Harvard University Press, 2009.

sincere; however, we are arguing that the Internal Market project created a particular research spirit, one where the instrumental use of law and the legal system dominated over any other possible objective. 'Stand and stare' was certainly not the credo Europe offered to its scholars. The outcome of the integration process was fixed in the sense that being very critical towards the integration process was an unwelcome message. Perhaps this is also part of the reason why groundbreaking research projects undertaken in the 1990s were executed outside Europe, mainly in the U.S.[68]

4. Integration without law

After completion of the Internal Market, the European Commission had to monitor the implementation process at the Member State level. Moreover, the newly adopted over 300 EU laws needed to be enforced. It is in this context that the notion of multi-level governance arose. It required a thorough management of who should be responsible for what in the Internal Market or European polity.[69] The most visible sign of the changing paradigm was the White Paper on Governance adopted in 2002.[70]

We will not argue that the Internal Market programme yielded 'European Governance'. Indeed, one might even claim that both concepts emerged more or less simultaneously and that European governance has deeper and older roots (see e.g. hereafter the so-called 'New approach') than the White Paper suggests. What is relevant here is the structural deficit in the capacity of the EU to promulgate rules and its lack of capacity and competence to enforce them.[71] As the Commission originally held executive power only in the fields

68. The most striking evidence is the research project run by M. Cappelletti, who was a professor at Stanford Law School and the EUI in Florence, who designed the project and J.H.H. Weiler, today Professor at NYU, who joined and who shaped the project which until today stands a landmark in the research landscape. See 'Integration Through Law', M. Cappelletti, M. Seccombe & J. Weiler (eds), Vol. 1, Book 1, Berlin-New York: Walter de Gruyter, 1986.
69. W. van Gerven, The European Union: A Polity of States and People, Hart Publishing: Oxford 2005.
70. European Governance, COM(2001) 428 final.
71. There is considerable discussion of the roots within the doctrine; see Ch. Joerges/M. Everson u.a., The European Turn to Governance and unanswered Questions of Legitimacy: Two Examples and Counterintuitive Suggestions, in Ch. Joerges/B. Strath/P. Wagner (Hrsg.), The Economy as Polity: The Political Constitution of Contemporary Capitalism, 2005, p. 159; O. de Schutter, The implementation of fundamental rights through the open method of co-ordination, in O. de Schutter/S. Deakin (eds.), Social rights and market forces: is the open method of co-ordination of em-

of competition and agricultural policy, it is not surprising that it was here that the idea was born to establish committees uniting the expertise of national and EC officials.[72] From the midst 1980s onwards, one might therefore identify a growing awareness of the European Commission to use and to test regulatory techniques which are not just copying national instrumental laws, but introduce new modes of law-making and enforcement which fit into the category of multi-level governance. The 1984 New Approach to Technical Standards and Regulations eventually led to the adoption of 'comitology' in 1987.[73] The former document and its interplay with comitology are paradigmatic in the coming together of Internal Market policy and what was later termed 'governance'. The New Approach and 'comitology' served as a blueprint for similar concepts, the 2001 Lamfalussy procedure, the Open Method of Co-ordination (OMC) launched in 2000 and last but not least co-regulation in 2002. The Lamfalussy procedure established a four-step law-making and law enforcement mechanism in the field of financial services, which combines binding European standard-making at the first two levels and non-binding rule-making at the third level via national regulatory agencies, which must enforce the rules as well.[74] Completion of the Internal Market yielded a paradigm shift in EU law-making in order to overcome a number of negative side effects of globalization. Especially the Lisbon Council promoted inter alia *social inclusion* as a means to compensate those citizens, workers, consumers who are not able to meet the challenges resulting from a globalizing economy and run the risk to be cut off from the labour market and the consumer market. Social exclusion, this is the overall message, shall be overcome. So the transition from the Internal Market to globalization yielded the need to respond to social concerns and was an important driving force behind the introduction of the European social model.

The European social model is supposed to form a solid basis for the transformation of the EU into a knowledge economy. However, national legal systems also need to be adapted as part of an active welfare state to ensure that work pays, to secure long-term sustainability in the face of an ageing population, to promote social inclusion and gender equality, and to provide quality health services. More specific with regard to the information society, differ-

ployment and social rights the future of social Europe?, 2005, p. 279; M. Dawson, The OMC and the European Economic Constitution, 2007, PhD EUI Florence.

72. E. Vos, The rise of committees, (1997) 3 European Law Journal, p. 211.
73. Directive 99/468/EC, OJ L 184, 17.7.1999, 23.
74. Th. M.J. Möllers, Lamfalussy-Verfahren und Europäisches Wirtschaftsrecht, ZEuP 2008, 480.

ent means of access must prevent from info-exclusion. The combat against illiteracy must be reinforced. Special attention must be given to disabled people.[75]

Especially the OMC and the 'Social dialogue'[76] operate in those areas of social policy, where the European Union has no competences. National governments remain the key actors, able to control the process. In particular the OMC does not produce binding results and exclusion of the ECJ was vital for its establishment. There is now a rich academic debate on the success or failure of the OMC, on the practical effects, on the role and function of Member States, the European Commission and on the NGOs, and on the impact on European integration.[77]

For the community of legal scholars throughout Europe, however, all these attempts remained for a long time widely unnoticed, as they took place in rather remote areas of EU law and did not (yet) reach the higher level of a more general debate on implementation and enforcement. All this changed after the launch of the 2002 White Paper on Governance. It changed not only the political landscape, but also reshaped the research agenda.

Governance led to a far-reaching politicization of law-making and enforcement, politicization here being understood as circumventing or overruling 'law' as the decisive means for shaping the European integration process. Traditional legislation became less popular to the advantage of self-regulation,[78] co-regulation[79] and other 'new' modes of governance.[80] And

75. At p. 3.
76. The European social dialogue refers to discussions, consultations, negotiations and joint actions involving organizations representing the two sides of industry (employers and workers). It takes two main forms – a tripartite dialogue involving the public authorities, and a bipartite dialogue between the European employers and trade union organizations. It has resulted in over 300 joint texts by the European social partners, which are included in a database.
77. For an overview of the arguments, M. Dawson, 2009. For a critical account, see in particular D. Trubek & L. Trubek, Hard and Soft Law in the Construction of Social Europe: the Role of the Open Method of Co-ordination, European Law Journal 11 (2005), p. 343.
78. F. Cafaggi (ed.) Reframing self-regulation in European private law, 2006.
79. A. Héritier/S. Eckert, New modes of governance in the shadow of hierarchy: self-regulation by industry in Europe, RSCAS 2007/20.
80. Colin Scott has argued that many of the new modes of governance are not really new and as far as they are new, they are often not all that innovative; 'Governing Without Law or Governing Without Government? New-ish Governance and the Legitimacy of the EU'. European Law Journal, 15 (2):160; see more comprehensively F. Cafaggi/H.

politics and political scientists 'replaced' law and lawyers in many of these new areas. Legislative studies (Gesetzgebungslehre), once dominated by jurists/public lawyers, lost terrain to new disciplines, such as regulation and governance,[81] where political scientists now rule the game.[82] New sub-fields emerged, such as risk regulation, ICT-regulation, energy and transport regulation, and so on. What all these fields have in common is that, as far as law still plays a role, doctrinal legal research is usually replaced by multidisciplinary law and ... approaches requiring different methods and theories.

'Integration through law' of course did not come to an end, but as the dominant paradigm it was replaced by 'integration without law'.[83] Political scientists were upgraded and lawyers were downgraded. That this has repercussions also for legal practice can be demonstrated by referring to the involvement of political scientists in the law-making process. A key element of the 2002 White Paper on Governance is the better-regulation programme.[84] An important part of this programme is the introduction of ex ante evaluation and impact assessments, which should forestall the adoption of new rules. Impact assessments are in practice often executed by political scientists (or economists), lawyers play an auxiliary role only. Their competence is needed to fill in templates designed by political scientists and economists. Also the task of the legal service of the European Commission in the legislative drafting process is changing more and more into a role of offering technical-legal assistance.

From the late 1990s onwards, legal scholarship was also faced with the theoretical implications of integration without law. The new modes of governance raise first and foremost a problem of legitimacy. How can the drift away from established law-making procedures, from traditional sets of regulatory instruments, from hard judicial and/or administrative enforcement to

Muir Watt (eds.), Making of European Private Law: Governance Design, 2008; F. Cafaggi/H. Muir Watt (eds.), The regulatory functions of European private law, 2009

81. See the journal Regulation & Governance that mentions political scientist as its first target group.
82. See for example the ECPR standing group on regulatory governance: http://regulation.upf.edu/.
83. Ch. Joerges, Integration durch Entrechtlichung? Ein Zwischenruf, ZERP-Diskussions-papier 1/2007.
84. S. Weatherill, Better regulation, Oxford, Hart, 2007.
84. There is a huge academic debate in this area; see more generally Weimar, 2007 as well as various publications from Joerges, inter alia with Everson, in Joerges/Strath/Wagner (eds.), 2005, pp. 159 et seq. and on the legitimacy of soft law, L. Senden, Soft Law in European Community Law, 2006.

softer forms be given democratic legitimacy? The normative side of this academic debate is whether governance may only be democratically legitimated if basic procedural requirements, such as transparency, participation and accountability, are safeguarded and if the enforceability of these parameters is secured via individual or collective rights.[85]

These are of course all interesting and highly relevant questions, but where is the legal research about what all this means for the development of positive law? What happens for example as soon as parties disagree on the interpretation of codes of conducts, certification schemes, covenants or other hybrid forms of governance? What 'rule of recognition' should the EJC adopt in order to determine if and when these rules are (ir)relevant for the legal system? Or what is (or will be) the function of impact assessments, Internet consultations, and other better regulation tools for the ECJ in the interpretation of directives and regulations once a conflict arises about how EU law has to be applied or enforced?[86] At the beginning of the new millennium, integration without law dominated not only legal practice but also legal scholarship. If and as far as lawyers embarked on topics related to regulation and governance, they were faced with the methodological problems and the theoretical approaches in political science. Again we can witness herd behaviour. Legal scholarship silently shifted its focus, without much resistance. Unfortunately, little has been written on the relationship between law and political science,[87] about why the shift occurred, what the possible methodological implications resulting there from are, whether the quality of multidisciplinary research has suffered from translation problems between different disciplinary approaches.

5. Integration beyond law

Integration through law and integration without law are in a way self-explanatory. Integration beyond law deserves a deeper investigation. It is only against this background that the tendency towards herd behaviour in EU-legal

85. This is the argument Hans-W. Micklitz made in 'The Politics of Judicial Co-operation', p. 479 et seq.
86. See A.C.M. Meuwese, Impact assessment in EU Lawmaking, Alphen a/d Rijn: Kluwer Law International, 2008, and A. Alemanno, The Better regulation initiative at the judicial gate: A trojan horse within the Commission's walls or the way forward?, European Law Journal 2009, Vol. 15, nr. 3, p. 396 versus R. Munday, In the wake of 'good governance': impact assessments and the politicisiation of statutory interpretation', Modern Law Review 2008, nr. 3, pp. 385-412.
87. But see K.J. Alter/R. Dehousse/G. Vanberg, Law, Political Science and EU Legal Studies: An interdisciplinary Project? European Union Politics 2002, p. 113.

scholarship and the impact of integration beyond law on legal methodology become clearer.

We are referring here to the current state of EU law, EU methodology and EU legal scholarship. The lacking distance makes it more difficult to so clearly structure mainstream thinking. However, we would identify two developments emerging from the idea of 'integration beyond law'. First, there is the efficiency paradigm dating back to the Lisbon declaration in 2000. Second, we have seen a paradoxical acceleration of the constitutionalization process in the aftermath of the 2005 French and Dutch 'no' to the EU Constitution. Where one would expect EU institutions, such as the ECJ, to be more careful and reserved in their lawmaking ambitions, almost the opposite seems the case; the credo appears to be: 'full speed ahead' with the integration process and with the constitutionalization of EU law with or without a formal constitution.

Why then 'integration beyond law'? Where is the 'beyond'? Or hypothesis is that the current integration paradigm can no longer be associated to one dominant ideology. It is the combination of the aim to become 'the most competitive and most dynamic knowledge-based economy' in the world, as formulated in the Lisbon agenda, with the need to redress the negative consequences of globalization that stamp the European integration process. Constitutionalization beyond the borders of the Lisbon treaty ('creeping constitutionalization')[88] will probably be necessary to guide the future integration process, which has no clear border or horizon. Constitutionalization turns into a substitute for a formal constitution. Fundamental and human rights, to be located somewhere in between 'law' and 'politics' have already gained and may gain an ever stronger impetus, legally and politically (ideologically). We believe to observe that the current trend in legal scholarship may be caught in the paradigm of integration beyond law that enshrines the main stream paradigms of 'efficiency in law' and 'constitutionalization through fundamental and human rights', and that poses new challenges to the methodology of law.

Let us begin with the first strain. The efficiency doctrine is linked to what might be called the economization of European law, a process that started with the ECJ using the market freedoms to build a European legal order separate and distinct from the national orders. Economization of the legal order has found its most prominent expression in the concept of the European Eco-

88. G. Teubner, Constitutionalism and transnational governance, in: Christian Joerges, Inge-Johanne Sand and Gunther Teubner, eds., Oxford Press, pp. 3-28, 2004.

nomic Constitution, a concept borrowed from post-war Germany.[89] A strong competition law should shield the private law society (Privatrechtsgesellschaft) against regulatory intrusion guided by various policy purposes, be they industrial, social or environmental policies. The concept of a European Economic Constitution introduced economic theory into the way in which law should be used in the European integration process, here in down-grading regulatory law but likewise requesting strong legal rules to guarantee market freedoms and freedom of contract. However, the introduction of economics into the European integration process may unfold various effects on the role and function of law in the integration process. Economics may strengthen the role of law, but economics may also undermine the role of law. There is a hidden link between ordo-liberalism requesting a tight legal frame and law & economics putting the role and function of law into question (Posner), which definitely deserves more attention. Ordo-liberalims opens the floodgate for economics into law. Seen this way the Internal Market Programme, in combination with various Treaty amendments, turned law into a regulatory tool, not to 'shield' the private law society but to 'shape' private law society. The underpinning economic ideology enshrined in the Internal Market programme was the suggested set of market failures of a 'Common Market' that could not further European integration and that could not yield the necessary social dimension. The concept of the European Economic Constitution outlasted the regulatory wave in the aftermath of the Internal Market programme, in a somewhat revised form though. But the story of economization went on, though in a new form. Law and regulation became subject to one major ideology – economic efficiency. Here law is not upgraded, but submitted to a yardstick, one which fits to the law & economics type of thinking. Here is the gate through which the herd of law & economics lawyers could enter the backyard of (European) law.

The 2000 Lisbon Council declaration, although not an official legally binding document, heavily affected the spirit of the law-making process in the EU, in its content and its procedure. Despite its soft character the Lisbon Council 2000 must be regarded as the backbone of the economic efficiency doctrine till today, at least the one which is favoured and advocated for by the European Commission, while traces of it can also be found in the case law of

89. D. Gerber, Constitutionalising the Economy: German Neo-Liberalism, Competition Law and the 'New' Europe, AJCL 1994, p. 25.

the ECJ.[90] In the presidential conclusion of the Lisbon Council decision we may find the following statement:

> 'An effective framework review and improvement based on the Internal Market Strategy endorsed by the Helsinki Council, is essential if the full benefits of market liberalization *are to be reaped* (emphasis added). Moreover, fair and uniformly applied competition and state aid rules are essential for ensuring that business can thrive and operative effectively on a level playing field in the internal market.' [91]

The so-called 'new economic approach' (state aid,[92] competition[93] and consumer contracts[94]) could have been understood as a revival and reinvigoration of the Internal Market programme, though in light of the 21st century[95] it has taken on a slightly different connotation. In short, the European Commission shapes[96] *industrial* policy through state aid law, competition law and consumer law, to mention just a number of key areas.[97] The downgrading of competition policy raised much concern with German academics who fear for

90. St. Smismans, From Harmonisation to coordination? EU law in the Lisbon governance architecture, Journal of European Public Policy forthcoming.
91. At p. 5.
92. See Kroes, Commissioner for Competition Policy, The refined economic approach in state aid law: a policy perspective, 21st September 2006.
93. H. Ulrich (ed.), The Evolution of European Competition Law, 2006.
94. The very same thinking may be found in COM (2006) 744 final, Review of the Consumer Acquis; see Micklitz, Der gemeinschaftsrechtliche Verbraucherschutz-Acquis. Rechtspolitischer Überblick und Zukunftsperspektiven, in Wagner/Wedl, Bilanz und Perspektiven zum europäischen Recht, Nachdenkschrift anlässlich 50 Jahre Römische Verträge, 2007, pp. 293-323; first condensed in the Draft on Consumer Rights COM (2008) 614 final, thereto H.-W. Micklitz/N. Reich, Crónica de una Muerte Anunciada: The Commission Proposal for a Directive on Consumer Rights, CMLR 46 (2009) 471-519; see for broader perspective K. Soper/F. Trentmann (eds.), Citizenship and Consumption, 2008. The EU is about to adopt the Consumer Rights Directive, but limited to a revision of the Directive 85/577/EEC on doorstep selling and Directive 97/7/EC on distant selling.
95. COM (2007) 724 final, 20.11.2007.
96. A prominent candidate is certainly the field of regulated markets; see H.-W. Micklitz, The Visible Hand of European Private Law, in Yearbook of European Law 2009, volume 28, P. Eeckhout/T. Tridimas (eds.), 2010, p. 3.
97. One could easily think of other policy areas, such as environmental policy, where the European Commission uses emission standards to urge the German car industry to engage in the production of small cars.

the European Economic Constitution.[98] Tied to the efficiency doctrine, it seems as if these fears are justified to a certain extent.

A new initiative of the European Commissioner for industry and entrepreneurship to submit draft laws to an EU competivity test fits all too well into such a perspective.[99] Here it is not the law providing a framework for competition, but competition setting the boundaries for law(s). Another visible expression of the new economic approach is the much-favoured concept of full harmonization. Full harmonization is claimed to increase economic efficiency. Consumer law here stands at the forefront of the debate and may serve as an example of paradigmatic importance:[100]

> 'The Green Paper on Consumer Protection (COM 2001 531 final) set out options for the further harmonization of rules on commercial practices, either on a case-by-case basis or supplementing this through framework legislation. There is also a need to review and reform existing EU consumer protection directives, to bring them up to date and progressively adapt them from minimum harmonization to 'full harmonization' measures. The Green Paper and the Commission's strategy on services (2000 888) make it clear that the simple application of mutual recognition, without harmonization, is not likely to be appropriate for such consumer protection issues. However, provided a sufficient degree of harmonization is achieved, the country of origin approach could be applied to remaining questions'.

The incriminated draft on consumer rights is written within the spirit of the Lisbon Council, of shifting regulation from minimum to maximum harmonization, of increasing economic efficiency of consumer protection to the benefit of traders and service providers. This vision might fail, but what remains is the powerful attempt to submit a particular area of European policy, which is said to represent the social dimension of the Internal Market, to the dominance of economic efficiency. A similar type of thinking might be found in the discussion around the European Civil Code. The solution the European

98. J. Drexl, Wettbewerbsverfassung, in: von Bogdandy, Armin/Jürgen Bast (Hrsg.): Europäisches Verfassungsrecht, 2. Aufl. Dordrecht etc., Springer, 2009, p. 905.
99. http://www.europeanvoice.com/article/imported/draft-laws-to-be-put-to-eu-competitivity-test/69238.aspx
100. OJ C 137, 8.6.2002, 2.

Commission seems to have in mind should and must meet the efficiency rhetoric.[101]

The increasing importance of economic efficiency led to major changes in legal scholarship and legal research in European law. Europe legal scholarship seen as whole has been relatively reluctant to integrate law and economics into its research design, at least until recently. It is fair to assume that contrary to the United States, law and economics does not represent the mainstream thinking in European scholarly research. The inner reason might indeed be that legal doctrine in Europe is traditionally much deeper anchored in legal science and scholarly research than in the United States.[102] However, here again the wind seems to change. The European Commission is shifting the focus more and more to using law and economics type of thinking for shaping and testing the feasibility of European rule making. Even the DCFR has been submitted to a 'economic efficiency test'.[103] And again the academic herd seems to follows suit. Today good scholarly research often seems to require familiarity with law & economics. This is particularly true whenever information or tort turn up as potential regulatory tools. Whilst there is nothing to criticize here, as legal scholars have to be acquainted with mainstream thinking, the basic assumptions of law and economics, the theoretical preconceptions behind this major strain in legal scholarship today, often remain unscrutinised.[104]

The second current mainstream results from the constitutionalization process. On the surface there is a link between the increasing attention given to new forms of governance in the EU, the initial project to adopt a European Constitution and the ever stronger drift towards constitutionalization via fundamental and human rights. One might even wonder whether the human rights' rhetoric must also be regarded as a late heritage of the 1968 revolt/revolution. Looking back, fundamental rights and human rights have gained ground in scholarly legal research in the last decades. Today they begin to dominate legal scholarship in whatever area of the law, including pri-

101. See Website of DG Justice on the expert committee that is currently reviewing the DCFR http://ec.europa.eu/justice/policies/consumer/policies_consumer_intro_en.htm
102. K. Grechenig/M. Gelter, Divergente Evolution des Rechtsdenkens – Von amerikanischer Rechtsökonomik und deutscher Dogmatik, RabelsZ 72 (2008), p. 513.
103. See G. Wagner (ed), The Common Frame of Reference, A View from Law and Economics, 2009.
104. But see E.J. Mestmäcker, A Legal Theory without Law, Posner v. Hayek on Economic Analysis of Law, 2007. One might wonder whether the question to be raised should not be whether law and economics is downgraded in practices to an economic instrument without legal theory behind.

vate law which in the ordo-liberal thinking should be kept separate from the constitutional order.[105]

Let us roughly reconstruct the European constitutionalization from scratch. The ECJ started speaking of a constitutional charter in Les Verts in 1986.[106] However, it never used the word Constitution with a big 'C'.[107] The White Paper on Governance enhanced a scholarly debate on how the constitutionalization process should and might look like. L. Azoulai[108] distinguished four forms of constitutionalization: 1) federalization, 2) multipluralism, 3) conflictual constitutionalization and 4) dualistic constitutionalization in an attempt to structure the current debate. K. Tuori uses the metaphor of the many constitutions of Europe very much in line with constitutional pluralism but going beyond that debate in looking in the substance of the different constitutions, e.g. the political, the economic and the social constitution. The big 'C' was introduced via the political debate in the constitutional assembly.

The 'failure' of the Constitution deprives us of the need to discuss whether the project could be regarded as a constitution at all. What remains, however, and what seems to be the most important outcome of the Treaty of Lisbon is the integration of the Charter of Fundamental Rights into the European legal order. Secondary community law will now have to be tested whether it complies with fundamental rights. The opinion of the Advocate General Kokott[109] sheds light on the potential of the Charter. It is not difficult to predict that the academic attention will focus on the constitutionalization process, in its various forms and its potential impact on the legal system per se.

The fundamental rights are dominating and will dominate scholarly research. Just like economic efficiency human rights issue are omnipresent to-

105. E.J. Mestmäcker, E. Böhm, Canaris, and the recent research in Constitutionalisation of Private Law, Cherednychenko, Fundament Rights, Contract Law and the Protection of the Weaker Party, A Comparative Analysis of the Constitutionalisation of the Contract Law with Emphasis on Risky Financial Transactions, 2008; Ch. Mak, Fundamental Rights in European Contract Law, A Comparision of the Impact of Fundamental Rights on Contractual Relationships in Germany, the Netherlands, Italy and England, 2008; A. C. Ciachhi/G. Brüggemeier/G. Commandé (eds.), Fundamental Rights and Private Law in the European Union, Volume I and II, Comparative Analysis of Selected Case Patterns, Cambridge University Press 2010.
106. ECJ, 26.9.1984, Case 294/83 [1986] ECR 1339 at 23
107. N. Walker, Big 'C' or small 'c', ELJ 2006, 12.
108. Intégration juridique et légitimité, in L. Fontaine (dir.), *Droit et légitimité*, collection 'Droit et justice', Bruylant, Bruxelles, forthcoming.
109. AG Kokott, 30.9.2010, ECJ, Case C-236/09 – Test Achats, nyr.

day in scholarly research. Good scholarly research is hardly unthinkable without giving due account to the human rights dimension. The situation resembles to the economic efficiency doctrine. Whilst there is little to say against such a pressure on the scope of scholarly research, a lot has to be said on the sometimes even unreflected instrumentalization of human rights. Scholarly research turns on the question whether this and that 'right' should and must be understood as a subjective enforceable right – and not be left in the realms to politics – and once the existence of a right has to be identified – how far the newly established human or fundamental right can be stretched. What is missing is a deeper reflection of the role and function of human rights and fundamental rights in a European legal order, and not in the European legal order alone.[110]

6. An interim remark

The analysis of herd behaviour in European legal scholarship should be understood as a lesson on how legal scholarship might be caught in one major understanding of how the law can be used for all sorts of social, political and economic purposes. It is the blatant and unquestioned instrumentalization of law over the last decades in whatever form which raises our concern as legal scholars. The instrumental use of law as a means to shape the European integration process has left deep traces in legal scholarship and in legal methodology. The solution is not to return to the past, to set aside the instrumental use of law and to understand law as a formal system that should not be inflicted with politics and economics, a system that stands on its own, disconnected and a-political. The 1968-1986 paradigm taught us the political character of the law, in both directions, as a means to transform and change society or as a means to preserve and conserve society. Whilst the 1968 'revolution' started a process in scholarly legal research to disclose ideological preconceptions, it has itself triggered a new ideology, one which first overstretched the belief in 'law' and then 'undermined' the belief in law. The instrumental use of law yielded the need for legal methods that could cope with the law and ... disciplines, be they law and politics, or law and economics, just to mention those which had the major impact on European scholarly research. Much, maybe too much emphasis has been put on the law and ... disciplines, on the somewhat helpless search for a legal method, which allows

110. There are exceptions to the rule. A. Sen, Elements of a Theory on Human Rights, Philosophy and Public Affairs, 2004, 315; H. Collins, The Constitutionalisation of Private Law as a Path to Social Justice in H.-W. Micklitz (ed.), The Many Faces of Social Justice in Private Law, Elgar, forthcoming.

for the integration of non-legal disciplines into the legal system.[111] What has gone somewhat lost in the overall mainstream is the role and function of legal doctrine. The second part of the paper is meant to analyse how legal doctrine might be revitalized against the backdrop of the law and disciplines.

III. Ways out

1. The role and function of legal methods

1.1. Why methods: globalization and legal education

The first reason why we need a European debate on a European methodology results from the Europeanization of legal education. Both the Bologna process with its mutual recognition of credits and the Erasmus/Socrates programme grant system has stimulated student mobility throughout Europe. But since legal scholarship and teaching have always had close ties with legal practice, the recognition directives 89/48/EEC and 98/5 EEC, allowing lawyers established in one Member State to practise law in another one under their own academic title have probably been even more important in creating a European legal market.[112] What we can witness today is a growing competition between law schools in offering students an education that prepares them for an international career. These law schools are responding to the demands of the market where multi-national law firms, multinational corporations, but also NGOs are becoming increasingly active in setting up offices in different Member States and competing with each other in order to recruit the best young lawyers with a diverse and multinational training.[113]

An essential part of the training and education of lawyers who want to pursue an international career will be European law. As Miguel Maduro has argued, it is today no longer possible to teach contract law, consumer law or environmental law, to name just a few, without at least some basic knowledge about the nature and function(s) of EU law, its unique system, its general principles and methods of interpretation developed by, among others, the CFI

111. See the analysis of V. Nourse and G. Shaffer, Varieties of New Legal Realism: Can A New World Order Prompt a New Legal Theory?, Cornell law review vol. 95 (2009) pp. 61-139.
112. N. Reich, Recent trends in European legal education: the place of the European Law Faculties Association 21 Penn St Int'l L Rev, 2002, pp. 21-38.
113. See for example, G. Morgan and S. Quack, Institutional Legacies and Firm Dynamics: The Growth and Internationalisation of UK and German Law Firms, Organization Studies 26 (12): pp. 1765-1785.

and ECJ.[114] EU law cuts across through traditional boundaries of private and public law; EU law is both and does not care about national legal thinking in boxes and categories.[115] Simultaneously, however, it is not enough for students to acquire 'just' a minimum understanding of how EU law works. Because of the fact that EU law and national law are becoming more and more intertwined, the challenge is to develop a better understanding of different sorts of legal arguments deriving from both national and EU law. In most law suits before national courts, European courts and international arbitrations in which a dispute over EU law plays a role, for example, require a firm knowledge of at least two, but more often three or more, legal systems.

In reality most of the research in nationally bound legal subjects takes a vertical perspective, in that legal scholars just pick out of the 'supreme' legal order the bits and pieces they need for the understanding of the problem at stake. The EU legal order, however, is a horizontal order that rests on the 27 vertical national legal orders, which necessarily implies to look into the European dimension of each and every question concerned and does not fit to the particular national context in which the European question arises.

Even if one does not believe in convergence of legal systems or an ongoing process of European integration, it seems hard to deny that, for instance, methods and techniques of comparative law have an important role to play in facilitating intercultural legal communication between both practicing lawyers and academics in order to build bridges across jurisdictions and between domestic legal traditions. Therefore, as Esin Örücü has stated, research has to go beyond 'juxtaposing, contrasting and comparing'. This strengthens the call for comparative lawyers to be trained in interdisciplinary research problems, to have knowledge of and familiarity with different legal cultures, to have a good command of languages, knowledge of history, economics and politics, and also to receive training in methodology'.[116] Unfortunately though, most handbooks do explain how difficult comparative legal research is but offer little guidance on how to do it. Could it perhaps be that we do not really have

114. M. Maduro, The Europeanization and Globalisation of Law, Contraditorio, Policy Paper 10/1, February 2010, p. 5. (see: http://www.contraditorio.pt/admin/ source/files/ 1276200432-PolicyPaper10_01_LegalEducationandthe Europeanizationand Globalisation ofLaw-Original.pdf).

115. See, N. Reich, The public/private divide in European law in H.-W. Micklitz/F. Cafaggi (eds.), European Private Law after the Common Frame of Reference, 2010, p. 56; L. Azoulai, Sur un sens de la distinction public/privé dans le droit de l'union européenne, RTD eur. 48 (2010), 853.

116. Esin Örücü, Looking at convergence through the eyes of a comparative lawyer, EJCL, Vol. 9.2 2005, p. 11.

a well-developed methodology of comparative law yet because we as researchers rely so heavily on the craftsmanship, the common sense and practical wisdom that is given centre-stage in law school? The rising importance of comparative history[117] could provide promising ground for linking history and law into a joint concept.

Notwithstanding this, one of the major benefits of making lawyers and legal scholars familiar with methods of comparative law could be that it pushes the analysis of legal problems to broader levels of abstraction.[118] After all, comparative law is not first and foremost about finding similarities and differences but about explaining *why* there are different answers to (functional) equivalent legal questions and *what* the argumentation is behind those answers. The quest for explanations guides legal researchers in a natural way towards hypothesis and theory-building. As we will argue hereafter, this is exactly where both legal scholarship and legal practice can benefit from it. Comparative law opens new perspectives on European law and questions. Add to this that, especially in many smaller European countries, the academic forum is too limited for a broad scholarly debate on European law-related issues and the fact that there is still no relatively 'unified, cross national community' of scholars specialized in European law,[119] and one will understand the importance of comparative research for building bridges between legal scholars.

1.2. Why methods: Americanization of EU law? What about Europeanization of American law?

In the early 1990s, Wolfgang Wiegand reported about the growing importance of a 'reception of American law in Europe'.[120] Wiegand even went as far as comparing the Americanization of European law with the medieval reception of Roman law throughout Europe, which started in Bologna in the eleventh century. He concluded, among other things, that the political and economic dominance of the U.S., the spread of the English language in sci-

117. There is even a journal under that title, comparative history, which provides an account for the research undertaken.
118. John C. Reitz, How To Do Comparative Law, 46 AM. J. COMP. L. 617 (1998), pp. 625-626.
119. B. de Witte, 'European Union Law: A Unified Academic Discipline?' (EUI Working Papers RSCAS no 34, 2008) Retrieved from: http://cadmus.eui.eu/dspace/handle/1814/10028).
120. Wolfgang Wiegand, The Reception of American Law in Europe, J. COMP. L. 229 (1991), Vol. 39, nr. 2 pp. 229-248.

ence,[121] together with the fact that lawyers occupying leading positions in academia, law firms, major banks and private industry increasingly display a strong leaning towards American legal thinking. Wiegand believed that would have fundamental effects on European law even if the powerbase of the U.S. were going to fade because of the rise of other economic super powers.

Whilst most legal scholarship is focusing on some sort of comparison between national law and EU law or between EU law and U.S. law, we do not know whether and to what extent Americanization of the legal systems in Europe has really taken place, and where and how. There is some evidence that the OECD served as a catalyst for the transferral of U.S. law to Europe, in particular in fields such as environmental law and consumer law. After 1990, however, the EU got more and more involved in external relations and took gradually over a similar task, though in a more discrete form in that the EU used the American legal order as a blueprint and channelled regulatory models through the common law systems to continental Europe. The liberalization and privatization of former public services may serve as evidence for such a transformation process. But again, even where such an influence is hard to neglect, we do not know exactly how the European legal order differs from its counterpart, whether the legal transplants work only in one direction or whether the EU law also influences the U.S. legal system and be it in a rather remote form.

Even for those who do not believe in the Americanization of European law because of tremendous cultural differences and deviating styles of regulation and litigation,[122] which lead to differences in the application even if the legal system resemble each other at the first hand sight, it is hard to deny that European legal scholarship as such has undergone major changes over the last thirty years. Comparative legal analysis under exclusion of U.S. law has become hard to justify. But the changes reach beyond the formal broadening of the subject matter under investigation. In an eloquent article in honour of Sir Francis Jacobs, former Advocate General at the ECJ, Anthony Arnull convincingly argues that, since the 1980s, European scholars of EU law have clearly travelled part of the way down the path that moves away from legal

121. L. Borghans & F. Cörvers, The Americanization of European Higher Education and Research, Research Centre for Education and the Labour Market, Maastricht University, NBER Working Paper No. w15217, August 2009.(http://papers.ssrn.com/sol3/papers.cfm?abstract_id=1454933##)

122. Robert A. Kagan, Globalization and Legal Change: The Americanization of European Law, Regulation & Governance, Vol.1, no. 2 (2007) pp. 99-120.

technicalities, which is followed by academics across the Atlantic, who often display a dismissive attitude towards traditional doctrinal legal analysis.[123]

We would not deny such a finding, but we would argue that contrary to the U.S., in Europe there is no mainstream legal scholarship that shies away from legal dogmatics. Quite to the contrary, we would very much insist on the side-by-side of two different strains of legal scholarship, one which is still tied to legal dogmatics and another one that reaches beyond legal dogmatics and follows the current main stream trend in focusing on law and economics, and increasingly also on law and other disciplines.

The big question remains, however, if this trend is the result of Americanization of European law or of intra-European developments which have their roots in the Member States, in internationalization more in general, or in a growing competition between law and (other) social sciences for research funding requiring clarity about what distinguishes fundamental legal research from applied research, to name just a few possible explanations.

2. Have European legal scholars to learn from American empiricism? Or have American legal scholars to learn from European legal dogmatics?

The dominant perspective is that European scholars look to the U.S. as a source of inspiration. There is this well-known bonmot that the U.S. is always five-ten years ahead of us and that the EU is still following American trends when these have already lost pace in the US and are replaced by new patterns of legal scholarship. The more serious question is whether Richard Posner's plea to enhance legal dogmatics brings U.S. legal scholarship closer to Europe, in that Europe preserved a tradition that has lost ground in U.S. scholarship.

One lesson that European legal scholars can learn from experiences in the U.S. is that there is a lot of added value in the introduction of multidisciplinary law and ... approaches on top of a tradition of sophisticated doctrinal research as long as this does not lead to self-indulgence and the tendency to neglect or disparage legal scholarship that is unfashionable for the time being.[124]

An interesting case in point of both innovation and naivety is the rise of empirical legal scholarship in the U.S. From a European perspective this

123. A. M. Arnull, 'The Americanization of EU law scholarship', in A. M. Arnull, P. Eeckhout and T. Tridimas (eds.), Continuity and Change in EU Law: Essays in Honour of Sir Francis Jacobs (OUP, 2008), pp. 415-431 (424).

124. Ibid, p. 431.

looks like a revitalization of the so-called Rechtstatsachenforschung as founded by Max Weber in the 1920s and as reinvigorated in the 1970s in most Western European democracies. Seen this way, behavioural economics is just a variant of what has been called Verhaltensforschung in the 1920s and 1970s. As Lawless, Rubbenolt and Ulen noticed, American legal scholars have done much borrowing from other disciplines lately in order to enrich their theoretical understanding of the law with two major results for the legal academy.[125]

First, successful interdisciplinary approaches have led to an explosion of attention for empiricism from law professors keen on illuminating under researched questions, such as judicial biases, adverse effects of laws and regulations, and matters of causation like the (unintended) behavioural effects of strict liability regimes. Second, this attention resulted in also borrowing research methods and techniques from other disciplines, such as economics, sociology, psychology, biology and political science.

Especially this second trend has had a number of unintended side effects that do not concern the quantity of empirical legal research but relate to the average quality of that work. V. Nourse and G. Shaffer have forcefully demonstrated[126] that all these investments into empirical research did not find their way into a legal methodology that allows for a using of social facts in the interpretation of the legal system.

What legal scholarship did, however, is to reveal the methodological weakness of empirical research undertaken under the new regime. That serious concerns exist regarding the quality of empirical legal research in the U.S. is shown in a seminal article by Lee Epstein and Gary King, two experts in research methodology who studied around 350 journal articles with empirical ambitions published in American law journals between 1990 and 2000, including 50 of the most cited articles according to the SSRN legal scholarship network. The overall conclusion of Epstein and King was that 'the current state of empirical legal scholarship is deeply flawed'.[127] While they admit that some articles in law reviews are better than others, the authors claim that every single one of them violated at least one of the methodologi-

125. Robert M. Lawless, Jennifer K. Robbenolt, Thomas S. Ulen, Empirical Methods in Law, Aspen Publishers, New York 2010, pp. 3-4.
126. Varieties of New Legal Realism: Can A New World Order Prompt a New Legal Theory?, University of Minnesota Law School, Legal Studies Research Paper Series, Research Paper No. 09-17.
127. Lee Epstein & Gary King, The Rules of Inference, 69 U. Chi. L. Revd.1, p. 6 (2002).

cal rules of inference that guide empirical research, such as rules on data collection, causation, replicability, etc.[128]

As could be expected, Epstein and King's article aroused a lot of debate. Some opponents accused them of violating their own rules of inference.[129] Others claimed that many of the methodological ills that they attributed to legal scholarship, such as explaining in detail how cases are coded or how data are archived, are problems that are certainly not exclusive to legal scholarship.[130] This objection is a strange one since it is hard to comprehend how methodological pitfalls in other disciplines could ever make up for similar shortcomings in scholarly legal publications. Perhaps even stranger, though, is the critique by two well-known Harvard law professors that 'particular versions of the truth' ventilated in journal articles that are tendentious when taken separately may, at the systemic level, produce close approximations of the truth because advocacy legal scholarship will probably raise criticism of 'opposing camps'.[131] This is a peculiar way of arguing that there is not so much wrong with empirical legal scholarship. Epstein and King refute this argument convincingly by noting that adversary scholarship might work in theory in the sense that in the end anything is possible, but that they have never seen examples of academic disciplines trying to make progress through such an adversial approach.[132] In fact, the argument that the validity of empirical legal articles depends on the exposition by fellow scholars of a one-sided or coloured presentation of empirical evidence seems to support Epstein and King's claim that too many lawyers engaged in scholarly legal work behave more like advocates than as independent researchers who are willing to be surprised by reality.

Is there no truth whatsoever in the critique that Epstein and King treat all empirical legal research too much alike? Perhaps there is. Jan Smits has, for example, argued that one could regard law as a 'normative-empirical' science in which existing legal systems are sources of law.[133] National laws and court

128. Ibid p. 17. The rules of inference are worked out in parts III-VIII of the article.
129. Frank Cross, Michael Heise & Gregory C. Sisk, Above the Rules: A Response to Epstein and King, 69 U. CHI. L Rev 135 (2002).
130. Richard L. Revesz, A Defense of Empirical Legal Scholarship, 69 U Chi L Rev 169, p. 184 (2002).
131. Jack Goldsmith and Adrian Vermeule, Empirical Methodology and Legal Scholarship, 69 U Chi L Rev 153, 156 (2002).
132. Lee Epstein & Gary King, A Reply, U Chi L Rev 69, 194 (2002).
133. Jan M. Smits, Redefining Normative Legal Science: Towards an Argumentative Discipline, in F. Coomans, F. Grünfeld & M. Kamminga (eds.), Methods of Human Rights Research, Antwerpen-Oxford: Intersentia, 2009, pp. 45-58.

decisions can then be treated as empirical data, according to Smits, in order to explain how different arguments are being used to respond to certain legal questions and problems.[134] If we view empiricism in this way, Epstein and King's strict demands of replicability may simply go too far because the collection of data is not first and foremost a matter of finding the truth. According to Smits, legal research should be about dealing with (conflicting) arguments that have been tested elsewhere in practice and comparative law becomes an empirical endeavour.[135]

Even if one does not share Smit's liberal opinion about what counts as empirical legal research,[136] it is still possible to have fundamental doubts about the extent to which it is possible or desirable to apply empirical methods to answer legal questions. Interesting in this respect is Robin Feldman's observation that law's fascination with science in order to make law and legal research more 'neutral' reaches back at least two hundred years in American legal history.[137] She describes how throughout history American legal scholars have always cast doubts about whether law is capable of resolving difficult social and moral conflicts and there has been a constant hope that science can do better. The attention for empirical research by legal realists, members of the critical legal studies movement and adherents of new legal realism is closely related to this fixation on scientific methods. According to Feldman, there is a constant return to the same well, despite the fact that scientification has never succeeded in rescuing legal scholars from the discomfort and uncertainties that go along with legal research.[138]

Does the latter imply that European legal scholars better refrain from empirical or socio-legal research? The answer is definitely no. There is nothing wrong with interdisciplinary approaches and applying social-science research methods on legal questions as such. On the contrary, we would say. European law can benefit tremendously by paying close attention to, for example, political sciences in order to get more grip on the legal politics (Rechtspolitik)

134. Jan Smits, Omstreden rechtswetenschap, BJU, Den Haag 2009, p. 114.
135. Ibid, p. 160.
136. The problem is that laws, court decisions and scholarly legal publications have no direct link with the real world but only an indirect one in the sense that only after the implementation or enforcement of legal rules, law's impact becomes clear. This explains why there can be such a thing as a gap between the law in the books and the law in action.
137. Robin Feldman, The Role of Science in Law, Oxford University Press 2009.
138. Robin Feldman, Law's Misguided Love Affair with Science, MINN. J.L. SCI. & TECH. 2009;10(1): 95-116 (97, 115).

that play such an important and role in law and policymaking.[139] However, we may not forget that doctrinal legal expertise is often crucial in order to be able to raise the right questions and determine which variables should be tested in attempting to explain a particular legal phenomenon.[140] Moreover, one has to realise that normative questions concerning how the law should read can never be fully answered through empirical or socio-legal research. One will always need interpretation and argumentation to bridge the gap between facts and norms.

Is this what American legal scholarship can learn from European legal scholarhip – a more balanced going together of legal dogmatics with extra-legal empirical research? In the U.S. hardcore law & economics is on the decline, which, however, never gained the same ground in Europe as legal dogmatics rested in place for the good and for the bad.[141] European legal scholarship is not following the different mainstreams of legal scholarship to the same extreme as it happens in the U.S. Nobody would claim the death of legal dogmatics or the death of empirical research. There are ups and downs too, but the ups and the downs are less high, respectively less low. It is true legal dogmatics is back on the agenda, here termed the revival of legal formalism. On the other hand, however, there are more and more legal scholars that engage into social empirical legal research that reaches beyond law. The problem we see is that empirical legal research in Europe is discredited by the attempts of the European Commission to equate empirical analysis with impact assessments. It suffices to contrast the superficial analysis of collective actions in Europe[142] as initiated by the European Commission with the carefully and methodologically sound analysis of US class actions.[143] In so far

139. Karen J. Alter, Renaud Dehousse, Georg Vanberg, Law, Political Science and EU Legal Studies, European Union Politics, Volume 3 (1): 113-136 (126) 2002.
140. Matthias Siems, The Taxonomy of Interdisciplinary Legal Research: Finding the Way Out of the Desert' Journal of Commonwealth Law and Legal Education 7 (2009): 5-17.
141. K. Grechenig/M. Gelter, Divergente Evolution des Rechtsdenkens – Von amerikanischer Rechtsökonomik und deutscher Dogmatik, RabelsZ 72 (2008), 513.
142. 'Evaluation of the effectiveness and efficiency of collective redress mechanisms in the European Union'; http://ec.europa.eu/consumers/redress_cons/finalreportevaluationstudypart1-final2008-11-26.pdf and the problems faced by consumers in obtaining redress for infringements of consumer protection legislation, and the economic consequences of such problems' http://ec.europa.eu/consumers/redress_cons/docs/finalreport-focusgroup2-final.pdf.
143. See e.g. T. Eisenberg/G. Miller/E. Sherwin, Arbitration's Summer Soldiers: An Empirical Study on Arbitration in Consumer and Non-Consumer Contracts, 41 U. Mich. Law

Europe remains behind the U.S. standards on empirical legal research. One may nevertheless recognize a stronger approximation of scholarly research in these two parts of the world, which allows for a stronger exchange of ideas in both directions.

3. What is doctrinal legal research and why is it still important for the study of European law?

It is difficult, if not impossible, to come up with one generally accepted definition of doctrinal legal research in Europe. The characteristics of legal doctrine are certainly not identical in every country. The role that legislation or precedents fulfil in legal dogmatics is, for example, obviously not identical in common law and civil law countries. Nevertheless, there appear to be some core features that most doctrinal research has in common, both in European countries and even across the Atlantic in the U.S. The most important ones are:

- In doctrinal work, arguments are derived from authoritative sources, such as existing rules, principles, precedents, and scholarly publications.
- The law somehow represents a system. Through the production of general and defeasible theories, legal doctrine aims to present the law as a coherent net of principles, rules, meta-rules and exceptions, at different levels of abstraction.[144]
- Decisions in individual cases are supposed to exceed arbitrariness because they have to (be) fit into the system. Deciding in hard cases implies that existing rules will be stretched or even replaced but always in such a way that in the end the system is coherent again.

Contested is the view whether doctrinalists need to take an internal perspective in studying the law. Undoubtedly many scholars still do it, but it is exactly this feature that is nowadays often considered to be too narrow. That is why so many think it should be replaced by a 'law in context' approach. Other views on what doctrinal legal research entails have evolved over the years. In the past most scholars associated legal doctrine first and foremost with a faithful and consistent application of legal rules and principles by the judiciary. According to Emerson Tiller and Frank Cross, however, academics

Reform, 871 (2007-2008), J. Coffee, Law and The Market, The Impact of Enforcement, http://cbe.anu.edu.au/capitalmarkets/papers/COFFEE-CAPITAL-MARKETS.pdf

144. A Pecznick, A Theory of Legal Doctrine, Ratio Juris, Volume 14, Issue 1, pp. 75-105 (2001).

increasingly recognize that law is not applied with perfect neutrality.[145] This, however, is not really new for European scholars who are familiar with the methodological discussions in the aftermath of 1968. Again we would like to point to J. Esser. How the law is found and shaped is influenced by many internal and external (societal) factors, including personal biases and preconceptions, judicial ideology and socio-economic consequences of court decisions (Folgenorientierung). This again is an old issue, widely discussed in the 1970s and 1980s.[146]

While we started this paper with the assertion by Posner jr. that doctrinal legal research is dead in the U.S., Rubin and Freeley claim that a new doctrinal approach emerged in the U.S., which is a product of both judicial ideology and pre-existing legal principles upon which judges must build their argumentation.[147] They believe that, not in the least because of the multidisciplinary research with respect to judicial lawmaking, both legal scholars and social scientists increasingly recognize the independent significance of legal doctrine. Social scientist may remain more focused on what is the driving force behind judicial outcomes, but there is a growing awareness that doctrine is certainly not irrelevant, according to Rubin and Freeley. The other way around, doctrinalists in the U.S. also seem to have learned to understand and appreciate how important extralegal influences on court decisions can be and why it is better to realise this than to try to hide it.[148] The same holds true for European scholarship, where Maduro has shown how the role of the European Court of Justice is increasingly impacted by, and needs to be adapted to, a context of constitutional pluralism and multiplicity of legal sources.[149]

What can we say with respect to the development of European doctrinal legal research? First of all, we should make clear at the outset that there is no

145. Emerson H. Tiller & Frank B. Cross, What is Legal Doctrine?, Northwestern University Law Review Vol. 100, No. 1, (2006) pp. 517-534 (522).
146. E. Schmidt, Der Umgang mit Normtatsachen im Zivilprozeß, in FS Wassermann (1985), S. 807.
147. Edward Rubin & Malcolm Feeley, Creating Legal Doctrine, 69 S. Cal. L. Rev 1989 (1996).
148. Emerson H. Tiller & Frank B. Cross, What is Legal Doctrine?, Northwestern University Law Review Vol. 100, No. 1, (2006) pp. 517-534 (522) at p. 527.
149. Miguel Maduro, Interpreting European Law: Judicial Adjudication in a Context of Constitutional Pluralism, 1 EUR. J. LEG. STUD. (Dec. 2007), available at http://www.ejls.eu/.

'methodological ius commune Europaeum'.[150] There are, and always have been, many different doctrinal traditions in the Member States of the EU. However, the story does not end here. First of all, each and every Member State has to deal with a growing plurality of legal sources since EU law and European human rights law are increasingly pervading both public and private law in the Member States. This has a direct influence on the methodology of legal research since the interpretation of national legal rules is more than ever before affected by multiple legal sources, on multiple levels of government (e.g. International treaties, Council of Europe/ECHR, primary and secondary EU law, including the interpretation of EU law by the ECJ, and national law). Not only national courts and local governments, but also legal scholars, increasingly have to interpret national law in accordance with EU law and European legal doctrine.

Secondly, EU law knows its own system and fundamental principles. In many cases that system deviates from the Member States' legal systems. Hence EU law irritates an autonomous systematization of national law. So not only do doctrinalists have to learn to find the right sources of EU law, which is not always easy because EU law is also increasingly a combination of hard and soft law (e.g. co-regulation), but they also have to understand the distinct features of the EU legal system. One of those features is that the EU legislature(s) sometimes deliberately uses ambiguous language in order to reach a compromise between conflicting Member States. Other typical features are the autonomous interpretation of legal concepts by the ECJ and the relative insignificance, compared to the situation in most Member States, of legal history, travaux preparatoires, and legal doctrine itself as a source of law.

The aforementioned challenges the idea of guaranteeing certainty through a consistent application of legal methods. There is no longer one pyramid-like organized national legal system in which judges and legal scholars function as 'gatekeepers' who are supposed to guard and maintain the consistency of the system. Instead a plurality of legal systems ('an archipelago instead of an island') has developed in which hierarchy plays a less prominent role[151] and the interpretation of EU law in country A can affect the way how the law in country B should be applied with the preliminary rulings procedure of the

150. J. Smits, The Europeanisation of national legal systems: some consequences for legal thinking in civil law countries, in M. van Hoecke (ed.), Epistemology and Methodology of Comparative Law, Oxford: Hart Publishing 2004, pp. 229-245 (229).

151. Especially with respect to constitutional law, the idea of a 'constitutional dialogue' between several 'highest' courts (ICJ, ECHR, ECJ, national Supreme Courts) is gaining terrain.

ECJ functioning as an intermediary. The other side of the coin is that EU institutions increasingly use comparative law methods in the drafting of new EU law and in the decision-making by the ECJ.[152] Comparative law, using a doctrinal approach, is important for EU lawmakers in order to assess ex ante some of the implications of new European rules for the different Member States.

We believe there are also more fundamental reasons why doctrinal legal research will become of growing importance for EU law. A vigorous debate between Armin von Bogdandy and Matthias Kumm on the past and future of European (constitutional) scholarship demonstrates this.[153] Von Bogdandy has argued that a European legal research area is emerging and that due to the fact that European law has long passed the stage of occasional 'irritation' of national legal systems, a European doctrinal legal scholarship is likely to occur sooner or later.[154] He believes the litmus test for a common European scholarship should not be the emergence of more comprehensive and fragmented doctrinal patterns. Instead, the best response to growing heterogeneity of legal sources should be matched with a strengthening of theoretical (and so we add methodological) components, where possible drawn from the common European heritage in legal theory and spurred by transnational scientific legal communities.

Kumm, from his part, claims that it is misleading to characterize mainstream European legal scholarship as 'doctrinal constructivism' as Bogdandy does. According to him, European scholars in the course of history have rejected three extremes in legal scholarship trying to reduce it to its moral, its empirical/factual, or its formal/conceptual dimension.[155] If anything characterizes European legal scholarship, Kumm argues, it would be the continuous attempts to integrate the formal, the empirical and the moral dimensions of law. At the same time, he acknowledges: 'There might not be much agreement on how, exactly, the various elements complement one another and

152. K. Lenaerts, Interlocking Legal Orders in the European Union and Comparative Law, International & Comparative Law Quarterly, (2003), 52: 873-906.
153. A. Von Bogdandy, The past and promise of doctrinal constructivism: A strategy for responding to the challenges facing constitutional scholarship in Europe, ICON, July 2009, pp. 364-399. M. Kumm, On the past and future of European constitutional scholarship, ICON, July 2009, pp. 401-415.
154. Von Bogdandy ibid, p. 399.
155. P. 407.

why.'[156] We believe Kumm is right in pointing to disagreement here, but wonder whether this is not where methodology should come into the picture?

Kumm seems to admire the methodological pluralism in the U.S., where he feels legal scholars to a large extent apply the methodologies of other disciplines to law.[157] As we have demonstrated above by referring to the debate on methodology in empirical legal scholarship, this is exactly where the problems in U.S. legal scholarship have come to the surface; lawyers neglecting the rules of inference that accompany the methods and techniques of the social sciences. We also have serious doubts whether the answer to this is the outsourcing of legal research to scholars with a non-legal background, as Kumm argues is already taking place in the elite law schools in the U.S. We believe it is just as impossible to undertake good multidisciplinary or empirical research without a proper understanding of legal doctrine as it is to conduct solid doctrinal research with at least some knowledge of facts and fact finding. One needs this understanding, not in the last place, in order to be able to raise the right questions without making a mockery of law and legal theory. If the opposite were true, things would be a lot easier and there would probably not have been such a long history of frictions between legal formalism, naturalism and (new) legal realism in the U.S. and in Europe.

4. An agenda for revitalization of European doctrinal research

One of the great advantages of the study of European law from a methodological viewpoint is that it does not have this long history of battles between formalism, naturalism and legal realism. Moreover, traditional doctrinal legal scholarship is already changing because of the Europeanization of different legal fields. This should facilitate in making our spirits ready for a revitalization of doctrinal legal research with more emphasis on methodology (!) *and* theory (!).

We do not have the illusion that we can come up with a simple blueprint for a European methodology of law and legal research. What we will sketch hereafter are some thoughts and ideas that need further research and debate. We sincerely believe, however, that such a methodology debate is useful and necessary and should not be postponed simply because it implies a willingness to take a long ride on a bumpy and winding road. 'Reflexion auf Eigenes Tun' is never easy, but European law has a lot to gain from it. Having said

156. P. 408.
157. P. 410.

this, what are some of the implications of the revitalization of European law we are supposing?

1. European legal research, doctrinal or not doctrinal should start with a disclosure of ideological preconceptions. This is the major lesson we can learn from the instrumental use of law in the aftermath of 1968, by legal leftist lawyers who intended to change society via law and by rightist lawyers who intended to preserve the status quo or even wanted to turn the clock back to the 19th century. Emphasis has to be put on 'disclosure', as we all start as legal scholars from preconceptions in our research. What is needed is a constant process of 'Selbstvergewisserung' and of 'Hinterfragen' of these pre-conceptions, whatever they are. This will not be possible without having a sound background in legal methodology, which cannot be understood without reference to legal theory. Methodology determines how one looks at legal problems. It sets the 'rules of the game'. An interesting case in point is the debate on the legal origins thesis – the thesis that legal origin impacts economic growth and the common law is better for economic growth than the civil law – challenging traditional approaches to comparative law that have not paid much attention to the economic consequences of legal regimes and how these can be explained.[158]
2. European doctrinal legal research should be *freed from the role model and research methods of the judge* as its sole point of reference and look for answers to the question what can be the added value of a legal scholarship that goes beyond being a service for legal practice.[159] We believe this indicates that academic legal research should primarily be engaged with trying to understand what is behind the law on a certain subject, why lawmakers operate as they do, why they look for legal answers to (certain) societal problems instead of pursuing alternatives to law, and why the law says what it says instead of pondering about how the answer to a legal problem can be embedded in the legal system. Legal practitioners are ca-

158. R. Michaels, Comparative Law by Numbers, Legal Origins Thesis, Doing Business Reports, and the Silence of Traditional Comparative Law, 57 AM. J. COMP. L. 765-795 (2009), M. Siems, The End of Comparative Law', Journal of Comparative Law 2: (2007) 133-150.
159. J.B.M. Vranken, Exploring the Jurist's Frame of Mind, Kluwer Law International, Deventer 2006.

pable of doing the latter, but they are usually not interested or do not have the time to look for the answers to these 'why' questions.[160]

3. Since European lawmakers are increasingly emphasizing the importance of *evidence-based law-making* (impact assessments, consultations, expert advice etcetera), a doctrinal legal scholarship that wants to stay in touch with legal practice without being lured into 'herd behaviour' should start *asking critical questions*, such as: how is the empirical evidence on which new EU laws are being based collected and what guarantees are build into the process to prevent 'policy-based evidence making'? What are, or should be, the legal consequences if EU institutions neglect their own rules, guidelines and procedures for law-making and facilitate integration without or beyond law? What 'rules of recognition' could or should the ECJ apply when deciding over the question whether alternative modes of governance are legally relevant and how can the legitimacy of those rules can be assessed?
4. If consensus can be reached, now or in the future, about the importance of a 'law in context' approach as, for instance, advocated by Francis Snyder, the founding father and editor in chief of the European Law Journal, this needs to be reflected in legal education in order to ascertain that lawyers and legal researchers are cognisant of the most important parameters of political science, law & economics, comparative law and empirical legal research methods. We can quote Kyle and Hutchinson here, who have stated: '*More extensive training needs to be offered in fundamental research.* This is 'Research deigned to secure a deeper understanding of law as a social phenomenon, including research on the historical, philosophical, linguistic, economic, social or political implications of law.' [...] Fundamental research, which can include empirical and social science models, needs to be part of the graduating lawyers' research skills and attributes.'[161]
5. It is of vital importance that the introduction to these other *'non-legal' research methodologies does not replace the training in doctrinal research but come on top of that training and that they are taught in combination with doctrinal methods.* Again this is a lesson to be drawn from the revision of legal education initiated in the aftermath of 1968 in many Euro-

160. M. McConville and W. Hong Chui (ed.), Research Methods for Law, Edinburgh University Press: Edinburgh 2007, p. 2.
161. K. Burns and T. Hutchinson, The impact of 'empirical facts' on legal scholarship and legal research training, The Law Teacher, Vol. 43, No. 2, July 2009, pp. 153-178 (159).

pean countries.[162] If one of the major problems of doctrinal research(ers) is that they do not possess a good understanding of how normative and empirical arguments interact, then that is exactly what we should work on. As far as we are concerned, this should not imply that we want to turn law students into amateur social or political scientists or economists, but they should at least be able to understand (some of) the language and methods that other (social) sciences apply in order to learn more about the value, validity and reliability of non-doctrinal research methods and techniques. Moreover, law students should be taught how facts and fact finding play a role in legal decision making in, for example, teleological interpretation, considerations of proportionality and subsidiarity in the interpretation and application of European law and in 'Normkonkretisierung' or the filling in of open norms and legal principles.[163]

6. For doctrinal research itself the latter means raising awareness as to what methodology actually entails and why it is particularly important for those scholars who focus on European law in their research. We believe that especially European legal scholarship can no longer rely on the informal 'elephant paths' earlier generations may (or may not) have laid down for others to follow. The plurality of sources on which European law rests, the interrelation between national and European law, the blurring of the public private divide in EU law and the introduction of new modes of government and governance have made the system extremely complex, fluid and unstable. Moreover, the instrumentalization of European legal scholarship has led to a lack of critical distance towards the object of legal research. In combination these developments underline the importance of methodological rules that can help to *filter out poor research and function as 'a mediator between the researcher's subjective beliefs and opinions* and the data and evidence that he or she produces through research.'[164]
7. Revitalization entails, among other things: *more attention from legal scholarship for the advantages of a solid research design, with special attention for the formulation of a good research question/hypothesis*, which:

162. See the experience in Germany with the so-called Einstufige Juristenausbildung, E. Schmidt, Theorie/Praxis-Verknüpfung und künftige Einheitsausbildung, DRiZ 1982, 47.
163. Niels Petersen, Braucht die Rechtswissenschaft eine empirische Wende?, Max Planck Institute for Research on Collective Goods, Bonn 2010/10. Http://www.coll.mpg.de/pdf_dat/2010_10online.pdf.
164. M. McConville and W.H.Chui (eds), Research Methods for Law, Edinburgh: Edinburgh University Press, 2007, p. 22.

challenges researchers to embed their research in a scholarly debate by showing on whose shoulders they stand and where they deviate from mainstream thinking; explains what the theoretical relevance of their research is, in other words, what doctrinal positions or other theories are being attacked, adjusted or strengthened, or how certain developments in positive law can be explained or predicted; highlights ones research aim with respect to what will be added to the existing body of knowledge on the subject, and to explain what methods or techniques will be used to answer the research question and justifies why this approach is suitable for that purpose.

8. A revitalized doctrinal European legal scholarship should not be mistaken for 'methodological fetishism' or for a strict separation between methods of legal scholarship and methods of law and policymaking. On the contrary, if 'policy' means 'a course of action adopted or proposed by an organization or person, more specifically an action which implies a choice of one action among others',[165] especially doctrinalists should be interested in the parallels and disparities between methods of law-making by EU institutions and methods of legal research. Both doctrinal legal scholars and lawmakers increasingly have to overcome similar sorts of 'translation problems', such as giving legal meaning to facts and empirical evidence, making sense of what foreign legal concepts learn for the EU legal context ('Member States as laboratories') and assessing the credibility of a steadily growing amount of electronic legal sources. What are the underlying values and methods that guide these policy choices? How can legal scholars and lawmakers avoid 'tunnel vision', overcome cognitive biases (e.g. misperceiving risks) and how do they balance intuition and practical wisdom with counter intuitiveness and a consistent application of methods?

To be continued ...

165. W. van Gerven, Politics, Ethics & the Law, Legal Practice & Scholarship, LSE Law, Society and Economy Working Papers 20/2008, p. 20.

The Importance of the Instruments Provided for in the Treaties for Developing a European Legal Method

Wulf-Henning Roth

§ 1. Introduction

The topic of this paper is addressed to the instruments provided for in the European Treaties that may be regarded as important for the development of a European legal method. In the following we will – firstly – address the issue of the interpretation of international conventions that may present analogous problems (under § 2), and then go on to ask what makes European Union law special – the notion of the Union as a Union based on law (§ 3 I; '*Rechtsgemeinschaft*') and the judicial architecture at the Union level (§ 3 II), with special emphasis on the preliminary ruling procedure (§ 3 III). In this system, the individual – to some extent – is attributed the role of a private attorney general (§ 4). Basic principles of Union law play an important role (§ 5). We conclude by stressing the fact that in the European judicial architecture the European Court of Justice (ECJ) takes a central role in interpreting Union law[1] and thereby in developing a European legal method (§ 6).

At the outset, three caveats have to be made:

(1) The discussion on (the development of) a 'European legal method' could be understood not only as dealing with the interpretation, application and development of law by the judiciary, but also to extend to the law-making process by the legislature (or as the case may be: the executive). Discussing the method of European legislation, we might observe that legislation is often strongly determined by a functional approach, giving rise to what may be de-

1. This term is in the following used interchangeably with 'Community law', 'European law' and 'European Union law'.

scribed as piece-meal legislation.[2] This kind of legislation has found its critics in the private law arena, but this and other issues of good legislation[3] are beyond the topic of this paper.

(2) Other contributions of this conference will deal with what is meant by 'European legal method'. 'Legal method' as used in the context of this presentation shall not refer to a method to legislate; it rather refers to the method of interpretation, application and development of law by the judiciary. In this regard, the discussion on a 'European' legal method[4] has to be kept apart from approaches we are accustomed to in the national legal orders. Keeping the European methodology apart from national traditions does, however, not imply that there may not be a common ground between European and national legal methods: A short glance at the interpretative methods used by the European Court of Justice (ECJ) reveals that, to a certain extent, the approach taken will ring quite familiar in the ears of many lawyers from the Member States (though, of course, there are also important deviances). As far as the Court refers to language of the provision,[5] its context,[6] to some degree also to the preparatory materials,[7] and with special emphasis the object or purpose of the legislative act[8] as *topoi* for its interpretation, the Court's methodology

2. See e.g. Roth, Transposing 'Pointillist' EC Guidelines into Systematic National Codes – Problems and Consequences, Eur. Rev. Priv. Law 10 (2002) 761.
3. Timmermans, How can one improve the Quality of Community Legislation? CMLRev 34 (1997) 1229; see also various contributions in Weatherill (ed.), Better Regulation (2007).
4. This topic has recently attracted a lot of attention in German academic quarters; see e.g. Adrian, Grundprobleme einer juristischen (gemeinschaftsrechtlichen) Methodenlehre (2009); Dederichs, Die Methodik des EuGH (2004); Jahrbuch Junger Zivilrechtswissenschaftler 2009: Europäische Methodik: Konvergenz und Diskrepanz europäischen und nationalen Privatrechts (2009); Hager, Rechtsmethoden in Europa (2009); Henninger, Europäisches Privatrecht und Methode (2009); Höpfner/Rüthers, Grundlagen einer Europäischen Methodenlehre, Archiv für civilistische Praxis 209 (2009) 1; Müller/Christensen, Juristische Methodik, Bd. II – Europerecht (2003); Riesenhuber (ed.), Europäische Methodenlehre, 2nd ed. (2010).
5. ECR C-5/05, *Joustra*, ECR 2006, I-11075, para. 41; C-203/09, *Volvo Car* (n.y.r.), para. 39.
6. ECR Case 135/83, *Abels*, ECR 1985, 469, para. 36; C-381/08, *Car Trim* (n.y.r.), para. 47.
7. ECR C-336/03, *easyCar*, ECR 2005, I-1947, para. 20; C-203/09, *Volvo Car* (n.y.r.), para. 40.
8. ECR C-481/99, *Heininger*, ECR 2001, I-9945, para. 46; C-489/07, *Pia Messner*, ECR 2009, I-7315, para. 20.

does not offer much surprise. Nevertheless – as the Court has pointed out in its *C.I.L.F.I.T.* judgment – the interpretation of Community law presents some characteristic features (and particular difficulties),[9] such as

- its multilingual nature whereby the different languages have to be regarded as equally authentic,
- the use of concepts that are peculiar to Community law,
- and the need to interpret traditional national concepts in the light of the specific objectives of Community law with the need to give them a different autonomous meaning.[10]
- Moreover, the Court has given the *effet utile* principle particular weight and strength.[11]

(3) Discussing 'a' European legal method tends to imply that there is a one-fits-all method that may be applied to all areas of European law. This is probably a somewhat problematic oversimplication: It is suggested that the approach taken with regard to constitutional issues is somewhat different from that applied in competition law, and, all the more, legislative acts devoted to the harmonizing of Member State laws: The very policies involved in these divergent fields of law will necessarily influence and shape the legal method applied.[12] Moreover, the interpretation of European Union law is necessarily influenced, explicitly or impliedly, by the (activist or passive) role that the European Court of Justice plays in relation to the Member States in their function as masters of the Treaties, and, with regard to secondary Union law, in relation to the Union institutions involved in the legislative procedure.

9. ECR Case 283/81, *C.I.L.F.I.T.*, ECR 1982, 3415, para. 17.
10. ECR C-188/03, *Junk*, ECR 2005, I-885, para. 29
11. ECR C-129/94, *Ruiz Bernáldez*, ECR 1996, I-1829, para. 19; C-537/03, *Katja Candolin*, ECR 2005, I-5745, para. 28; C-453/99, *Courage*, ECR 2001, I-6297, para. 25-26.
12. See for questions of methodology, as applied in different fields of law (like contract law, labour law, competition law, capital market law and company law), the contributions in Riesenhuber (ed.) (fn. 4), p. 487.

§ 2. As a comparison: the interpretation of international conventions

I. Article 31 of the Vienna Convention of 1969

The Vienna Convention on the Law of Treaties,[13] which codifies rules of public international law, contains some rules on the interpretation of international treaties: Article 31 states that a treaty must be interpreted in good faith in accordance with the ordinary meaning to be given to its terms in their context and in the light of its object and purpose.[14] Language being the starting point, Article 33 (1) of the Vienna Convention provides with regard to a treaty with more than one authentic language version that the different authentic language versions stand on the same footing,[15] and, as Article 33 (3) sets forth, the terms in the different languages should be presumed to have the same meaning. Where there remains a conflict between different language versions, the provision has to be interpreted in the light of its purpose and goal. The latter point sounds very familiar to a lawyer trained in European law.[16] Most recently, in its *Walz* judgment applying this method of interpretation with respect to the terms 'préjudice' and 'dommage' in the Convention of Montreal,[17] the ECR started from the proposition – again sounding familiar – that the terms have to be given a uniform and autonomous interpretation, notwithstanding the different meanings given to that concept in the domestic laws of the States Parties to that convention.[18]

II. Deficiencies

This is not to say that Union law has to be interpreted in the same way as international conventions. Indeed, there are important differences such as, as a matter of principle, the relevance of subsequent practice of the Contracting States in the interpretation of a convention.[19]

However, most importantly, with regard to international treaties, there is no guarantee for a really autonomous and uniform interpretation of the in-

13. Signed in Vienna, May 23rd 1969.
14. See ECJ C-63/09, *Axel Walz* (n.y.r.), para. 23 with further references.
15. Except for the case that one language version is attributed priority.
16. For an in-depth analysis of the rules set forth by the Vienna Convention, see e.g. Gardiner, Treaty Interpretation, 2008, p. 141.
17. The terms are used without distinction with the terms 'dano' and 'damage' in other authentic language versions.
18. ECJ C-63/09, *Walz* (n.y.r.), para. 21.
19. As to this notion, see Gardiner (fn. 16), p. 225.

strument as long as there is no institution which is competent to give an authoritative interpretation. For instance, any student of the Vienna Sales Law Convention of 1980 will be familiar with the fact that the interpretation of the Convention in different jurisdictions may follow different paths.[20] And a still more striking example may be taken from the European arena: The Convention on the Law Applicable to Contractual Obligations ('Rome Convention') of 1980,[21] in its Article 18, contains an obligation for the courts of the Contracting States to strive for a uniform interpretation of the Convention, which more or less implies an obligation to take notice of the case law of the courts of the other Contracting Partners. However, experience of some thirty years will easily reveal that the national courts have more or less ignored this obligation and rather preferred to follow their own legal and interpretative traditions.[22]

It is to be concluded that despite the claim for an autonomous interpretation of international conventions and treaties, such a uniform application and interpretation without an 'international' and efficiently working enforcement mechanism may to a certain extent remain a goal that may be striven for, but that will not be reached in daily practice.

§ 3. What makes the Union Treaties special?

There are two basic features that make the European Treaties 'special' vis-à-vis international treaties and conventions, and that call for developing a 'European legal method':

- First: the notion of the European Union as a 'Union based on the rule of law' (*Rechtsgemeinschaft*) (under I.);
- and second: The enforcement mechanisms established on the Union/ Community level (under II.) and on the national level (under III.).

20. See for an intriguing comparative study that deals with the application of CISG Convention by US and German courts Merlin, Gesetzesauslegung in den USA und in Deutschland, 2005, p. 322.
21. O.J. 1998 C 27/34.
22. E.g. concerning the proper law of a contract concluded with a commercial agent, see Bundesgerichtshof 11.2.1988, Neue Juristische Wochenschrift 1988, 1466: domicile of the commercial agent; Cour de cassation 15.5.2001, Revue critique 2002, 86 (with comment P. Lagarde); 25.11.2003, Revue critique 2004, 102 (with comment P. Lagarde): seat of the undertaking.

I. A Union based on the rule of law

We may, firstly, recall the judgment *van Gend en Loos* in which the ECJ has postulated that the EEC is not merely an international treaty just creating mutual obligations between the contracting states, but that the Community constitutes *a new legal order* of international law by which the States have limited their sovereign rights, and by which the States have conferred rights on the individuals that were meant to be protected by the Court of Justice,[23] and, by way of the notion of direct applicability, by the national courts as well.[24]

On this basis the Court developed its vision, put forward in *Les Verts v. Parliament*, that the European Economic Community has to be regarded '... as a Community based on the rule of law, inasmuch as neither its Member States nor its institutions can avoid a review of the question whether the measures adopted by them are in conformity with the basic constitutional charter, the Treaty, ...'.[25] The Court emphasized that the Treaty has '... established a complete system of legal remedies and procedures designed to permit the Court of Justice to review the legality of measures adopted by the institutions ...', and it goes without saying: of measures adopted by the Member States as well. It is this concept of a Community based on the *rule of law*[26] that has inspired the development of Community law in the last forty or fifty years.[27]

Though it is true that the ECJ has, in its case law, extended and refined the concept of the Community as a *Rechtsgemeinschaft*,[28] it is the EEC Treaty itself that has laid the major foundations for the need to interpret Community law, and thereby to develop a legal method that takes regard of the specific features of Community law: The EEC Treaty has created institutions – Council, Parliament, and the Commission – with competences the use of which would necessarily lead to 'constitutional' conflicts. The Treaty – from its inception – was meant to be the framework for solving those conflicts on the horizontal level between the institutions of the Community on the one hand,

23. ECJ Case 26/62, *Van Gend en Loos*, ECR 1963, 1 (under II.B.); see the comments by Pescatore, de Witte, Mayer and Halberstam in: Maduro/Azoulai (eds.), The Past and Future of EU Law, 2010, p. 3.
24. ECJ Case 26/62, *Van Gend en Loos*, ECR 1963, 1 (under II.B.).
25. ECJ Case 294/83, *Les Verts*, ECR 1986, 1339, para. 23.
26. See Art. 2 TEU and the references to the rule of law in the Preamble of the Treaty; see also *Lecourt*, L'Europe des Juges, 1976, p. 221 with reference to *Hallstein.*
27. Tridimas, The General Principles of EU Law, 2nd ed. 2006, p. 52.
28. ECJ C-402/05 P and C-415/05 P, *Yassin Abdullah Kadi*, ECR 2008, I-6351, para. 281.

and to solve conflicts of interest and competence between the Community and the Member States.

II. Enforcement mechanisms at the Community level

By establishing Community institutions with competences on the one hand and providing for a Court to supervise the use of these competences on the other, the EEC Treaty, from its inception, has arguably gone beyond a mere international treaty. The EEC Treaty has instituted three kinds of enforcements proceedings that put the Court into a position to give the Treaty provisions a binding interpretation.

(1) By giving jurisdiction to the ECJ to review the legality of Community acts – based on Article 230 EC/Article 263 TFEU – by an *action for annulment*,[29] the Treaty offers an important instrument for enforcing the concept of the 'rule of law' on the one hand, and for an effective supervision of the principle of conferred powers that is still basic for the Union today (Article 5 (2) TEU) on the other. Questions of competence have to be regarded as inherently *constitutional questions*. The Court, by interpreting the Treaty, needs a vision of the relationship between the Community institutions and their competences,[30] which it has to work out – requiring a specific legal method based on the very essentials, but also on the specifics of the European Treaties – a 'European legal method'.

(2) Whereas, under public international law, the enforcement of treaty obligations is usually left to the Contracting States, the EEC Treaty, from its inception, has provided for another important control instrument *sui generis*: the *infringement proceedings*[31] which may be brought by the Commission against a Member State (ex Article 226 EC/Article 258 TFEU). Infringement proceedings give the Court of Justice an opportunity to interpret basic provisions of the Treaties, e.g. to determine the scope and the meaning of the fundamental freedoms and their impact on the law of the Member States. Thereby these proceedings offer the Commission the chance to ask the Court to deal with important, but yet unresolved issues of European law, and to develop the law further.

29. E.g. Arnull, The European Union and its Court of Justice, 2nd ed., 2006, p. 53.
30. As for the notion of institutional balance, see e.g. ECJ Case 138/79, *Roquette Frères*, ECR 1980, 3333, para. 33; Jacqué, The Principle of Institutional Balance, C.M.L.Rev. 41 (2004) 383.
31. Arnull (fn. 29), p. 34.

(3) A third control mechanism at the Community level relates to the jurisdiction of the European courts for *actions for damages*[32] brought by individuals, concerning unlawful acts by Community institutions (ex Article 288 (2) EC/Article 340 TFEU). This enforcement instrument gives the Courts the competence to develop a European law of torts in the area of Union liability and at the same time to deal with Union law provisions that are supposed to be infringed.

It goes without saying that the European Treaties, by attributing jurisdiction to the ECJ (and the General Court) in these cases, provide for an enforcement mechanism that is meant to lead to *a uniform and consistent application* of the Treaties. Beyond the claim that provisions in an international treaty have to be attributed an *autonomous meaning,* it is the very institution of a Community court that guarantees a uniform interpretation of Community law. As such the jurisdiction of the Community courts in the matters described above provide the basis for developing a specific European legal method.

III. The preliminary ruling procedure

The perhaps most important instrument for the ECJ to get involved in the interpretation and development of European law, and thereby creating and applying a European legal method, is the preliminary ruling procedure, based on Article 267 TFEU.

1. The importance of the procedure

If one starts from the assumption, as the ECJ did in *van Gend en Loos*, that the Community could be conceived as a *new legal order* of international law which created not only obligations for the Member States, but also rights and obligations for individuals which, based on the notions of direct effect and direct applicability, could be pursued in the national courts, it becomes quite apparent that this assumption puts much of the responsibility of applying European law on the national courts.

National courts have to deal with European law in a number of ways:

- They are, on the basis of the directly applicable Treaty provisions such as Art. 101 and 102 TFEU, and of directly applicable regulations, obliged to apply European law in national proceedings; the rights and obligations of

32. Kapteyn & VerLoren van Themaat, The Law of the European Union and the European Communites, 4th ed. 2008, p. 473; Tridimas (fn. 27), p. 477.

individuals are directly derived from European law. Insofar it may be said that national courts act as 'Community' courts enforcing Community law-based rights and obligations.

- Given the supremacy of European law, they have to interpret national law in conformity with European law, or even to leave it unapplied in a case where a conflict with European law is unavoidable.[33] In such a setting it is the function of the national courts to supervise national law and administrative acts for their conformity with European law.[34]
- Moreover, national courts deal with European law, though in a more indirect fashion, when and where they are obliged to interpret national legal provisions in conformity with the aims and standards set forth by a directive:[35] The courts thereby enforce the goals of a directive on the one hand, and, on the other hand, supervise, and perhaps correct, the fulfilment of the obligation to transpose a directive into national law by the national legislature.

These questions will be raised in court proceedings on the national level. It goes without saying that within this legal framework national courts play a central role and therefore carry a great responsibility in the correct enforcement of European law. However, this *decentralized* application and enforcement of European law carries with it a fundamental problem: National courts will quite naturally be inclined to interpret European law according to their legal traditions, thereby creating the danger that European law will be interpreted and applied differently in the various Member States.

The instrument to ensure a uniform interpretation of Community law by the *national courts* is, of course, the preliminary ruling procedure, based on Article 267 TFEU. Without exaggeration, it may be said that this procedure plays a most fundamental role in the European legal system: It is meant to ensure that European primary and secondary law, as far as possible, have the same effect within all the Member States of the Union,[36] and it moves the European Court of Justice into a position where it exerts utmost influence on

33. Most recently: ECJ C-429/09, *Günter Fuß* (n.y.r.), para. 40.
34. The function to enforce directly applicable (though unwritten) European tort law is mixed with the supervisory function where national courts deal with damage claims based on the *Francovich* case law; see e.g. Tridimas (fn. 27), p. 498.
35. ECJ C-12/08, *Mono Car Styling*, ECR 2009, I-6653, para. 60; for an extended discussion see e.g. Roth, Die richtlinienkonforme Auslegung, in: Riesenhuber (ed.) (fn. 4), p. 393.
36. ECJ C-137/08, *VB Pénzügyi Lízing* (n.y.r.), para. 28.

the decentralized application of European law on the national level. In this decentralized enforcement system the existence of the preliminary ruling procedure also creates a strong incentive for a uniform interpretation of European law, and thereby for the development of a European legal method.

The preliminary ruling procedure has been of particular importance in the development of European Community law: It was by a request of a national court that fundamental principles of Community law such as direct effect,[37] the supremacy of Community law,[38] and the 'general principles', such as fundamental rights,[39] have been established and worked out by the Court. But the preliminary ruling procedure is essential not only for the observance of primary Union law by the national courts, but also for the application of European secondary law: The *Societas Europaea*, based on a EU regulation,[40] needs, as far as this regulation extends, a uniform treatment in civil proceedings all over Europe. The Societas Europaea would not be accepted by the business community as a viable instrument if the provisions of the SE regulation were given a different interpretation by national courts, with the consequence that the meaning and impact of particular provisions would vary from Member State to Member State. Uniform treatment can, of course, only be guaranteed where a mechanism like the preliminary ruling procedure is present and effective.

2. The cooperation with national courts

It is worthy to note that the ECJ, in its adjudication dealing with the application of the preliminary ruling procedure, stresses the context of *cooperation* in which the reference procedure takes place,[41] on the one hand, and the *instrumental function* of the reference procedure on the other hand.[42]

The ECJ has interpreted Article 267 TFEU as an instrument for a 'dialogue'[43] with the national court making the reference which may not be im-

37. ECJ Case 26/62, *Von Gend en Loos*, ECR 1963, 1.
38. ECJ Case 6/64, *Costa v. ENEL*, ECR 1964, 585.
39. ECJ Case 29/69, *Stauder v. Ulm*, ECR 1969, 419 (right of property).
40. Regulation (EC) No. 2157/2001 of October 8th 2001, O.J. 2001 L 294/1.
41. ECJ C-467/08, *Padawan* (n.y.r.), para. 21; C-137/08, *VB Pénzügyi Lízing* (n.y.r.), para. 28.
42. The protection of the coherence of the system of judicial protection in the Union is served by the *duty* for all national courts to refer a question of validity of a Union act to the Court of Justice, see ECJ C-461/03, *Gaston Schul-Douane*, ECR 2005, I-10513, para. 22.
43. ECJ C-210/06, *Cartesio*, ECR 2008, I-9641, para. 91; C-137/08, *VB Pénzügyi Lízing* (n.y.r.), para. 29.

pinged upon by procedural mechanisms of national law,[44] be it also constitutional law.[45] This, of course, may seem self-evident in as far as national courts are under a *duty* to ask for a preliminary ruling, as are courts of last resort according to Article 267 (3) TFEU.

However, the Court has been also anxious to strengthen the position of national courts that enjoy discretion to make a reference according to Article 267 (2) TFEU:

- The ECJ has more than once stressed that national courts have the widest discretion in referring matters to the ECJ provided that the preconditions of Article 267 TFEU are met, and they may exercise their discretion at whatever stage of proceedings they feel appropriate. As a consequence, this discretion cannot be restricted by national procedural law which makes the ruling of a higher court on matters of European law binding on the lower court.[46] Moreover, lower courts stand under the obligation to disregard rulings of a higher Court if those are not consistent with European Union law.[47]
- In case that a provision of national law is in conflict with European Union law, the national judge has to leave the provision unapplied. This obligation cannot be touched upon by a national procedural provision (even of constitutional flavour) which transfers this power to a higher (or a constitutional) court.[48]
- To ensure the effectiveness of the Article 267 TFEU procedure, national procedural law cannot restrict the discretion (or even obligation) to make a reference in a setting in which a national provision may be considered unconstitutional as well. Even when national procedural law makes it obligatory to refer a question of unconstitutionality to a specialized national (constitutional) court, the national judge does not lose its right (under Article 267 (2) TFEU) or escape its obligation (under Article 267 (3) TFEU)

44. Most recently: ECJ C-173/09, *Elchinov* (n.y.r.), para. 27.
45. ECJ C-188/10 and C-189/10, *Melki* (n.y.r.), para. 52.
46. ECJ Case 166/73, *Rheinmühlen*, ECR 1974, 33; C-173/09, *Elchinov* (n.y.r.), para. 26-27 with further references.
47. ECJ C-173/09, *Elchinov* (n.y.r.), para. 30.
48. ECJ Case 106/77, *Simmenthal*, ECR 1978, 629, para. 24; C-314/08, *Filipiak* (n.y.r.), para. 81.

to refer a question on the interpretation or validity of EU law to the European Court of Justice.[49]

Article 267 TFEU, as interpreted by the ECJ, has established a system of judicial protection that is designed to achieve a uniform interpretation of European Union law. This goal is quite obviously effectuated by the abovementioned case law that is meant to bolster the power of the national judge to cooperate with the ECJ in a *direct manner* thereby ensuring a uniform application of European law.

3. The C.I.L.F.I.T. *doctrine*

The goal to reach a uniform interpretation of European law in all Member States has also strongly inspired the case law concerning the *obligation* for courts of last resort to ask for a preliminary judgment (Article 267 (3) TFEU), and the search for potential restrictions to this obligation. As is well-known, the ECJ, in its *C.I.L.F.I.T.* judgment, has developed a rather restrained view of any inherent limitations of the obligation to refer:[50] It held that an obligation to make a reference is only excluded in a case where the correct application of Community law was 'so obvious as to leave no scope for any reasonable doubt as to the matter in which the question raised is to be resolved'. Whether the correct application of Community law may be considered as being 'so obvious' also has to be viewed from the standpoint of the courts of the other Member States and the ECJ, thereby taking also into account 'the characteristic features of Community law and the particular difficulties to which its interpretation gives rise.'[51] The Court, in its case law up till today, has not yet softened its position on this issue. It is submitted that the ECJ still regards it of utmost importance to reduce the danger that European Union law becomes subject to divergent interpretations in the Member States.

IV. The role of national courts

In as far as European primary law and regulations are directly applicable, national courts are important actors in the application of European Union law. This role has been strengthened to a considerable extent by the case law of the ECJ with regard to the application of directives by national courts. Ac-

49. ECJ C-188/10 and 189/10, *Melki* (n.y.r.), para. 45.
50. For a discussion of this judgment, see the contributions of Edward, Craig, Sarmiento and Sweet in Maduro/Azoulai (eds.) (fn. 23), p. 171.
51. ECJ Case 283/81, *C.I.L.F.I.T.*, ECR 1982, 3415, para. 16-17.

cording to Article 288 TFEU and to settled case law,[52] directives – in contrast to regulations – are binding only on the Member States, and they cannot impose obligations on an individual: Whereas a provision in a directive may, under certain conditions, be applied vertically (in the relationship between the individual and the State) in favour (but not to the disadvantage) of an individual,[53] a directive cannot be directly applied horizontally as between individuals. This is even the case where a provision in a directive may be regarded as a clear, precise and unconditional provision seeking to confer rights and/or obligations on individuals.[54]

Taken this as the starting point, the ECJ has developed the obligation of national courts, and indeed all national authorities, to interpret national law in conformity with the goals and provisions set forth in a directive. This obligation is analogous to the principle of interpretation according to which a national court has to apply national law 'in conformity'[55] with primary Union law.[56] This obligation may be based on Article 288 TFEU,[57] and it has, in the past, also been based on the general duty of a Member State, set forth in Article 4 (3) TEU (ex Article 10 EC), 'to take all appropriate measures, whether general or particular,' to achieve the result envisaged by the directive. Based on this duty the ECJ held that '... when applying national law, ... the national court has to interpret that law ... as far as possible, in the light of the wording and the purpose of the directive so as to achieve the result it has in view and thereby comply with the third paragraph of (ex) Article 189 of the Treaty'[58] (now Article 288 (3) TFEU).

In contrast to a *direct* application of a provision in a regulation, the obligation, based on Article 4 (3) TEU,[59] to interpret national law in conformity with a directive leads to an *indirect* effect of a directive. However, this obligation nevertheless amounts to a most powerful instrument to get national courts engaged in the enforcement of European Union law; and, indeed, the contrast between a direct application of a directive provision and its indirect effect by way of interpreting national law in accordance with the directive

52. E.g. ECJ C-12/08, *Mono Car Styling*, ECR 2009, I-6653, para. 59.
53. E.g. ECJ Case 8/81, *Becker*, ECR 1982, 71; C-188/89, *Foster*, ECR 1990, 3348; most recently C-429/09, *Günter Fuß* (n.y.r.), para. 35-40.
54. ECJ C-12/08, *Mono Car Styling*, ECR 2009, I-6653, para. 59.
55. See ECJ C-188/10 and C-189/10, *Melki* (n.y.r.), para. 50.
56. Craig, The legal effect of directives: policy, rules and exceptions, Eur.L. Rev. 34 (2009) 349 (357).
57. ECJ C-12/08, *Mono Car Styling*, ECR 2009, I-6653, para. 60.
58. ECJ C-91/92, *Faccini Dori*, ECR 1994, I-3325, para. 26.
59. Most recently ECJ C-429/09, *Günter Fuß* (n.y.r.), para. 39.

should not be exaggerated: It becomes crucial only in a case where a *contra legem* interpretation of national law is barred by national law.[60]

The duty to interpret national law in accordance with a directive becomes an effective instrument for enforcing European Union law in a uniform manner if taken together with the preliminary reference procedure: Thereby the European Court of Justice again moves into a central position for the interpretation and development of European law – and thereby for the development of a specific European legal method.

§ 4. The individual as 'instrument'

Discussing the 'instruments' provided for by the Treaties that enable the development of a European legal method puts the spotlight on the system of judicial supervision set up by the Treaties. However, it is as important to take a look at the role of the individual in this system of judicial protection – and the instruments that may help to make the judicial system of supervision, and the goal of a uniform interpretation of European Union law, more effective.

I. Direct applicability

To begin with, the notion of *direct applicability* of primary Union law has to be conceived as a most important *enforcement device*: The individual who, before a national court, may call on European Union law to have conflicting national law disapplied may be regarded as an 'attorney general' acting in the interest of the European Union: Though an individual, in the proceedings before a national court, will normally and primarily follow his/her natural self-interest, the proceedings will at the same time serve the purpose of effective enforcement of Union law when, in a case of conflict, national law remains unapplied by a national court.

II. The fundamental freedoms as individual rights and their scope

Together with the notion of direct applicability, the ECJ, from the beginnings of its case law, has conceived the fundamental freedoms not merely as provisions that define the *structure* of what was to become the 'common market' (and later on: 'the single market'). Rather, the Court has conceived the fun-

60. The Court, in a number of judgments, has taken the view that national courts are bound by the interpretative methods recognized by national law and that European Union law cannot serve as the basis for an interpretation of national law *contra legem*; ECJ C-12/08, *Mono Car Styling*, ECR 2009, I-6653, para. 61.

damental freedoms essentially as *individual rights*, e.g. of the traders importing and exporting goods,[61] or of undertakings providing services on an interstate level. Such an approach is not self-evident at all. However, construing the fundamental freedoms not merely as *obligations* of the Member States as Contracting Partners of the EEC Treaty, but also as *rights* on which individuals can call before a national court, conceives the individual as an *instrument* to effectively enforce European law in the arena of national courts – besides the means of the Commission to institute infringement proceedings.

Such a concept has been developed in the judgment *van Gend en Loos* in which the Court expressly said that 'the vigilance of the individuals concerned to protect their rights amounts to an effective supervision in addition to the supervision entrusted by (ex) Articles 169 and 170 to the diligence of the Commission and the Member States.'[62] From the very beginning the Court has interpreted the Community Treaties in such a way as to integrate not only the Member States, but also the individuals into the legal system. In its *Francovich*[63] and *Courage*[64] judgments the Court sums up this concept in the following sentences:

> 'It should be borne in mind ... that the EEC Treaty has created its own legal system, which is integrated into the legal systems of the Member States and which their courts are bound to apply. The subjects of that legal system are not only the Member States but also their nationals. Just as it imposes burdens on individuals, Community law is also intended to give rise to rights which become part of their legal patrimony. Those rights arise not only where they are expressly granted by the Treaty but also by virtue of obligations which the Treaty imposes in a clearly defined manner both on individuals and on the Member States and the Community institutions ...'.

This attribution of rights to individuals under the fundamental freedoms case law and, based thereupon, the enforcement of European Union law by actions brought by those individuals becomes all the more important when and where the *scope* of the fundamental freedoms is interpreted in an *expansive manner*, e.g. when freedom to provide services is not only conceived as a 'right' of the provider of the service to offer a service across state boundaries, but also as a

61. ECJ Case 8/74, *Procureur du Roi* v. *Dassonville*, ECR 1974, 837.
62. ECJ Case 26/62, *Van Gend en Loos*, ECR 1963, 1 (under II.B.).
63. ECJ C-6/90 and C-9/90, *Francovich*, ECR 1991, I-5357, para. 31.
64. ECJ C-453/99, *Courage*, ECR 2001, I-6297, para. 19.

'right' of a (potential) *recipient* to receive a service on a non-discriminatory basis (in the State where the service provider is located),[65] and moreover unrestrained by measures of the Member State where the recipient resides.[66]

Another example for such an expansive interpretation of the fundamental freedoms might be their application to actions and measures taken by private associations or organisations,[67] or even just by private undertakings:[68] a problem widely discussed in the academic arena under the heading of 'horizontal' application of the fundamental freedoms.[69] Again, the 'horizontal' application has to be conceived as a powerful instrument in the hands of individuals to enforce European Union law vis-à-vis other actors in the market.[70] On this background the preliminary rulings procedure will have to be used to develop the necessary standards for a uniform horizontal application of the freedoms in the Member States.[71]

III. Remedies: The right to compensation of damages

The ECJ has empowered the individual in its role as 'private attorney' with another powerful instrument to enforce Union law by creating the remedy of compensation of damages that ensues from a failure to comply with the Treaties: The creation of this remedy will in most cases lead to a reference, and thereby give the ECJ the chance to interpret Union law again.

1. State liability

In its *Francovich* judgment the ECJ once more relied on the contention that the Treaty has to be interpreted in such a way as not only to create obligations for the Member States, but also to give rise to rights that individuals may rely upon. The Court called on the *effet utile* principle, claiming that the full effectiveness of Community rules would be impaired if the individuals could not

65. ECJ C-45/93, *Commission v. Spain*, ECR 1994, I-911, para. 10.
66. ECJ Case 286/82 and 26/83, *Luisi Carbone*, ECR 1984, 377, para. 10; C-384/93, *Alpine Investments,* ECR 1995, I-1141, para. 30; C-158/96, *Kohll*, ECR 1998, I-1931, para. 33.
67. ECJ Case 36/74, *Walrave*, ECR 1974, 1405; C-415/93, *Bosman*, ECR 1995, I-4921.
68. ECJ C-281/98, *Angonese*, ECR 2000, I-4139; C-94/07, *Raccanelli*, ECR 2008, I-5939.
69. See for an analysis of the case law of the ECJ and a proposal to deal with the problem: Roth, Privatautonomie und die Grundfreiheiten des EG-Vertrages, in: Festschrift für Medicus (2009), p. 393.
70. ECJ C-438/05, *Viking*, ECR 2007, I-10779.
71. See for one of the most recent judgments ECJ C-325/08, *Olympic Lyonnais* (n.y.r.).

obtain redress in case that their Treaty rights were infringed.[72] The Court claimed that the existence of State liability were 'inherent in the system of the Treaty,'[73] and that the same result could be deduced from ex Article 5 EEC Treaty (now Article 4 (3) TEU), which requires the Member States to take 'all appropriate measures ... to ensure fulfilment of their obligations under Community law'.[74] General principles of Union law like Article 4 (3) TEU and the effet utile principle serve as the basis for effectively enforcing Union law rights by individuals in national courts: Individuals as self-interested persons who serve as 'private attorney general' and thereby act in the interest of the Union to effectively enforce Union law whereby the uniform interpretation of which is secured by the preliminary ruling procedure.

2. Damage claims in competition cases

Basically the same approach has been taken by the ECJ with regard to damage claims in competition cases. Starting from the general aim of undistorted competition as set forth in ex Article 3 (1) lit. g EC, ex Article 81 and 82 EC (Article 101, 102 TFEU) have been interpreted as fundamental provisions that do not only produce 'direct effects between individuals', but also 'create rights for the individuals concerned which national courts must safeguard.'[75] The principle of full effectiveness, so the ECJ concludes, 'would be put at a risk if it were not open to any individual to claim damages for loss caused to him by a contract or by conduct liable to restrict or distort competition.'[76] The Court thereby establishes *a second route* of competition law enforcement, besides the enforcement by the EU Commission and the national competition authorities. The protection of competitors and/or suppliers, customers, and consumers set forth in Article 101 and 102 TFEU is being transformed into a right of the affected individuals with constitutional flavour that national courts have to effectively safeguard by providing a compensation remedy for losses caused by anticompetitive behaviour.

At the same time the Court underlines the function of the right of an individual to claim compensation for damages as 'private attorney general': 'Indeed, the existence of such a right strengthens the working of the Community competition rules and discourages agreements or practices ... which are liable

72. ECJ C-6/90 and C-9/90, *Francovich*, ECR 1991, I-5357, para. 33-34.
73. ECJ C-6/90 and C-9/90 (fn. 72), para. 35; C-429/09, *Günter Fuß* (n.y.r.), para. 45.
74. ECJ C-6/90 and C-9/90 (fn. 72), para. 36.
75. ECJ C-453/99, *Courage*, ECR 2001, I-6297, para. 23; see also para. 25.
76. Para. 26.

to restrict or distort competition.'[77] And the Court goes on to state that 'actions for damages before the national courts can make a significant contribution to the maintenance of effective competition in the Community.'[78]

At this point it becomes evident that the ECJ has again created a legal remedy for an intensified enforcement of European Union law that, of course, calls for a uniform interpretation and application of European competition law by the national courts. The creation of the compensatory remedy is built on the existence of the preliminary ruling procedure, and on the assumption that the national courts will make use of this procedure leading to an intensified, but uniform application of European competition law.

§ 5. Basic principles of European law as 'instruments'

The preliminary ruling procedure would not work without some basic principles of European law that have already been mentioned: *Direct effect* and *direct applicability* of primary Union law and regulations as well as the *supremacy* of Union law are at the very basis of an efficient working of the reference procedure and the application of European law by national courts. Without direct applicability and supremacy as basic principles of European law, the national courts would simply apply national law, and, hopefully, just take note of European law as public international law with its obligations derived therefrom. Accordingly, the legal principles of direct effect, direct applicability and of supremacy may also be regarded as 'instruments' to engage the national courts in the business of enforcing European law, and taken together with the preliminary ruling procedure, as an effective enforcement mechanism for the development of European law and its uniform application in the courts of the Member States. They may be viewed as an expression of the principle of *practical effectiveness* (*effet utile*) which the Court, from its early days on, has been eager to apply.[79]

In a more substantive vein stand the goals, values and general principles that the Community is meant to pursue and to which it is bound. It is true that the goals set forth in ex Article 2 EC become relevant only in connection with specific provisions in the Treaties,[80] but they have to be taken as important factors in the interpretation of these provisions. To give one example or two:

77. Para. 27.
78. Para. 27.
79. E.g. ECJ Case 14/68, *Walt Wilhelm*, ECR 1969, 1, para. 6.
80. ECJ C-484/08, *Caja de Ahorros* (n.y.r.), para. 46.

In *Albany* the ECJ had to deal with the question whether certain restrictions of competition inherent in collective agreements between organisations representing employers and workers may be caught by ex Article 81 EC. Turning to ex Article 3 (1) lit. j EC and ex Article 2 EC, the Court was anxious to stress that the Community was meant to follow a policy in the social sphere, ensuring a high level ... of social protection;[81] on this basis the Court limited the scope of application of ex Article 81 EC excluding collective agreements meant to improve conditions of work and employment.[82] And in *Viking* the ECJ, dealing with the issue whether a collective action by a labour union may be caught by freedom of establishment, stressed the point that the European Community had developed a social dimension which has to be taken into consideration when applying the fundamental freedoms.[83] Apart from ex Article 2 EC, the ECJ has developed general principles of Union law,[84] most importantly the fundamental rights, that have to be taken into account when primary (and secondary) Union law is to be interpreted. In case the application of these general principles may lead to a conflict with other Treaty provisions, the need for a European method to solve such a conflict becomes obvious.[85]

§ 6. The importance of a centralized authority for the interpretation of European law

This paper shall be concluded with some general observations concerning the existence of a centralized judicial authority and its importance for a uniform interpretation of European Union law and the development of a European legal method. As has been described, the EEC Treaty has, from the outset, provided for the necessary procedural instruments to put the ECJ into the position to deal with fundamental issues of Treaty interpretation and application.

(1) The Court has the function of a truly *constitutional court* to clarify the competences of the Union institutions (on the horizontal level), as well as to delineate the competences of the Union vis-à-vis the Member States, and to

81. ECJ C-67/96, *Albany*, ECR 1999, I-5751, para. 54.
82. Para. 59.
83. ECJ C-438/05, *Viking*, ECR 2007, I-10779, para. 79.
84. Tridimas (fn. 27), p. 59; Arnull (fn. 29), p. 335.
85. See the opinion of AG Trstenjak, C-271/08, *Commission* v. *Germany* (n.y.r.), para. 186-199.

circumscribe the duties of the Member States to cooperate with the Union and among themselves (Article 4 (3) TEU). These functions have been expressly attributed to the ECJ from the outset (ex Article 164, 169, 170, 173 EEC Treaty), functions that can only be fulfilled by a centralized judicial institution, interpreting the Treaty provisions, and thereby developing a European legal method.

(2) The same may said with regard to the Treaty provisions dealing with the European common market, like e.g. the fundamental freedoms and the competition provisions. The development of an efficient common market presupposes that the interpretation of the fundamental freedoms is not dependant on potentially varying interpretations by national courts inspired by (protective) interests and (legal) traditions prevailing in the respective Member States. It seems to be essential for the functioning of a common market that a quasi-federal institution like the ECJ has jurisdiction to deal with those issues, and to develop standards and principles that are binding on the national courts leading to a uniform application of the Treaties throughout the Union.

(3) From its beginning, the EEC has been an *open-ended* legal order with many gaps and unresolved problems, and therefore with a need to develop general principles of law, based on common principles of the legal orders of the Member States. The attribution of competence to the Council and the Commission to administer the European agricultural market has by necessity created the need to develop a European administrative law, with such fundamental principles as proportionality,[86] legal certainty, and the protection of legitimate expectations.[87] Moreover, the lack of a charter of fundamental rights in the original EEC Treaty could not seriously be interpreted as *carte blanche* for the institutions of the Community as being not bound by any fundamental rights. Quite to the contrary: Ex Article 164 EEC Treaty (now Article 19 TEU) has created the obligation for the Court of Justice to ensure that in the interpretation and application of the Treaty 'the law is observed'. This provision has, from the outset, put the Court into the position to develop the unwritten 'general principles' and fundamental rights to which the Community institutions must be regarded to be bound. The development of these principles presupposes the development of a European legal method as inherent in the obligation of the Court to ensure that 'the law is observed'.

86. Tridimas (fn. 27), p. 193.
87. Tridimas (fn. 27), p. 242.

Where Did the Spirit and Its Friends Go? On the European Legal Method(s) and the Interpretational Style of the Court of Justice of the European Union

Ulla Neergaard and Ruth Nielsen

1 Introduction

1.1 Legal Method in the Very Early Years

Already the very first preliminary ruling of the Court of Justice – rendered all the way back in the spring of 1962 – refers not only to the 'letter', but also to the 'spirit' and 'purpose' of the provision under scrutiny, *i.e.* Article 267 TFEU.[1] In its classic and still thought-provoking second preliminary ruling, *van Gend en Loos*, introducing the direct effect doctrine, which was rendered already in the beginning of 1963, it is also stressed in the argumentation that the 'spirit' and the 'objective' is of importance, but also that:[2]

> 'To ascertain whether the provisions of an international treaty extend so far in their effects it is necessary to consider the spirit, the general scheme and the wording of those provisions. The objective of the EEC Treaty, which is to establish a common market, the functioning of which is of direct concern to interested parties in the Community, implies that this treaty is more than an agreement which merely creates mutual obligations between the contracting states ...'

The argumentation is then followed by, among others, a thorough reference to Article 267 TFEU, and it is stated that the Community constitutes a new

1. Case 13/61 *de Geus/Bosch* [1962] ECR p. 45.
2. Case 26/62 *van Gend en Loos* [1963] ECR p. 1.

legal order of international law. In addition, the risk of ineffectiveness of a given provision is given weight.

In the ninth preliminary ruling, constituting an equally and deservedly famous case, *Costa* v *ENEL*, concerning the establishment of supremacy, a similar focus on the 'spirit' and the 'purpose' may be observed, but also:[3]

> 'By contrast with ordinary international treaties, the EEC Treaty has created its own legal system which, on the entry into force of the Treaty, became an integral part of the legal systems of the member states and which their courts are bound to apply ... The integration into the laws of each member state of provisions which derive from the Community, and more generally the terms and the spirit of the Treaty, make it impossible for the states, as a corollary, to accord precedence to a unilateral and subsequent measure over a legal system accepted by them on a basis of reciprocity, such a measure cannot therefore be inconsistent with that legal system, the executive force of Community law cannot vary from one state to another in deference to subsequent domestic law, without jeopardizing the attainment of the objectives of the Treaty set out in Article 5(2) [now in principle Article 4 TEU] and giving rise to the discrimination prohibited by Article 7 [now Article 18 TFEU] ... The precedence of Community law is confirmed by Article 189 [now Article 288 TFEU], whereby a regulation 'shall be binding' and 'directly applicable in all Member States'. This provision which is subject to no reservation, would be quite meaningless if a state could unilaterally nullify its effects by means of a legislative measure which could prevail over Community law.' [4]

Thus, somehow, in the first ten to fifteen years or thereabout, the CJEU was rather explicit with regard to what kind of normative material could be relied upon when interpreting EU law and what was characteristic of its interpretational style. In our view, the legal method[5] applied by the CJEU seemed more

3. See Maduro, Miguel Poiares and Azoulai, Loïc: The Past and Future of EU Law. The Classics of EU Law Revisited on the 50th Anniversary of the Rome Treaty, Hart Publishing 2010, where both *van Gend en Loos* and *Costa* v *ENEL* are designated as 'classic' judgments (a definition thereof is found at p. xiii).
4. Case 6/64 *Costa* v *ENEL* [1964] ECR p. 585.
5. In accordance with the Danish (Nordic) tradition, which is based on a modified and diluted form of Scandinavian legal realism, we use the expression 'legal method' as referring to the doctrine of the sources of law and their interpretation;; see the general project description for the European Legal Method-project at http://www.cbs.dk/forskning/institutter_centre/institutter/law/menu/forskningsprojekter#ELM1 See on

transparent[6] and explicit in this very first period of existence than in later years. In general terms, one can say that the place of law in European societies has for centuries been somewhere between imagination and power.[7] The early Court seemed to demonstrate considerable judicial imagination when interpreting primary law.[8] We are in this essay interested in detecting and analysing – at least some of – the changes which might have occurred.

1.2 Research Question(s)

On this background, the primary research question of the present essay is whether the views regarding the legal methods (judicial methods) used by the CJEU for justifying its decisions that for years have been regarded as 'truths' in legal literature may be considered as 'real truths' and whether they still can be considered as 'truths' today (2011).

Scandinavian Legal Realism Ross, Alf: Ret og Retfærdighed, Copenhagen 1953, translated into English as: On Law and Justice, London 1958. See also Nielsen, Ruth: Legal Realism and EU law, in Koch, Henning, Karsten Hagel-Sørensen, Ulrich Haltern and Joseph H.H. Weiler (eds.): Europe – The New Legal Realism, Copenhagen 2010.

6. There is probably a difference between lawyers with a common law background and a civil law background in assessing what is transparent and what is the opposite of transparent. Lasser, Mitchel: Judicial deliberations: a comparative analysis of judicial transparency and legitimacy, Oxford 2009, p. 3 states: 'Common Law judicial decision-making – the American comparative story goes – carries such great legitimacy precisely because of its great transparency. Individually signed opinions (including concurrences and dissents), the disclosure of judicial votes, the forthright recognition of interpretive difficulties, the candid discussion of judicial legal development, and public judicial debate over substantive policy issues combine to foster judicial accountability and control, to encourage democratic debate and deliberation, and thus to accord well-deserved legitimacy to American judicial power. Civilian judicial decision-making – the American comparative story continues – lacks appropriate legitimacy precisely because it lacks sufficient transparency. Civilian judicial decisions consist of little more than cryptic and technical judicial fiats. They offer monolithic, unsigned, collegial judgments that refuse to disclose judicial votes, prohibit concurrences or dissents, and shun the overt discussion of policy in favor of syllogistic – or at least highly deductive – statements that downplay, if not mask or ignore, all meaningful judicial interpretive work.' In the early years CJEU judgments looked rather like French judgments and may look fairly intransparent to a common law observer.
7. Cf. Unger, Roberto: What Should Legal Analysis Become?, London/New York 1996, freely available at http://www.law.harvard.edu/faculty/unger/english/whatsa.php, p. 26.
8. We use the term primary EU law as referring to the Treaties and general principles and fundamental rights.

We have chosen to focus on the following classic legal science 'truths' about the CJEU's judicial method and their later development:

1. *The application of the teleological method as justification in interpretations (see further section 2);*
2. *Reference to uniformity in EU law as the goal of interpretations under Article 267 TFEU (see further section 3);*
3. *The application of Article 4 TEU as justification in interpretations (see further section 4); and*
4. *The application of general principles and fundamental rights as justification in interpretations (see further section 5).*

We do not consider these as an exhaustive account of 'truths'. However, we think that as a whole they are sufficiently representative. We estimate that all of these 'truths' may be said to have a certain degree of basis in the early EU law literature. [9] They are often also taken for granted in later literature. In other words, there might be a herd mentality – or self-generating mentality – concerning these, so that authors tend to repeat more or less uncritically what has been stated in earlier works.[10] Thus, our primary focus will be on documenting how they have been applied/developed/deviated from over the years in the case law of the CJEU and whether they can be considered 'truths' of today (2011).

Our terminology in this essay is determined/limited by the legal dogmatic framework we have chosen. When we speak of 'truths' and 'real truths', it only refers to whether the views are in accordance with what can be deduced from the CJEU's judicial practice or a legal dogmatic analysis of it. Observers using other theoretical and methodological starting points than the one we have chosen would probably be interested in other aspects in order to qualify

9. See on the methods applied by the CJEU in the early period *e.g.* Pescatore, Pierre: L'ordre juridique des communautés européennes. Etude des sources du droit communautaire, originally from 1975, re-published Bruxelles 2006; Lecourt, Robert: L'Europe des juges, originally from 1976, re-published Bruxelles 2008; Brown, L. Neville & Tom Kennedy: The Court of Justice of the European Communities, London 2000 Part Four; Arnull, Anthony: The European Union and its Court of Justice, Oxford 2006; Gulmann, Claus: Methods of Interpretation of the European Court of Justice, Scandinavian Studies in law 1980, p. 187, http://www.scandinavianlaw.se/pdf/24-8.pdf with extensive citations in particular from the writings of Pescatore and Lecourt; and Koopmans, Thijmen: The Birth of European Law at the CrossRoads of Legal Traditions, The American Journal of Comparative Law 1991, p. 493.
10. See the essay in the present volume by Micklitz, Hans and Rob van Gestel.

a statement as a truth. By justification we mean the reasons the CJEU states in support of its rulings in the texts of the judgments.

We use the term *literal interpretation* as referring to an interpretation primarily based on the wording and syntax of the provision under interpretation. By *historical interpretation* we refer to interpretations where the interpreter looks for the (subjective) intention of the historical legislator, *i.e.* the author of the provision (Treaty provision or secondary legislation) under interpretation. In historical interpretation considerable weight is often put on the preparatory works (*travaux préparatoires).* The relative importance of literal and historical interpretation depends on the drafting traditions in the legal system under interpretation, in particular whether it uses preambles in its legislation. Nordic legislation, for example, usually does not have preambles. Statements that are placed in the preambles in EU legislation are in Nordic legislation found in the preparatory works. Historical interpretation is therefore traditionally more important when interpreting national law in these countries than when interpreting EU law, where a literal interpretation of the preambles will often show views that could only be found by historical interpretation of the preparatory works in Nordic law. In *systematic interpretation* the interpreter refers to the place of the provision under interpretation in the legal act and/or in the legal system it is part of. In *teleological interpretation* the focus is on the objective *telos* of the provision under interpretation; see further below in section 2.

In comparative works on interpretation,[11] it has been common to state that arguments from the historical legislator's intent were/are far less frequently encountered in the UK than in continental European countries. After the UK's entry into the EU, UK law is interpreted in a more purposive way both in the sense referred to in historical interpretation (the intention of the EU legislator or the intention of the UK legislator to transpose a particular piece of EU law into UK law with the same meaning as intended by the EU legislator) and in the sense referred to in teleological interpretation, which takes the objective aim of the law under interpretation into account. In English language literature the term 'purposive interpretation' is sometimes used in a way that somewhat blurs the difference between historical and teleological interpretation compared to the use of that distinction in the continental (including the Nordic) literature.[12] In this essay we follow the continental (Nordic) tradition and try to make it clear whether a purpose referred to is the his-

11. See MacCormick, Neil and Robert S. Summers (eds.): Interpreting Statutes. A Comparative Study, Aldershot 1991, p. 472.
12. See for example Larenz, Karl und Claus-Wilhelm Canaris: Methodenlehre der Rechtswissenschaft, Berlin 1995, p. 141 *et seq.*

torical legislator's purpose or the purpose that in the view of the interpreter (the judge/the CJEU) is the objective aim (purpose) of the provision under interpretation.

1.3 Background Theory (Critical Legal Positivism)

An author's choice of research questions, terminology in which to express them and method for examining them is probably always deeply influenced by his or her *Vorverständnis* (preconception) of the subject.[13]

We take inspiration from Tuori's theory of critical legal positivism.[14] Tuori has argued for a critical version of legal positivism as the basis for legal scholarship. He presents the normative and practical faces of law as a multi-layered phenomenon within which there is an important role for critical legal dogmatics in furthering law's self-understanding and coherence. This theory forms in our view the most elaborate version of modern Nordic legal positivism and can, in our view, be seen as a further development of Scandinavian legal realism.[15] Critical legal positivism presents itself as a further development of legal positivism. It builds on other theories such as Kelsen's Pure Theory of Law (*Reine Rechtslehre*),[16] Hart's theory of law[17] and the institutional theory of law developed by MacCormick.[18]

1.3.1 The Different Layers of Law

According to critical legal positivism, law and its changes should be examined on three levels: the surface level of the law; the legal culture; and the deep structure of law.

13. Esser, Josef: Vorverständnis und Methodenwahl in der Rechtsfindung, Frankfurt 1972.
14. Tuori, Kaarlo: Critical Legal Positivism, Aldershot 2002.
15. See on Scandinavian Legal Realism Alf Ross: Ret og Retfærdighed, Copenhagen1953, translated into English as On Law and Justice, London 1958. See also Nielsen, Ruth: Legal Realism and EU law in Koch, Henning, Karsten Hagel-Sørensen, Ulrich Haltern and Joseph H. H. Weiler (eds.): Europe – The New Legal Realism, Copenhagen 2010.
16. Kelsen, Hans: Introduction to the Problems of Legal Theory (A Translation of the First edition of Reine Rechtslehre 1934), Oxford 1992.
17. Hart, H. L. A.: The Concept of Law, Oxford 1994.
18. See furher MacCormick, Neil and Ota Weinberger: An Institutional Theory of Law. New Approaches to Legal Positivism, Dordrecht 1986; Weinberger, Ota: Law, Institution and Legal Politics, Fundamental Problems of Legal Theory and Social Philosophy, Dordrecht 1991; Bengoetxea, Joxerramon: Institutions, Legal Theory and EC Law, Archiv für Rechts- und Sozialphilosophie 1991, p. 195; and MacCormick, Neil (ed.): Constructing Legal Systems. 'European Union' in Legal Theory, Dordrecht 1997.

The surface level of the law comprises various pieces of legislation as well as the text of judgments. The legal culture constitutes the middle or mediating level of law. Tuori uses the term deep structure of law to name the common core of a distinct historical type of law, for example modern law. Viewed in this way, legal development starts at the surface level and then gradually over a number of years settles down as deeper layers of law. Legal history is thus a process of sedimentation.

Expressed in the terminology of critical legal positivism, the present essay examines developments at the surface level of law and discusses their sedimentation into the legal culture. We regard legal method as part of the expert legal culture.

In regard to the theme of the present essay, the obvious weakness of Tuori's theory on critical legal positivism is that it has been developed on the basis of national (Western) law without taking much notice of EU law and its interaction with the law of the EU Member States. Multi-layeredness in the EU legal order is different from multi-layeredness of national law and dependant on other processes than sedimentation. We believe that our analysis of developments in the CJEU's judicial method over time can show something about the specific character of the multi-layeredness of the EU legal order.

1.3.2 The Two Faces of Law: Law as a Legal Order and Law as Legal Practices

Critical legal positivism sees law as having two faces. It can be approached as a symbolic normative phenomenon, as a *legal order*, on the one hand, and as a set of specific social practices, as *legal practices*, on the other hand. The most important legal practices are law-making, adjudication and legal research practices. Expressed in the terminology of this theory the present essay is an example of one legal practice (research practice) studying another legal practice (judicial practice). There are thus two variants of legal method at stake in the present essay: we use a legal research method for studying the CJEU's judicial method.

The two aspects of law – law as a legal order and law as legal practices – are in constant interaction. Legal practices could not exist without legal norms. The legal order defines certain social practices as legal, as for example law-making or adjudication (constitutive legal norms) and guide the conduct of the agents of these practices. The legal method (understood as the sources of law and the way they are interpreted) to be used by the CJEU is part of the valid law (*geltendes Recht*) in the multi-layered legal order applicable in the territory of the EU Member States. Seen from the perspective of legal positivism, nothing is law just because the CJEU says so. A judgment from CJEU is primarily a statement of the legal ideology of the CJEU and lacks the factual dimension of law that from a positivist perspective is necessary in order for a normative system to be valid law, unless a national legal/state system chooses to add a factual dimension to the statements of the CJEU. The highest courts in the Member States only accept the case law of the CJEU as valid law as long as it applies an acceptable legal method (judicial method). This can be illustrated by the reaction of the German *Bundesarbeitsgericht* and *Bundesverfassungsgericht* to the CJEU's *Mangold* judgment,[19] which has met with heavy criticism for overstepping the borderline between law and policy but was accepted by the German courts partly because the *Mangold* judgment was deemed to be correct from a methodological point of view. The *Bundesarbeitsgericht* followed the CJEU's judgment in *Mangold* in a judgment from 2006 against Honeywell, where it stated that the CJEU's *Mangold* judgment was (emphasis added):[20]

> '... *methodisch vertretbar* und hält sich daher im Rahmen der dem Europäischen Gerichtshof bei der Auslegung des Primärrechts eröffneten Rechtserkenntnismöglichkeiten ...'

In July 2010, the German *Bundesverfassungsgericht* in rejecting a constitutional complaint (*'Verfassungsbeschwerde'*) against the *Honeywell* judgment of the *Bundesarbeitsgericht* stated that (emphasis added):[21]

> 'Dem Gerichtshof [*i.e.* CJEU] ist auch die Rechtsfortbildung im Wege *methodisch gebundener Rechtsprechung* nicht verwehrt.'

In *Brasserie de Pecheur*, the CJEU expressed a similar view. It stated (emphasis added):[22]

> 'Since the Treaty contains no provision expressly and specifically governing the consequences of breaches of Community law by Member States, it is for the Court, in pursuance of the task conferred on it by Article 164 of

19. Case C-144/04 *Mangold* [2005] ECR p. I-9981.
20. Urteil vom 26.4.2006, 7 AZR 500/04, http://juris.bundesarbeitsgericht.de/cgi-bin/rechtsprechung/document.py?Gericht=bag&Art=en&sid=7748175819924172abf091c3a364e945&nr=11198&pos=0&anz=1.
21. BVerfG, 2 BvR 2661/06 vom 6.7.2010, http://www.bverfg.de/entscheidungen/rs20100706_2bvr266106.html.
22. Case C-46/93 and C-48/93 *Brasserie du pêcheur* [1996] ECR p. I-1029, Para. 27.

> the Treaty of ensuring that in the interpretation and application of the Treaty the law is observed, to rule on such a question *in accordance with generally accepted methods of interpretation*, in particular by reference to the fundamental principles of the Community legal system and, where necessary, general principles common to the legal systems of the Member States.'

Law as a *legal order* could also not exist without *legal practices*, which are responsible for its production and reproduction. The term *legal system* is used in critical legal positivism to cover both of the law's two aspects (legal order and legal practices).

1.3.3 Combination of an Insider-Perspective and an Outsider-Perspective in Legal Dogmatics

According to critical legal positivism, legal research practice is of a double character. It is at the same time both legal practice (and as such part of the legal system) and research practice (and as such part of the (social or humanistic science) research community). Legal research practice as a legal practice participating in the development of the legal system often uses practically the same methods of interpretation as the CJEU's judicial method, which is the object studied by the research. We also do that in this essay.

In the EU's early period, there was considerable personal overlap between EU law as judge-made law and EU law as '*Professorenrecht*'.[23] Today (2011), there is a greater distance between the career paths of judges and legal scholars and between a judicial and an academic way of looking at EU law and more diversity in academic research on EU law.

1.3.4 Other Theoretical Approaches

Other authors choose to view EU law in light of other background theories. Groussot,[24] in an analysis of the contribution of the CJEU to the development

23. Leading academic writers as for example Lecourt and Pescatore were judges/presidents of the CJEU for a period.
24. See on theoretical aspects Bengoetxea, Joxerramon: The Legal Reasoning of the European Court of Justice, Oxford 1993; Bengoetxea, Joxerramon: Legal Reasoning and the Hermeneutic Turn in the Law – Remarks on the European Court of Justice in Ulla Neergaard, Ruth Nielsen and Lynn Roseberry (eds.): The Role of Courts in Developing a European Social Model – Theoretical and Methodological Perspectives, Copenhagen 2010; and Groussot, Xavier: Creation, Development and Impact of the General Principles of Community Law: Towards a jus commune europaeum?, Lund

of general principles in EU law, raises the question whether the CJEU is a Dworkinian court. Our answer to that question is no. In a general textbook on EU law that for a number of years was the leading Danish textbook on EU law, Gulmann and Hagel-Sørensen state that:[25]

> 'Seen from a Nordic legal positivist perspective the CJEU's case law contains clear natural law elements.'

We will not look further into the CJEU's methods in a natural law perspective in this essay.

1.4 Our Research Method

In this essay, we take an evolutionary approach both to our case material from the surface level of the legal order and to the understanding of it in academic legal literature at the surface and medium levels of the law.

1.4.1 Legal Dogmatic Research and Other Social and Humanistic Science Studies of Law

There are marked differences between the methods and practices used for answering research questions in legal dogmatic research (doctrinal legal research) and the methods used in other social or humanistic sciences studying EU law as an object.[26] A reason for this lies in the research questions. In legal

2005, p. 192 – a shorter version is published under the title General Principles of Community Law, Amsterdam 2006.

25. Translated by Neergaard and Nielsen. See the Danish original Gulmann, Claus and Karsten Hagel-Sørensen: EU-ret, Copenhagen 1995, p. 155, note 22. The original reads: 'Set fra en nordisk, retspositivistisk synsvinkel indeholder EF-Domstolens praksis klare naturretlige elementer'. In the Nordic legal positivist tradition, leading writers – as for example Alf Ross – have expressed strong criticism of natural law. A main point in this criticism was/is that any view can be defended by natural law arguments. Ross thus wrote: 'Like a harlot, natural law is at the disposal of everyone.' See Ross, Alf: On Law and Justice, London 1958 (English translation of Ret og Retfærdighed, Copenhagen1953), p. 261. The Danish original reads: 'Som en skøge er naturretten til rådighed for enhver', Ret og Retfærdighed, p. 343.
26. See for example the analysis of the debate on an EU Constitution from a rhetorical perspective in Just, Sine Nørholm: The Constitution of Meaning – A Meaningful Constitution?, Copenhagen 2005, where the author *inter alia* uses newspaper articles as material, and the analysis of Article 267 TFEU references from a political science perspective in Wind, Marlene: The Nordics, the EU and the Reluctance Towards Supranational Judicial Review, Journal of Common Market Studies 2009, p. 1039,

dogmatic research, the central questions can be boiled down to questions about valid law. The research question(s) in this essay could also be framed as being whether the four truths we look into in more detail in the following sections are valid EU law. As Tuori points out legal (dogmatic) research approaches the law from a participant's perspective while social science research approaches the law from an external observer's perspective.

It is necessary to use different methods to answer different research questions. In dogmatic studies of law, the questions relate to what is valid law, and the material examined in order to arrive at an answer is a normative material (the sources of law), which is read and interpreted in accordance with the expert legal culture. The legal method(s) applied in dogmatic legal research have common traits with the scholastic methods developed in early natural law theory, where a statement was regarded as true when it could be traced back to an authoritative source.[27] The focus on valid law is characteristic both of judges in the exercise of their functions as judges and for academic legal research irrespective of whether it is based on natural law theory or a legal theory which can be seen as positivistic. When EU law is approached from other professional perspectives, for example from a political science perspective, the focus of interest will typically not be valid law but some other aspects, as regards political scientists some kind of policy or political phenomenon. Political scientists and their interest in seeing EU law as a *multi-level governance system* have played a major role in the soft law development since the Treaty of Amsterdam. It is beyond the scope of this essay to clarify the differences (and perhaps similarities) between a legal dogmatic view of EU law as a *multi-layered legal order* and a political science view of EU as a *multi-level governance system.*

1.4.2 Identification of the Material (Case Law and Literature) We Examine

We use the expression 'legal method' as referring to the doctrine of the sources of law and their interpretation.[28] We examine which kind of normative material (for example the ECHR, principles common to the legal tradi-

where the author examines what judges do (not by reading their judgments but) by sending them questionnaires.

27. See Martijn Hesselink: A European Legal Method? On European Private Law and Scientific Method, European Law Journal 2009, p. 20.
28. See the general project description for the European Legal Method-project at http://www.cbs.dk/forskning/institutter_centre/institutter/law/menu/forskningsprojekter#ELM1.

tions of the Member States[29] or precedents[30]) and what sort of argumentative patterns (for example teleological interpretation or literal interpretation) the CJEU uses. In its judgments, the CJEU does usually not refer to legal literature and never to literature on legal theory.

Our analysis is based on a sample of judgments from the CJEU. We have made a systematic review of preliminary references from 1958-72 and from 2008-10. In the last period we only look at rulings delivered by the Grand chamber. The period between the years 1958-72 is referred to as the early period.[31] 1972 is chosen as the final year to be included because since 1973 new Member States have continued to join the EU, which in itself is assumed to constitute a natural delimitation of a first period of the CJEU's life. The period between the years 2008-10 is referred to as the most recent case law.[32] As mentioned, the first reference for a preliminary ruling dates back to 1961. In the early years of the EU, there were only few references, but since the early 1970s the number of references has grown considerably.[33] In the first years, the CJEU answered any question a national court had chosen to refer, but since *Foglia* it has tightened its practice on admissibility.[34] Since *Telemarsicabruzzo,*[35] the CJEU normally dismisses poorly framed references as

29. Koopmans, Thijmen: The Birth of European Law at the CrossRoads of Legal Traditions, The American Journal of Comparative Law 1991, p. 493 concludes: 'Personally, I am tempted to think that the Court of Justice has become one of the major sources of legal innovation in Europe not only because of its position as the Community's judicial institution, but also because of the intellectual strength of its comparative methods.' By comparative method Koopmans in that paper refers to the CJEU's practice of picking up elements from the law of one or more Member State(s) and using them as building blocks in developing an interpretation of EU law; see further below in section 5.
30. See Koopmans, Thijmen: *Stare decisis* in European Law, in O'Keefe, David and Henry G. Schermers: Essays in European Law and Integration, Kluwer 1982 and below in section 3.
31. It comprises 160 preliminary rulings in cases brought before the CJEU 1958-72, *i.e.* from Case 13/61 to Case 87/72.
32. It comprises 40 preliminary rulings referred to the CJEU from 2008-10 and decided before the end of 2010, *i.e.* from Case C-46/08 to Case C-357/09.
33. See the statistics on the development from 1952-2007 in the ECJ Annual Report 2007, p. 97.
34. Case 244/80 *Foglia/Novello* [1981] ECR p. 3045; see further Barnard, Catherine and Eleanor Sharpston: The Changing Face of Article 177 References, Common Market Law Review 1997, p. 1113.
35. Case C-320/90, C-321/90 and C-322/90 *Telemarsicabruzzo and others* / [1993] ECR p. I-393.

inadmissible.[36] The total number of preliminary references to the CJEU from 1961 to 2009 is 6,620.[37] The Founding Treaties provided for the possibility of forming chambers, either to undertake certain preparatory inquiries or to adjudicate on particular categories of cases. Due to the now very large amount of preliminary rulings rendered by the CJEU, it has not been possible to include more than three years of judgments to examine. We have selected preliminary rulings because these cases are often of general importance[38] and tend to show more about the interplay between EU law and national law in the Member States than judgments resulting from other types of procedures.

In addition to the abovementioned sample of preliminary rulings, we use a number of other judgments, both preliminary rulings and other types of judgments in the following sections selected on the basis of our intuitive knowledge of existing relevant case law.

We also only use a limited selection of literature which we have found illustrative. All these limitations are made due to the concern of realistically accomplishing the examination, as it has been considered not feasible to examine the total amount of case law and literature. Nevertheless, it is our belief that the material we have selected is after all sufficiently representative to build a certain idea of the answers to our research question(s). However, it is self-evident that the answers reached should be viewed in light of the limitations made.

1.5 Structure of the Analysis

In what follows, each 'truth' will be further explained/defined and a certain idea of its role in literature will be given. However, the primary focus will be on how they have been applied over the years in the case law of the CJEU and whether they are indeed also 'truths' of today. The overall benefit of this approach would hopefully be to gain an impression of the evolution of the European legal method as provided by the CJEU itself, including an impres-

36. See further Morten P. Broberg and Fenger, Niels: Preliminary References to The European Court of Justice, Oxford 2010, p. 302.
37. See Statistics of judicial activity of the Court of Justice 2009, p. 101 at http://curia.europa.eu/jcms/upload/docs/application/pdf/2010-05/ra09_stat_cour_final_en.pdf. The Court of Justice of the European Union consists of three courts: the Court of Justice, the General Court (created in 1988 as the Court of First Instance) and the Civil Service Tribunal (created in 2004). Since their establishment, approximately 15 000 judgments have been delivered by the three courts; see the website of the CJEU at http://curia.europa.eu/jcms/jcms/Jo2_6999/.
38. Cf. Llorens, Albertina Albors: The European Court of Justice, More than a Telelogical Court, Cambridge Yearbook of European Legal Studies 1999, p. 373.

sion of what may be said to constitute the main present day (2011) truths about CJEU's legal method.

There are thus four sections (2-5) in this essay, one for each of the above 'truths'. In each section there are subsections with the following headings:

1. Understanding/definition of the truth in question
2. The sources of law of relevance for the truth in question
3. Acceptance in literature of the truth as a real truth
4. The early case law
5. The development in the case law
6. The most recent case law
7. Preliminary conclusions.

Finally, in section 6, we will sum up our conclusions on the basis of all the analyses made.

2 The First Truth: Application of the Teleological Method as Justification in Interpretations

2.1 Understanding/Definition of the First Truth

The English Lord Denning has in *Bulmer Ltd.* v *Bollinger SA* noted among others the following about the CJEU's legal method:[39]

> 'All the way through the Treaty there are gaps and lacunae. These have to be filled in by the judges, or by regulations or directives. It is the European way ... Seeing these differences, *what are the English courts to do when they are faced with a problem of interpretation*? They must follow the European pattern. No longer must they argue about the precise grammatical sense. They must look to the purpose and intent ... They must divine the spirit of the Treaty and gain inspiration from it. If they find a gap, they must fill it as best they can ...'

Hereby, the importance of the 'purpose' in EU law is so – almost emotionally – emphasised by one of the most influential legal actors in the UK. This element in EU law is often referred to as the teleological method, which is one of the more important among several interpretational methods applied by the

39. [1974] Ch 401, 425.

CJEU over the years.[40] At times, it may be referred to under different headings, for instance 'purposive interpretation'[41] or 'teleological interpretation'.[42]

The method has long and deep roots in EU law. According to the historian Rasmussen, the Commission had an important and seminal role in the launching of the teleological method, as it was its policy to persuade the CJEU to 'assume the role of a Supreme Court and adopt ... not a narrow textual reading but an 'organic interpretation' determined also by the wide-reaching objective of the Common Market' and that its legal service had long recommended the 'teleological mode'. [43]

Several 'insiders' have over the years explained about the interpretational style of the CJEU. For instance, Chevallier (attaché of the CJEU) already in 1964-65 – although not explicitly making reference to the term 'teleological method' – stressed the importance of objectives and the spirit of the Treaty. Also, among others he remarked that:[44]

> 'Generally speaking, it can be said ... that the Court tries to discover the thinking of the authors of those texts of Community law it is called upon to interpret. The thinking of the author of a text may be sought in different ways, ranging from the analytic to the synthetic; in other words one may base oneself upon the letter or upon the spirit of the text, which involves a whole hierarchy of criteria, running, when it is a question of construing a treaty, from a meticulous examination of its wording to a study of the results which would flow from various interpretations ...'

40. For instance, in (Advocate General of the CJEU) Maduro, Miguel Poiares: Interpreting European Law – Judicial Adjudication in a Context of Constitutional Pluralism, Working Paper IE Law School WPLS08-02, 05-02-2008, p. 3, it is stated: 'Legal interpretation at the Court of Justice is governed by text, context and telos or purpose.'
41. (Judge of the CJEU) MacKenzie Stuart, Lord: The European Communities and the Rule of Law, The Hamlyn Lectures, Twenty-Ninth Series, Stevens & Sons 1977, p. 76.
42. This term has been critisised by *e.g.* Hartley, Trevor: The Foundations of the European Union Law, Oxford University Press 2010, p. 72.
43. Rasmussen, Morten: Constructing and Deconstructing 'Constitutional' European Law. Some Reflections on how to study the history of European law, in Koch, Henning, Karsten Hagel-Sørensen, Ulrich Haltern and Joseph H. H. Weiler (eds.): Europe. The New Legal Realism, Djøf Publishing, 2010 pp. 639-660, on pp. 644 and 648 in particular.
44. Chevallier, Roger-Michel: The European Court in Its Interpretation of Community Law, Common Market Law Review 1964-65, p. 23.

Pescatore (judge at the CJEU), however, was very explicit about the importance of the teleological interpretation, and defined it back in 1971 in the following manner:[45]

> 'As regards *teleological interpretation*, this is based on the consideration of the objectives assigned to the Community. Contrary to a widespread idea, this is not simply 'one method among others'. The rule of law being by its nature a provision with a certain objective, the teleological method is, in the last analysis, the decisive criterion of every legal interpretation. This is doubly true in the context of treaties, which proceed by laying down objectives rather than substantive rules. It is not surprising, then, that this method has proved particularly fertile, especially in the sphere of fundamental problems of an economic, commercial, and fiscal character which the Court of Justice has been required to resolve ... In view of these methods of interpretation, the case law of the Court of Justice has become within the Community framework a powerful factor for development of Community law in the direction of the objectives, both immediate and distant, assigned to the building of Europe.'

Another of the early writers/insiders to be mentioned is Lecourt (president of the CJEU), who has stated in 1976:[46]

45. Pescatore, Pierre: The Law of Integration. Emergence of a new phenomenon in international relations, based on the experience of the European Communities, A.W. Sijthoff 1974, pp. 88-89. Also see Pescatore, Pierre: Les objets de la Communauté Européenne comme principes d'interprétation dans la jurisprudence de la Cour de Justice. Contribution a la doctrine de l'Interprétation téleogique des traités internationaux, in Miscellanea W.J. Ganshof van der Meersch, II, Bruylant 1972, pp. 325-363; and Pescatore, Pierre: L'ordre juridique des Communautés Européennes. Étude des sources du droit communautaire, originally from 1975, re-published 2006 (Bruyllant).
46. Lecourt, Robert: L'Europe des Juges, originally from 1976, re-published Bruxelles 2008 (Bruylant), pp. 235-236. Much later, it is, for instance, defined in Brown, L. Neville and Tom Kennedy: The Court of Justice of the European Communities, Sweet & Maxwell 2000, p. 339, in the following manner: 'The term teleological is applied to an interpretation which is based upon the purpose or object of the text facing the judge. This approach, which is increasingly favoured by the Court, is peculiarly appropriate in Community law where, as we have seen, the Treaties provide mainly a broad programme or design rather than a detailed blue-print. In setting forth the grand design the Treaties, both in their preambles and in certain Articles, express the objectives of the Communities in very general terms; in turn, these objectives are

> 'Si le Traité de Rome confie à la Cour la mission d'assurer le respect du droit dans l'interprétation et l'application du Traité, ce n'est certainement pas pour l'inviter à en négliger les objectifs, mais pour l'inciter à les sauvegarder et les prendre pour guide de son interprétation. Aborder le droit communautaire sans être conscient de cet impératif serait se condamner à ne voir dans les traités que des dispositions internationales ordinaires à interpréter restrictivement en face de règles nationales ordinaires à interpréter restrictivement en face de règles nationales occupant la totalité du terrain juridiques. Peu de choses sépareraient alors les Traités communautaires de simples traités de commerce associant sans plus des Etats entre eux. Ainsi serait négligée toute l'infrastructure institutionnelle et la vocation normative permanente pour ne voir dans les traités que des dispositions figées, statiques, justiciables seulement d'une interprétation exégétiques et formelle. Ainsi, par un caractéristique renversement d'objectifs, dans les matières transférées à la Communauté, la norme communautaire deviendrait l'exception, d'interprétation stricte. Seraient du coup méconnus les fondements des Traités, la volonté de leurs auteurs et les buts progressifs qu'ils se proposaient d'atteindre. D'un traité-cadre on ferait ainsi un traité bloqué. Ce n'est qu'après s'être pénétré de l'importance d'un tel préalable à quoi tout, dans les Traités, est subordonné, qu'il sera possible de dégager les méthodes d'interprétation spécifiques à un droit communautaire. C'est de ce préalable que découle l'æuvre du juge qui vient d'être analysée. Le sens de sa mission était d'autant moins douteux que ces traités s'ouvrent sur des préambules singulièrement descriptifs des buts visés. Comme les textes de ces traités sont, le plus souvent, des dispositions générales énoncant des principes assortis de règles plus illustratives qu'exhaustives, ils ne pouvaient que confier à la prudence du juge le soin d'en dégager les implications juridiques ... Rudolf von Ihering avait naguère observé que 'le but est le créateur du droit'.'

A third of the early writers/insiders to be mentioned is Kutscher (judge of the CJEU), who – also in 1976 – wrote:[47]

knit together by the underlying assumption that they will lead eventually to an economic and political union.'

47. Kutscher, H.: Methods of interpretation as seen by a judge at the Court of Justice, Judicial and Academic Conference 27-28 September 1976, Court of Justice of the European Communities, Reports, Luxembourg 1976, p. I-39.

> 'The special nature of the Community, which must be regarded, not as an association of States subject to international law, but as a community *sui generis* is orientated to the future and designed with a view to the alteration of economic and social relationships and progressive integration, rules out a static and requires a dynamic and evolutionary interpretation of Community law. The Community judge must never forget that the Treaties establishing the European Communities have laid the foundations of an ever closer union among the peoples of Europe and that the High Contracting Parties were anxious to strengthen the unity of their economies and to ensure their harmonious development (Preamble to the EEC Treaty). The principle of the progressive integration of the Member States in order to attain the objectives of the Treaty does not only comprise a political requirement; it amounts rather to a Community legal principle, which the Court of Justice has to bear in mind when interpreting Community law, if it is to discharge in a proper manner its allotted task of upholding the law when it interprets and applies the Treaties. How else should the Court of Justice carry out this function which it has been assigned except by an interpretation of Community law geared to the aims of the Treaty, that is to say, one which is dynamic and teleological?'

As an example of a view stated in more recent time, it may be mentioned that Maduro wrote – with a different perspective – the following about the understanding of the method while he was still an Advocate General at the CJEU:[48]

> 'Teleological interpretation in EU law does not, therefore, refer exclusively to a purpose driven interpretation of the relevant legal rules. It refers to a particular systemic understanding of the EU legal order that permeates the interpretation of all its rules.' In other words, the Court [h]as not simply been concerned with ascertaining the aim of a particular legal provision. It also interpreted that rule in the light of the broader context pro-

48. Maduro, Miguel Poiares: 'Interpreting European Law – Judicial Adjudication in a Context of Constitutional Pluralism', Working Paper IE Law School WPLS08-02, 05-02-2008, p. 3. On the 'meta-teleological' method, also see *e.g.* Lasser, Mitchell: 'Anticipating Three Models of Judicial Control, Debate and Legitimacy: The European Court of Justice, the Cour de cassation and the United States Supreme Court', Jean Monnet Working Paper 1/03, NYU School of Law. This author also – on p. 44 – speaks of 'meta' purposes, which are understood as: '... the purposes, values or policies underlying not so much the particular piece of legislation at issue, but those underlying the EU and its legal structure *as a whole.*'

vided by the EC (now EU) legal order and its 'constitutional telos'. There is a clear association between the systemic (context) and teleological elements of interpretation in the Court's reasoning. It is not simply the telos of the rules to be interpreted that matters but also the telos of the legal context in which those rules exist. We can talk therefore of both a teleological and a meta-teleological reasoning in the Court ...'

The teleological method has certain roots in national law.[49] In some Member States the legal systems have to some degree been familiar with the teleological method, whereas in others the familiarity therewith has been fairly absent. This may also have had an influence on how the CJEU's application thereof has been received in each of the individual Member States.[50]

The rationale justifying a decision by referring to the goal or purpose of the rule in general has been explained by Feteris as being found in considering legal rules as an instrument for realising certain legal, social and economic goals.[51] The author further explains that the meaning of a legal rule should be established on the basis of the good the rule aims to promote or the evil it seeks to avert and that legal rules are designed to promote certain goals

49. In fact, the roots of the concept are even wider. Thus, at Wikipedia (consulted on 8 November 2010) it is among others explained: 'A telos (from the Greek τέλος for 'end', 'purpose', or 'goal') is an end or purpose, in a fairly constrained sense used by philosophers such as Aristotle. It is the root of the term 'teleology', roughly the study of purposiveness, or the study of objects with a view to their aims, purposes, or intentions. Teleology figures centrally in Aristotle's biology and in his theory of causes. It is central to nearly all philosophical theories of history, such as those of Hegel and Marx. One running debate in contemporary philosophy of biology is to what extent teleological language (as in the 'purposes' of various organs or life-processes) is unavoidable, or is simply a shorthand for ideas that can ultimately be spelled out non-teleologically. Philosophy of action also makes essential use of teleological vocabulary: on Davidson's account, an action is just something an agent does with an intention ... that is, looking forward to some end to be achieved by the action.'
50. In addition, the teleological method is closely related to the *effet utile* principle. See *e.g.* Lasser, Mitchel: Judicial Deliberations. A Comparative Analysis of Judicial Transparency and Legitimacy, Oxford University Press 2004, pp. 207-208; Brown, L. Neville and Tom Kennedy: The Court of Justice of the European Communities, Sweet & Maxwell 2000, p. 343; or Slynn, Gordon: The Court of Justice of the European Communities, International & Comparative Law Quarterly 1984, pp. 409-429.
51. Feteris, Eveline T.: The Rational Reconstruction of Weighing and Balancing on the Basis of Teleological-Evaluative Considerations in the Justification of Judicial Decisions, Ratio Juris 2008, p. 483.

and values that are considered essential from the perspective of justice or public good.[52]

Altogether, many different understandings/definitions exist, however, all with a common core.

2.2 The Sources of Law of Relevance for the First Truth

On this background, the attention should be turned to the objectives themselves; here limited to those present in primary law.[53] The birthmarks of the EU as to be found in the establishment of the original European Economic Community pursuant to the Treaty of Rome, which entered into force on 1 January 1958, were – as the name itself already indicates – largely only of an economic character. In the Preamble, the idea of some kind of integration was presented, as it among others is stated that the Founders are determined to establish the foundations of an ever closer union among the European peoples. Article 2 EEC determined that:

> 'The Community shall have as its task, by establishing a common market and progressively approximating the economic policies of Member States, to promote throughout the Community a harmonious development of economic activities, a continuous and balanced expansion, an increase in stability, an accelerated raising of the standard of living and closer relations between the States belonging to it.'

In the succeeding Article 3 EEC, it was stated that for the purposes set out in the preceding Article, the activities of the Community shall include various more specific ones, which are then listed.

Regarding the development in the subsequent years, it is worth mentioning that with the Treaty of Maastricht, which entered into force 1 November 1993, the name of the Community became altered into the European Community, whereby the term 'Economic' became excluded. This step definitely had at least a symbolic importance. From then on came two parallel formulations of objectives, namely in the EC Treaty and in the EU Treaty respectively. Article 2 EC now stated:

52. *Ibid.*
53. In what follows, space does not allow for a full account of the objectives over the time, but rather only the main elements of the development. Also, a limitation is made to objectives of primary law and not *e.g.* secondary law as well.

> 'The Community shall have as its task, by establishing a common market and an economic and monetary union and by implementing the common policies or activities referred to in Articles 3 and 3a, to promote throughout the Community a harmonious and balanced development of economic activities, sustainable and non-inflationary growth respecting the environment, a high degree of convergence of economic performance, a high level of employment and of social protection, the raising of the standard of living and quality of life, and economic and social cohesion and solidarity among Member States.'

In the succeeding Articles 3 and 4 EC, various more concrete objectives were stated. In the EU Treaty references in the Preamble were made to certain 'integrationist' aspects, such as: 'a new stage in the process of European integration'; 'the process of creating an ever closer union among the peoples of Europe'; and advancing 'European integration'. In Article 1 EU a similar reference to the creation of 'an ever closer union among the peoples of Europe' was stipulated. Article 2 EU listed several objectives, among others:

> '... to promote economic and social progress which is balanced and sustainable, in particular through the creation of an area without internal frontiers, through the strengthening of economic and social cohesion and through the establishment of economic and monetary union, ultimately including a single currency in accordance with the provisions of this Treaty ...'

The same pattern may – to be short – be said to continue with the Treaty of Nice (entered into force 1 February 2003) and the Treaty of Amsterdam (entered into force 1 May 1999). With the Treaty of Lisbon (entered into force 1 December 2009), many significant changes arrived. Regarding values, Article 2 TEU stipulates that:

> 'The Union is founded on the values of respect for human dignity, freedom, democracy, equality, the rule of law and respect for human rights, including the rights of persons belonging to minorities. These values are common to the Member States in a society in which pluralism, non-discrimination, tolerance, justice, solidarity and equality between women and men prevail.'

It seems most noteworthy that 'a highly competitive social market economy' should play an explicit and significant role.[54] The context in which this concept is found in, namely Article 3(3) TEU should therefore be stated in its entirety:

> 'The Union shall establish an internal market. It shall work for the sustainable development of Europe based on balanced economic growth and price stability, a highly competitive social market economy, aiming at full employment and social progress, and a high level of protection and improvement of the quality of the environment. It shall promote scientific and technological advance. It shall combat social exclusion and discrimination, and shall promote social justice and protection, equality between women and men, solidarity between generations and protection of the rights of the child. It shall promote economic, social and territorial cohesion, and solidarity among Member States. It shall respect its rich cultural and linguistic diversity, and shall ensure that Europe's cultural heritage is safeguarded and enhanced.'

In the FEU Treaty many objectives are still to be found. In addition, the Charter on Fundamental Rights contains objectives of importance.

To sum up on the development regarding objectives, it is very clear that the amount of objectives has increased. Also, the directions these point to have become more and more diverse. In fact, nowadays, the formulations of the objectives have become so heterogenous that they may in certain situations be counteracting so that the attempt to realise one objective may be in conflict with the realisation of another. Also, there has been a development from only more economic aims to also more political and ideological objectives. In this regard, it is worth stressing that a social dimension has become more and more important. As seen, there is also a development towards an inclusion of values. It may be claimed that these may be given impact on an equal footing with objectives in an application of the teleological method. All these changes may affect the application of the teleological method. It may be assumed that it could be more difficult to use the teleological method with so many competing aims (and values). Finally, an 'integrationist' element has been given weight in the Treaty texts over the years. This has a certain degree

54. On this subject, see *e.g.* Azoulai, Loïc: The Court of Justice and the Social Market Economy: The Emergence of an Ideal and the Conditions for Its Realization, Common Market Law Review 2008.

of relevance here, as the objectives of the EU have often been seen as having in common the overall aim of 'integration' or 'unity'.[55]

2.3 Acceptance in Literature of the First Truth as a Real Truth

Especially in section 2.1, but to a certain degree also in section 2.2, above, references were made to examples of literature which may be read as a clear

55. For instance, Bredimas wrote back in 1978: 'There are certain ideas which have furnished decisive themes in lots of cases before the Court, such as equality of treatment, non-discrimination, economic interpenetration, mutual solidarity, free circulation, economic and legal unity. Judge [Pescatore] [Footnote omitted], in a most illuminating survey, remarks that all those objectives are encompassed by the idea of unity, precisely because they all aspire towards the idea of unity of Western European Nations. In a word, they aspire to transcend nationalism and subordination to absolute state sovereignty towards a common achievement.' Bredimas, Anna: Methods of Interpretation and Community Law, North-Holland Publishing Company 1978, p. 72. Bredimas also quotes (on p. 74) Constantinesco for his view all the way back in 1963 on Community law as economic law. Also see *e.g.* (judge of the CJEU) Edward, David: The European Court of Justice – Friend or Foe, address 18 July 1996; see http://law.du.edu/documents/judge-david-edward-oral-history/1996-the-european-court-of-justice.pdf, pp. 67-68, where he states: 'The so-called 'integrationist agenda' is in the treaties. No-one who spends ten minutes reading the treaties can be in the slightest doubt about that. Like or not, that agenda is political. The Court, interpreting the treaties, cannot ignore the agenda the member states have set for themselves.' Further, see Mann, Clarence J.: The Function of Judicial Decision in European Economic Integration, Martinus Nijhoff 1972, p. 233: 'As a matter of method, therefore, the Court has adopted essentially a teleological approach to Treaty interpretation. It decides in terms of known Treaty interpretation, but these in turn unfold in light of the 'new objects or vistas' revealed through the operation of the Treaties.[Footnote omitted] This approach accords with the evolutionary quality of Community law, based not as the United Nations on 'orders or coordination' but rather on 'orders of integration.'[Footnote omitted] The Community legal orders are designed not only to attain certain stated economic objectives, but to do so in an effort to integrate the substantially competing economies of the Member States. Integration is to be accomplished, moreover, not merely by the enlisted cooperation of national governments, but also through a disciplined procedural and institutional framework of government which is profoundly constitutional in nature.' Finally, see *e.g.* (president at the CJEU) Due, Ole: EF-Domstolens retspraksis som integrationsfremmende faktor, Juridisk Tidsskrift ved Stockholms Universitet 1992, årg. 3/1991-92, p. 412; (judge at the CJEU) Lenaerts, Koen: Interlocking Legal Orders in the European Union and Comparative Law, International and Comparative Law Quarterly 2003, p. 879; or Pescatore, Pierre: Les objets de la Communauté Européenne comme principes d'interprétation dans la jurisprudence de la Cour de Justice. Contribution a la doctrine de l'Interprétation téleogique des traités internationaux, in Miscellanea W.J. Ganshof van der Meersch, II, Bruylant 1972, p. 361.

acceptance of the truth as a real truth. It should be understood that early and leading commentators were in fact judges, who in this way had a very severe influence on the 'marketing' of the truth. In what follows, this point of departure will be further examined, followed by a more general further examination of the literature.

One way of understanding the significance of the double role of some of the judges is by making reference to Neville Brown and Kennedy, who in explaining the importance of the teleological method refer to the fact that Pescatore (judge at the CJEU) as well as Kutscher (president at the CJEU) have expressed that the teleological and contextual methods assume greater importance than the historical or literal methods.[56] In this way, it has generally been assumed that the method has played a large role in the interpretations accomplished by the CJEU. The authority of indications of the interpretational style of the CJEU is thus often given higher weight if such derive from an 'insider'.[57]

The method has often been critisised for, among others, creating legal activism, and consequently in larger terms for being problematic in respect of democracy and legitimacy terms.[58] The critical voices often belong to persons who are in favour of reliance on legal texts (such as constructivism and originalism) and/or persons who do not agree with the European project and its implications.[59] For instance, in an important paper Neill has critically observed that:[60]

56. Brown, L. Neville and Tom Kennedy: The Court of Justice of the European Communities, Sweet & Maxwell 2000, p. 340.
57. To this should be added that especially (judge at the CJEU) Pescatore is said to have given name to a school ('the Pescatore School') which is seen as probably the most important and influential till this day. See Weiler, Joseph H. H.: Hjalte Rasmussen. Nemo propheta in patria sua, in Koch, Henning, Karsten Hagel-Sørensen, Ulrich Haltern and Joseph H. H. Weiler (eds.): Europe. The New Legal Realism, Djøf Publishing 2010, p. XIII.
58. As Due, Ole: EF-domstolens fortolkningsmetoder og Wienerkonventionen om Traktatretten, in Festskrift til Ulf Bernitz, Europarättslig Tidsskrift 2001, pp. 74-75, states: 'Når Domstolens fortolkning udsættes for generel kritik, vedrører denne normalt dem meget udstrakte brug af Fællesskabets formål som fortolkningselement.'
59. See *e.g.* Maduro, Miguel Poiares: 'Interpreting European Law – Judicial Adjudication in a Context of Constitutional Pluralism', Working Paper IE Law School WPLS08-02, 05-02-2008, pp. 5-6.
60. Neill, Patrick: The European Court of Justice: A Case Study in Judicial Activism, August 1995, European Policy Forum, Frankfurter Institut, p. 47. Also see *e.g.* Hartley, Trevor C.: The European Court, judicial objectivity and the constitution of the

> 'The methods of interpretation adopted by the ECJ appear to have liberated the Court from the customarily accepted discipline of endeavouring by textual analysis to ascertain the meaning of the language of the relevant provision ... From the beginning the Court has sought out the spirit of the various texts and their underlying scheme. Furthermore, the Court believes that it has a responsibility to act, as it were, as a motive force pushing the Community forward towards the goals enshrined in the preambles to the successive Treaties ... that it fails to respect fundamental rights. Acting from this perspective the Court has, for example, felt entitled through its case law to read an unwritten bill of rights into Community law, this being, according to a member of the Court, 'the most striking contribution which the Court has made to the development of a constitution for Europe' [Footnote omitted] In commenting on this process, a distinguished comparative lawyer notes that the judges of the Court of Justice 'are claiming for themselves the legitimacy and capacity to do what the framers did not even think of doing, and what the political branches of the Communities do not even try to undertake'.'

Also, Gulmann, who later on became a judge at the CJEU, wrote in 1980 that: 'In my opinion, the most pertinent topic for discussion is whether the Court of Justice exaggerates the importance of the teleological method of interpretation, considering that the decisive objectives taken into account are those expressed in the preamble and the first few articles of the treaties ... One may ask whether it is acceptable that the Court should regard itself as the only true guardian of the Community ideas – ideas laid down just after the war during a period when the world looked quite different from what it is today.' [61]

European Union, Law Quarterly Review 1996, p. 95: 'I[t] is becoming more and more widely recognised that the Court of Justice of the European Communities, generally known as the European Court, sometimes interprets provisions of the Treaties contrary to the natural meaning of the words used,[footnote omitted] an activity to which the phrase 'judicial legislation' may justifiably be applied. Moreover, the court's refusal to accept the natural meaning of Treaty provisions has not occurred on an ad hoc or random basis: it has taken place in pursuance of a settled and consistent policy of promoting European federalism, a policy which includes the extension of the powers of the court itself.'

61. Gulmann, Claus: Methods of Interpretation of the European Court of Justice, Scandinavian Studies in Law 1980, pp. 202-203. Also see Rasmussen, Hjalte: On Law and Policy in the European Court of Justice. A Comparative Study in Judicial Policymaking, Martinus Nijhoff Publishers 1986, which represents a seminal work on activism

However, defences of the method are also often seen and heard. For instance, reference could be made to the abovementioned expression by Lord Denning at least with regard to putting forward an understanding of the need for the method. Also, as another example it may be mentioned that Due (president of the CJEU) has put forward statements in the same direction.[62]

of the CJEU. On p. 380, Rasmussen with regard to the teleological method, among others, stated that: 'By the invention of a *teleological inevitability*, the Court sought to deprive European political leaders of the opportunity of controlling the pace and rhythm of the movement toward the ultimate common goal: the realization of dreams about a 'United States of Europe', which inspired men like *Jean Monnet*. Albeit that dream might still be shared by many, intervening social social changes might legitimately have induced them to disagree with *Monnet* that the dream should have become reality by 1980 ...' Also see, among others, Rasmussen, Hjalte: European Court of Justice, GadJura 1998.

62. Due, Ole: EF-Domstolens retspraksis som integrationsfremmende faktor, Juridisk Tidsskrift ved Stockholms Universitet, 1992, p. 412. The debate on this aspect of teleological method is long, harsh, and with many contributions. See further *e.g.*: Aberavon, Lord Howe of: Euro-justice: yes or no? European Law Review 1996, pp. 187-198; Arnull, Anthony: The European Union and its Court of Justice', Oxford University Press 2006, p. 620 and the following; Arnull, Anthony: The European Court and judicial objectivity: a reply to Professor Hartley, Law Quarterly Review 1996, pp. 411-423; Brown, L. Neville and Tom Kennedy: The Court of Justice of the European Communities, Sweet & Maxwell 2000, p. 340; Cappelletti, Mauro: Is the European Court of Justice 'running wild'? European Law Review 1987, pp. 3-17; Edward, David: Judicial Activism – Myth or Reality? *Van Gend en Loos, Costa v ENEL and the Van Duyn* family revisited, in Campbell, A.I.L. and M. Voyatzi (eds.): Legal Reasoning and Judicial Interpretation of European Law. Essays in Honour of Lord MacKenzie-Stuart, Trenton Publishing 1996, pp. 29-67; (Judge of the CJEU) Lenaerts, Koen: Some Thoughts About the Interaction Between Judges and Politicians in the European Community, Yearbook of European Law 1992, pp. 1-34; Maduro, Miguel Poiares: 'Interpreting European Law – Judicial Adjudication in a Context of Constitutional Pluralism', Working Paper IE Law School WPLS08-02, 05-02-2008, p. 5; (Judge at the CJEU) Pescatore, Pierre: Jusqu'où le juge peut-il aller trop loin?, in Rosenløv, Jens and Kirsten Thorup (eds.): Festskrift til Ole Due. Liber Amicorum, G.E.C. Gads Forlag 1994, pp. 299-338; Schermers, Henry G.: Judicial Protection in the European Communities, Kluwer 1976, p. 13 and the following; Schmid, Christoph U.: From *Effet Utile* to *Effet Neolibéral*. A Critique of the New Methodological Expansionism of the European Court of Justice, in Rainer Nickel (ed.): Conflict of Laws and Laws of Conflict in Europe and Beyond. Patterns of Supranational and Transnational Juridification, ARENA Report No 1/09, RECON Report No 7 2009, pp. 423; (Judge of the CJEU) MacKenzie Stuart, Lord: The European Communities and the Rule of Law, The Hamlyn Lectures, Twenty-Ninth Series, Stevens & Sons 1977, p. 76 and the following; Tridimas, Takis: The Court of Justice and judicial activism, European Law Review 1996, pp. 199-210; and de Waele, Henri:

Altogether, it seems rather clear that the truth must be considered as a real truth in the sense that some version of a teleological method exists, at least if 'real' means that documentation can be found in literature including explicit statements even from CJEU judges.

2.4 The Early Case Law

As mentioned above in section 1, the CJEU in one of its early classic judgments, *van Gend en Loos* from 1963, introducing the direct effect doctrine, referred to the 'objective' – viewed as the establishment of a common market – of the EEC Treaty as an important element in the basis for its finding.[63] Also in the other early classic judgment mentioned above in section 1, *Costa* v *ENEL* from 1964, concerning the establishment of supremacy, there is a similar focus on the 'objectives' (those in Article 5(2) EEC (now in principle substituted by Article 4 TEU); and more generally 'of the Treaty')).[64] Therefore, already at this early stage, the teleological method is severely present as a justification for the introduction of absolutely fundamental principles.

Besides the reference to these two judgments as documentation as to the existence of the teleological method in the early case law, a more systematic examination of the preliminary rulings from 1958-73 has been conducted. For this purpose, the teleological method is here limited to be understood as a legal argumentation/reasoning implying that the literal meaning of a provision – if any – may be playing less of a role if the reference to objectives of the Treaty(/ies) may be said to imply that. Therefore, the examination has concentrated on seeing to which degree an explicit reference to the objectives of the Treaty is made.

On the surface, objectives may have a role to play in the argumentation in the cases of the sample.[65] However, perhaps somewhat surprisingly – viewed in light of the widespread acceptance of the existence of the teleological method – in the large majority of the cases the objectives of the Treaty are not mentioned. Out of the 160 preliminary rulings from this early period, in fact

The Role of the European Court of Justice in the Integration Process: A Contemporary and Normative Assessment, Hanse Law Review 2010, pp. 3-26. Finally, as a recent example, the Danish judge at the CJEU, Lars Bay Larsen, is quoted for having said that the CJEU is not 'politicizing' and 'activistic', as this is fairly wrong as the real problem simply is that the quality of law from the legislators is so flawed. See Louise Wendt Jensen: EU-dommer: 'Lovgiverne burde lovgive mere præcist', djøfbladet 2010, Number 20, pp. 30-32.

63. Case 26/62 *van Gend en Loos* [1963] ECR p. 1.
64. Case 6/64 *Costa* v *ENEL* [1964] ECR p. 585.
65. See section 1.4.2 above.

only a rather small share makes explicit reference to the terms 'object(ive)', 'purpose', 'spirit', 'intent' or 'aim' of the Treaty as such (rather than of *e.g.* individual Treaty provisions or secondary law). Thus, as a consequence only a very few cases may be viewed as implying that the literal meaning of one or more provisions – if any – may be playing less of a role due the reference to Treaty objectives.

Also, in a very large share of cases there is in other respects made reference to these terms, *i.e. e.g.* in respect of the objectives, *etc.*, of individual Treaty provisions or secondary law. In this regard, objectives, *etc.*, do in fact play a significant role in this early period in the sense that objectives are mentioned often, but most frequently not the least as serving a purpose of 'leverage' in interpretations. At times, it may even have the opposite result, namely that the CJEU states that a given interpretation would be to give the provision in question a scope exceeding its purpose, which in the view of the CJEU is not acceptable. The reference may also, more simply, play the role of explaining to the readers of the judgment what the piece of law in question is about through an explanation of its objectives, *etc.*

Altogether, there is no doubt that the first truth was established very early in the case law of the CJEU. Thus, it seems rather clear that the truth must be considered as a real truth, at least if 'real' means that documentation as to its existence can be found in the early case law. However, importantly, the use of the teleological method as defined above (*i.e.* objectives of the Treaty and implying a more 'non-literal' interpretation) only occurred in a fairly limited amount of cases. Those cases are also the ones which generally have 'famous status' and are continuously referred to in literature. When students and others only read these in fact unusual cases from the early period, the impression gained as to the methods used by the CJEU is actually somehow delusional.[66]

66. In the same direction, see Albors Llorens, Albertina: The European Court of Justice, More than a Teleological Court, Cambridge Yearbook of European Legal Studies 1999, p. 374, who states: 'Thus, a comparatively small number of decisions from across the Court's vast case law has been chosen [in most studies] to either substantiate the accusation that the Court 'indulges in creative jurisprudence' [footnote omitted] or to support the view that 'in its case law the Court has not exceeded its powers. [footnote omitted]' But to be fair to the Court, its judgments need to be taken with a temporal and substantive context, rather than in isolation.' Also, on p. 398 it is stated: 'The debate as to whether or not the Court's judgments are influenced by a wish to further its own perception of the Treaty objectives will surely rumble on. But whichever view one takes of the Court's work, it is too facile to generalise on the basis of a few de-

2.5 The Development in the Case Law

In what follows, the analysis will focus on a few examples of the CJEU's application of the teleological method in the period between the early period and the period consisting of the most recent case law. Only one important case has been selected from each of the decenniums beginning with the 1970s. Hereby, the analysis naturally cannot be more than simply illustrative, rather than exhaustive.

From the 1970s, *Defrenne-II* from 1976 has been selected for further analysis. It may be viewed to represent a 'classic' judgment which may be taken as an indication of general acceptance of importance.[67] It primarily concerns the interpretation of what was then Article 119 of the Treaty on equal pay.[68] The judgment, among others, results in horizontal direct effect of the provision and has cast a very long and needed shadow.[69] In the case, the CJEU famously states that the Community is not merely an economic union,

cisions randomly selected from more than forty years of case law. A more rigorous approach, based on a systematic analysis of the Court's case law in different areas, would do it more justice. The comparatively few judgments where it has reached a seemingly dramatic result must not obscure the careful and painstaking interpretative task carried out by the Court in the majority of its decisions.' It may be added that Albors Llorens' analysis and ours vary a bit, especially because the material included is not completely identical. Although both analyses include preliminary rulings, the time span included in ours is slightly shorter. Also, Albors Llorens includes a smaller amount of cases, as she has selected three areas of law, where we have included all the cases in the selected period. Nevertheless, the results of the two examinations appear with regard to frequency of the use of the teleological method rather identical. With regard to the issue of judicial activism, it is not the primary aim of the present essay to examine that. For other limited studies on the teleological method, see *e.g.* Lord, Kenneth M.: Bootstrapping an Environmental Policy from an Economic Covenant: The Teleological Approach of the European Court of Justice, Cornell International Law Journal 1996, pp. 571-606; and Mazzarella, David: The Integration of Aviation Law in the EC: Teleological Jurisprudence and the European Court of Justice, Transportation Law Journal 1991-1992, pp. 353-372.

67. Maduro, Miguel Poiares and Loïc Azoulai: The Past and Future of EU Law. The Classics of EU Law Revisited on the 50th Anniversary of the Rome Treaty, Hart Publishing 2010.
68. Case 43/75 *Defrenne* [1976] ECR p. 455, Paras. 7-14.
69. As expressed by Sharpston, Eleanor: The Shock Arrive in Force: Horizontal Direct Effect of a Treaty Provision and Temporal Limitation of Judgments Join the Armoury of EC Law, in Maduro, Miguel Poiares and Loïc Azoulai: The Past and Future of EU Law. The Classics of EU Law Revisited on the 50th Anniversary of the Rome Treaty, Hart Publishing 2010, p. 264.

but also one which follows social objectives. On the basis of a purposive interpretation, the CJEU reaches its conclusion on equal pay and thereby the case constitutes a major step towards equal treatment of men and women.[70]

From the 1980s, *CILFIT* from 1981 has been selected for further analysis. This case also represents a 'classic' judgment which as mentioned may be taken as an indication of general acceptance of importance.[71] In fact, one of the strongest expressions of the CJEU – with regard to the legal method it claims that it applies – is found in *CILFIT:* 'Finally, every provision of Community law must be placed in its context and interpreted in the light of the provisions of Community law as a whole, regard being had to the objectives thereof and to its state of evolution at the date on which the provision in question is to be applied.' [72] References to this sentence are found again and again in legal textbooks on EU law. It is clearly understood that regard has to be made to the objectives, but in fact here very widely understood, as it is the objectives of 'Community law as a whole'.

From the 1990s, *Albany* shall be briefly touched upon. At the overall level, this case concerned the interpretation of Articles 85, 86 and 90 of the EC Treaty (later Articles 81 EC, 82 EC and 86 EC, and now Articles 101, 102 and 106 TFEU) in relationship to compulsory membership of pension fonds. In the argumentation of the CJEU, objectives seem to play a rather important role.[73] In fact, the outcome of *Albany* clearly seems based on the application of objectives as decisive.[74] However, it could be claimed that the objectives here are not used as leverage, but rather the opposite.

Among cases rendered in the New Millenium, *Laval* (from 2007) has been selected as a representative case of interest to the present analysis.[75] The case was rendered by the Grand Chamber, which in itself is an indication of significance. *Laval* may in brief be said to concern the conflict between the free

70. Simon, Denys: SABENA is dead, Gabrielle Defrenne's case is still alive: the old lady's testament ..., in Maduro, Miguel Poiares and Loïc Azoulai: The Past and Future of EU Law. The Classics of EU Law Revisited on the 50th Anniversary of the Rome Treaty, Hart Publishing 2010, p. 266.
71. Maduro, Miguel Poiares and Loïc Azoulai: The Past and Future of EU Law. The Classics of EU Law Revisited on the 50th Anniversary of the Rome Treaty, Hart Publishing 2010.
72. Case 283/81 *CILFIT* [1982] ECR p. 3415, Para. 20.
73. Case C-219/97 *Drijvende Bokken* [1999] ECR p. I-06121, Paras. 41-47.
74. From the 1990s reference may also be made to *e.g.* Case 333/97 *Deutscher Rundfunkanstalten* [1999] ECR p. I-07599, Para. 27.
75. Another interesting case from this decade is Case C-224/98 *D'Hoop* [2002] ECR p. I-06191, on union citizenship. See in particular Paras. 28 and 32.

movement of services and the right of collective action – and related thereto the protection of workers, where the former may in simplified terms to be viewed as a tool in reaching economic aims and the latter an element in social purposes. The argumentation of the case is long and complicated. For the present purposes, it suffices to emphasise that in its judgment, the CJEU determines:[76]

> 'It should be added that, according to Article 3(1)(c) and (j) EC, the activities of the Community are to include not only an 'internal market characterised by the abolition, as between Member States, of obstacles to the free movement of goods, persons, services and capital', but also 'a policy in the social sphere'. Article 2 EC states that the Community is to have as its task, inter alia, the promotion of 'a harmonious, balanced and sustainable development of economic activities' and 'a high level of employment and of social protection'.
>
> Since the Community has thus not only an economic but also a social purpose, the rights under the provisions of the EC Treaty on the free movement of goods, persons, services and capital must be balanced against the objectives pursued by social policy, which include, as is clear from the first paragraph of Article 136 EC, inter alia, improved living and working conditions, so as to make possible their harmonisation while improvement is being maintained, proper social protection and dialogue between management and labour.'

This represents a clear indication of objectives, and the thinking of the CJEU in the direction of at least a double aim, *i.e.* a Community having both an economic and a social purpose. This may be understood in the direction of a social market economy somehow already being of importance, *i.e.* before the entering into force of the Treaty of Lisbon. However, the indication of the aims is not truly applied in the argumentation of the CJEU in a teleological manner. They are referred to, but do not in actual fact play any severe role on the explicit level as to the outcome of the case, where in fact it may be claimed – again in simplified terms – that the free movement of services 'wins' over the right of collective action. To this should be added that in the case the interest of the free movement of services is formulated at the EU level whereas the interest of the protection of workers is defined at the national level. So in a way, the 'integration' element as mentioned above may

76. Case C-341/05 *Laval* [2007] ECR p. I-11767, Paras. 104-105.

be viewed as the true 'winner'. It also seems to be an example of how much more difficult it may become to find guidance in the objectives when they as explained above are in conflict with one another (as the economic and social purposes often will be).[77]

Altogether, from this interim period, it is possible to find examples of cases where objectives have a certain importance. However, the teleological method in the sense defined above is not necessarily present in these.

2.6 The Most Recent Case Law

Looking at the (rather limited) sample of forty preliminary rulings rendered by the Grand Chamber in recent years, we estimate that references to objectives of the Treaties are only seldom made. More importantly, an explicit application of the teleological method as defined above is difficult to detect. Yet, it is still so that references to objectives of *e.g.* Treaty provisions and secondary law take place fairly often. Thus, in most cases some kind of reference to objectives can be detected.

In addition, it may be stressed that it is still possible to find more general guidelines (á la *CILFIT* referred to above) as to the interpretational style perceived applied by the CJEU itself, which still includes a reference to aims. For instance, in *TNT Express*, the CJEU stated that: 'According to settled case law, in interpreting a provision of European Union law it is necessary to consider not only its wording but also the context in which it occurs and the objectives pursued by the rules of which it is part ...' [78]

It may also be observed that as far as we can see, the 'spirit' of the Treaties is not referred to. However, it may be stressed that this observation is only based on the examined sample.[79]

77. In the same direction, see Case C-438/05 Viking [2007] ECR p. I-10779, especially Paras. 78-79.
78. Case C-533/08 *TNT Express* 4 May 2010 (n.y.r.), Para. 44. Also see *e.g.* Case C-66/08 *Kozłowski* [2008] ECR p. I-6041, Para. 42, where the CJEU stated that: 'It follows from the need for uniform application of Community law and from the principle of equality that the terms of a provision of Community law which makes no express reference to the law of the Member States for the purpose of determining its meaning and scope must normally be given an autonomous and uniform interpretation throughout the Union, having regard to the context of the provision and the objective pursued by the legislation in question ...'
79. However, in Case C-480/08 *Teixeira* 23 February 2010 (n.y.r.), Para. 83, there is a reference to the spirit of EEC regulation 1612/68: 'According to that judgment, to make the application of Article 12 of that regulation subject to an age-limit or to the

Among the cases in the sample, an illustrative example of the role of objectives is *Metock*. At the overall level, it concerns third country nationals' rights of entry and residence. In the case, there are clearly references to aims.[80] The 'integration' element explained about above is clearly of importance, although not filling out lacunae as such, but rather as a directive as to which result is preferable.

2.7 Preliminary Conclusions

The first of the abovementioned truths, *i.e.* the application of the teleological method as justification in interpretations, has been examined above. It has been demonstrated that the method is considered to have an important role to play in many different and complex legal contexts, however, especially when introducing new and dramatic principles of EU law. Without any doubt, the analysis shows that the method has indeed been powerful in certain cases. Altogether, it may be claimed that the old truth was a real truth, at least in certain parts of the case law.

Whether this truth is still a truth of today is likely to have to be answered in the positive, however, with several modifications. The overall finding that the truth still has a certain value today may be considered supported by the fact that references to objectives still take place in significant cases such as *Laval* and *Metock*. In addition, one objective above all, that of the 'integration' element might still be viewed as a guiding star, however, probably often only at the implicit level.

One modification to be mentioned stems from the fact that Treaty objectives are likely not any longer to have the same strength in interpretations as the single most important factor in deciding an outcome. In other words, objectives do not seem to have a very strong role in filling out lacunae or in implying that the literal meaning of a provision – if any – may be playing less of a role if the reference to objectives of the Treaty(/ies) may be said to imply that. Another modification is that while the heterogeneity, the complexity and the amount of aims have increased over the years, so have the lacunae in EU law decreased over the same period of time, thus at the same time making it more difficult to use the teleological method – at least in the abovementioned understanding – as well as the CJEU not being in the same need thereof. A third modification of great impact concerns the fact that many cases – also very important ones with great impact on the contours of future law (including

status of dependent child would conflict not only with the letter of that provision but also with its spirit (*Gaal*, paragraph 25).'

80. Case C-127/08 *Metock* [2008] ECR p. I-06241, Paras. 67-68 and 88-89.

for instance several of the so-called classic cases) – do not include references to objectives and do not on the explicit level include the teleological method.

Therefore, it might be correct when Maduro emphasises that: 'Reasoning through telos will be an increased necessity in the context of a pluralistic legal order. Such pluralism tends to increase the textual ambiguity of legal provisions and to enhance the potential for conflicting legal norms.' However, this may not necessarily be detectable in the case law of the CJEU.[81] Also, when Gulmann predicted in 1980 that there is '... little reason to believe that the Court of Justice will change its methods of interpretation in the years to come', there are indicators now showing that with regard to the teleological method certain changes have indeed occurred.[82]

3 The Second Truth: Reference to Uniformity in EU Law as the Goal of Interpretations under Article 267 TFEU

3.1 Understanding/Definition of the Second Truth

According to some legal theories, a legal order cannot exist without uniformity.[83] If one takes such a view, it is almost a truism that the task of the CJEU to ensure that in the interpretation and application of the Treaties the law is observed, see Article 19 TEU, entails that it is the goal of interpretations under Article 267 TFEU to promote uniformity in EU law. There has, however, been much debate in later years on pluralism and diversity in EU law.[84] The development of the EU legal order has, for example, given rise to much debate about constitutional pluralism.[85] In that context one can discuss various possible ways of understanding the character of and relations between legal systems in the European Union, in particular, whether there is one EU legal system distinct from and in addition to the national legal systems (the 27+1

81. Maduro, Miguel Poiares: 'Interpreting European Law – Judicial Adjudication in a Context of Constitutional Pluralism', Working Paper IE Law School WPLS08-02, 05-02-2008.
82. Gulmann, Claus: Methods of Interpretation of the European Court of Justice, Scandinavian Studies in Law 1980, p. 204.
83. See Prechal, Sacha and Bert van Roermund (Eds.): The Coherence of EU Law – The Search for Unity in Divergent Concepts, Oxford 2008.
84. There is abundant literature; see for example Modéer, Kjell-Åke: The Historical Roots of European Legal Culture, JFT (Tidskrift utgiven av Juridiska Föreningen i Finland) 2010, p. 493.
85. See Walker, Neil: The Idea of Constitutional Pluralism, Modern Law Review 2002, p. 317.

model), or whether it is better to conceive of EU law merely as an aspect of Member States' legal systems (the 27 model), or whether we should think of there being but one single EU legal system of which Member States' 'national legal systems' are in some sense sub-systems (the one Big system model).[86] If one takes the latter view (the one Big system model), uniformity cannot stand alone as a description/analysis of the present situation but must be combined with diversity.

As appears from sections 1 and 2, it was characteristic of the classic CJEU judgments applying a systematic and teleological method of interpretation in the early period that the Court looked for the spirit permeating the EU legal order as a whole. In the early period Article 267 TFEU was not only seen as a means to ensure uniformity in the interpretation of specific pieces of EU legislation but also as a means to facilitate uniformity in the EU legal order as a whole. The Treaty of Rome was seen as a framework treaty that was of a different kind than an ordinary international trade agreement in that the Treaty of Rome established an institutional infrastructure and permanent norm-setting organs and procedures with a view to promoting an ever closer union between the people of Europe and the gradual development of a more and more integrated common market. Today, the CJEU expresses itself in a much more limited way and seldom (or never) says anything about the grand design of the whole EU legal order. If one looks only at particular provisions in primary or secondary EU legislation, for example one article in a regulation, it is uncontroversial to assume that it should be given a uniform interpretation across the Member States.

3.2 The Sources of Law of Relevance for the Second Truth

3.2.1 Treaty Provisions – Diversity as a Positive Value since the Treaty of Maastricht

According to Article 267 TFEU (ex Article 234 EC and before that Article 177 EEC):

> 'The Court of Justice of the European Union shall have jurisdiction to give preliminary rulings concerning:

86. See Dickson, Julie: How Many Legal Systems? Some Puzzles Regarding the Identity Conditions of, and Relations Between, Legal Systems in the European Union, http://papers.ssrn.com/sol3/papers.cfm?abstract_id=1279612 (University of Oxford Legal Research Paper Series, Paper No 40/2008). See also Hesselink, Martijn: The Common Frame of Reference as a source of European private law, Tulane Law Review 2009, p. 919 and the same author's contribution in this volume.

> (a) the interpretation of the Treaties;
> (b) the validity and interpretation of acts of the institutions, bodies, offices or agencies of the Union;
>
> Where such a question is raised before any court or tribunal of a Member State, that court or tribunal may, if it considers that a decision on the question is necessary to enable it to give judgment, request the Court to give a ruling thereon.
> Where any such question is raised in a case pending before a court or tribunal of a Member State against whose decisions there is no judicial remedy under national law, that court or tribunal shall bring the matter before the Court.
> If such a question is raised in a case pending before a court or tribunal of a Member State with regard to a person in custody, the Court of Justice of the European Union shall act with the minimum of delay.'

As appears there is no mention of uniformity of EU law in the wording of Article 267 TFEU. The idea that Article 267 TFEU has something to do with ensuring uniformity in the interpretation of EU law is a product of the CJEU's teleological and systematic interpretation of Article 267 TFEU and of the understanding of EU law and the preliminary reference procedure in academic literature in the early period (the 1960s and 1970s), which was linked to facilitating the development of the common/internal market and to conceiving of the EU legal system as distinct from and in addition to the national legal systems of EU Member States and as having a fairly limited substantive scope centred around the hard-core economic objectives of the EU.

Article 19 TEU (ex Article 220 EC/164 EEC) provides that the CJEU shall ensure that in the interpretation and application of the Treaties the law is observed. The EU/FEU Treaties contain no provision on which legal method the CJEU shall apply when interpreting the Treaties or secondary law. They hereby differ from the United Nations (UN) system where Article 38 of the Statute of the ICJ (International Court of Justice) lists the sources of law the ICJ shall apply in its interpretations.[87]

87. See the ICJ's website at http://www.icj-cij.org/. The International Court, whose function is to decide in accordance with international law such disputes as are submitted to it, shall apply: a. international conventions, whether general or particular, establishing rules expressly recognized by the contesting states; b. international custom, as evidence of a general practice accepted as law; c. the general principles of law recognized by civilized nations; d. subject to the provisions of Article 59, judicial decisions

Since the adoption of the Treaty of Maastricht, diversity has been treated as a positive value in the Treaties.[88] In the Treaty of Maastricht the then Article 128 EC (now Article 167 TFEU) provided (emphasis added):

> 'The Community shall contribute to the flowering of the cultures of the Member States, while respecting their national and regional *diversity* and at the same time bringing the common cultural heritage to the fore.'

Today (2011), 'United in diversity' is the motto of the European Union.[89] The Treaty of Lisbon does not contain provisions on a motto for the Union, but Article 4(3) TEU has been amended into (emphasis added):

> 'Pursuant to the principle of sincere cooperation, the Union and the Member States shall, *in full mutual respect*, assist each other in carrying out tasks which flow from the Treaties.'

As pointed out by Hesselink,[90] the idea of 'mutual respect' introduced by the Treaty of Lisbon could be regarded as a 'countervailing principle', which could provide a basis for legal diversity. There are also a number of specific provisions in TEU and TFEU that express a positive attitude to diversity.[91] In a present day (2011) perspective, a teleological interpretation of Article 267 TFEU in light of the scheme of the Treaties will thus have to acknowledge both uniformity (coherence) and diversity in EU law as objectives.

3.2.2 Links between Uniformity/Diversity and Different Sources of Law/Styles of Interpretation

If the particular source of law (legal material) at issue in a case is unwritten, as for example some general principles of law, or if a written text is drafted in

and the teachings of the most highly qualified publicists of the various nations, as subsidiary means for the determination of rules of law.

88. Modéer, Kjell-Åke: The Historical Roots of European Legal Culture, JFT (Tidskrift utgiven av Juridiska Föreningen i Finland) 2010, p. 493.
89. This motto was proposed in Article I-8 of the draft Treaty on a Constitution for EU. The EU uses this motto today; see http://europa.eu/abc/symbols/motto/index_en.htm even though the Constitutional Treaty failed to be ratified in all Member States and therefore never came into force.
90. See his contribution in the present volume.
91. See Article 3(3) TEU (aim of the Union) and the following Articles in TFEU: 152 (social partners), 165 (education and vocational training), 167 (culture), 191 (environment) and 207 (common commercial policy).

a very fragmentary and open style as is partly the case with the constituent Treaties, the interpreter (the judge) is left with a wider scope of discretion than if the interpretation is about a clear text with well-defined concepts as is often the case in regard to secondary law. If there are many interpreters of EU law, for example both the CJEU and all national courts applying EU law, using sources of law and styles of interpretation that give a wide discretion to the interpreter will reduce the uniformity of EU law. If one compares the questions referred to the CJEU with the answers given by the CJEU, there is often a shift in focus towards primary law. When a referring court asks whether a particular provision in secondary law should be interpreted as meaning this or that, the CJEU often answers by telling the referring court some general truths about primary law, for example that there is a general principle that can be used to solve the problem in the case at hand. This may be seen as an example of a civil law way of reasoning. The CJEU constructs general primary law rules at a high level in the hierarchy of the sources of law and then deduces the result in the individual case from the general rule. Koopmans states about civil law in relation to EU law:[92]

> '... the French tradition favors a deductive method of reasoning: it infers its rules from broad maxims, and its solutions to legal problems from those rules, preferably by a chain of logically correct deductions.'

The CJEU tends to favour general sources of law over specific rules, *e.g.* the ECHR over labour specific rules such as ILO conventions and recommendations.[93]

A considerable share of the preliminary rulings is about the interpretation of secondary law. In EU law literature they have not attracted much attention, especially not in the early period. If one looks in Pescatore's book on the European legal order from 1975, one only finds references to 17 preliminary rulings, mainly cases about primary law. The early Court's reputation as a creative, dynamic court very much rests on its use of constructive methods of interpretation (systematic and teleological methods) in early preliminary rulings on primary law. In regard to interpretation of secondary law, the CJEU

92. Koopmans, Thijmen: The Birth of European Law at the CrossRoads of Legal Traditions, The American Journal of Comparative Law 1991, p. 493
93. For a criticism of the CJEU's scant regard for ILO conventions, see O'Higgins, Paul: Some problems of enforcement of rights under the Community Charter of Fundamental Social Rights of Workers in Vogel-Polsky, Eliane (ed): Quel avenir pour l'Europe sociale: 1992 et après?, Bruxelles 1992, p. 73.

has always primarily applied literal and historical methods of interpretation. One of the reasons why the methods of interpretation differ as between primary law and secondary legislation is presumably the difference in drafting style. The Treaties establish only fragments of a legal order. Most of the CJEU's innovative contribution consists in constructing missing parts of the legal order that applies in the territories of EU Member States. Most of the concepts used in the Treaties are not explicitly defined in the Treaties whereas most key-concepts used in secondary legislation are defined explicitly and often rather precisely in that legislation.[94] There is therefore a much stronger basis for literal interpretation of secondary law than of primary law. Another difference between the two parts of law is the difference in availability of preparatory works. One of the main differences between interpretation of Treaty texts and secondary legislation is that the CJEU usually does not try to find the intention of the drafters of the Treaties but often refers to the intended meaning of the authors of secondary legislation as it is stated in the preparatory works.

3.2.3 Stare Decisis in EU Law

In the first years references in CJEU judgments to case law were unusual. The reason could be that only few cases were decided. In cases where a referring court asked a question that had already been answered, the CJEU just referred to its previous answer.[95] Reference by the CJEU to its own previous case law has become common-place, not only in cases where there is settled case law but also references to previous judgments where there are a number of judgments which might be slightly relevant. The CJEU is not bound by its previous decisions but in practice it does not often depart from them.[96] Commentators from England are often quite critical of the CJEU's way of using case law. Arnull thus states:[97]

94. The concept of pay in the equal pay provision in Article 157 TFEU (ex Articles 141/119 EC) is, however, defined. This concept/definition was at issue in Case 80/70 *Defrenne-I* [1971] ECR p. 445; see below in section 3.7.
95. See for example 28/62 *Da Costa en Schaake* [1963] ECR p. 31.
96. See generally Arnull, Anthony: Owning up to fallibility: Precedent and the Court of Justice, Common Market Law Review 1993, p. 247; and Koopmans, Thijmen: *Stare decisis* in European Law, in O'Keefe, David and Henry G. Schermers: Essays in European Law and Integration, Kluwer 1982.
97. Arnull et al: Wyatt and Dashwood's European Union Law, London 2006, p. 409. See also Arnull, Anthony: Owning up to fallibility: Precedent and the Court of Justice, Common Market Law Review 1993, p. 247.

'... references to [the Court's] previous decisions became commonplace, but the analysis of them remained superficial and selective by the standards of English court. The reader of the Court's judgments will be struck by the fact that previous decisions are often only cited by the Court where they support its argument. Authorities which point the other way are sometimes not mentioned at all, and sometimes even presented as if they support the line the Court has chosen to take.'

The CJEU gives itself a very free discretion to pick and choose among the hundreds of judgments that potentially could be relevant. That practice leads to low transparency and provides space for diversity in the interpretation of EU law.

3.2.4 Different Languages

The linguistic diversity of EU law can limit its uniformity.[98] In its *CILFIT* case law, the CJEU has held that the national courts of last instance are only free to omit references for a preliminary ruling after looking at the different language versions.[99]

It is not only EU legislation that exists in many languages. The same applies to CJEU judgments. It may be questioned whether the CJEU judgments in different languages can be regarded as expressing a uniform answer to the questions referred to the Court. In the national (Swedish) part of the *Laval* Case, it has been argued that the CJEU judgment in that case does not lay down the same rule in the English language version and the continental language versions of the judgment.[100] In brief, the English language version states that what the trade unions did is contrary to EU law, but the continental language versions rather state that a legal system that allows the trade unions to do what they did is contrary to EU law.[101] The main proceeding in the *Laval* Case was a suit by a Latvian contractor who had won a contract for re-

98. See Prechal, Sacha and Bert van Roermund (Eds.): The Coherence of EU Law – The Search for Unity in Divergent Concepts, Oxford 2008.
99. Case 283/81 *CILFIT* [1982] ECR p. 3415.
100. Case C-341/05 *Laval* [2007] ECR p. I-11767.
101. The English language version states: 'Article 49 EC and ... are to be interpreted as precluding a trade union, in a Member State ... from attempting, by means of collective action ... to force a provider of services ...'. The French (and similarly the German and Swedish versions) states: 'Les articles 49 CE et ... doivent être interprétés en ce sens qu'ils s'opposent à ce que, dans un État membre ..., une organisation syndicale puisse tenter de contraindre ...'

building a Swedish school against two (small) Swedish trade unions,[102] which in accordance with Swedish law had taken – under Swedish law lawful – collective actions against him with a view to raising the wages from Latvian to Swedish level. Laval claimed damages from the trade unions (not from the Swedish state which was not a party to the case before the Swedish Labour Court). The trade unions argued that it was the Swedish state's responsibility not the trade unions' if Swedish law was contrary to EU law. On 2 December 2009, the Swedish Labour Court handed down its judgment.[103] With four votes over three, it ruled that it followed from EU law that the trade unions should pay damages to Laval. The Labour Court held that a duty for the trade unions to pay damages to Laval could not be based on Swedish law, but the Swedish Labour Court found a basis for such a liability in EU law directly applied.[104] The Swedish Labour Court cited the English language version of the CJEU's *Laval* judgment in support of its ruling. The trade unions argued that it should have used the continental (including the Swedish) version of the judgment.[105]

3.3 Acceptance in Literature of the Second Truth as a Real Truth

In the early period the view that uniformity of interpretation of EU law was desirable or necessary was, as mentioned, closely related to the use of the teleological method of interpretation combined with the view that the relevant goal was construction of a common/internal market. Lecourt thus stated:[106]

> 'Comment concevoir une unité de marché entre Etats sans les soumettre ... á une même loi'

102. The umbrella organisation Swedish LO (the Confederation of trade unions) was not party in *Laval*.
103. http://www.arbetsdomstolen.se/upload/pdf/2009/89-09.pdf. An unofficial translation by Erik Sjödin of the Swedish Labour Court's judgment in *Laval* into English may be found at the labour law portal http://arbetsratt.juridicum.su.se/.
104. It stated (translated by Neergaard and Nielsen): 'It must be regarded as clarified that there is a general principle of Community law according to which damages should be due even between private individuals in case of an infringement of a Treaty provision with horizontal direct effect. That ... is clear from the Raccanelli case.'
105. Swedish was the procedural language of the case.
106. Lecourt, Robert: L'Europe des juges, originally from1976, re-published Bruxelles 2008, p. 222.

Pescatore expressed the desirability of uniformity in a somewhat different manner, not so closely linked to the internal market, in that he stated that Article 267 TFEU was a means to:[107]

> '... assurer l'unité du droit communautaire, son efficacité, son dynamisme, som 'genie' propre, c'est-á-dire son originalité et sa conformité aux buts de la construction européenne.'

The purpose for EC/EU (creation of a common market) which the CJEU and the academic literature in the early period read into the original EC Treaty was thus interpreted as requiring uniformity in the interpretation of EU law, and Article 267 TFEU was seen as a mechanism for providing such uniformity. In later times diversity has been much discussed; see above in section 3.1.

There is abundant literature on preliminary references looking at more or less the same material as we are using from different angles and employing different methods. Nearly all textbooks on EU institutional and/or constitutional law contain chapters or sections on Article 267 TFEU.[108] There are also monographs on preliminary rulings, and many academic articles.[109] Most of these works deal with the interpretation of Article 267 TFEU and discuss questions such as which bodies may or must refer questions to the CJEU, when will a preliminary case be admissible, *etc.* In the early period there were also a considerable number of accounts of the methods applied by the CJEU when applying Article 267 TFEU (then Article 177 EEC).[110]

107. Pescatore, Pierre: L'ordre juridique des communautés européennes. Etude des sources du droit communautaire, originally from1975, re-published Bruxelles 2006, p. 215.
108. See for example Hartley, T.C.: The Foundations of European Union Law, Oxford 2010, p. 287.
109. See for example Andenas, Mads: Article 177 references to the European Court: policy and practice, London 1994; and Broberg, Morten P. and Niels Fenger: Preliminary References to The European Court of Justice, Oxford 2010.
110. On the methods applied by the CJEU in the early period, see Pescatore, Pierre: L'ordre juridique des communautés européennes. Etude des sources du droit communautaire, originally from 1975, re-published Bruxelles 2006; Lecourt, Robert: L'Europe des juges, originally from1976, re-published Bruxelles 2008; Brown, L. Neville and Tom Kennedy: The Court of Justice of the European Communities, London 2000 part Four; Arnull, Anthony: The European Union and its Court of Justice, Oxford 2006; Gulmann, Claus: Methods of Interpretation of the European Court of Justice, Scandinavian Studies in law 1980, 187, with extensive citations in particular from the writings of Pescatore and Lecourt; and Koopmans and Thijmen: The Birth

3.4 The Early Case Law

Before 1973 all preliminary rulings were plenary rulings, *i.e.* decided by seven judges.[111] The fact that all preliminary rulings were decided by the same small group of judges and that the number of cases was so low that it is likely that these judges effectively knew all cases decided by the CJEU added to the uniformity of the CJEU's interpretations in the period before 1973. Already in its first preliminary ruling, the CJEU, with reference to the spirit of Article 267 TFEU, took the view that a harmonising of interpretation is the purpose of Article 267 TFEU.[112] The same view was expressed in other early judgments. As the CJEU stated in *Rheinmühlen* (emphasis added):[113]

> 'Article 177 [now Article 267 TFEU] is essential for the preservation of the community character of the law established by the Treaty and has the object of ensuring that in all circumstances this law is *the same* in all states of the Community.'

In the CJEU's early case law, the CJEU accorded an interpretative monopoly to itself. Centralisation of the power to interpret EU law adds to its uniformity. The preliminary reference procedure helps all legal actors, in particular judicial bodies, in the EU to interpret EU law in the same way and avoid or overcome its fragmentation into (27) different legal systems when meeting national law. de Witte has argued that the crucial doctrinal novelty of *Van Gend en Loos*[114] was that the question whether a specific Treaty provision has direct effect is to be decided centrally by the CJEU, not decentrally by various national courts.[115] This centralisation of the competence to interpret EU law very much adds to its uniformity.

of European Law at the CrossRoads of Legal Traditions, The American Journal of Comparative Law 1991, p. 493.

111. The original Article 165 EEC provided: 'The Court of Justice shall sit in plenary session. It may, however, form chambers, each consisting of three or five Judges, either to undertake certain preparatory inquiries or to adjudicate on particular categories of cases in accordance with rules laid down for these purposes. Whenever the Court of Justice ... has to give preliminary rulings on questions submitted to it pursuant to Article 177, it shall sit in plenary session.'
112. Case 13/61 *de Geus/Bosch* [1962] ECR p. 45.
113. Case 166/73 *Rheinmühlen Düsseldorf* [1974] ECR p. 33, Para. 2.
114. Case 26/62 *van Gend en Loos* [1963] ECR p. 1.
115. Cf de Witte, Bruno: The Continuous Significance of Van Gend en Loos, in Maduro, Miguel Poiares and Loïc Azoulai (eds.): The Past and Future of EU Law: The Clas-

3.5 The Development in the Case Law

In 1996, the CJEU took the view that the EU did not have competence under Article 352 TFEU (ex Article 308/235) to adhere to the ECHR.[116] The Court stated that respect for human rights is a condition of the lawfulness of Community law but accession to the ECHR would entail a substantial change in the then existing Community system for the protection of human rights in that it would entail the entry of the Community into a distinct international institutional system. Today (2011) there is a clear legal base in Article 6 TEU for EU accession to the ECHR. If and when the EU accedes to the ECHR, the CJEU will lose the interpretative monopoly in fundamental rights cases that it has enjoyed since the early part of the Community period.

The question whether there is or should be uniformity in the intepretation of EU law can be seen as a question whether different treatment/discrimination on grounds of nationality and other criteria is allowed. The EU has pursued a strong non-discrimination agenda since the mid-1970s and has, at EU level, given high priority to anti-discrimination.

Until 1 May 1999 (the coming into force of the Treaty of Amsterdam), there were only explicit EU legislation on non-discrimination on grounds of nationality and sex, and as far as gender was concerned mainly in employment and occupation. After 2000, broader bans on discrimination on a number of grounds and in other areas, including goods and services have been adopted,[117] and the general principle of equal treatment and non-discrimination has been further developed.

Direct or indirect discrimination on grounds of nationality is mainly relevant in connection with free movement on the internal market. In broad terms restrictions and/or discriminations may be justified by reference to two different groups of legitimate aims: either the Treaty-based exceptions from the free movement provisions, in particular public policy, public security or public health, or by reference to all the overriding reasons relating to the public interest that are accepted in the case law of the CJEU following *Dasson-*

sics of EU Law Revisited on the 50th Anniversary of the Rome Treaty, Hart Publishing 2010, p. 9.

116. Opinion 2/94 [1996] ECR p. I-1759.

117. See the Ethnic Equality Directive, 2000/43/EC, which prohibits ethnic discrimination in nearly all sectors of society, the Employment Framework Directive, 2000/78/EC, which prohibts discrimination on grounds of religion, age, disability and sexual orientation in employment, and the goods and services directive, 2004/113, which prohibits sex discrimination in the access to and supply of goods and services.

ville[118] and *Cassis de Dijon*,[119] for example consumer protection and protection of workers.

In *Gebhard*,[120] the CJEU held that national measures liable to hinder or make less attractive the exercise of fundamental freedoms guaranteed by the Treaty such as freedom of establishment must fulfil four conditions: they must be applied in a non-discriminatory manner; they must be justified by imperative requirements in the general interest; they must be suitable for securing the attainment of the objective which they pursue; and they must not go beyond what is necessary in order to attain it.

In regard to the requirement that the restriction must be necessary in order to be justified, it is sometimes argued that if a restriction is not applied uniformly in different Member States this difference between the Member States indicates that the restriction is not necessary. In an infringement case against Italy,[121] the Commission requested the CJEU to declare that by maintaining an obligation to contract, which was imposed on all insurance undertakings operating in the field of third-party liability motor insurance, Italy had failed to fulfil its obligations under Articles 49 TFEU (ex Article 43 EC) and 56 TFEU (ex Article 49 EC). The Commission argued that other Member States than Italy had less restrictive systems for obtaining the same results as the Italian legislation was claimed to be pursuing. The Commission thus argued that diversity among the Member States and lack of uniformity indicated that a measure did not meet the requirement of necessity and therefore could not be justified. The CJEU rejected this argument. It held (emphasis added):

> '.... it should be borne in mind that rules of a Member State do not constitute a restriction within the meaning of the EC Treaty solely by virtue of the fact that other Member States apply less strict, or more commercially favourable, rules to providers of similar services established in their territory.'

The general view is that direct discrimination can only be justified on grounds of the Treaty-based legitimate aims, while indirect discrimination and nondiscriminatory restrictions can be justified on the basis of all the overriding reasons relating to the public interest. These may – as appears from the above – vary from country to country. Seen in a uniformity/diversity perspective, the abundant case law of the CJEU on justification of discrimina-

118. Case 8/74 *Procureur du Roi* v *Benoît and Gustave Dassonville* [1974] ECR p. 837.
119. Case 120/78 *Rewe* v *Bundesmonopolzentralverwaltung* [1979] ECR p. 649.
120. Case C-55/94 *Gebhard* [1995] ECR p. I-4165.
121. Case C-518/06 *Commission* v *Italy* [2009] ECR p. I-3491.

tion/restrictions on the free movement on the internal market is an example of wide-ranging acceptance of diversity. The mere fact that it differs from country to country which restrictions are considered necessary is not enough to render a restriction unlawful as a matter of EU law.

In 1957, the then EC Treaty contained only one single provision (Article 119 EEC Treaty, now Article 157 FEU) on gender discrimination, namely the principle of equal pay between men and women for work of equal value. The equal pay provision in Article 119 EEC was inserted in the Treaty on the demand of France, which believed that there was stricter rules on equal pay in France than in some of the other original Member States of the EU and wanted a uniform level of equal pay protection in order to protect businesses established in France against distortion of competition. EU sex discrimination law thus started on an uniformity agenda directed towards ensuring the economic aims of the early Community/EU internal (common) market.

Since the mid 1970s, a large number of directives prohibiting sex discrimination have been adopted. Most of them were replaced by the recast directive on gender equality in employment in 2006.

The adoption of the Treaty of Amsterdam 1997, which entered into force on 1 May 1999, marked a turning point in the development of EU discrimination law. The Treaty of Amsterdam introduced important innovations. It incorporated the requirement of mainstreaming gender equality in Article 8 TFEU (ex Article 3(2) EC). It also introduced Article 19 TFEU (originally Article 13 EC), which became the legal basis for an expanded anti-discrimination regime prohibiting discrimination not only on grounds of nationality and gender but also on grounds of ethnic origin, religion, age, handicap and sexual orientation. There has been a shift in emphasis over time from an economic to a fundamental rights perspective; see further below in section 5.

The CJEU has played an important role in the field of equal treatment between men and women, in particular in the period from the 1970s to the 1990s. Since 2000 the EU legislator has played the leading role in the development.

The three *Defrenne* Cases[122] dealt with various aspects of the original equal pay provision in the Treaty. In *Defrenne-I* the Court held that a retirement pension established within the framework of a social security scheme laid down by legislation falls outside the scope of the equal pay provision in the Treaty.

In *Defrenne-II*, the CJEU held that Art. 119 EEC (now Article 157 TFEU) had direct effect as binding for private employers and that the equal pay pro-

122. Case 80/70 *Defrenne-I* [1971] ECR p. 445; Case 43/75 *Defrenne-II* [1976] ECR p. 455; and Case 149/77 *Defrenne-III* [1978] ECR p. 1365.

vision in the Treaty not only had the original economic aim of securing equal competition between employers established in different Member States but had a double aim, both economic and social.

In *Defrenne-III*, Defrenne – a female air hostess – tried to rely on the equal pay provision in the Treaty against a sex discriminatory dismissal practice of her employer, The referring court asked whether the principle of equal pay laid down by article 119 EEC may be interpreted as requiring general equality of working conditions for men and women, so that the insertion into the contract of employment of an air hostess of a clause bringing the contract to an end when she reaches the age of 40 years, it being established that no such limit is attached to the contract of male cabin attendants who carry out the same work, constitutes discrimination prohibited by the said provision. The CJEU held that the equal pay provision should not be applied to dismissal on grounds of sex.

The referring court also asked whether, apart from the specific provisions of Article 119 EEC, Community law contained any general principle prohibiting discrimination based on sex as regards the conditions of employment and working conditions of men and women. The CJEU replied that the principle of non-discrimination on grounds of sex was a fundamental right, but since the *Defrenne-III* Case was about a problem (dismissal) that at the material time of the case was outside the scope of EU law, EU law on fundamental rights could not be relied upon; see the following citation from the CJEU's answer:[123]

> 'The court has repeatedly stated that respect for fundamental personal human rights is one of the general principles of community law, the observance of which it has a duty to ensure.
>
> 27. There can be no doubt that the elimination of discrimination based on sex forms part of those fundamental rights ...
>
> 30. On the other hand, as regards the relationships of employer and employee which are subject to national law, the community had not, at the time of the events now before the belgian courts, assumed any responsibility for supervising and guaranteeing the observance of the principle of equality between men and women in working conditions other than remuneration.'

123. Para. 26.

In the infringement case against Denmark on grounds of the first Danish Equal pay Act,[124] the CJEU struck down a traditional element in the Nordic legal method,[125] namely the reliance on preparatory works of statutory laws as insufficient in connection with implementation of the Equal pay Directive. The CJEU held that Denmark had failed to fulfil its obligations under the EEC Treaty by placing part of the Directive's provisions in the preparatory works of the Danish Equal pay Act. It argued that the principles of legal certainty and the protection of individuals require an unequivocal wording which would give the persons concerned a clear and precise understanding of their rights and obligations and would enable the courts to ensure that those rights and obligations are observed.

The *Deutsche Telekom* Cases on equal pay were about violations by a German employer (Deutsche Telekom) of the equal pay principle by excluding German part-time workers from pension schemes.[126] Because most part-time workers in Germany are women, such exclusion is indirect sex discrimination in violation of the equal pay rules in both EU law and national German law. The German rules apply to periods from the coming into force of the German *Grundgesetz* in 1949. Article 157 TFEU (ext art. 119 EC and 141 EC) is only directly applicable against employers in regard to equal pay in periods

124. Case 143/83 *Commission* v *Denmark*, [1985] ECR p. 427.
125. In the Nordic countries, preambles are typically not used when drafting legislation. Many legal actors in these countries regard the preparatory works of legislation as a functional equivalent to preambles. The Nordic legislators' habit of placing some rules or observations about the law in the preparatory works of statutes and the importance attached to preparatory works as a source of law have given rise to two infringement cases brought by the Commission against Denmark and Sweden before the CJEU in connection with implementation of directives. In addition to the infringement case against Denmark, the Commission took proceedings against Sweden in Case C-478/99 *Commission* v *Sweden* [2002] ECR p. I-4147 on the implementation of the Directive on unfair terms in consumer contracts (93/13/EEC), where Sweden had implemented the non-mandatory part of the Directive in the preparatory works and not in the text of the implementing Act. Denmark and Finland had done the same and intervened in the case in support of Sweden. The Advocate general stated (emphasis added): 'The Commission claims that the importance of the preparatory work has declined as a result of Sweden's accession to the European Union, but the Swedish Government contests that assertion. *It is possible that the preparatory work for a law is still an important source of law in the Nordic countries.*' The CJEU dismissed the Commission's application.
126. Case C-50/96 *Schröder* [2000] ECR p. I-743; Case C-270/97 *Sievers* [2000] ECR p. I-929; and Joined cases C-234/96 and C-235/96 *Vick et al* [2000] ECR p. I-799.

after 8 April 1976; see *Defrenne-II*.[127] In *Barber*, a special time limitation at 17 May 1990 was fixed for pension matters.[128] The workers in the *Deutsche Telekom* Cases claimed equal pay for periods for which they had such a claim under German law but not under EU law. The employer Deutsche Telekom asserted that EU law on equal pay – Article 157 TFEU – should be interpreted as a maximum provision in order to protect German employers from distortion of competition by being treated by stricter equal pay standards than employers estalished in other EU countries. Deutsche Telekom did therefore not accept that it should respect the equal pay principle in pension matters for periods before 17 May 1990. As appears from the above, German law was more favourable for discriminated women than EU law, *i.e.* their fundamental right not to be discriminated against was better protected by German law than by EU law; see below in section 5 on the German *Solange* doctrine, according to which Germany only accepts the supremacy of EU law as long as it does not detract from the German fundamental rights protection.

The CJEU held that the equal pay provision in Article 157 TFEU [then Article 119 EC] does not preclude provisions of a Member State which lay down a principle of equal treatment by virtue of which part-time workers are entitled to retroactive membership of an occupational pension scheme and to receive a pension under that scheme, notwithstanding the risk of distortions of competition between economic operators of the various Member States to the detriment of employers established in the first Member State. The application of national law cannot be held to be contrary to the principle of non-discrimination on grounds of nationality merely because other Member States allegedly apply less strict rules. Moreover, the economic aim pursued by Article 157 TFEU [then Article 119 EC], namely the elimination of distortions of competition between undertakings established in different Member States, is secondary to its social aim, which constitutes the expression of a fundamental human right not to be discriminated against on grounds of sex; see on fundamental rights below in section 5 where also *Mangold* is discussed.

One of the innovations in discrimination law delivered by the CJEU is the evolution of the concept of indirect discrimination. Indirect discrimination is in the directives adopted after 2000 defined as occurring where an apparently neutral provision, criterion or practice would put persons of one sex or a person affected by one of the other protected grounds (ethnicity, age, religion, sexual orientation or disability) at a particular disadvantage compared with

127. Case 43/75 *Defrenne-II* [1976] ECR p. 455.
128. Case 262/88 *Barber* [1990] ECR p. I-1889.

persons of other groups, unless that provision, criterion or practice is objectively justified by a legitimate aim, and the means of achieving that aim are appropriate and necessary. Indirect discrimination is concerned with the effects of a certain treatment and takes into account everyday social realities. For instance, less favourable treatment of part-time workers will often amount to indirect discrimination against women because most part-time employees in some (but not all) EU countries are women. Compared to the case of direct discrimination, the possibilities for justification of indirect discrimination are much broader. The current definition of indirect discrimination was first laid down in the Ethnic Equality Directive. In the proposal for that directive,[129] the Commission referred to the definition developed by the CJEU in *Flynn*.[130] The justification possibility is designed in the same way as the principle of proportionality and like that principle provides a scope for taking diversity between the Member States into account.

As appears from the above, the CJEU has allowed departures from uniformity, for example in its case law on justification of discriminations/restrictions on free movement and on indirect sex discrimination.

3.6 The Most Recent Case Law

In the latest years, uniformity is mainly referred to in CJEU cases on general principles and fundamental rights, including citizens' rights, and with reference to questions about the interpretation of specific pieces of EU legislation. As examples from our sample of cases from 2008-2010, *Kozłowski*, *Mantello* and *Deutschland* v *B and D* may be mentioned. In *Kozłowski*, the CJEU stated (emphasis added):[131]

> 'It follows from the need for uniform application of Community law and from the principle of equality that the terms of *a provision of Community law* which makes no express reference to the law of the Member States for the purpose of determining its meaning and scope must normally be given an autonomous and uniform interpretation throughout the Union, having regard to the context of the provision and the objective pursued by the legislation in question (see, by analogy, Case C-195/06 Österreichischer Rundfunk [2007] ECR I-8817, paragraph 24 and case-law cited).'

129. COM (99)566.
130. Case C-237/94 *Flynn* [1996] p. I-2617.
131. Case C-66/08 *Kozłowski* [2008] ECR p. I-6041.

In *Mantello* on the European arrest warrant, the CJEU stated (emphasis added):[132]

> 'In that regard, the concept of 'same acts' in Article 3(2) of the Framework Decision cannot be left to the discretion of the judicial authorities of each Member State on the basis of their national law. It follows from the need for uniform application of European Union law that, since that provision makes no reference to the law of the Member States with regard to that concept, the latter *must be given an autonomous and uniform interpretation throughout the European Union* (see, by analogy, Case C-66/08 Koszłowski [2008] ECR I-6041, paragraphs 41 and 42). It is therefore an autonomous concept of European Union law which, as such, may be the subject of a reference for a preliminary ruling by any court before which a relevant action has been brought, under the conditions laid down in Title VII of Protocol No 36 to the Treaty on the Functioning of the European Union on transitional provisions.'

In *Deutschland* v *B and D* on minimum standards for the grant of refugee status, the CJEU stated (emphasis added):[133]

> 'It should nevertheless be borne in mind that where the questions referred by national courts concern the interpretation of a provision of Community law, the Court is in principle obliged to give a ruling. In particular, neither the wording of Articles 68 EC and 234 EC nor the aim of the procedure established by Article 234 EC indicates that those responsible for framing the EC Treaty intended to exclude from the jurisdiction of the Court references for a preliminary ruling on a directive in the specific case where the national law of a Member State refers to the content of provisions of an international agreement which have been re-stated in that directive, in order to determine the rules applicable to a situation which is purely internal to that State. In such a case, it is clearly *in the interests of the European Union that, in order to forestall future differences of interpretation, the provisions of that international agreement which have been taken over by national law and by EU law* should be given a uniform interpretation, irrespective of the circumstances in which they are to apply (see, by analogy,

132. Case C-261/09 *Mantello* 16 November 2010 (n.y.r.), Para. 38.
133. Joined cases C-57/09 and C-101/09 9 November 2010 (n.y.r.), Para. 71.

Joined Cases C-175/08, C-176/08, C-178/08 and C-179/08 Salahadin Abdulla and Others [2010] ECR I-0000, paragraph 48).'

Thus, in recent years uniformity is referred to in connection with the interpretation of particular provisions.

3.7 Preliminary Conclusions

Our focus in this section has been on showing how the early truth about uniformity in EU law as a whole as the goal of Article 267 TFEU interpretations has developed in the changing contexts over time. Many legal theories stress that all interpretation is contextual,[134] and practically all EU law scholars (irrespective of their theoretical/methodological standpoints) regard the CJEU's interpretative style as contextual. In this section we have shown that in later periods – especially after the adoption of the Treaty of Maastricht in the early 1990s – Article 267 TFEU is no longer associated with uniformity in the interpretation of EU law as a whole and with the internal market and the view that EU law is a legal system distinct from and in addition to the national legal systems of EU Member States to the same degree as in the early period (the 1960s and 1970s). In regard to EU law as a whole, Article 267 TFEU may now be seen as a framework for judicial interaction between the national courts in the EU and the CJEU where they can unite in their legal diversity with a view to ensure the *coherence* of EU law[135] as a multilayered legal order.[136] That is particularly so if one conceives of EU law as a single EU legal system of which Member States' national legal systems are in some sense sub-systems.[137] In a growing number of cases, the CJEU has linked uniformity to general principles and fundamental rights rather than to the internal

134. In regard to Scandinavian legal realism, see for example Ross, Alf: On Law and Justice, London 1958 (English translation of Ret og Retfærdighed, Copenhagen 1953) Chapter 4.
135. Cf. Prechal, Sacha and Bert van Roermund (eds.): The Coherence of EU Law. The Search for Unity in Divergent Concepts, Oxford 2008.
136. Cf. Sabel, Charles F. and Oliver Gerstenberg: Constitutionalising an Overlapping Consensus: The CJEU and the Emergence of a Coordinate Constitutional Order, European Law Journal 2010, p. 511.
137. See Dickson, Julie: How Many Legal Systems? Some Puzzles Regarding the Identity Conditions of, and Relations Between, Legal Systems in the European Union, http://papers.ssrn.com/sol3/papers.cfm?abstract_id=1279612 (University of Oxford Legal Research Paper Series, Paper No 40/2008). See also Hesselink, Martijn: The Common Frame of Reference as a source of European private law, Tulane Law Review, 2009, p. 919; and the same author's contribution in this volume.

market; see further below in section 5. In regard to the interpretation of particular provisions in individual pieces of EU secondary legislation, the CJEU refers to 'the need for uniform application of EU law' in much the same way as it has always done.

Over the years, the EU has developed both in the direction of a more and more integrated internal market and in the direction of more and more expansion – geographically, across legal and non-legal cultures, different interest groups, linguistically, *etc.*[138] There has been a tension between the aims of integration and expansion. The increased expansion of the EU has led to increased diversity (from 4 to 23 languages, from a civil law legal order to a legal order comprising both civil law and common law countries, *etc.*).

The very considerable *growth in number of cases* has also resulted in a situation where many cases are decided by judges who have not participated in many of the other cases decided by the CJEU, which may lead to decreasing (internal) uniformity in the interpretations provided by the CJEU.

The legal order applicable in the territory of the EU Member States is increasingly a *multi-layered* legal order with mutual embeddedness between normative material stemming from the national level and the EU level. That leads to variations depending on which national system is in issue and thereby some reductions in the uniformity of interpretation. In particular, the principle of proportionality and the concept of indirect discrimination have been used in this context. These principles are discussed further in section 5.

There is a shift in emphasis in the application of Article 267 TFEU from the early period where the CJEU's interest was focused on uniformity as a means to promoting the internal market and a role for itself as a central court with interpretative monopoly to the later stages where there is more scope for diversity and more focus on fundamental rights including citizens' rights; see further below in section 5.

In academic literature written by authors with a background in political science, it has become usual since the early 1990s to state that European politics has been reshaped in recent decades by a dual process of centralization and decentralization known as multi-level governance.[139]

In case law and legal literature, the legal order formed by EU law in interplay with national law has been seen as a multi-layered legal order since the

138. It is not so much the CJEU through its case law as the EU legislator through adoption of harmonising secondary legislation that has created the internal market.

139. See Hooghe, Liesbet and Gary Marks: Multi-level governance and European integration, 2001 and Hooghe, Liesbet: The European Commission and the integration of Europe – images of governance, Cambridge 2001.

early period. The CJEU has since the early period held that a number of EU law provisions are directly applicable[140] in the Member States with supremacy[141] over national law. In addition EU law comprises a number of provisions with only indirect effect on national law. The legal order applicable in the territory of the EU Member States thus has both an EU law aspect and a national law aspect. The interplay between national and EU aspects of this legal order gives it a multi-level character and has done that increasingly during the 50 years of the EU's existence. In 1975, Pescatore, in a chapter on the relation between EU law and national law, stated that EU law:[142]

> '... fait partie integrante de l'ordre juridique applicable sur le territoire national éntendu que, tout en déployant cet effet, il conserve sa nature propre et son autonomie.'

The fundamental rights perspective has been strengthened over the years; see on this aspect below in section 5.

In recent years there has been growing interest in legal literature in discussing various possible ways of understanding the character of and relations between legal systems in the European Union; see above in section 3.1.[143] In the early period the CJEU expressed itself, for example in *Costa* v *ENEL*, in a manner that seems to indicate that EU law was seen as an autonomous system distinct from and in addition to the national legal systems. Since the early period we have not found clear indications in CJEU case law on how many legal systems the CJEU thinks there are in the European Union.

140. See Case 26/62 *van Gend en Loos* [1963] ECR p. 1.
141. See Case 6/64, *Costa* v *ENEL* [1964] ECR p. 585.
142. Pescatore, Pierre: L'ordre juridique des communautés européennes. Etude des sources du droit communautaire, originally from1975, re-published Bruxelles 2006, p. 187.
143. See Dickson, Julie: How Many Legal Systems? Some Puzzles Regarding the Identity Conditions of, and Relations Between, Legal Systems in the European Union, http://papers.ssrn.com/sol3/papers.cfm?abstract_id=1279612 (University of Oxford Legal Research Paper Series, Paper No 40/2008). See also Hesselink, Martijn: The Common Frame of Reference as a source of European private law, Tulane Law Review 4 2009, p. 919 and the same author's contribution in this volume.

4 The Third Truth: Application of Article 4 TEU as Justification in Interpretations

4.1 Understanding/Definition of the Third Truth

As seen in the quotation above of *Costa* v *ENEL*, concerning the establishment of supremacy, the CJEU justified the outcome on, among others, Article 5(2) EEC (now in principle substituted by Article 4 TEU), as it held that: '... the executive force of Community law cannot vary from one state to another in deference to subsequent domestic law, without jeopardising the attainment of the objectives of the Treaty set out in Article 5(2) ...' [144] The provision has been perceived as *e.g.* containing a duty of solidarity,[145] or as a duty of loyal cooperation.[146] It has been referred to as the most important 'general principle' of Community law.[147] For the present purposes, the third truth will be understood as a legal argumentation/reasoning using Article 4(3) TEU in an overreaching manner so as to engender *e.g.* fundamental principles of EU law.[148]

4.2 The Sources of Law of Relevance for the Third Truth

The original wording of Article 4 TEU in the shape of Article 5 EEC in the Treaty of Rome was:[149]

> 'Member States shall take all appropriate measures, whether general or particular, to ensure fulfilment of the obligations arising out of this Treaty or resulting from action taken by the institutions of the Community. They shall facilitate the achievement of the Community's tasks.
>
> They shall abstain from any measure which could jeopardise the attainment of the objectives of this Treaty.'

144. Case 6/64, *Costa* v *ENEL* [1964] ECR p. 585.
145. See *e.g.* Rasmussen, Hjalte: EU-ret i kontekst, pp. 423-425; or Ross, Malcolm: Promoting Solidarity: From Public Services to a European Model of Competition?, CML Rev. 2007, pp. 1057-1080.
146. See e.g. Case C-446/05 *Doulamis* [2008] ECR p. I-1377, Para. 19.
147. Temple Lang, John: Article 10 EC – The Most Important *'General Principle'* of Community Law, in Bernitz, Ulf, Joakim Nergelius, Cecilia Cardner in association with Xavier Groussot: General Principles of EC Law in a Process of Development, Kluwer Law International 2008, pp. 75-113.
148. In the same direction, see *e.g.* Accetto, Matej and Stefan Zleptnig: The Principle of Effectiveness: Rethinking Its Role in Community Law, European Public Law 2005, p. 386.
149. The Treaty of Rome entered into force in 1958.

With the Treaty of Amsterdam, the provision became renumbered as Article 10 EC.[150] Today, the exact wording of Article 4(3) TEU has – after the entering into force of the Treaty of Lisbon – become:[151]

> 'Pursuant to the principle of sincere cooperation, the Union and the Member States shall, in full mutual respect, assist each other in carrying out tasks which flow from the Treaties.
>
> The Member States shall take any appropriate measure, general or particular, to ensure fulfilment of the obligations arising out of the Treaties or resulting from the acts of the institutions of the Union.
>
> The Member States shall facilitate the achievement of the Union's tasks and refrain from any measure which could jeopardise the attainment of the Union's objectives.'

Hereby, the provision has moved from one Treaty to another,[152] and the content of the provision has for the first time truly been changed, however, apparently not too much in substance, except for the obvious addition which the first sentence constitutes.[153] The provision of today may from the wording itself be seen as referring to four general obligations: 1) the obligation of the Union and the Member States to assist each other in carrying out tasks which flow from the Treaties; 2) the obligation of the Member States to take any appropriate measure; 3) the obligation of the Member States to facilitate the

150. The Treaty of Amsterdam entered into force in 1999.

151. The Treaty of Lisbon entered into force in 2010.

152. *I.e.* instead of being situated in what used to be the EC Treaty which now in principle is the Treaty on the Functioning of the EU, it is now situated in the EU Treaty. In the EC Treaty it was situated in a Part concerning 'Principles'. In the EU Treaty it is situated in a Part concerning 'Common Provisions'.

153. Declaration 3 to the Treaty of Nice, which entered into force in 2003, expressed the following about the principle inherent in the first sentence of Article 4(3) TEU: 'The Conference recalls that the duty of sincere cooperation which derives from Article 10 of the Treaty establishing the European Community and governs relations between the Member States and the Community institutions also governs relations between the Community institutions themselves. In relations between those institutions, when it proves necessary, in the context of that duty of sincere cooperation, to facilitate the application of the provisions of the Treaty establishing the European Community, the European Parliament, the Council and the Commission may conclude interinstitutional agreements. Such agreements may not amend or supplement the provisions of the Treaty and may be concluded only with the agreement of these three institutions.'

achievement of the Union's tasks; and 4) the obligation of the Member States to refrain from any measure which could jeopardise the attainment of the Union's objectives. Among these, the first three obligations may be viewed as positive, and the fourth as negative in character. The former group is thus characterised by being general duties for action, whereas the latter one is a general duty against action.

4.3 Acceptance in Literature of the Third Truth as a Real Truth

The exact extent of the provision's scope has for long been surrounded with uncertainty and great doctrinal disagreement.[154] It is not necessarily possible to find too much guidance from the CJEU, as illustrated by the following sentence which at least in some years was designated the role of being the CJEU's point of departure when interpreting Article 5(2) EC: 'This provision lays down a general duty for the Member States, the actual tenor of which depends in each individual case on the provisions of the Treaty or on the rules derived from its general scheme.'[155] This sentence illustrates the opposite meanings attributed to the provision: either a strict interpretation only giving the provision life whenever interacting with other Treaty provisions (understood from the first part of the sentence); or a wide interpretation allowing for an understanding of the provision that is derived from general principles, explicitly or implicitly, appearing in the Treaties or secondary legislation (understood from the second part of the sentence).

Probably because the provision has the potential of a wide scope – or due to its history and wording – some authors have in earlier times claimed that it is without independent legal force and that its content should depend on provisions elsewhere in the Treaty or arising from Community measures.[156] In this regard, Schermers and Pearson have argued that: 'It is also clear that by itself it has no independent legal force, but must be read in conjunction with

154. See *e.g.* Constantinesco, Vlad: L'article 5 CEE, de la bonne foi à la loyalité communautaire, in Liber Amicorum Pierre Pescatore, Baden-Baden 1987, p. 99.

155. See Constantinesco, Vlad; L'article 5 CEE, de la bonne foi à la loyalité communautaire, in Liber Amicorum Pierre Pescatore, Baden-Baden 1987, p. 110; and Case 78/70 *Deutsche Grammophon* [1971] ECR p. 497.

156. See *e.g.* Temple Lang, John: Community Constitutional Law: Article 5 EEC Treaty, Common Market Law Review 1990, p. 646; or Constantinesco, Vlad, L'article 5 CEE, de la bonne foi à la loyalité communautaire, in Liber Amicorum Pierre Pescatore, Baden-Baden 1987, p. 110.

other provisions in order to establish its concrete application' [157] This approach may for instance be viewed as supported to some degree by a case such as *Banchero*, where it is stated that: 'Article 5 requires Member States to carry out their obligations under Community law in good faith. It is, however, settled case law that this provision cannot be applied independently when the situation concerned is governed by a specific provision of the Treaty.'[158] Thus, it has been claimed that it is mainly applied as a supportive provision when interpreting other Treaty provisions. Others have rather claimed that it has independent legal force. In this regard, reference may for example be made to Due (president of the CJEU), who has expressed the following:[159]

> 'Dans plusierus des cas déjà cites, on peut se demander si l'article 5 a joué le role d'un element d'interprétation à l'égard de la disposition spécifique ou s'il n'a pas plutôt constitué la base juridique veritable d'une obligation ne pouvant être déduite de ladite disposition. Dans les exemples qui suivent, il s'agit clairement de ce dernier cas de figure.'

Today, the second position seems to most adequately cover the role actually played by the provision. Therefore, it may be considered important both in a combination with other provisions and by itself.[160]

The provision was, as a point of departure, originally thought of as having been written as an *obiter dictum*,[161] and consequently without independent legal force. It is the expression of a widely acknowledged principle of international law that Treaties should be respected, *i.e.* the principle *pacta sunt servanda*, which is expressed in Article 26 of the Vienna Convention on the Law of Treaties.[162] It has originally also been viewed as containing a political

157. See Schermers, Henry G. and Patrick J. Pearson: Some Comments on Article 5 of the EEC Treaty, in Baur, Jürgen F.; Klaus J. Hopt and Peter K. Mailänder (eds.): Festschrift für Ernst Steindorff zum 70. Geburtstag am 13. März 1990, Berlin 1990, p. 1377.
158. See Case C-387/93 *Banchero* [1995] ECR p. I-4683, Para. 17.
159. Due, Ole: Article 5 du Traité CEE. Une disposition de caractère fédéral?, in Collected Courses of the Academy of European Law, Florence 1991, Vol. II, Book 1, p. 27.
160. See *e.g.* Gulmann, Claus and Karsten Hagel-Sørensen: EU-ret, Jurist- og Økonomforbundets Forlag 1995, pp. 57-58.
161. See Schermers, Henry G. and Patrick J. Pearson: Some Comments on Article 5 of the EEC Treaty, in Baur, Jürgen F.; Klaus J. Hopt and Peter K. Mailänder (eds.): Festschrift für Ernst Steindorff zum 70. Geburtstag am 13. März 1990, p. 1363.
162. See *e.g.* Gulmann, Claus and Karsten Hagel-Sørensen: EU-ret, Jurist- og Økonomforbundets Forlag 1995, p. 57. The mentioned Article 26 states: 'Every treaty in force is binding on the parties to it and must be performed by them in good faith.'; see Suy,

principle or a rule of interpretation.[163] This point of departure also explains the first of the two mentioned positions on the understanding of the provision. However, this has changed over the years, and an author like Ross has stated: '... [I]t is clear that Article 10, whatever its authors may have intended fifty years ago, is no empty rhetoric or fluffy aspirational code for EU club members. It is instead a fundamental statement about the mediation of relations between key institutional actors in conduct of parts of the Treaties ...' [164] In the same direction, *e.g.* Rasmussen has noted that: '... leaving aside for a moment the fact that the drafters did not intend that Article 5's solidarity obligation to be legally binding at all, the Court's ever wider construction of the legally binding scope of that provision drew many Member States into unwitting breaches of Community law.' [165]

So the very, very seminal truth was in fact rather different from the formulation of the truth as stated in this essay. Still, we think that the change came so early that it makes sense to assert that the truth about the provision was viable from very early on. This will be understood also *e.g.* from the reference above to *Costa* v *ENEL* and reference *e.g.* to Temple Lang, who has asserted that: 'Article 5 has the effect of transferring competence over certain areas of law from the Member States to the Community.'[166] Accetto and Zleptnig have even more to the point stated that the provision: '... has played a highly important role in the development of Community law, as the Court used it in

Eric, Corpus Iuris Gentium – A Collection of Basic Texts on Modern Interstate Relations, Acco Leuven, 1996, pp. 99-120. In addition, reference may also be made to the UN Charter, Article 2(2): 'All Members, in order to ensure all of them the rights and benefits resulting from membership, shall fulfil in good faith the obligations assumed by them in accordance with the present charter'; see Suy, Eric: Corpus Iuris Gentium – A Collection of Basic Texts on Modern Interstate Relations, Acco Leuven, 1996, pp. 13-33. In German law there is a similar, but not identical, constitutional principle concerning *Bundestreue*; see Schermers, Henry G. and Patrick J. Pearson: Some Comments on Article 5 of the EEC Treaty, in Baur, Jürgen F.; Klaus J. Hopt and Peter K. Mailänder (eds.): Festschrift für Ernst Steindorff zum 70. Geburtstag am 13. März 1990, Berlin, 1990, p. 1360. Generally, the principle has in other legal contexts been given a rather 'black letter law' meaning; see Neergaard, Ulla: Solidaritetsprincippet som trylleformular, in Nielsen, Ruth (ed.): Julebog 1999, p. 75 ff.

163. *Ibid.* p. 423.
164. Ross, Malcolm: Promoting Solidarity: From Public Services to a European Model of Competition?, Common Market Law Review 2007, p. 1062.
165. Rasmussen, Hjalte: European Court of Justice, GadJura 1998, p. 99.
166. Temple Lang, John: Article 5 of the EEC Treaty: The Emergence of Constitutional Principles in the Case Law of the Court of Justice, Fordham International Law Journal 1987, p. 504.

an overreaching manner so as to engender several fundamental principles of Community law.'[167] The provision has grown in significance over the years and is now often seen as filling up holes of Community law.[168] It has had a significant role in many different areas of law, such as for example the state action doctrine, the obligation of consistent interpretation in relation to domestic laws, and the principle of State liability in damages.[169]

Altogether, it seems rather clear that the truth must be considered as a real truth, at least if 'real' means that documentation can be found in literature including explicit statements even from 'insiders'.

4.4 The Early Case Law

Only the second of the two very early classic cases mentioned above in section 1, namely *Costa* v *ENEL*, makes explicit reference to what is now Article 4 TEU.[170] This case is the first of all the preliminary rulings where the provision is applied. Here the provision is given a significant role, as it as mentioned above is used as a lever for the introduction of the principle of supremacy. Thus, the provision is in our opinion very clearly used as leverage for one of the outcomes of the case, namely the dramatic establishment of the principle of supremacy. Hereby the foundation of the provision as a rather particular provision was also laid, thus in fact launching the third truth which is under scrutiny here.

167. Accetto, Matej and Stefan Zleptnig: The Principle of Effectiveness: Rethinking Its Role in Community Law, European Public Law 2005, p. 386. Also see *e.g.*: Biering, Peter, Jens Hartig Danielsen, Nina Holst-Christensen and Karsten Hagel-Sørensen: EU-Karnov, Thomson Reuters Professional 2010, Vol. 1, p. 81: 'Ikke desto mindre har bestemmelsen væsentlige praktiske virkninger. Dette skyldes for det første, at Domstolen i vidt omfang har brugt bestemmelsen til støtte for resultater, der nok kunne udledes af andre traktatbestemmelser eller af traktaternes almindelige system, men hvor der på grund af resultatets vidtgående karakter kunne være brug for en supplerende begrundelse. Det skyldes for det andet, at bestemmelsen i et vist omfang er brugt som grundlag for pligter for medlemsstaterne i tilfælde, hvor det er vanskeligt i traktaterne eller i den afledte EU-ret i øvrigt at finde grundlag for sådanne pligter.'
168. See *e.g.* Due, Ole: Article 5 du Traité CEE. Une disposition de caractère fédéral?, in Collected Courses of the Academy of European Law, Florence, 1991, Volume 2, Book 1, p. 35; and Prechal, Sacha: Case C-374/89, Commission v. Belgium, Judgment of the Court of 19 February 1991, not yet reported, Common Market Law Review 1992, pp. 371-379; and Temple Lang, John: The Duties of National Authorities Under Community Constitutional Law, European Law Review 1998, pp. 109-131.
169. See further section 4.5 below.
170. Case 26/62, *van Gend en Loos* [1963] ECR p. 1; and Case 6/64 *Costa* v *ENEL* [1964] ECR p. 585.

Besides the reference to this judgment as documentation as to the existence of the third truth in the early case law, a more systematic examination of the preliminary rulings from 1958-73 has been conducted.[171] The impression gained is that the provision in the early years is only seldom applied, and not really as a lever as such. It might be that some of these cases become support for the later important development of Article 4 TEU as an unusual provision. Nevertheless, the most important basis for the claim of the old truth must be considered largely to constitute of *Costa* v *ENEL*.

4.5 The Development in the Case Law

As pointed out above, the provision has had a significant role to play in many different areas of law. For the sake of limitation, here, it is only its role in the areas of: 1) the state action doctrine (section 4.5.1.); 2) the principle of State liability in damages (section 4.5.2.); and 3) the obligation of consistent interpretation in relation to domestic laws (section 4.5.3.), which will be scrutinised further in the present section.[172] These areas have a sufficient degree of difference as well as a sufficient degree of importance to give an overall impression of the truth in action.

4.5.1 The State Action Doctrine

For many years, the CJEU has interpreted what before the entering into force of the Lisbon Treaty used to be a combined reading of Articles 3(1) litra g), 10, and 81 (and at times also Article 82) EC, thereby imposing an obligation on Member States not to adopt measures that might deprive Article 81 EC of

171. See section 1.4.2 above.

172. Article 4 TEU is applied in quite a lot of different situations. Examples of cases of relevance in other areas than those dealt with here could be: Case 44/84 *Hurd* [1986] ECR p. 29; Case 85/85 *Commission* v *Belgium* [1986] ECR p. 1149; Case 190/87 *Moormann* [1988] ECR p. 4689; Case 235/87 *Matteucci* [1988] ECR p. 5589; Case 68/88 *Commission* v *Greece* [1989] ECR p. 2965; Case 8/88, *Germany* v *Commission* [1990] ECR p. I-2321; Case C-251/89 *Athanasopoulos* [1991] ECR p. I-02797; Case C-348/93 *Commission v Italy* [1995] ECR p. I-673; Case C-129/96 *Inter-Environnement* [1997] ECR p. I-7411; Case C-265/95 *Commission* v *France* [1997] ECR p. I-6959; Case C-186/98 *Nunes* [1999] ECR p. I-4883; Case C-112/00 *Schmidberger* [2003] ECR p. I-5659; Case C-453/00 *Kühne & Heitz* [2004] ECR p. I-837; Joined Cases C-387/02, C-391/02 and C-403/02 *Berlusconi* [2005] ECR p. 3565; Case C-415/03 *Commission* v *Greece* [2005] ECR p. I-3875; Case C-432/05 *Unibet* [2007] ECR p. I-2271; Case C-2/06 *Kempter* [2008] ECR p. I-411; and Case C-246/07 *Commission* v *Sweden*, 20 April 2010 (n.y.r.).

its effectiveness or prejudice its full and uniform application.[173] Thus, in this area of law, Article 4 TEU has played a rather significant role. The area has – among many names – been referred to as the state action doctrine.[174] The general principle established by the CJEU was expressed in *Leclerc* in the following words:[175]

> 'Whilst it is true that the rules on competition are concerned with the conduct of undertakings and not with national legislation, Member States are none the less obliged under the second paragraph of Article 5 of the Treaty not to detract, by means of national legislation, from the full and uniform application of Community law or from the effectiveness of its implementing measures; nor may they introduce or maintain in force measures, even of legislative nature, which may render ineffective the competition rules applicable to undertakings.'

This joined interpretation of the provisions in question has been seen by the majority of legal scholars as an attempt to bridge a claimed harmful gap between central competition aims and rules and national anti-competitive measures. The central competition rules are often interpreted as based on the premise that the unrestrained interaction of competitive forces will yield the greatest possible efficiency in the use of economic resources, thereby obtaining the maximum economic welfare. On the other hand, national anti-competitive measures usually hinder competition. For instance, Member States often place price or production controls upon selected businesses in order to correct perceived market failures, such as excessive rivalry. In general, because it is often difficult for companies to raise prices collusively, the economic effect of a national measure will overcome the effect of an ordinary price agreement. This occurs because members and non-members of the cartel are restrained from undercutting the agreed price after an agreement has

173. Article 3(1) litra g) is not really in existence any longer, whereas Article 10 in substance is now Article 4 TEU and Article 81 EC is now Article 101 TFEU. See for a recent analysis Gerard, Damien: EU Competition Policy after Lisbon: Time to Review the 'State Action Doctrine'?, Journal of European Competition Law & Policy 2010, pp. 202-210.
174. See further *e.g.* Neergaard, Ulla: Competition & Competences. The Tensions between European Competition Law and Anti-Competitive Measures by the Member States, DJØF Publishing, 1998; and Neergaard, Ulla: Medlemsstaternes loyalitetsforpligtelse, in Caroline Heide-Jørgensen, et al (eds.): Konkurrenceretten i EU, Jurist- og Økonomforbundets Forlag 2009, pp. 1129-1156.
175. Case 229/83 *Leclerc* [1985] ECR p. 1, Para. 14.

become law. Accordingly, the general principle is seen as a strengthening of the Community's concern for free competition and a weakening of the Member States' concern for their right to economic intervention. At the same time, this general principle is seen as pointing in the direction of an increased level of centralisation at the cost of local self-determination. The truism of Article 101 TFEU only being applicable to private companies has in its application together with the other provisions transformed its function so that measures enacted by the Member States are also in danger of condemnation.

The first of the cases of some relevance is *Walt Wilhelm*, which can be seen as representing a very initial step towards the formulation of the general principle governing the interaction of what then were Articles 3(g), 5(2), and 85 EC, as quoted above. It was decided already in 1969.[176] In this case no national law was challenged directly, but it is of particular relevance to the present analysis in that the CJEU established the principle which would become the 'grandmother' of the principles governing the interaction of the three provisions, and which is likely to be understood as what has been referred to as the *effet utile* principle.[177] This was the principle that Member States must neither introduce nor retain measures capable of prejudicing the practical effectiveness of the Treaty[178] or its full and uniform application.[179] Although what was then Article 5 EEC was mentioned in the preliminary questions, the CJEU did not itself refer thereto in explicit terms. The principles were stated in the context of deciding the relationship between competition law at the Community level and competition law at the state level, *i.e.* the more traditional relationship between these two levels of competition law. In *INNO*, which was decided in 1977, the CJEU more explicitly supported its reasoning on the basis of what was then Article 5 EEC.[180]

Walt Wilhelm and *INNO* may be considered as the two of the primary cases leading up to the abovementioned *Leclerc* Case from 1985, which may be considered as the truly founding case regarding the state action doctrine. Although the CJEU in that case established the abovementioned general principle, it did in fact conclude:[181]

176. See Case 14/68 *Walt Wilhelm* [1969] ECR p. 1.
177. This was, *inter alia*, referred to in *Leclerc*.
178. See *Walt Wilhelm*, Para. 6.
179. See *ibid.*, Para. 9.
180. Case 13/77 *INNO* [1977] ECR p. 2115, Paras. 30-34.
181. Case 229/83 *Leclerc* [1985] ECR p. 1, Para. 20.

'It is thus apparent that the purely national systems and practices in the book trade have not yet been made subject to a Community competition policy with which the Member States would be required to comply by virtue of their duty to abstain from any measure which might jeopardize the attainment of the objectives of the Treaty. It follows that, as Community law stands, Member States' obligations under Article 5 of the EEC Treaty, in conjunction with Articles 3(f) and 85, are not specific enough to preclude them from enacting legislation of the type at issue on competition in the retail prices of books, provided that such legislation is consonant with the other specific Treaty provisions, in particular those concerning the free movement of goods.'

So, at the concrete level, the actual strength of the provision was reduced when compared with the content of the general principle. Then, in the short period between the years 1987-1989, the CJEU unambigously held that a government measure violated the three provisions. The cases in which this happened are *Vlaamse Reisbureaus*, *Aubert* and *Ahmed Saeed.*[182] Hereby, the doctrine demonstrated its potential 'teeth'. Since then, less 'bite' has come from this doctrine. Fairly many cases have in fact followed, but the CJEU tends to base its rulings in this area on its precedence, no longer truly spending too much interpretational energy on what is now Article 4 TEU.[183] This may be illustrated by reference to the fairly recent *Doulamis* Case, rendered in 2008.[184] Reference can with the same purpose also be made to the even more recent *Sbarigia* Case, where the CJEU ruled:[185]

'As regards, secondly, Articles 81 EC and 82 EC, although it is true that they are concerned solely with the conduct of undertakings and not with laws or regulations emanating from Member States, those articles, read in conjunction with Article 10 EC, which lays down a duty to cooperate, none the less require Member States not to introduce or maintain in force

182. Case 311/85 *Vlaamse Reisebureaus* [1987] ECR p. 3801; Case 136/86 *Aubert* [1987] ECR p. 4789; and Case 66/86 *Ahmed Saeed* [1989] ECR p. 803.
183. For an examination of this case law, see *inter alia* Neergaard, Ulla: Competition & Competences. The Tensions between European Competition Law and Anti-Competitive Measures by the Member States, DJØF Publishing 1998; and Neergaard, Ulla: Medlemsstaternes loyalitetsforpligtelse, in Caroline Heide-Jørgensen, et al (eds.): Konkurrenceretten i EU, Jurist- og Økonomforbundets Forlag 2009, pp. 1129-1156.
184. Case C-446/05 *Doulamis* [2008] ECR p. I-1377, Paras. 18, 19 and 24.
185. In Case C-393/08 *Sbarigia* 1 July 2010 (n.y.r.), Paras. 31-32. It should be noted that the reference to the aim provision has disappeared.

> measures, even of a legislative or regulatory nature, which may render ineffective the competition rules applicable to undertakings (see *Cipolla and Others*, paragraph 46 and case-law cited).
>
> In that regard, however, it is quite obvious that the national legislation at issue in the main proceedings, relating to the possible grant of an exemption in relation to the opening periods of a pharmacy located in a specific municipal area of the municipality of Rome, cannot, in itself or by its application, affect trade between Member States within the meaning of Articles 81 EC and 82 EC ...'

Thus, the impression today of the doctrine is that the potential strength – it in fact has – in turning down anti-competitive state measures has not truly been brought into reality. Furthermore, the individual role of Article 4 TEU as leverage in interpretations is not significant in the same manner as in the early years, where the content of the doctrine was shaped.

4.5.2 The Principle of State Liability in Damages

The Treaties have never contained any provisions regarding Member State liability in damages. Nevertheless, the CJEU has established such a principle as valid law. The founding case in that regard is *Francovich*, which was decided in 1991. The case is rightly designated as a classic case by Maduro and Azoulai.[186] After having established that it follows that the principle whereby a State must be liable for loss and damage caused to individuals as a result of breaches of Community law for which the State can be held responsible is inherent in the system of the Treaty, what was then Article 5 of the Treaty was referred to as supplementary basis for this new obligation:[187]

> 'A further basis for the obligation of Member States to make good such loss and damage is to be found in Article 5 of the Treaty, under which the Member States are required to take all appropriate measures, whether general or particular, to ensure fulfilment of their obligations under Community law. Among these is the obligation to nullify the unlawful consequences of a breach of Community law (see, in relation to the analogous provision of Article 86 of the ECSC Treaty, the judgment in Case 6/60 Humblet v Belgium [1960] ECR 559).

186. Maduro, Miguel Poiares and Loïc Azoulai: The Past and Future of EU Law. The Classics of EU Law Revisited on the 50th Anniversary of the Rome Treaty, Hart Publishing 2010.
187. Joined Cases C-6/90 and C-9/90 *Francovich* [1991] ECR I-5357, Paras. 35-37.

> It follows from all the foregoing that it is a principle of Community law that the Member States are obliged to make good loss and damage caused to individuals by breaches of Community law for which they can be held responsible.'

Thus, the provision is the only Treaty provision as such which plays the role of basis for the claim of the existence of the principle of State liability in damages. To us, it therefore seems rather clear that the provision here is applied as leverage in the unusual interpretation delivered in the case. As explained by Baquero Cruz, some commentators have not surprisingly contested the legitimacy and soundness of *Francovich*: 'They argued that it had no basis whatsoever in the Treaty, that the reasoning was insufficient, that the Court was overstepping its competences, encroaching into the competences of the Community legislator and implicitly revising the Treaty. The leading English handbook continues to describe this judgment as 'the most dramatic and distinctive of the Court's interventionist rulings'.[188] The subsequent judgments developing *Francovich* have been said to tone down the doctrine, which could otherwise have had rather far-reaching consequences.[189] Regarding what is now Article 4 TEU, the same line of argumentation, however, seems upheld. For instance, reference may be made to the second very important case in this area of law, *Braisserie du Pêcheur* from 1996.[190] Here, reference is in a similar manner made to the principle of full effectiveness and to what is now Article 4 TEU. In addition, it can be noticed that it has now become possible for the CJEU to support the doctrine on Article 215 EC, which it then does.

The third very important case in this area of law is often considered to be *Köbler*, decided in 2003.[191] This case concerned an infringement attributable to a national court and the *Francovich* doctrine. Here, what is now Article 4 TEU is rather remarkably no longer explicitly present in the argumenta-

188. Baquero Cruz, Julio: *Francovich* and Imperfect Law, in Miguel Poiares Maduro and Loïc Azoulai: The Past and Future of EU Law. The Classics of EU Law Revisited on the 50th Anniversary of the Rome Treaty, Hart Publishing 2010, pp. 419-420.
189. Ruiz-Jarabo Colomer, Damaso: Once Upon a Time – *Francovich*: From Fairy Tale to Cruel Reality?, in Poiares Maduro, Miguel and Loïc Azoulai: The Past and Future of EU Law. The Classics of EU Law Revisited on the 50th Anniversary of the Rome Treaty, Hart Publishing 2010, p. 409.
190. Joined Cases C-46/93 and C-48/93 *Brasserie du Pêcheur* [1996] ECR p. I-1029, Para. 4.
191. Case C-224/01 *Köbler* [2003] ECR p. I-10239.

tion.[192] The same tendency is traceable in two rather recent cases. Reference may be made to *Danske Slagterier* from 2009[193] and to *Transportes Urbanos* from 2010, where it is stated in the latter:[194]

> 'In order to answer that question, it is to be recalled at the outset that, in accordance with settled case-law, the principle of State liability for loss and damage caused to individuals as a result of breaches of European Union law for which the State can be held responsible is inherent in the system of the treaties on which the European Union is based ...'

Both cases – rendered by the Grand Chamber – document that what is now Article 4 TEU is apparently no longer referred to.[195]

In sum, the *Francovich* doctrine ended up being less far-reaching than originally thought of by many. However, also the role of what is now Article 4 TEU changed in the case law developing the doctrine. Thus, today it does not seem to have an individual and explicit role in this area of law. Rather, it seems to have disappeared out of the case law, at least at the explicit level.

4.5.3 The Principle of Conforming Interpretation

The obligation of consistent interpretation should largely be understood in the context of directives not having horizontal direct effect. Through this obligation, an alternative tool by which individuals may rely on directives against another individual has been developed.[196] The principle is also known as the principle of indirect effects or the principle of consistent interpretation.[197] It

192. Case C-224/01 *Köbler* [2003] ECR p. I-10239, Paras. 30-36.
193. Case C-445/06 *Danske Slagterier* [2009] ECR p. I-2119, Para. 19.
194. Case C-118/08 *Transportes Urbanos*, 26 January 2010 (n.y.r.), Para. 29.
195. About the *Francovich* doctrine's general importance estimated over time, reference may be made to Ruiz-Jarabo Colomer, Damaso: Once Upon a Time – *Francovich*: From Fairy Tale to Cruel Reality?, in Miguel Poiares Maduro and Loïc Azoulai: The Past and Future of EU Law. The Classics of EU Law Revisited on the 50th Anniversary of the Rome Treaty, Hart Publishing 2010, pp. 411-412. Other examples of cases of relevance are: Case C-392/93 *British Telecommunications* [1996] ECR p. I-1631; Case C-5/94 *Hedley Lomas* [1996] ECR p. I-2553; Case C-127/95 *Norbrook Laboratories* [1998] ECR p. I-01531; Joined cases C-178/94, C-179/94, C-188/94, C-189/94 and C-190/94 *Dillenkofer* [1996] ECR p. I-04845; Case C-424/97 *Haim* [2000] ECR p. I-05123; and Case C-173/03 *Traghetti del Mediterraneo* [2006] ECR p. I-5177.
196. See *e.g.* Steiner, Josephine, Lorna Woods and Christian Twigg-Flesner: EU Law, Oxford University Press 2006, p. 107.
197. *Ibid.*

may – in simplified terms – be regarded as an interpretative tool to be applied by domestic courts interpreting national legislation which conflicts with a directive (primarily) in the same area.[198] Its importance may be understood from the following stated by Chalmers, Davies and Monti:[199]

> 'Direct effect has, in the last twenty years, become merely one route amongst others through which individuals may invoke EU law in national courts. It is arguable, indeed, that it is no longer even the predominant doctrine in that regard – this may be the doctrine of indirect effect. As the development of direct effect has faltered, the doctrine of indirect effect has expanded. Back in 1998, an empirical study found that it was deployed more widely in British courts than direct effect.[footnote omitted] Despite the greater academic attention that is generally given to direct effect, it has therefore been argued persuasively that indirect effect 'is currently the main form of ensuring effect of Directives whether correctly, incorrectly or not transposed at all' ...'

The principle is considered as launched in 1984 in *von Colson and Kamann*, where the following was stated:[200]

> 'However, the Member States' obligation arising from a directive to achieve the result envisaged by the directive and their duty under Article 5 of the Treaty to take all appropriate measures, whether general or particular, to ensure the fulfilment of that obligation, is binding on all the authorities of Member States including, for matters within their jurisdiction, the courts. It follows that, in applying the national law and in particular the provisions of a national law specifically introduced in order to implement directive no 76/207, national courts are required to interpret their national law in the light of the wording and the purpose of the directive in order to achieve the result referred to in the third paragraph of Article 189.'[201]

Quite clearly, Article 4 TEU plays the role of leverage for the hereby launched obligation to interpret a national law in the light and the purpose of

198. *Ibid.*
199. Chalmers, Damien, Gareth Davies and Giorgio Monti: European Union Law, Cambridge University Press 2010, p. 294.
200. See further about the principle in *e.g.* Neergaard, Ulla and Ruth Nielsen: EU Ret, Thomson Reuters 2010, pp. 235-240.
201. Case 14/83 *von Colson* [1984] ECR p. 1891, Para. 26.

the directive in question. In addition, reference is made to what was then Article 189 of the Treaty.

Since *von Colson and Kamann*, several cases have followed up on it. For instance, in the often referred to *Marleasing*, rendered in 1990, the CJEU states:[202]

> 'In order to reply to that question, it should be observed that, as the Court pointed out in its judgment in Case 14/83 Von Colson and Kamann v Land Nordrhein-Westfalen [1984] ECR 1891, paragraph 26, the Member States' obligation arising from a directive to achieve the result envisaged by the directive and their duty under Article 5 of the Treaty to take all appropriate measures, whether general or particular, to ensure the fulfilment of that obligation, is binding on all the authorities of Member States including, for matters within their jurisdiction, the courts. It follows that, in applying national law, whether the provisions in question were adopted before or after the directive, the national court called upon to interpret it is required to do so, as far as possible, in the light of the wording and the purpose of the directive in order to achieve the result pursued by the latter and thereby comply with the third paragraph of Article 189 of the Treaty.'

Yet another illustrative case is *Faccini Dori* from 1994.[203] Moving up in time, it makes sense to make reference to *Pfeiffer* from 2004.[204] Heading on to the most recent judgments in the area, it seems clear that *von Colson and Kamann* continues to be used as point of reference, but not necessarily what is now Article 4 TEU. For instance, reference may be made to *Kücükdeveci*.[205] Also *Accardo* is of interest as the CJEU states:[206]

> 'It is true that the Member States' obligation arising from a directive to achieve the result envisaged by that directive and their duty to take all appropriate measures, whether general or particular, to ensure the fulfilment of that obligation are binding on all the authorities of the Member States including, for matters within their jurisdiction, the courts (see, inter alia,

202. Case C-106/89 *Marleasing* [1990] ECR p. I-4135, Para. 8.
203. Case C-91/92 *Faccini Dori* [1994] ECR p. I-3325, Para. 26.
204. Joined Cases C-397/01 to C-403/01 *Pfeiffer* [2004] ECR p. I-8835, Paras. 110 and 113-114.
205. Case C-555/07 *Kücükdeveci* 19 January 2010 (n.y.r.), Paras. 47-48.
206. Case C-227/09 *Accardo* 21 October 2010 (n.y.r.), Para. 49.

Case 14/83 *von Colson and Kamann* [1984] ECR 1891, paragraph 26, and *Kücükdeveci*, paragraph 47 and the case-law cited).'

In sum, the overall impression of this area – in which Article 4 TEU has played a significant role – is that it has continued to develop with a long line of case law.[207] Thus, the obligation keeps developing with the effect of larger and larger impact. For a very long period of time, the CJEU continuously referred to this provision. Also, it is noteworthy that often what is now Article 288 TFEU – as well as the system of the Treaty – has been referred to as additional support. In very recent years, however, the reference to Article 4 TEU is not necessarily always included as precedents seem to play a much more important role.

4.5.4 Summing Up Regarding the Development in the Case Law

The analysis of the three selected areas shows that Article 4 TEU has been powerful as leverage in interpretations. Three very different principles have been established with the provision as an important basis – principles which in fact have not even been codified in the Treaties at present. All three principles may also be viewed as having in common somehow being based on a rationale of EU law having to be obeyed by the Member States – *i.e.* ensuring the effectiveness of the EU law – which makes a certain degree of sense in relationship to Article 4 TEU as basis. It may also be noticed that the provision in this way was particularly of importance in a rather short period of time, *i.e.* only seven years (namely the 1980s and the very early beginning of the 1990s – *Leclerc* was rendered in 1985, *Francovich* in 1991, and *von Colson and Kamann* in 1984).

Based on the analysis of the present section, it seems that once a derived principle has been established, the role of Article 4 TEU often diminishes and the precedent(s) in question are often used as the dominating authority/basis. In the state action doctrine, it still has a place in the case law in the sense that it is mentioned, but in the state liability doctrine, reference to the provision appears not to be made anymore. In the area concerning the principle of conforming interpretation, the picture is not completely clear

207. Further examples of cases of relevance in this area are: Case 79/83 *Harz* [1984] ECR p. 1921; Case 80/86 *Kolpinghuis* [1987] ECR p. 3969; Case C-334/92 *Miret* [1993] ECR p. I-6911; Case C-160/01 *Mau* [2003] ECR p. I-4791; Case C-212/04 *Adeneler* [2006] ECR p. I-6057; and Case C-105/03 *Pupino* [2005] ECR p. I-5285.

4.6 The Most Recent Case Law

Looking at the (rather limited) sample of forty preliminary rulings rendered by the Grand Chamber in recent years, we estimate that the same tendency is present. In fact, it seems as if Article 4 TEU is only actively referred to by the CJEU in one single case.[208] Thus, in *ČEZ* the CJEU included the provision in relation to the obligation to interpret national law in a manner which ensures compliance with Community law.[209]

4.7 Preliminary Conclusions

The third of the abovementioned truths, *i.e.* the application of Article 4 TEU as justification in interpretations, has been examined above. It has been demonstrated that the provision has had an important role to play in many different and complex legal contexts. On the basis of the analysis, it may be concluded that the old truth was a real truth. Also, it may be concluded that it is still a truth today, however, primarily only in situations where the CJEU would establish new (often revolutionary) principles, *etc.*, because in such situations there may still be a need of leverage. As explained above in section 4.5, it seems that once a derived principle has been established, the role of Article 4 TEU often diminishes as the precedent(s) in question often take over the role as authority/basis. The examination of the sample has shown that measured quantitatively, the provision in the selected cases is only seldom applied, and when this happens, only seldom as a lever in interpretations.

5 The Fourth Truth: Application of General Principles and Fundamental Rights as Justification in Interpretations

5.1 Understanding/Definition of the Fourth Truth

Since the early period some general principles, notably the principles of proportionality, equality, legal certainty and protection of legitimate interests have been recognised in Community law/EU law.[210] The constitutional prin-

208. In addition, it may be mentioned that in Case C-118/08 *Transportes Urbanos*, 26 January 2010 (n.y.r.), which is mentioned above, no reference to Article 4 TEU is made, although it is part of the *Francovich* doctrine. Also, in Case C-169/08 *Sardegna* [2009] ECR p. I-10821, the national court makes reference to the provision, but the CJEU does not.

209. Case C-115/08 *ČEZ* [2009] ECR p. I-10265, Paras. 138 and the following.

210. See generally on general principles and fundamental rights Bernitz, Ulf, Joakim Nergelius and Cecilia Cardner (eds.): General principles of EC law in a process of devel-

ciples of direct effect and supremacy were developed in the 1960s in *Van Gend en Loos* and *Costa* v *ENEL*. Since the early 1970s, the EU has recognised fundamental rights as part of the general principles of EU law. General principles of law are thus a major source of European Union law. The trend is generally that general principles and fundamental rights play a more prominent role today (2011) than they did 40 or 50 years ago. As an example, the proposal for the Directive on equal treatment in the access to and supply of goods and services may be mentioned.[211] The Commission explicitly stressed that the EU approach to gender equality in law has developed over time, so that the original emphasis on equal pay and on avoiding distortions of competition between businesses established in different Member States has been replaced by a concern for equality as a fundamental right.

Some of the methods of interpretation used by the CJEU, notably literal, historical, teleological and systematic interpretation; see above in the previous sections, are usually regarded as traditional methods of interpretation in civil law countries and are well-known from interpretation of national law. The CJEU's development of general principles as part of its interpretative function is to a higher extent a new legal method which plays a much stronger role in the EU legal order than in national law.[212] That has to do with the interplay between national, international and supranational elements in the development and functioning of general principles in the EU legal order; see below in section 5.2 on the sources of law of relevance.

In EU law, the term 'general principle' is manifold. General principles and fundamental rights have been classified in many different ways.[213] In addition, it is often an open question what exactly can be considered a general principle. As Advocate General Mazak expressed it in *Masdar* (emphasis added):[214]

opment, Kluwer 2008; Bernitz, Ulf and Joakim Nergelius (eds.): General principles of European community law, Kluwer 2000; Groussot, Xavier: Creation, Development and Impact of the General Principles of Community Law: Towards a jus commune europaeum?, Lund 2005 (a shorter version is published under the title General Principles of Community Law, Amsterdam 2006); and Tridimas, Takis: The General Principles of EU Law, Oxford 2006.

211. COM(2003)657 p. 2. The proposal resulted in Directive 2004/113/EC on equal treatment for men and women in the access to and supply of goods and services.
212. Cf. Martijn Hesselink's contribution in this volume.
213. See Tridimas, Takis: The General Principles of EU Law, Oxford 2006, p. 2 *et seq*; and Groussot, Xavier: General Principles of Community Law, Amsterdam 2006.
214. Case C-47/07 *Masdar* [2008] ECR p. I-09761.

> '... as is generally the case with general principles of law as a legal source, until there is settled case-law on the matter discussing the concrete content of such a principle can be very much *like discussing the shape of a ghost.*'

5.2 The Sources of Law of Relevance for the Fourth Truth

General principles in EU law are derived from various sources, of which the most important are the legal systems of the Member States, international conventions, in particular ECHR, and to a lesser extent the constituent Treaties. Until the Treaty of Lisbon came into force (1 December 2009), general principles developed in the case law of the CJEU have constituted the main basis on which EU fundamental rights law have been developed. Since the coming into force of the Treaty of Lisbon, the EU is due to become a Party to the ECHR,[215] and the EU Charter of Fundamental Rights has acquired the same legal value as the Treaties (TEU and TFEU). The Charter contains 50 'rights, freedoms and principles' without identifying which of its provisions are rights, which are freedoms and which are principles. There are seven chapters in the Charter: Title I. Dignity; Title II. Freedoms; Title III. Equality; Title IV. Solidarity; Title V. Citizens' Rights; Title VI. Justice; and Title VII. General Provisions.[216]

5.2.1 National Law, Evaluative Comparative Method

It is often stated both in legal literature and in CJEU cases that the CJEU uses a comparative method, *i.e.* looks at the different principles and fundamental rights existing in national law to find inspiration for EU law on general principles and fundamental rights. AG Leger thus stated in *Commission* v *CCRE*:[217]

> 'As we know, to establish the existence of a general principle of Community law, the Court carries out a comparative examination of national legal

215. From the ECHR side, such accession has been made possible by the addition of a Protocol No 14, which has now entered into force following ratification by Russia. A new second paragraph was added to Article 59 of the Convention, reading 'The European Union may accede to this Convention'. Its explanatory memorandum noted that all necessary modifications to the Convention required by such accession could be brought about either by an amending protocol to the Convention or by means of an accession treaty to be concluded by the EU.
216. On the Commission's plans concerning the Charter after the coming into force of the Lisbon Treaty, see COM(2010)573, Strategy for the effective implementation of the Charter of Fundamental Rights by the European Union.
217. Case C-87/01 *P* [2003] ECR p. I-7617, Para. 64.

systems. In this connection, it is unanimously agreed[218] that the Court does not seek to determine the arithmetrical average of national laws or to fall into line with the lowest common denominator. On the contrary, the Court takes a critical approach[219] and gives the answer which is most appropriate in relation to the structure and aims of the Community.'[220]

On the same subject Hartley writes:[221]

> 'When the Court looks to national law for inspiration, it is not necessary that the principle should be accepted by the legal systems of all the Member States. It would be sufficient if the principle were generally accepted by the legal systems of most Member States, or if it was in conformity with a trend in the Member States, so that one could say that the national legal systems were developing towards it.[222] It must again be emphasized, however, that whatever the factual origin of the principle, it is applied by the European Court as a principle of EU law, not national law.'

218. Leger's note reads: 'See, in particular, the Opinion of Advocate General Lagrange in the case of Hoogovens v High Authority, cited above, ECR 284; the Opinions of Advocate General Roemer in the case of Duraffour v Council, cited above, ECR 532 and 533, in Case 5/71 Zuckerfabrik Schoppenstedt v Council [1971] ECR 975, 991, and in Joined Cases 63/72 to 69/72 Werhahn Hansamühle and Others v Council [1973] ECR 1229. 1258 and 1259; and the Opinion of Advocate General Slynn in the case of AM & S Europe v Commission, cited above, ECR 1648 to 1650. Among academic writings, see H. Kutscher, cited above, p. I-29; J.-V. Louis, L'ordre juridique communautaire, Brussels, Office for Official Publications of the European Communities, sixth ed., paragraph 87; P. Pescatore, cited above, pp. 654 and 655; and J.-V. Louis, G. Vandersanden, D. Waelbroeck and M. Waelbroeck, Commentaire J. Megret, Le droit de la CE, vol. 10, La Cour de justice, les actes des institutions, éditions de l'université de Bruxelles, Brussels 1993, second ed., p. 155.'
219. Leger's note reads: 'Opinion of Advocate General Roemer in the case of Zuckerfabrik Schõppenstedt v Council, cited above, ECR 991'.
220. Leger's note reads: 'See *Internationale Handelsgesellschaft* cited above, paragraph 4.'
221. Hartley, T. C.: The Foundations of European Union Law, Oxford 2010, p. 142.
222. Hartley's note reads: 'See Hoogovens v. High Authority, Case 14/61, [1962] ECR 2 53 at 283-4, where Advocate General Lagrange said that the Court is not content to adopt the common denominator between the different systems but 'chooses from each of the Member States those solutions which, having regard to the objects of the Treaty, appear to it to be the best'.'

Koopmans concludes under the heading 'A TWO-WAY INFLUENCE':

> '... the Court of Justice has become one of the major sources of legal innovation in Europe not only because of its position as the Community's judicial institution, but also because of the intellectual strength of its comparative methods.[223] National courts take heed to the Court's way of reasoning. As a result, we sometimes see that legal principles which have made their way from the national legal systems to the Court's case law, in order to be transformed into principles of Community law, make their way back to the national courts. This happens, of course, not only because of their willingness to adopt a certain method of law finding; besides, national courts are often under an obligation to apply rules of Community law.'

A distinction is often drawn between a minimalist, a maximalist and evaluative approach to the use of comparative method in developing general principles and fundamental rights.[224] Under the CJEU case law, it is not required that a general principle or fundamental right must be accepted in all the national systems in the EU or that only the best national solution can be accepted as an EU principle. The CJEU uses an evaluative approach and discerns generally accepted principles underlying national law in the Member States.

5.2.2 International Law, in Particular ECHR

All EU countries are members of the United Nations, ILO and the Council of Europe. France ratified the ECHR Convention in 1974. It was only after that that the ECHR has been ratified by all EU Member States. The ECHR was first specifically referred to by the CJEU in 1975 in *Rutili*[225] and has since been quoted by the Court on numerous occasions.[226] In a case on annulment

223. Koopman's note reads: 'See P. Pescatore, 'Le recours dans la jurisprudence de la Cour de Justice des Communautes europeennes a des normes deduites de la comparason des droits des Etats membres,' Revue trimestrielle de droit commercial 337 (1980).'
224. See for example Groussot, Xavier: Creation, Development and Impact of the General Principles of Community Law: Towards a jus commune europaeum?, Lund 2005, p. 88 *et seq*.
225. Case 36/75 *Rutili* [1975] ECR p. 1219.
226. See further Coppel, Jason and Adian O'Neill: The European Court of Justice: Taking Rights Seriously?, Common Market Law Review 1992, p. 669.

of a Commission decision, the CJEU referred to the case law of the European Court of Human Rights and stated:[227]

> 'It must be added that the Court of Justice, in paragraphs 274 to 276 of the judgment in Limburgse Vinyl Maatschappij and Others v Commission, observed that since the judgment in Orkem v Commission there have been further developments in the case-law of the European Court of Human Rights which the Community judicature must take into account when interpreting the fundamental rights. The Court of Justice stated however in that regard that those developments were not such as to put in question the statements of principle in Orkem v Commission.'

Compared to the ECHR the EU Charter on Fundamental Rights goes much further in protecting economic and social rights.[228] The content of the solidarity provisions in the Charter draws heavily on the Council of Europe Revised Social Charter from 1996 to which there are many references in the Explanatory remarks. All 27 EU Member States are signatories to the Revised Social Charter from 1996, but twelve of them have not ratified this convention and have consequently never been bound by it under public international law.[229]

There is generally only scant reference to ILO conventions in EU law.[230] That has been criticised in the literature.[231] In *Laval*[232] and *Viking*,[233] the

227. Case C-301/04 P *Commission* v *SGL Carbon AG* [2006] ECR p. I-5915, Para. 43.
228. The ECHR offers some protection of economic and social rights. In Airey v Ireland (Application no. 6289/73, judgment of 9 October 1979), the ECtHR stated (emphasis added): 'Whilst the Convention sets forth what are essentially civil and political rights, many of them have implications of a social or economic nature. The Court therefore considers, like the Commission, that *the mere fact that an interpretation of the Convention may extend into the sphere of social and economic rights should not be a decisive factor against such an interpretation; there is no water-tight division separating that sphere from the field covered by the Convention.*'
229. Austria, Czech Republic, Denmark, Germany, Greece, Hungary, Latvia, Luxembourg, Poland, Slovakia, Spain and the United Kingdom.
230. Eight ILO Conventions have been identified by the ILO's Governing Body as being fundamental to the rights of people at work, irrespective of levels of development of individual Member States. They are grouped into four categories: 1) Freedom of Association; 2) Abolition of Forced Labour; 3) Equality; and 4) Elimination of Child Labour.
231. O'Higgins, Paul: Some problems of enforcement of rights under the Community Charter of Fundamental Social Rights of Workers in Vogel-Polsky, Eliane (ed.): Quel avenir pour l'Europe sociale: 1992 et après?, Bruxelles 1992, p. 73.
232. Case C-341/05 *Laval* [2007] ECR p. I-11767.

CJEU did, however, refer to ILO Convention 87 as a basis for considering the right to take collective action as a fundamental right. *Laval* has been widely criticised for tipping the balance between market freedoms and the fundamental right to take collective action in favour of market freedoms. It may be argued that the limited right to take collective action accepted by the CJEU in *Laval* falls short of the level of protection of the right to strike provided by ILO Convention 87. It has been suggested that the Swedish government in *Laval* should have invoked Article 351 TFEU (ex Article 307 EC) and contended that the Swedish (and Danish) rules on strikes are necessary to comply with duties undertaken under public international law before membership of the EU and therefore according to Article 351 TFEU (ex Article 307 EC) take precedence over EU law.[234]

In the Charter on Fundamental Rights and the explanations referred to in the Charter that set out the sources of its provisions, there is no explicit reference to ILO conventions. The eight fundamental ILO conventions are, however, all ratified by all 27 EU countries.[235] Consequently they are 'international obligations common to the Member States'. For that reason they have become more binding as a matter of EU law and not only of international law since the Treaty of Lisbon entered into force.

5.2.3 Treaties (TEU, TFEU and the EU Charter of Fundamental Rights)

The original Treaty of Rome 1957 did not contain specific provisions on the protection of fundamental rights. Article 6 EU was first included in the EU Treaty (the Treaty of Maastricht), signed in 1992, and was subsequently amended by the Treaty of Amsterdam in 1997 and the Treaty of Lisbon which substantially revised Article 6 EU which now (post Lisbon) reads:

233. Case C-438/05 *Viking* [2007] ECR p. I-10779.
234. See Ronnie Eklund: A Swedish Perspective on Laval, Comparative Labor Law and Policy Journal 2008, p. 551, compare Case C-158/91 *Levy* [1993] ECR p. I-4287 and Case C-13/93 *Minne* [1994] ECR p. I-371, where France and Belgium successfully defended with the help of Article 307 EC their commitments under ILO Convention 89 on Night Work for Women Employed in Industry, which the CJEU later found to be contrary to the provisions of the Equal Treatment Directive (76/207EEC).
235. Eight ILO Conventions have been identified by the ILO's Governing Body as being fundamental to the rights of people at work, irrespective of levels of development of individual Member States. They are grouped into four categories: 1) Freedom of Association, 2) Abolition of Forced Labour, 3) Equality and 4) Elimination of Child Labour. See further Neergaard, Ulla & Ruth Nielsen: Blurring Boundaries: From the Danish Welfare State to the European Social Model? p. 59, http://papers.ssrn.com/sol3/papers. cfm?abstract_id=1618758.

> 'The Union recognises the rights, freedoms and principles set out in the Charter of Fundamental Rights of the European Union of 7 December 2000, as adapted at Strasbourg, on 12 December 2007, which shall have the same legal value as the Treaties.
>
> The provisions of the Charter shall not extend in any way the competences of the Union as defined in the Treaties.
>
> The rights, freedoms and principles in the Charter shall be interpreted in accordance with the general provisions of Title VII of the Charter governing its interpretation and application and with due regard to the explanations referred to in the Charter, that set out the sources of those provisions.'

When the Treaties are used as a basis for declaring general principles and fundamental rights, the CJEU usually uses systematic and teleological interpretation; see Tridimas who in 2008 stated:[236]

> 'It is mainly on the basis of a systematic and teleological interpretation of the founding treaties that the Court has construed the inclusion of fundamental rights in the Community law system.'

Article 4 TEU (ex Article 10 EC) is often cited in this context.[237] The fundamental rights perspective is also decisive in the EU Charter of Fundamental Rights.

5.3 Acceptance in Literature of the Fourth Truth as a Real Truth

It is generally accepted in academic literature that general principles of EU law play an important role in the CJEU's jurisprudence, especially in its more creative and expansive parts. In the literature it has been discusssed what is characteristic of the adjudicative model followed by the CJEU in developing general principles and fundamental rights. Groussot distinguishes between a rights and a consensus model.[238] A judge following a rights model is inspired by Dworkin's theory of law and focuses on securing individual's rights in ac-

236. See Arnull, Anthony, Piet Eeckhout and Takis Tridimas: Continuity and Change in EU Law. Essays in Honour of Sir Francis Jacobs, Oxford 2008, p. 125.
237. See Temple Lang, John: Article 10 EC – The most important 'General Principle' of Community Law in Bernitz, Ulf, Joakim Nergelius and Cecilia Cardner (eds.): General principles of EC law in a process of development, Kluwer 2008, p. 75. See also above in section 4.
238. Groussot, Xavier: Creation, Development and Impact of the General Principles of Community Law: Towards a jus commune europaeum?, Lund 2005, p. 186 *et seq*.

cordance with justice and fairness.[239] A judge following a consensus model focuses on delivering judgments that can be expected to be accepted by the community he/she functions in as representing its values.

In our view, the CJEU primarily follows a consensus model.[240] As is well known, the EU protection of general principles and fundamental rights has been developed in dialogue with the highest national courts partly as a means to ensure their acceptance of the supremacy of EU law over national law. The German *Bundesverfassungsgericht* has only accepted that EU law takes precedence over German law as long as (*Solange*) EU law protects fundamental rights as well as German law does. As Weiler has stated:[241]

> 'The surface language of the Court in Stauder and its progeny is the language of human rights. The deep structure all about supremacy ... [It was] an attempt to protect the concept of supremacy threatened because of the apparent (largely theoretical) inadequate protection of human rights in the original Treaty.'

In 1967, the German *Bundesverfassungsgericht* held that a constitutional complaint (*Verfassungsbeschwerde*) against regulations adopted by the Council and the Commission of the EC/EU was not admissible under German law. It added, however, (emphasis added):[242]

> 'Die Entscheidung beschränkt sich auf den Ausspruch, daß das Bundesverfassungsgericht nicht unmittelbar mit der Verfassungsbeschwerde gegen Verordnungen des Rates und der Kommission der EWG angerufen werden kann.
>
> Nicht entschieden ist damit, ob und in welchem Umfang das Bundesverfassungsgericht im Rahmen eines zulässigerweise bei ihm anhängig gemachten Verfahrens *Gemeinschaftsrecht an den Grundrechtsnormen des Grundgesetzes messen kann.*'

239. See Dworkin, Ronald: Taking rights seriously, Cambridge Mass. 1977.
240. A rights model is broadly in line with a natural law approach to law while the consensus model is more in line with legal positivism; see above in section 1 on critical legal positivism as the background theory we have chosen. Authors choosing to look at the law through the lenses of natural law theory will probably see the CJEU as more of a Dworkinian court than we do.
241. Cited from Coppel, Jason and Adrian O'Neill: The European Court of Justice: Taking Rights Seriously?, Common Market Law Review 1992, p. 669.
242. BVerfGE 22, 293.

The German *Bundesverfassungsgericht* addressed its relation to the CJEU in 1974 in the *Solange-I* decision. The *Bundesverfassungsgericht* reserved the right to review the compatibility of EU law with the German Constitution as long as the integration process had not progressed so far that EU law also receives a catalogue of fundamental rights decided on by a parliament and of settled validity, which is adequate in comparison with the catalogue of fundamental rights contained in the German Constitution.[243] In its *Solange-II* decision from 1986, the *Bundesverfassungsgericht* modified its *Solange-I* decision and noted in its *Solange-II* decision that a measure of protection of fundamental rights had been established in the case law of the CJEU concerning fundamental rights, which in its conception, substance and manner of implementation is essentially comparable with the standards of fundamental rights provided for in the *Grundgesetz*. The *Bundesverfassungsgericht* therefore changed its '*Solange-I* formula' into the following: the *Bundesverfassungsgericht* would no longer review secondary EU law on the basis of German fundamental rights norms as long as the European Communities, and in particular the case law of the European Court, generally ensure an effective protection of fundamental rights as against the sovereign powers of the Communities which is to be regarded substantially similar to the protection of fundamental rights required unconditionally by the Constitution, and insofar as they generally safeguard the essential content of fundamental rights.[244]

243. The German original reads: 'Solange der Integrationsprozeß der Gemeinschaft nicht so weit fortgeschritten ist, daß das Gemeinschaftsrecht auch einen von einem Parlament beschlossenen und in Geltung stehenden formulierten Katalog von Grundrechten enthält, der dem Grundrechtskatalog des Grundgesetzes adäquat ist, ist nach Einholung der in Art. 177 EWGV geforderten Entscheidung des Europäischen Gerichtshofes die Vorlage eines Gerichts der Bundesrepublik Deutschland an das Bundesverfassungsgericht im Normenkontrollverfahren zulässig und geboten, wenn das Gericht die für es entscheidungserhebliche Vorschrift des Gemeinschaftsrechts in der vom Europäischen Gerichtshof gegebenen Auslegung für unanwendbar hält, weil und soweit sie mit einem der Grundrechte des Grundgesetzes kollidiert.' See BVerfGE 37, 271 – *Solange-I*.

244. The German original reads: 'Solange die Europäischen Gemeinschaften, insbesondere die Rechtsprechung des Gerichtshofs der Gemeinschaften einen wirksamen Schutz der Grundrechte gegenüber der Hoheitsgewalt der Gemeinschaften generell gewährleisten, der dem vom Grundgesetz als unabdingbar gebotenen Grundrechtsschutz im wesentlichen gleichzuachten ist, zumal den Wesensgehalt der Grundrechte generell verbürgt, wird das Bundesverfassungsgericht seine Gerichtsbarkeit über die Anwendbarkeit von abgeleitetem Gemeinschaftsrecht, das als Rechtsgrundlage für ein Verhalten deutscher Gerichte oder Behörden im Hoheitsbereich der Bundesrepublik Deutschland in Anspruch genommen wird, nicht mehr ausüben und dieses Recht

On 30 June 2009, the German *Bundesverfassungsgericht* assessed the compatibility of the Treaty of Lisbon with German law, judging that there are no decisive constitutional objections to the German Act Approving the Treaty of Lisbon.[245]

5.4 The Early Case Law

In the earliest period the CJEU refused to review Community law in the light of national constitutional principles. In 1959 in *Stork*, a German applicant contended that a decision of the High Authority was invalid because it violated the German constitution (*Grundgesetz*/Basic Law).[246] The CJEU held (emphasis added):

> '... under article 8 of the Treaty the high authority is only required to apply community law. It is not competent to apply the national law of the Member States. Similarly, under article 31 the court is only required to ensure that in the interpretation and application of the treaty, and of rules laid down for implementation thereof, the law is observed. It is not normally required to rule on provisions of national law. Consequently, the high authority *is not empowered to examine a ground of complaint which maintains that, when it adopted its decision, it infringed principles of German constitutional law* (in particular articles 2 and 12 of the basic law).'

Since 1970, the CJEU has developed a case law on fundamental rights as part of Community/EU law. Starting in the late 1960s, increasing concern was expressed in the courts of Germany and Italy on the question as to whether the fundamental rights guaranteed in their national constitutions were recognised and protected within EU law. In response to the threat that national courts would opt for the supremacy of their own national constitutional provisions on fundamental rights protection, the CJEU held that the protection of fundamental rights was a general principle of EU law.

In 1969, in *Stauder*, the CJEU for the first time stated that fundamental rights were enshrined in the general principles of Community law and pro-

mithin nicht mehr am Maßstab der Grundrechte des Grundgesetzes überprüfen; entsprechende Vorlagen nach Art. 100 Abs. 1 GG sind somit unzulässig.' See BVerfGE 73, 339 – *Solange-II*, available at http://www.servat.unibe.ch/fallrecht/bv073339.html.

245. Judgment on 30 June 2009, Bundesverfassungsgericht, BVerfG, 2 BvE 2/08.
246. Case 1/58 *Stork & Cie.* v *ECSC High Authority* [1959] ECR p. 17.

tected by the Court.[247] In *Internationale Handelsgesellschaft* the reference to fundamental rights was expanded by the Court stating that respect for fundamental rights forms an integral part of the general principles of law protected by the CJEU and that these principles were inspired by the *constitutional traditions* common to the Member States.[248]

In 1974, the CJEU held in *Nold* that, in addition to Member States' constitutional traditions, *international conventions* could also supply guidelines which could be taken into consideration by the Court on matters concerning claims to fundamental rights.[249] In particular, the ECHR has a special significance in this respect.

In the early case law, general principles and fundamental rights were used in interpreting EU law and for review of EU law. General principles of EU law and fundamental rights were considered binding on the institutions of the EU in the exercise of their powers.

5.5 The Development in the Case Law

In the further development of EU law and fundamental rights, their field of application has been expanded to cover review of national law within the scope of EU law. In the early period the focus was on public law; in the later development the reach of EU general principles and fundamental rights has been expanded to private law. According to Article 51 of the EU Charter on fundamental rights, the Charter is, in addition to the institutions, bodies, offices and agencies of the Union, also addressed to the Member States but only when they are implementing Union law. That is meant as a codification of CJEU case law. In the Explanations to Article 51, it is stated (emphasis added) that:

> 'As regards the Member States, it follows unambiguously from the case-law of the Court of Justice that the requirement to respect fundamental rights defined in the context of the Union is only binding on the Member States when they act *in the scope of Union law* (judgment of 13 July 1989, Case 5/88 Wachauf [1989] ECR 2609; judgment of 18 June 1991, Case C-260/89 ERT [1991] ECR I-2925; judgment of 18 December 1997, Case C-309/96 Annibaldi [1997] ECR I-7493).'

247. Case 29/69 *Stauder* v *Ulm* [1969] ECR p. 419.
248. Case 11/70 *Internationale Handelsgesellschaft* [1970] ECR p. 1125.
249. Case 4/73 *Nold* [1974] ECR p. 491.

In its case law, the CJEU has required Member States to respect the fundamental rights not only when they transpose an EU rule into national law but also when they take measures that may hinder the free movement of persons, services and capital. In *Carpenter,* the CJEU thus stated that a Member State may invoke reasons of public interest to justify a national measure which is likely to obstruct the exercise of the freedom to provide services only if that measure is compatible with the fundamental rights whose observance the Court ensures.[250] In support of this interpretation, it referred to *ERT*[251] and *Familiapress.*[252] The CJEU has been confronted with the interface between free movement on the internal market and fundamental rights on a number of occasions and has held that free movement and fundamental rights must be balanced against each other. The one does not automatically take precedence over the other. In *Schmidberger,*[253] the CJEU created a framework for reconciling freedom of expression and free movement of goods, and in Omega Spielhallen[254] it held that the freedom to provide services does not preclude an economic activity from being prohibited on grounds of protecting public policy by reason of the fact that that activity is an affront to human dignity.

Member States must observe EU law general principles and fundamental rights when they implement EU law. In *Wachauf*, the CJEU held (emphasis added):[255]

> '... it must be observed that Community rules which, upon the expiry of the lease, had the effect of depriving the lessee, without compensation, of the fruits of his labour and of his investments in the tenanted holding would be incompatible with the requirements of the protection of fundamental rights in the Community legal order. Since those requirements are also *binding on the Member States when they implement Community rules*, the Member States must, as far as possible, apply those rules in accordance with those requirements.'

In 2005, *i.e.* before the coming into force of the Treaty of Lisbon (1 December 2009) when there were different rules in the first pillar (Community law) and in the second and third pillars, the CJEU held that fundamental rights, as

250. Case C-60/00 *Carpenter* [2002] p. I-6279, Para. 40.
251. Case C-260/89 *ERT* [1991] ECR p. I-2925 Para. 43.
252. Case C-368/95 *Familiapress* [1997] ECR p. I-3689, Para. 24.
253. Case C-112/00 *Schmidberger* [2003] ECR p. I-5659.
254. Case C-36/02 *Omega Spielhallen* [2004] ECR p. I-9609.
255. Case 5/88 *Wachauf* [1989] ECR p. 2609.

general principles of law, applied not only to the scope of Community law (the first pillar) as distinct from EU law (all three pillars) but also to areas covered by the third pillar; see *Pupino*.[256] After the coming into force of the Treaty of Lisbon, the distinction between the first pillar and the third pillar in EU law is no longer relevant.

In *Mangold*,[257] which is about age discrimination in employment, the referring court asked questions on the interpretation of the directive on fixed-term employment contracts[258] and the general framework directive for equal treatment in employment and occupation.[259] The national court wished to know whether – in the context of a dispute between private parties – those directives preclude a national rule like the then German legislation on fixed-term contracts that allowed the employer free discretion to enter into fixed term contracts with employees over 52 but required employers to have objective justifications for choosing fixed-term contracts (as different from employment contracts for an indefinite period) when the employee was under 52.

The fixed-term contracts directive does not directly govern the conclusion of the first fixed-term contract but only limits the use of successive fixed term contracts and prohibits discriminatory working conditions for employees on fixed-term contracts. The purpose of the framework directive for equal treatment in employment and occupation is to lay down a general framework for combating discrimination on the grounds of religion or belief, disability, age or sexual orientation as regards employment and occupation, with a view to putting into effect in the Member States the principle of equal treatment. The deadline for implementation of the Directive in Germany was 2 December 2006. The facts of the Mangold case, the employment in a private law firm of Mangold, who was over 52, on a fixed-term contract thus took place between the adoption of the general framework directive for equal treatment in employment and occupation and the date of its implementation in Germany.

The CJEU took the view that the general framework directive for equal treatment in employment and occupation does not itself lay down the principle of equal treatment in the field of employment and occupation. The purpose of the directive is according to the preamble '... to lay down a general framework for combating discrimination on the grounds of religion or belief, disability, age or sexual orientation'. The CJEU therefore held that the source of the actual principle underlying the prohibition of those forms of discrimination is to

256. Case C-105/03 *Pupino* [2005] ECR p. I-5285.
257. Case C-144/04 *Mangold* [2005] ECR p. I-9981.
258. 1999/70/EC.
259. 2000/78/EC.

be found in various international instruments and in the constitutional traditions common to the Member States. The principle of non-discrimination on grounds of age must thus – in the view of the CJEU – be regarded as a general principle of EU law. Where national rules fall within the scope of EU law, which was the case in *Mangold* because the contested German legislation was a measure implementing the fixed term contracts directive, general principles of EU law must be observed in national law. The CJEU did not explicitly refer to *Wachauf*, but its reasoning in *Mangold* on this point is in accordance with its ruling in *Wachauf*. The CJEU concluded in *Mangold*:

> 'Community law and, more particularly, Article 6(1) of Council Directive 2000/78/EC of 27 November 2000 establishing a general framework for equal treatment in employment and occupation must be interpreted as precluding a provision of domestic law such as that at issue in the main proceedings which authorises, without restriction, unless there is a close connection with an earlier contract of employment of indefinite duration concluded with the same employer, the conclusion of fixed-term contracts of employment once the worker has reached the age of 52.
>
> It is the responsibility of the national court to guarantee the full effectiveness of the general principle of non-discrimination in respect of age, setting aside any provision of national law which may conflict with Community law, even where the period prescribed for transposition of that directive has not yet expired.'

Mangold has given rise to much discussion and been met with heavy criticism. The German *Bundesarbeitsgericht* (Federal Labour Court) followed the CJEU's judgment in *Mangold* in a judgment from 2006 against Honeywell. A Constitutional Complaint against the Honeywell judgment of the *Bundesarbeitsgericht* claiming that the EU prohibition against age discrimination as interpreted in the German judgment in Honeywell was contrary to the German *Grundgesetz* (*i.e.* Constitution) has been raised. As mentioned in the Introduction, the CJEU judgment in *Mangold* was accepted by the German courts partly because the Mangold judgment was deemed to be correct from a methodological point of view. In July 2010, the German *Bundesverfassungsgericht* in rejecting the constitutional complaint (*'Verfassungsbeschwerde'*) against the *Honeywell* judgment of the *Bundesarbeitsgericht* also accepted the CJEU *Mangold* judgment as methodologically correct.

A point in *Mangold* that has attracted much criticism is that the CJEU jumps at its own discretion from a very vague and general level (a general ban on discrimination) to a much more specific level (prohibition against age discrimination). It is only true that a general principle of prohibition against age discrimination has support in various international instruments if one accepts that the CJEU is free to change level of abstraction at its discretion. There is only support for a specific ban on age discrimination in the constitutions of Finland and Portugal and no support for it in international conventions that are normally referred to in connection with general principles and fundamental rights. Five years before the judgment in *Mangold*, all the Member States had unanimously in the EU Council adopted the Employment Framework Directive, which prohibits age discrimination. If one sees the EU legal order as one big system comprising both national and supranational aspects, one can see the acts on Member States in EU institutions as expressions of which principles are accepted in the national legal orders, which in this model are in some sense sub-systems of the EU legal order. In *Kücükdevici,* the CJEU maintained its decision in *Mangold.*[260]

Member States are only under an obligation to observe EU fundamental rights within the scope of EU law. In *Kremzow*, the CJEU held that where national legislation is concerned with a situation which does not fall within the field of application of Community law, the Court cannot give interpretative guidance.[261] In *Vajnai,* the problem was whether a penal provision in Hungary prohibiting the use of symbols of the international labour movement on pain of criminal prosecution was compatible with the fundamental EU law principle of non-discrimination.[262] The question was put to the CJEU as to whether Article 6 EU, the Race Directive or Articles 10, 11 and 12 of the Charter of Fundamental Rights allow a person who wishes to express his political convictions by means of a symbol representing them to do so in any Member State. The CJEU rejected the question as inadmissible because the case concerned a purely internal situation in Hungary. Similarly, in *Polier*[263] the CJEU refused to answer a question about the compatibility of a French dismissal provision with the Charter[264] (and some international provisions).

260. Case C-555/07 *Kücükdevici* 19 January 2010 (n.y.r.).
261. Case C-299/95 [1997] ECR p. I-2629.
262. Case C-328/04 [2005] ECR p. I-8577.
263. Case 361/07, not reported, available in French at the CJEU website curia.europa.eu.
264. The question was: '[L]'ordonnance 2005-893 [...], qui autorise le licenciement du salarié pendant la période de consolidation de deux ans, prévue par le [CNE], sans indiquer la légitimité de la rupture et [...] sans information préalable au regard du droit européen, tel que défini dans la charte des droits fondamentaux [de l'Union européenne], qui précise [...] le droit des travailleurs à ne pas être licencié sans motif valable, [est-elle valide?]ECR.'

General principles of civil law were referred to in 2007 in *Société thermale d'Eugénie-les-Bains.*[265] In *Hamilton*, the question was about the interpretation of a provision in the doorstep-selling directive.[266] The CJEU held:

> '... the provision which governs the exercise of the right of cancellation – namely, Article 5(1) of the doorstep selling directive – provides, inter alia, that '[t]he consumer shall have the right to renounce the effects of his undertaking'. The use in that provision of the term 'undertaking' indicates, as Volksbank argued at the hearing before the Court, that the right of cancellation may be exercised as long as the consumer is not bound, at the time that the right is exercised, by any undertaking under the cancelled contract. That logic flows from one of the general principles of civil law, namely that full performance of a contract results, as a general rule, from discharge of the mutual obligations under the contract or from termination of that contract.'

One of the most important cases on general principles and fundamental rights from recent years is *Kadi.*[267] It has attracted many comments from different angles.[268]

5.6 The Most Recent Case Law

In the last few years, there are many examples of reference to general principles – both in cases decided by the Grand Chamber and in other cases – often with references to earlier case law or settled case law in recent years; see for example references to effective judicial protection[269] and to legal certainty in *Bressol.*[270] In *Draka,*[271] on the interpretation of the Regulation[272] on Judicial cooperation in civil matters, the CJEU stated (emphasis added):

> 'In that connection, the Court has first of all held that *the principle of legal certainty in the Community legal system* and the objectives of the Brussels

265. Case C-277/05 *Société thermale d'Eugénie-les-Bains* [2007] ECR p. I-6415.
266. Case C-412/06 *Hamilton* [2008] ECR p. I-2383.
267. Joined cases C-402/05 P and C-415/05 P *Kadi* [2008] ECR p. I-6351.
268. See Isiksel, N. Türküler: Fundamental rights in the EU after Kadi and Al Barakaat, European Law Journal 2010, p. 551 with further references.
269. Joined Cases C-145/08 and C-149/08 *Club Hotel Loutraki* 6 May 2010 (n.y.r.).
270. Case C-73/08 *Bressol* 13 April 2010 (n.y.r.).
271. Case C-167/08 *Draka* [2009] ECR p. I-03477, Para. 25.
272. (EC) No 44/2001.

Convention in accordance with Article 220 EC, which is at its origin, require in all Member States *a uniform application of the legal concepts and legal classifications developed by the Court in the context of that convention ...*'

The general principle of equal treatment is still referred to in the same way as it has been through all the years the EC/EU has existed; see *Uzonyi* where the CJEU stated:[273]

'In that regard, the Court has consistently held that the prohibition on discrimination in the context of the common agricultural policy is merely a specific expression of the general principle of equal treatment, which requires that comparable situations not be treated differently and different situations not be treated alike unless such treatment is objectively justified.'

There are also references to the principle of proportionality[274] and non-discrimination on grounds of age. In *Wetherspoon* on the interpretation of the first and sixth VAT Directives the CJEU stated (emphasis added):[275]

'When Member States establish or accept a particular method of rounding, they are obliged to observe the principles governing the common system of VAT, such as those of fiscal neutrality and proportionality. It does not, however, follow from observance of those *recognised principles of the Community legal system* that the question as to which specific method of rounding should be used is itself within the scope of Community law (Koninklijke Ahold, paragraph 32).'

In *Vodafone*, the CJEU stated:[276]

'According to settled case-law, the principle of proportionality is one of the general principles of Community law and requires that measures implemented through Community law provisions be appropriate for attaining the legitimate objectives pursued by the legislation at issue and must not go beyond what is necessary to achieve them (Joined Cases C 453/03, C

273. Case C-133/09 *Uzonyi* 30 September 2010 (n.y.r.).
274. Case C-365/08 *Agrana Zucker* 20 May 2010 (n.y.r.).
275. Case C-302/07 *Wetherspoon* [2009] ECR p. I-1467, Para. 33.
276. Case C 58/08 *Vodafone Ltd* 8 June 2010 (n.y.r.).

11/04, C 12/04 and C 194/04 ABNA and Others [2005] ECR I 10423, paragraph 68 and the case-law cited).'

5.7 Preliminary Conclusions

Over the years the CJEU has expanded the scope of application of EU law general principles and fundamental rights, in particular as a standard for review of national law, thereby constraining the freedom of Member States to exercise their discretion as they wish. The methodological tools used by the CJEU to discover general principles and fundamental rights are by and large the same today (2010) as in the early 1970s, compare for example the judgments in *Internationale Handelsgesellschaft* from 1970 and *Mangold* from 2005.

Compared to interpretation of national law, the CJEU's use of general principles and fundamental rights as justification represents a novel form of interpretation in that the CJEU usually applies an evaluative comparative approach where it draws inspiration from national and international elements in the EU legal order when interpreting EU law and applying it for review of EU law and national law within the scope of EU law.

6 Conclusions

In the early period the CJEU interpreted the Treaty of Rome as a framework Treaty that as stated in its preamble was intended to facilitate an ongoing development towards an ever closer union among the peoples of Europe and ever more integration, in particular with regard to the economic aspects of society. The Treaty of Rome was thus seen as basically different from (other) international trade treaties. The CJEU produced a limited number of judgments – which are now considered classics – where it exercised a creative, dynamic style of interpretation building on the above overall vision of the grand design of the EU construction.

The classic judgments are built on the classic truths we have examined in the essay. The classic cases were atypical in the sense that from a quantitative point of view, even in the first period, the CJEU in most cases interpreted EU law in a manner not very different from the way national courts – at least in the civil law part of Europe – would normally use. In the later development the CJEU tends to express itself in a more limited way and abstain from putting forward grand visions of the way the EU is developing or should develop and focus more on interpreting particular elements of EU law. In the interpretation of specific parts of EU law, it is still true to say that the CJEU applies a teleological method of interpretation taking account of the objective of the particular provisions under interpretation, however with certain modifications. It often strives to give a uniform interpretation to particular words or concepts, but it has also developed principles and concepts, for example the principle of proportionality and the concept of indirect discrimination, in a way that allows for considerable diversity from country to country. It still relies on Article 4(3) TEU but tends not to refer explicitly to it in support of interpretations which have been established in settled case law from the CJEU. General principles, in particular fundamental rights as part of the general principles of the EU, are increasingly being referred to in CJEU case law. Thus, with reference to the title of the present essay, the spirit and its friends are still there, however, in a somewhat changed setting.

In the early period the CJEU took a rather hierarchical approach – for example in establishing the doctrines of direct effect and supremacy – to the relationship between elements of the European legal order originating from the EU level and elements originating from the national level. In the later development it seems to be turning towards a more interactive, horizontal approach to the relationship between layers originating from EU actors and layers originating from national actors. It is not clear whether the CJEU as a colloquium sees the EU legal order as one big system comprising elements of both national and EU origin or as a distinct legal system in addition to the national legal systems.[277]

277. Individual judges have in articles expressed clear views on that point; see for example in favour of the 'one big system model' Koopmanns, Thijmen: The Theory of Interpretation and the Court of Justice, in O'Keefe, David and Antonio Bavasso (eds.): Judicial Review in European Union Law, The Hague 2000, p. 45.

A Toolbox for European Judges*

Martijn W. Hesselink

Whose toolbox?

From the CFR to an optional instrument and a legislator's toolbox
In July 2010 the European Commission's published a Green Paper on policy options for progress towards a European Contract Law for consumers and businesses.[1] This is the latest development in a process that started almost a decade ago, with the publication by the European Commission of its first communication on European Contract Law,[2] to be followed in 2003 by an Action Plan in which the Commission announced the elaboration by a network of academics of a 'common frame of reference' (CFR)[3] and the publication in 2009 of the academic Draft Common Frame of Reference (DCFR).[4] The Green Paper opens a new round of consultation on the desirability, nature and scope of an 'instrument of European Contract Law'[5] while at the same time an 'expert group' is working, for the Commission, on a draft of such an instrument.[6] As to the legal nature of the instrument, the Commission

* This article has been accepted for publication in the *European Law Journal*. I am grateful to the Editors of the *European Law Journal* for authorisation to publish it in this volume.

1. COM(2010) 348 final, 1.7.2010.
2. COM(2001) 398, 11.7.2001.
3. COM(2003) 68, 12.2.2003. See also Communication on European Contract Law and the revision of the *acquis*: the way forward, COM(2004) 651, 11.10.2004.
4. Ch. von Bar et al (eds), *Principles, Definitions and Model Rules of European Private Law; Draft Common Frame of Reference (DCFR); Outline Edition* (Munich: Sellier, 2009).
5. The term 'Instrument of European Contract Law' seems to have replaced the term 'Common Frame of Reference' which is no longer used in this new Green paper except to refer to the background of the current consultation or to the text of the DCFR.
6. See Commission Decision of 26 April 2010 setting up the Expert Group on a Common Frame of Reference in the area of European contract law, 2010/233/EU, *OJ* 27.4.2010, L105/109, in particular art. 2 (Task). For reasons of transparency I point out that I am a member of that group.

suggests seven options: publication of the results of the expert group (option 1); an official toolbox for the legislator, consisting of either a) a Commission act on a toolbox or b) an interinstitutional agreement on a toolbox (option 2); a Commission recommendation on European contract law (option 3); a regulation setting up an optional instrument of European contract law (option 4); a directive on European contract law (option 5); a regulation establishing a European contract law (option 6); and a regulation establishing a European Civil Code (option 7). One option does not exclude the other; several of them could overlap, for example the optional instrument and the toolbox.

From the order of presentation – number 4 naturally suggests the moderate or compromise option in contrast with more extreme alternatives – and from Vice-President Reding's public interventions, it is clear that the Commission's own preference is for the optional instrument (OI).[7] According to the Green paper, the optional instrument would be conceived as a 2nd regime in each Member State, thus providing the contracting parties with an option between two regimes of domestic contract law.[8] It would insert into the national laws of the 27 Member States a comprehensive and, as much as possible, self-standing set of contract law rules which could be chosen by the parties as the law regulating their contracts.[9] As the Commission points out, this set of contract law rules would form part of each Member State's national law also for the purposes of private international law.[10] The optional instrument on contract law would thus be similar to the European order for payment procedure[11] and the European company (*Societas Europea*),[12] although the comprehensiveness and self-standing nature (in the sense that references to national laws or international instruments should be reduced as much as possible)[13] that the European Commission hopes for is likely to be even more problematic in the case of general contract law than it has been for the European company.

7. See e.g. V. Reding, 'Making the most of the internal market: concrete EU solutions to cut red tape and to boost the economy', Speech/10/42, Brussels, 24 February 2010 (press release).
8. Green Paper, 8.
9. Green Paper, 10.
10. Green Paper, footnote 25.
11. Regulation 1896/2006 of 12 December 2006 creating a European order for payment procedure.
12. Regulation 2157/2001 of 8 October 2001 on the Statute for a European company (SE).
13. See Green Paper, 7.

Whether such an optional instrument will gain enough political support is still very much an open political question. The case is different for the legislator's toolbox (option 2). If an optional instrument is going to be adopted, it is not obvious that the Commission will see a great need to take any formal measures, like adopting a Commission act or negotiating an interinstitutional agreement concerning the toolbox. Nevertheless, it seems natural, in such a case, that, even without any formal act or agreement, the optional instrument would become an informal, but potentially equally (or even more) influential, source of inspiration for the European legislator. If, however, the political project of an optional instrument fails then, of course, a more official toolbox is the second best alternative for the Commission and other supporters of a more European contract law. And the idea of a legislator's toolbox is politically hardly controversial.[14] Therefore, in the three most realist scenarios – i.e. an optional instrument without an official toolbox, an official legislator's toolbox without an optional instrument, and an optional instrument plus an official toolbox – in all likelihood the instrument will effectively become a toolbox for the legislator, either formally or informally.[15]

A toolbox for judges?

If an instrument on European contract law (ECL instrument) becomes a toolbox for the European legislator, either formally or informally, the question arises what this will mean for courts. Obviously, if the parties to a contract opt into an optional instrument as provided for in an EU regulation, then judges will have to apply the instrument as the applicable law between the

14. For example, the House of Lords considers that 'the development of a form of 'toolbox' to assist European legislators would be useful both to aid mutual understanding of the diverse legal systems of the EU and to improve the quality of European legislation to which the law of contract is relevant.' (House of Lords (European Union Committee), *European Contract Law: the Draft Common Frame of Reference, Report with Evidence*, 12th Report of Session 2008-09, HL Paper 95.
15. In theory, it is possible that the European legislator would adopt both an optional instrument and (formally or informally) a toolbox, but would use different text versions of the common frame of reference for these different functions. That could lead to considerable confusion (if not chaos) while at the same time it is not clear what would be gained from such a decision or practice, in terms of coherence or otherwise. The only exception could be where the toolbox had a broader (personal, substantive, territorial) scope. Therefore, in the following I will assume that there will be one single text playing different potential roles one of which will be, in any case, the role of a toolbox (be it formal or informal) for the European legislator.

parties.[16] However, what will happen outside this case of formal applicability? May or should the instrument have other, more informal roles? What place, if any, does the instrument (optional instrument or legislator's toolbox) have in the toolbox of European judges? Could or should courts, like legislators, in certain contexts be inspired by the instrument when deciding cases, and if so, when and why?

The idea that a court might wish to take the ECL instrument as a source of inspiration, or even as a source of law, is not a fancy one. On the contrary, it seems likely that this text will be attractive (or even irresistible) in the eyes of judges, especially when they are confronted with gaps or ambiguities in the law that they have to apply.[17] It is a true *Fundgrube* for model rules on all sorts of subjects that might come in very handy when courts need to resolve hard cases on contracts.

An optional instrument on European contract law would derive formal legitimacy from the fact that it was adopted as a regulation by the European legislator following the usual procedure, through an initiative from the Commission and adoption, probably after amendments, by Council and Parliament. Issues could arise as to the legal basis, especially if the optional instrument would have a broad personal, material or territorial scope,[18] but that is part of the normal order of things when European legislation is adopted. The same goes for more fundamental legitimacy issues such as the still existing democratic deficit in the European Union. More specific legitimacy issues may be raised because of the private law nature of an optional instrument: it might be argued that private law has an essence (party autonomy or commutative justice) which should be respected or that it grows organically and that a legislator can at most codify it, not design it according to its political preferences. Such arguments are general; not in the sense that they apply to all EU legislation, but in the sense that they apply to all general private law legislation (in particular, civil codes), be it European or national. Also in this

16. There may be issues relating to internationally mandatory rules (*lois de police*) and public policy (*ordre public*), but I will leave these aside here.
17. Cf. H.-W. Micklitz, 'Failure or Ideological Preconceptions – Thoughts on Two Grand Projects: The European Constitution and the European Civil Code', EUI Working Papers LAW No. 2010/04, 9: 'The ECJ has formally no jurisdiction to refer to rules which were not taken over in the Lisbon Treaty, but it cannot be excluded that these rules may inspire the ECJ in its interpretation.'
18. Cf. M.W. Hesselink, 'An optional instrument on EU contract law: could it increase legal certainty and foster cross-border trade?', PE 425.642 (Brussels, 2010).

sense, therefore, an optional European instrument on contract law would be business as usual.[19]

The legislator's toolbox function also does not seem to raise particularly pressing legitimacy issues. If legislators are inspired by existing texts, and even if they decide to regard a text as an official toolbox, such an informal or indirect normative effect of such texts is not very problematic or controversial, it seems, in all cases where the final outcome is formal legislation. The reason is that legislators are free to choose their own sources of inspiration and their only accountability is vis-à-vis their electorate: if they make the wrong choices in the eyes of their constituents, they will not be re-elected.

However, for judges the case may be different. An informal or indirect normative effect of the ECL instrument on adjudication seems to be prima facie more problematic from a legitimacy point of view. Although today nobody believes that judges could be merely 'les bouches qui prononcent les paroles de la loi' anymore; the idea that the decisions of judges depend primarily on what they had for breakfast is not broadly accepted either. Judges are bound to apply the law. Certainly, they are allowed to further develop the law as well, but they are constrained by the existing sources or legal materials, and by recognised methods. All grand theories of adjudication, including the most sceptical ones, accept that judges are constrained, at least to some extent, by law.[20] Moreover, judges operate in a broader political context in which their actions are embedded and which pose further limits as well. This raises the question of how the text of the instrument, in cases where it has not been positively opted into by the contracting parties, can ever become a source of inspiration that a court is allowed or even obliged to take into ac-

19. It has been suggested by J.M. Smits, 'European Private Law and Democracy: A Misunderstood Relationship', M. Faure & F. Stephen (eds.), *Essays in the law and economics of regulation in honour of Anthony Ogus* (Antwerp-Oxford: Intersentia, 2008), pp. 49-59, that the main source of legitimacy in the case of an optional code would be party autonomy, because the code will only become applicable when the parties opt for it, and that no further legitimation is required. However, it is still the law that provides the option and it does so, probably, subject to some mandatory rules. Moreover, the legitimacy provided by choice may actually be weak in cases of unequal bargaining. See the criticism by consumer groups, available at http://www.europarl.europa.eu/webnp/cms/lang/en/pid/1483.
20. Cf D. Kennedy, *A Critique of Adjudication {fin de siècle}* (Cambridge, Massachusetts: Harvard University Press, 1997), 92: '[I]f the project of legal necessity is a Golden Bowl, no one has found the fatal flaw that would allow us to shatter it with a single blow. Successful critique is 'local,' even when the locality is a whole theory of judicial neutrality'. Therefore, we do not need to further explore the matter here.

count. How can such an informal or indirect effect of the instrument be accommodated within accepted legal methods? Or, addressing the same question from a different angle, what might be successful legitimation strategies available for a court that wishes to rely on the instrument as a source of inspiration. Or, to put it yet differently, is there a legitimate place for on ECL instrument within the developing European legal method?[21] That is the central question in this paper. I will discuss three main types of legitimation: new European legal methods, classical methods of interpretation, and political legitimation. The order will be from very strong, specifically European, via more general 'legal', to weaker, 'merely political' legitimation.[22] However, before discussing these different types of legitimation, we will have to clarify a question relating to the scope of a European legal method.

European legal method: nationalist, dualist and Europeanist perspectives

There is another dimension to the questions of whose method and whose toolbox. Are we only talking about the Court of Justice of the European Union (CJEU), or also about national judges when they are applying Union law, or even about national judges when they are not applying Union law? For the latter case, we can distinguish further between a) disputes that only partly turn on EU law, for the remaining non-EU part, b) disputes that do not turn on EU law but where the EU legislator has exclusive competence; c) cases that are not affected by existing EU law but where the EU has a shared competence; and d) cases where the EU legislator has no competence. In which cases could or should the instrument play a role as a source of inspiration for judges? Should these cases somehow be distinguished categorically, some of them being a matter of European legal method where the ECL instrument could play a role, while others remain subject exclusively to the national legal method of the forum?

There are at least three different ways of looking at European private law and European legal method, i.e. a nationalist, a dualist, and a Europeanist

21. See M.W. Hesselink, 'A European Legal Method? On European Private Law and Scientific Method', 15 *ELJ* 1 (2009), 20-45.
22. I am not suggesting that merely legal legitimacy is per se strong legitimacy, but simply that, as Weiler puts it, '[a]n institution, system, or polity, in most, but not all, cases, must enjoy formal legitimacy to enjoy social legitimacy' (J.H.H. Weiler, *The Constitution of Europe; 'Do the New Clothes Have an Emperor?' and Other Essays on European Integration* (Cambridge: Cambridge University Press, 1999), p. 81).

way.[23] In the nationalist perception, the Europeanisation of private law is a process that affects and modifies the national system of private law. In this perception, although most of private law is of domestic origin, an increasing part is of European extraction. The focus is on how to integrate these 'foreign' elements without upsetting the original system. In the Europeanist perception, in contrast, all private law in the European Union forms a single, gradually integrating system. The focus is on the interplay between the different levels of governance and on how the progressive coherence of the whole multi-level system and the gradual convergence of its components can be achieved. In this perception, an increasing part of European private law is regulated on the EU level, whereas a considerable part is still regulated on the national level (and a minor part on the global level) of the same system. Finally, in a dualist perception, on the territory of each Member State there are two systems: a national and a European one. Both systems are complementary and intertwined but nevertheless distinct. In other words, each Member State has its own national system of private law, in addition to which they together share a common European system of European Community private law. In this perception, the focus is, quite naturally, on tracing the exact borderline between the two systems.

In the nationalist perception, a European toolbox on contract law will probably be perceived as a potential further attack on the national legal system. The attitude towards it is likely to be formal: it is not binding law so it can be ignored.[24] In contrast, in the Europeanist perception, a common frame of reference or instrument on European contract law that guides us through a process of gradual and progressive convergence is exactly what we need at this moment. The strategy will be to emphasise its substantive quality and the need to go beyond formal limits towards the further Europeanisation of private law. Finally, the dualist will be mainly concerned with the question in which cases (a-d, above) exactly the European instrument could play a role.

23. See further M.W. Hesselink 'The Common Frame of Reference as a source of European private law', 83 *Tulane Law Review* 4 (2009), 919-971, 932-936. For a similar distinction, see J. Dickson, 'How Many Legal Systems? Some Puzzles Regarding the Identity Conditions of, and Relations Between, Legal Systems in the European Union' (Univ. of Oxford Legal Research Paper Series, No. 40, 2008), whose a) 'Part of member states' Legal Systems' model, b) 'Distinct EU legal system' model or '27 plus 1' model, and c) 'One Big Legal System' model, are roughly similar to what I call, respectively, the a) nationalist, b) dualist, and c) Europeanist perspectives.
24. On such formalist patterns of entrenchment, see D. Caruso, 'The missing view of the cathedral: the private law paradigm of European legal integration', 3 *ELJ* (1997), pp. 27-32.

These are three perceptions of the same phenomenon, i.e. of private law in Europe, neither of which can be said at the outset to be more true (positively) or more right (normatively). It is impossible to discuss the issue in a neutral fashion. As I have explained elsewhere, the dualist project, which is dominant in the German academic debate on a European method, seems pointless because it will eventually collapse into either nationalism or Europeanism.[25] The following account is inspired by a (moderately) Europeanist approach, which means in practical terms that I will include in my discussion cases where national judges could undertake a ECL instrument-friendly interpretation of national or could otherwise be inspired by the ECL instrument, even beyond the scope of (potential) EU legislation.

New European legal methods

Sincere cooperation and Europe-friendly interpretation

The most far reaching role in adjudication for an ECL instrument would exist if the general EU duty of sincere cooperation would require judges to always carry the instrument in their toolbox and to use it where they can. The idea would be that the duty of sincere cooperation would require Europe-friendly interpretation of national law, in a broad sense of favouring an ever closer Union, which in turn would translate into a duty of ECL-instrument-friendly interpretation in contract cases.

Article 4, Para 3 of the Treaty on European Union reads as follows:

> Pursuant to the principle of sincere cooperation, the Union and the Member States shall, in full mutual respect, assist each other in carrying out tasks which flow from the Treaties.
>
> The Member States shall take any appropriate measure, general or particular, to ensure fulfilment of the obligations arising out of the Treaties or resulting from the acts of the institutions of the Union.
>
> The Member States shall facilitate the achievement of the Union's tasks and refrain from any measure which could jeopardise the attainment of the Union's objectives.

25. See further Hesselink, op cit n 23.

The obligation of harmonious interpretation, which will be discussed in the next section, is often regarded as an example of the positive obligation contained in the second sentence,[26] but does the principle of loyal cooperation, maybe in its third sentence, also require ECL-instrument-friendly interpretation? It does not seem so. The reason is that the duty of sincere cooperation, or duty of (Community) loyalty[27] or 'fidelity principle' as it is sometimes called after American usage,[28] i.e. the constitutional equivalent of the private law duty of good faith, does not even imply any general obligation for the Member States of Europe-friendliness.[29] A profoundly Euro-sceptic government can be just as loyal to the Union as any other. Bogdandy speaks of a 'principle of the free pursuit of interests' which implies, among other things, that the Member States remain free to pursue their national interests in the European institutions, and which militates against the assumption of a principle of integration in favour of more Europe or more unity.[30] A fortiori, this means that Member States are not under a general obligation of Europe-friendly interpretation of their national law. Judges are allowed to pursue the interests of the national legal system, e.g. its internal coherence or its own underlying values. This seems to be even more strongly the case for subjects that are outside the scope of the EU competences. Moreover, the idea of 'mutual respect' (introduced by the Lisbon Treaty) could be regarded as a 'countervailing principle',[31] which could provide a basis for legal diversity and an additional argument against a duty originating in primary EU law to interpret national private law in a Europe- or ECL-instrument-friendly way.

Some Member States require Europe-friendliness as a matter of national (constitutional) law, either as part of a more general duty of promoting the

26. See e.g. Joined Cases C-397/01 to C-403/01 *Pfeiffer and Others* [2004] ECR I-08835 and Case C-106/89 *Marleasing v La Comercial Internacional de Alimentación* [1990] ECR I-04135 and C.W.A. Timmermans, in: P.J.G. Kapteyn et al (ed), *The Law of the European Union and the European Communities*, 4th ed. (Alphen a/d Rijn: Kluwer Law International, 2008), 149. Another explanation is the *effet utile* doctrine. See further below.
27. Kapteyn & VerLoren van Themaat (Timmermans), op cit n 26, 147.
28. Cf D. Halberstam, 'The Political Morality of Federal Systems' (2004) 90 *Virginia L. Rev.* 101, 104.
29. See A. von Bogdandy, 'Founding Principles', in: A. von Bogdandy & J. Bast (eds), *Principles of European Constitutional Law*, 2nd ed. (Oxford: Hart Publishing, 2010), 42.
30. Ibidem, pp. 37-38.
31. See D. Chalmers, G. Davies & G. Monti, *European Union Law*, 2nd ed (Cambridge: CUP 2010), 223.

development of the international legal order[32] or as a specific constitutional duty to contribute to construing the European Union. In Germany, the *Bundesverfassungsgericht* (*BVerfG*) held, in its Lisbon ruling, that a principle of openness towards European law (*Europarechtsfreundlichkeit*) follows from German Basic Law: 'The constitutional mandate to realise a united Europe, which follows from Article 23.1 of the Basic Law and its Preamble means in particular for the German constitutional bodies that it is not left to their political discretion whether or not they participate in European integration. The Basic Law calls for European integration and an international peaceful order. Therefore, not only the principle of openness towards international law, but also the principle of openness towards European law (*Europarechtsfreundlichkeit*) applies.'[33] However, it is not clear that all Member States accept, as a matter of national (constitutional law), a duty of Europe-friendly interpretation. Moreover, it does not seem that in any of these countries, including Germany, such a duty would go much further than a (strong) presumption of applicability in the Member State of EU law. And, although this will differ from Member State to Member State, in most if not all countries, including Germany, it would be a very long shot (indeed almost certainly too long) to derive from any such national general duty of Europe-friendliness a specific duty to interpret their contract law in conformity with the ECL instrument.

Soft harmonious interpretation?

National law must be interpreted in conformity with European Union law.[34] Could this requirement of 'harmonious interpretation' imply a duty (sometimes) to interpret national law in conformity with the instrument on European contract law? Although the CJEU sometimes speaks, very broadly, of 'the requirement for national law to be interpreted in conformity with European Union law', it is clear that this requirement only exists in relation to na-

32. The Dutch constitution limits this task to the executive. See Article 90 Basic Law.
33. *BVerfGE* 123, 267, no. 225. See also nr. 241. In the same sense the Mangold-follow-up decision, *BVerfG*, 2 BvR 2661/06 of 6.7.2010, no. 58. Although the English term 'openness towards European law' for the German 'Europarechtsfreundlichkeit' is the official English translation published by the court itself, 'openness towards' nevertheless seems to be somewhat weaker and more passive (less engaging) a concept than 'friendliness'.
34. Settled case law. See e.g. Case C-106/89 *Marleasing* v *La Comercial Internacional de Alimentación* [1990] ECR I-04135 and Joined Cases C-397/01 to C-403/01 *Pfeiffer and Others* [2004] ECR I-08835, para 114.

tional law within the scope of European Union law.[35] If the optional instrument is going to be introduced, as envisaged, via a regulation, then *effet utile* issues could arise, e.g. when national rules would somehow hinder an easy opting into the instrument. However, interpretation of national law in conformity with the optional-instrument-regulation would be limited, it seems, to disputes between parties who (claim to) have made a choice for the instrument as the applicable law to their contract. In contrast, if the ECL instrument is going to be adopted by the European legislator as a legislative toolbox, then that certainly could significantly extend the potential scope of the ECL instrument and of any interpretation in conformity with it. However, crucially, it is very doubtful that the legislator's toolbox, even in the case of an inter-institutional agreement to 'comply or explain',[36] would count as 'European Union law' in the sense of the CJEU's settled case law on harmonious interpretation.

Or could it be argued that the adoption of EU 'soft law', provided that it remains within the scope of EU legislative competence (art. 5 TEU), implies a duty for the national courts of 'soft harmonious interpretation'? For example, within the context of (regular) harmonious interpretation it may happen that the directive or other EU provision in question also has to be interpreted. If that directive was inspired by the ECL instrument in its capacity as a legislative toolbox, should not then the national court when interpreting that directive with a view to an interpretation of its national law in conformity with that directive take the ECL instrument into account as a judicial toolbox? Clearly, any recognition of such a duty of soft harmonious interpretation would only possess equally soft (i.e. relatively weak) legitimacy.

General principles of EU law

General principles of EU law and of civil law

In its *Mangold* decision the Court of Justice acknowledged the existence of a principle of non-discrimination on grounds of age which must be regarded as

35. See Case C-555/07 *Kücükdeveci* [2010] ECR I-00000, para 48.
36. This has been suggested as the possible content of on interinstitutional agreement on an ECL instrument: the Commission, European Parliament en Council would commit themselves in relation to all future legislation within the scope of the instrument, to comply with the instrument or explain why they (propose to) deviate from it. Clearly, this would be a very far reaching commitment, which potentially could make the instrument hugely influential.

a 'general principle of European Union law', and which, in turn, is a specific application of the general principle of equal treatment.[37] By reason of the principle of the primacy of European Union law, which extends also to the principle of non-discrimination on grounds of age, contrary national legislation which falls within the scope of European Union law must be disapplied. In *Kücükdeveci* the Court made clear that, unlike the directives that give expression to the principle which only have indirect horizontal effect, this principle of EU law has direct horizontal effect.[38] This case law is far from isolated. General principles of EU law play an important role in the Court's jurisprudence, especially in its more creative and expansive part.

In addition to the general principles of EU law, the court recently has also discovered general principles of civil law. In *Société thermale d'Eugénie-Les-Bains* the Court cites 'the general principle of civil law' that 'each contracting party is bound to honour the terms of its contract and to perform its obligations thereunder';[39] in *Hamilton* it mentions as 'one of the general principles of civil law' the principle that 'full performance of a contract results, as a general rule, from discharge of the mutual obligations under the contract or from termination of that contract'.[40] In *Messner*, the Court invoked 'the principles of civil law, such as those of good faith or unjust enrichment',[41] and in *Asturcom* it referred to the 'basic principles of the domestic judicial systems, such as protection of the rights of the defence, the principle of legal certainty and the proper conduct of procedure' and to 'the importance, both for the Community legal order and for the national legal systems, of the principle of res judicata',[42] while in *Audiolux* the Court rejected the existence of a 'general principle of Community law' on the protection of minority shareholders.[43]

It is not clear yet whether such principles could also have direct horizontal effect. What we do know, however, is that the general principles of EU only apply when a case falls within the scope of European Union law. Still, what

37. Case C-144/04 *Mangold* [2005] ECR I- 09981, paras 74 to 76.
38. Case C-555/07 *Kücükdeveci* [2010] ECR I-00000, para 56.
39. Case C-277/05 *Société thermale d'Eugénie-les-Bains* v *Ministère de l'Économie, des Finances et de l'Industrie* [2007] ECR I-06415, para 24.
40. Case C-412/06 *Annelore Hamilton* v *Volksbank Filder eG* [2008] ECR I-02383, para 42.
41. Case C-489/07 *Pia Messner* v *Firma Stefan Krüger* [2009] ECR I-07315, para 26.
42. Case C-40/08 *Asturcom Telecomunicaciones SL v Maria Cristina Rodríguez Nogueira* [2009] ECR I-09579, paras 35 and 38.
43. Case C-101/08 *Audiolux SA and Others* v *Groupe Bruxelles Lambert SA (GBL) and Others and Bertelsmann AG and Others* [2009] ECR I-09823.

exactly this means is less clear. In *Mangold*, the case was within the scope of EU law because the discriminatory national legislation was a measure implementing an EC directive, while in *Kücükdeveci* the national law came within the scope of EU law because the equal treatment directive should already have been transposed. But if these general principles are part of primary law, is it really necessary for the applicability of the principle that there be some *other* (secondary or other primary) EU law also applicable to the case, or could it suffice that the case be within the competences of the EU (following art 5 TEU)? Moreover, for these new general principles of civil law it is even not clear whether they are meant to be general principles of EU civil law or rather general principles which the courts ascribe, as it were, to the national law legal systems. And, in the former case, are they meant to be a specific subset of general principles of EU, in which case they would, somewhat surprisingly – in view of the not so fundamental nature of most them[44] – obtain constitutional status as primary EU law, or are they of a new kind, i.e. of unwritten secondary EU law?

The instrument on European contract law as general principles

Our specific question here is whether the ECL instrument could ever become a source of inspiration for formulating general principles of Union law or of civil law, in this sense. Strictly speaking this is not a matter of interpretation. As the Court pointed out for the general principles of Union law, these principles apply as a matter of the primacy of EU law.

Could an ECL instrument, be it as an optional instrument or in the form of a legislator's toolbox, serve as evidence, a restatement or a codification of general principle of civil law? In his Opinion in the *Hamilton* case, Advocate-General Poiares Maduro explicitly referred to the CFR. He pointed out that the placing of a time-limit on the exercise of a right is 'a principle common to the laws of the Member States'. 'That principle', he continued, 'might well ultimately appear at Community level in the context of the creation of a common frame of reference for European contract law.'[45] As a toolbox for European judges who are trying to develop European general principles of civil law, the instrument may certainly be convenient, especially when taking

44. See below.
45. Para 24. See also the Opion of Advocate General Trstenjak *Messner* (C-489/07), para 94, where she points out 'in passing' that the approach she advocates is similar to the one adopted by the DCFR.

into account that most judges in the CJEU do not specialise in private law.[46] The instrument may even prove to be irresistible.

Moreover, the DCFR is the next step in a tradition in which the predecessors, i.e. the Unidroit Principles of International Commercial Contracts (UP) and the Principles of European Contract Law (PECL), were referred to as 'principles'.[47] The equivalent rules in the DCFR are referred to as 'model rules'. The reason why the UP and the PECL avoided the term 'rules' was that it seemed inappropriate for a private initiative to claim to be producing legal rules. They never were meant to be principles in, for example, a Dworkinian sense.[48] It is not clear, however, that the Court's principles are meant to be understood as principles in a Dworkinian sense either. Dworkin distinguishes between rules and principles because of their dimension of weight. Many of the general principles of EU law seem to possess a similar quality.[49] However, at least some of the Court's general principles of civil law do rather look like (but may be not entirely the same as) rules. In that case, it could indeed make sense to take the instrument, which is merely the next step in the same tradition after the DCFR, as a source of inspiration.[50]

In addition to the model rules, the DCFR, at the explicit request of the European Commission,[51] also contains a 'principles' section. It is an open question whether a section like this will also be included in the instrument on

46. Notable exceptions include Verica Trstenjak and Marek Safjan.
47. H. Beale & O. Lando (eds.), *Principles of European Contract Law, Parts I and II, Prepared by The Commission on European Contract Law* (The Hague: Kluwer Law International, 2000) and *UNIDROIT Principles of International Commercial Contracts* (Rome: Unidroit, 2004).
48. See R. Dworkin, *Law's Empire* (Cambridge, Massachusetts: Harvard University Press, 1986). See, earlier, his *A Matter of Principle* (Cambridge, Massachusetts: Harvard University Press 1985).
49. In Case C-101/08 *Audiolux SA and Others* v *Groupe Bruxelles Lambert SA (GBL) and Others and Bertelsmann AG and Others* [2009] ECR I-09823 the Court pointed out that general principles of Community law have 'the general, comprehensive character which is naturally inherent in general principles of law' (para 50) and are not 'characterised by a degree of detail requiring legislation to be drafted and enacted at Community level by a measure of secondary Community law' (para 63). However, M. Safjan & P. Mikłaszewicz, 'Horizontal effect of the general principles of EU law in the sphere of private law', 18 *ERPL* (2010), 475-486, 480, assimilate the general principles of EU law to fundamental rights.
50. qIn the same sense J. Basedow, 'The Court of Justice and private law: vacillations, general principles and the architecture of the European judiciary', 18 *ERPL* (2010) 443-474. Contrast Micklitz, *Failure or Ideological Preconceptions*, op cit n 17, 20.
51. See The way forward, loc cit n 3.

European contract law. But if it will, then at first sight this section might seem to be an obvious source of inspiration for any more Dworkinian principles of civil law that the Court may wish to develop. However, on further examination the principles section in the DCFR is rather problematic.[52] First, because the drafters themselves changed the section quite radically between two editions (within one year), which seems very odd for principles of private law which are supposed to be fundamental. Secondly, because what the DCFR refers to as principles actually rather seem to be values. And of course there are better and more obvious sources for shared European values than the DCFR, the Nice Charter and the first articles of the TEU to start with.

So far, I have referred to the CJEU as the oracle of general principles of EU law and of general principles of civil law. However, an interesting question is whether only the CJEU is allowed to formulate them. In *Mangold* and *Kücükdeveci* the Court said that it had 'acknowledged' the existence of a principle of non-discrimination on grounds of age which must be regarded as a 'general principle of European Union law'. This expression suggests that the principle already (may have) existed before it was acknowledged by the CJEU. If this is true, could national courts also acknowledge European principles, even before the CJEU has done so? As a matter of expediency that might be quite risky because later on it may turn out that such a new Union principle did not really exist. Therefore, it may be safer for a national court to refer to the CJEU for a preliminary ruling. On the other hand, however, the Court underlined in *Kücükdeveci* that national courts are not under an obligation to refer to the CJEU before disapplying a national provision that is contrary to a principles of EU law.[53] Now, *Kücükdeveci* was decided after *Mangold*. Therefore, the national court could already know of the existence of the general principle. But suppose that these cases had come to the court in the reverse order. The mere fact that before *Mangold* the Court had not yet acknowledged its existence does not exclude that this principle already existed before as a general principle of EU and that therefore a national court should or could have disapplied a national provision contrary to that principle, and even without reference to the CJEU. And the same would apply to other principles of EU law that may exist already today, but which the court has not yet had the opportunity to recognise. These are important questions concerning

52. M.W. Hesselink, 'If you don't like our principles we have others. On core values and underlying principles in European private law: a critical discussion of the new 'Principles' section in the draft CFR', in: H.W. Micklitz et al. (eds.)(Oxford: Hart Publishing, forthcoming).

53. See para 54.

the nature of the principles of Union law and concerning the nature of European adjudication and European legal method: do EU courts merely discover or 'acknowledge' principles that were so far unknown or do they create new ones? How much legal realism (and centralism) is there in European law? Clearly, these questions are relevant also for the way in which (only centralised and top-down or also decentralised and bottom-up) the contract law rules from the ECL instrument may penetrate into European contract law in the shape of general principles of European Union (civil) law.

Traditional methods of legal interpretation

Could or should the forthcoming instrument on European contract law play a role in the context of more traditional types of legal interpretation? Such a role within acknowledged legal interpretation would legitimise some indirect normative force for the instrument. The canon of general methods of statutory interpretation in many Member States includes grammatical, historical, systematic, and teleological interpretation, although legal systems differ as to the degree to which they recognise and articulate each of these methods.[54] In addition, comparative interpretation is sometimes acknowledged as a separate method of interpretation.

Grammatical or 'literal' interpretation

Grammatical or literal or linguistic interpretation focuses on the wording and syntax of the legal provision under interpretation. It is an established method of statutory interpretation in the Member States.[55] It is also the starting point

54. For Germany, see explicitly *BVerfGE* 11, 126, 130 (17 May 1960). Similar, art. 3, para 1 of the Spanish *Código Civil.*
55. For Germany, see e.g. K. Larenz & C.-W. Canaris, *Methodenlehre der Rechtswissenschaft*, 3rd ed. (Berlin etc: Springer, 1995), 141; for France, see M. Fabre-Magnan, *Introduction générale au droit; Cours et méthologie* (Paris: PUF, 2009), 49 (*méthode exégétique*); for England, see J. Cartwright, *Contract Law; An Introduction to the English Law of Contract for the Civil Lawyer* (Oxford: Hart Publishing, 2007), 25 (golden rule); for Belgium, see *Dekkers-Wylleman Handboek Burgerlijk Recht*, Vol. I (Antwerp-Oxford: Intersentia, 2009), no. 37 (E. Dirix); for Spain, see L. Díez-Picazo & A. Gullón, *Sistema de Derecho Civil*, Vol. I (10th ed.) (Madrid: Tecnos, 2010), 166; for Austria, see *Koziol-Welser Bürgerliches Recht*, Vol I (H. Koziol), 11th ed. (Vienna: Manz 2000), 21, for Italy, see G. Alpa, *Manuale di diritto privato*, 4th ed. (Milano: Cedam, 2005), 116; for CISG, see S. Eiselen, 'Literal interpretation: the meaning of the words', in: A. Janssen & O. Meyer (eds.), *CISG Methodology* (Munich: Sellier, 2009), 61-89.

of interpretation by the CJEU.[56] This is expressed e.g. in the standard phrase that 'in interpreting a provision of Community law it is necessary to consider *not only* its wording but also the context in which it occurs and the objects of the rules of which it forms part'[57] and in the standard formula for harmonious interpretation where the court states that 'in applying national law, the national court called on to interpret it is required to do so, as far as possible, in the light of *the wording and* the purpose of the directive in question, in order to achieve the result pursued by the directive'.[58]

In the context of such 'literal' interpretation, the instrument could play a role when courts are trying to determine the meaning of certain terms used in EU legislation. So far, the CJEU seems to be reluctant to transpose the meaning of a term used in one piece of European legislation into another. For example, in the *Simone Leitner* case the Court refused to borrow the definition of 'damage' from the product liability directive for determining the meaning of the same concept in the package travel directive, in spite of the suggestion by its Advocate-General Tizzano to do so.[59] For that reason, it seems unlikely that the court would use the instrument as a source of inspiration for finding autonomous *general* European definitions of legal concepts. On the other hand, however, that was exactly one of the main reasons given by the European Commission in its 2003 Action Plan, and with specific reference to the example of the *Leitner* case, for introducing the idea a common frame of reference.[60] Moreover, at the explicit request of the Commission the DCFR, as it was published in 2009, consists of principles, model rules, and *definitions*. Indeed, there is a whole part of the book (called Annex) dedicated entirely to definitions of legal concepts. Especially, in the case of an official legislator's toolbox based on a 'comply-or-explain' interinstitutional agreement (see above), courts may assume, with some reason, that the meaning of a term contained in EU legislation in the area of private law after the adoption of the instrument is the one formulated in the instrument.

56. See e.g. M. Pechstein & C. Drechsler, 'Die Auslegung und Fortbildung des Primarrechts', in: K. Riesenhuber (ed.), *Europäische Methodenlehre; Handbuch für Ausbildung und Praxis* (Berlin: De Gruyter Recht, 2006), § 8, 18.
57. See e.g. Joined Cases C-402/07 and C-432/07 *Sturgeon and Others* [2009] ECR I-10923 and Case C-156/98 *Germany* v *Commission* [2000] ECR I-06857, para 50 (emphasis added).
58. Case C-555/07 *Kücükdeveci* [2010] ECR I-00000, para 48.
59. Opinion of Advocate General Tizzano in Case C-168/00 (*Simone Leitner v TUI Deutschland GmbH Co. KG*) of 20 September 2002, paras 29 to 33.
60. Action Plan, loc cit n 3, 62.

Historical interpretation

Historical interpretation focuses on the legislative history of the provision and pays particular attention to the *travaux préparatoires*. This is a well established method of interpretation in many Member States especially in relation to more recent legislation.[61] However, it is only rarely used by the Court of Justice.[62]

Could the instrument on European contract law come into play in the context of historical interpretation? Obviously, that would much rather be the case in its legislator's toolbox capacity than if it was only adopted as an optional instrument. In the case of a Commission decision or an inter-institutional agreement to use the instrument as a reference tool for improving the coherence and the quality of EU legislation,[63] a court applying that legislation may be interested in looking behind the text of the EU legislation to see where it came from. This could especially be the case if the Commission proposal or the Council and European Parliament materials explicitly referred to the toolbox, be it to the black letter text of the model rules, or even to the official comments belonging to the instrument.

This may be particularly relevant in the context of harmonious interpretation, both when it is clear that the national legislator has not properly transposed a directive and when determining *whether* the national legislator has properly fulfilled its implementation duty. However, on the other hand, in the context of harmonious interpretation, teleological interpretation is both more recurrent and also the more obvious method.

The national legislator, without being bound to do so, could also spontaneously decide to be inspired by the legislator's toolbox or even by the op-

61. See for Germany, Larenz & Canaris, *Methodenlehre*, op cit n 55, 149; for France, Fabre-Magnan, *Introduction générale*, op cit n 55, 49; for Belgium, *Dekkers-Wylleman* (Dirix), op cit n 55, 37; for Spain, Díez-Picazo & Gullón, *Sistema*, op cit n 55, 168; for Austria, *Koziol-Welser* (Koziol), op cit n 55, 23, for Italy, Alpa, *Manuale*, op cit n 55, 117; for the Netherlands, *Asser-Vranken*** (Zwolle: Tjeenk Willink, 1995), 14; for CISG, see U. Gruber, 'Legislative Intention and the CISG' in: A. Janssen & O. Meyer (eds.), *CISG Methodology* (Munich: Sellier, 2009), 91-111.
62. See e.g. M. Pechstein & C. Drechsler, 'Die Auslegung und Fortbildung des Primarrechts', in: K. Riesenhuber (ed.), *Europäische Methodenlehre; Handbuch für Ausbildung und Praxis* (Berlin: De Gruyter Recht, 2006), § 8, nr. 32. In Case C-478/99, *Commission* v *Sweden*, Para. 23, the Court took into account the fact that 'according to a legal tradition that is well established in Sweden and common to the Nordic countries, preparatory work constitutes an important aid to interpreting legislation', but that, of course, only meant the acknowledgment of a tradition in the Nordic countries.
63. See Green Paper, 9.

tional instrument, as a model. Such a model role is explicitly envisaged by the European Commission.[64] In such cases, a national court when interpreting autochthonous national law similarly may also wish to 'look behind' the text of national law in order to see what exactly it was in the instrument on European contract law that inspired the national legislator.

Systematic interpretation

Another conventional interpretation method is systematic interpretation. This means that courts construe a certain legal rule, not in isolation, but in the light of the broader set of rules (contained in the same article, section, statute or code) that it is part of or otherwise coheres with.[65] The systematic interpretation method also plays a considerable role in the decisions of the CJEU,[66] e.g. when the Court holds that something 'follows from the general scheme of the Community rules' ('ergibt sich aus der allgemeinen Systematik der Gemeinschaftsregelung', 'résulte de l'économie générale de la réglementation communautaire').[67] However, the limit seems to lie in the *effet utile* doctrine which follows from the purposive nature of the European Union and its legislation.[68]

Could the instrument on European contract law play any role in the context of systematic interpretation? The European Commission's Action Plan presented the CFR as a tool for making European contract law more coherent.[69] And the Commission's Green paper envisages the toolbox as an instrument for ensuring the coherence of legislation.[70] If the aim of the instru-

64. Green Paper, p. 4.
65. See for Germany, Larenz & Canaris, *Methodenlehre*, op cit n 55, 145; for France, Fabre-Magnan, *Introduction générale*, op cit n 55, 49; for the Netherlands, *Asser-Vranken***, op cit n 61, 118; for Spain, Díez-Picazo & Gullón, *Sistema*, op cit n 55, 167; for Austria, *Koziol-Welser* (Koziol), op cit n 55, 22; for Italy, Alpa, *Manuale*, op cit n 55, 116; for the CISG, U. Magnus, 'Tracing methodology in the CISG: dogmatic foundations', 33-59, in: A. Janssen & O. Meyer (eds.), *CISG Methodology* (Munich: Sellier, 2009), 48.
66. See Pechstein & Drechsler, *Auslegung*, op cit n 56, 23-27.
67. See e.g. Case C-389/93 *Anton Duerbeck GmbH v Bundesambt für Ernährung und Forstwirtschaft* [1995] ECR I-01509, para 28. As a recent example, see Joined Cases C-261/07 and C-299/07 *VTB-VAB* [2009] ECR I-02949, para 58.
68. Ibidem.
69. See the title of the plan: 'A More Coherent European Contract Law, an Action Plan', loc cit n 3.
70. See Green Paper, 8: 'Commission act on a 'toolbox': Drawing on the results of the Expert Group, the Commission could adopt an act (e.g. a Communication or Com-

ment is indeed to make the acquis more coherent and if the European legislator (either the Commission alone, through a decision, or together with the Council and the Parliament, in an inter-institutional agreement) adopts the instrument as an official toolbox and actually uses it as a tool for making the acquis become more coherent, then it could make sense for an interpreter of European legislation in the area of contract law to take the instrument into account as well, even beyond the text of the acquis, when conducting a systematic interpretation.[71] Indeed, to the extent that 'the general scheme' of the EU rules in the area contract law is increasingly determined by the instrument on European contract law, a systematic interpretation would be more naturally inspired by the system of the instrument. This would also be in line with a view according to which the instrument could play a pivotal role in a developing multi-level system of European private law.[72]

Teleological interpretation

Teleological or purposive interpretation means interpretation in accordance with the rationale of the provision (*ratio legis*) or the policy aim underlying the rule. Although this is also a well established method of interpretation in the Member States,[73] it is not traditionally used there very often in relation to general private law. The reason is that private law is not usually regarded as having any specific purposes other than the fair and just resolution of disputes between private parties. However, this is clearly different for the more recent specific parts of private law, such as labour contract law, landlord and tenant law, and consumer law, which all have a specific aim, i.e. the protection of weaker parties.

The situation is very different for EU law, including EU private law. Because of the functional and instrumental nature of the EU, and of its primary and secondary legislation, teleological interpretation plays a prominent role in the practice of the CJEU. The competences of the Union are governed by the

mission Decision) on European Contract Law to be used as a reference tool by the Commission to ensure the coherence and quality of legislation.'

71. This reasoning could be regarded as a specific application of the idea of determining the intention of the historical legislator (historical interpretation).
72. See Hesselink, op cit n 23, 932. On European private law as a developing multi-level system, see C. Joerges, 'The Impact of European Integration on Private Law: Reductionist Perceptions, True Conflicts and a New Constitutional Perspective', *European Law Journal* (1997), 378.
73. See for Germany, Larenz & Canaris, *Methodenlehre*, op cit n 55, 153; for Spain, Díez-Picazo & Gullón, *Sistema*, op cit n 55, 170; for Austria *Koziol-Welser* (Koziol), op cit n 55, 25; for Italy, Alpa, *Manuale*, op cit n 55, 116.

principle of conferral (art. 5 (1) TEU). And these competences are conferred upon the Union with a view to achieving certain aims.[74] Although the European Union has not only an economic but also a social purpose,[75] the most relevant legislative objective in the area of private law has been the construction and proper functioning of the internal market. Most of the contract law acquis was adopted on the basis of what is now Article 114 TFEU (ex 95 EC). Pursuant to the first paragraph of that provision, the European Parliament and the Council can adopt approximation measures which 'have as their *object* the establishment and functioning of the internal market'. For legislation whose legitimacy is so closely linked to a specifically defined *telos*, it is only natural that courts should resort to a teleological method of interpretation. Indeed, as we saw, the CJEU underlines in its judgments that in interpreting a provision of EU law 'it is necessary to consider not only its wording but also the context in which it occurs and the *objects* of the rules of which it forms part'.[76]

What role could an instrument on European contract law play in the context of teleological interpretation? Directives in the area of private law have as their stated purpose 'the approximation of laws concerning [a certain specific subject]',[77] or, since *Tobacco*,[78] 'to contribute to the proper functioning

74. See art. 5, para 2 TEU.
75. Case C-341/05 *Laval un Partneri Ltd v Svenska Byggnadsarbetareförbundet and Others* [2007] ECR I-11767, para 105.
76. Loc cit n 57. (emphasis added).
77. See art. 1, Directive 90/314/EEC (on package travel, package holidays and package tours); Art. 1, Directive 93/13/EEC (on unfair terms in consumer contracts); art. 1, Directive 94/47/EC (on the protection of purchasers in respect of certain aspects of contracts relating to purchase of the right to use immovable properties on a timeshare basis); art. 1, Directive 97/7/EC (on the protection of consumers in respect of distance contracts); and art. 1, para 1, Directive 1999/44/EC (on certain aspects of the sale of consumer goods and associated guarantees).
78. Case C-376/98 *Germany v European Parliament and Council of the European Union* [2000] ECR I-08419 (*Tobacco*), para 84). As is well known, in that case the Court underlined that a measure adopted on the basis of art 114 TFEU (then 100a EC) must genuinely have as its object the improvement of the conditions for the establishment and functioning of the internal market and that a mere finding of disparities between national rules is insufficient to justify art 114 TFEU as a legal basis. However, according to S. Weatherill, 'An ever tighter grip: the European Court's pro-consumer interpretation of the EC's directives affecting contract law' in: M. Andenas et al (eds), *Liber amicorum Guido Alpa: Private law beyond the national systems* (London: British Institute of International and Comparative Law, 2007), 1037-1055, 1042 '*Tobacco Advertising* increasingly looks like a highly atypical ruling'.

of the internal market and achieve a high level of consumer protection by approximating laws on' a given subject.[79] They aim to do so by instructing the Member States to introduce into their national laws rules, which are usually rather detailed, concerning the rights and obligations of private parties in relation to certain aspects of certain types of contractual relationships. However, when a doubt arises as to how exactly the Member States are to modify their laws (i.e. when a directive seems to contain an ambiguity or a gap), the stated purpose of approximating laws is of little assistance because, clearly, *any* interpretation which is given by the CJEU and followed by the Member States will lead to the approximation of laws. The problem is that the aim of approximating laws says nothing about the content of these laws. It says nothing, that is, about the rights and obligations that the parties to certain contracts should have in certain circumstances. The notion of a high level of consumer protection provides more substantive guidance because it has a meaning not merely as a public aim but also in relation to the horizontal, private law question of what the rights and duties of the parties should be. However, it is also not conclusive itself since the aim of a high level of protection does not in itself imply any aspiration to maximise consumer protection. Therefore, a rule of thumb to the effect that in case of doubt about the meaning of a directive, the interpretation most favourable to the consumer shall prevail (in analogy to the duty to interpret preformulated contract clauses in a pro consumer fashion)[80] cannot be derived from art 12 TFEU.

This lack of normative guidance is an inevitable consequence of the incongruence between the public and vertical nature and aims of directives, on the one hand, and their private law content, on the other. Indirect horizontal effect has changed this in the sense that individuals are now entitled to an interpretation of Member State law that is as much in conformity with EU directives as possible. If the directive clearly states that a private party should have a certain right or obligation then to the extent that national law allows this (i.e. no contra legem), the private party is entitled to that private law right. But when it is unclear what rights or obligations the directive requires the Member States to assure their citizens, i.e. when it comes to the interpretation of the directive itself, we are back at the same question: if the directive contains gaps or ambiguities in relation to what the rights and obligations of private parties should be, of what assistance are the stated aims of approxima-

79. See art. 1, Directive 2005/29/EC, (Unfair Commercial Practices Directive); art. 1, Proposal for a Directive of the European Parliament and of the Council on consumer rights, COM(2008) 614 final, 8.10.2008.
80. See art 5, Directive 93/13/EEC on unfair terms in consumer contracts.

tion of laws, improvement of the internal market and (to a certain extent) a high level of consumer protection going to be?

In recent years the CJEU has had to decide, among other things, whether a court must assess of its own motion whether a jurisdiction or arbitration clause is unfair;[81] whether a technical problem in an aircraft which leads to the cancellation or delay of a flight is covered by the concept of 'extraordinary circumstances';[82] whether in the case of withdrawal by a consumer from a distance contract a seller may claim compensation for the value of the use of the consumer goods by the consumer;[83] whether a seller who has sold consumer goods which are not in conformity with the contract may require the consumer to pay compensation for the use of the defective goods until their replacement with new goods;[84] whether a right of cancellation may be exercised no later than one month from the time at which the contracting parties have performed in full their obligations under a contract for long-term credit;[85] whether a payment by bank transfer may avoid or put an end to the application of interest for late payment only when that the sum due is credited to the account of the creditor within the period for payment;[86] whether the effect of cancellation of a loan agreement can be limited to the avoidance of that agreement, even in the case of investment schemes in which the loan would not have been granted at all without the acquisition of the immovable property;[87] and whether consumers, in principle, have a right to compensation for non-material damage resulting from the non-performance or improper performance of the services constituting a package holiday.[88] It seems difficult, and indeed artificial, to answer such questions having in mind only the

81. Case C-137/08 *VB Pénzugyi Lízing Zrt. v Ferenc Schneider* [2010] ECR I-00000, Case C-40/08 *Asturcom Telecomunicaciones SL v Christina Rodriguez Nogueira* [2009] ECR I-00000, Case C-243/08 *Pannon GSM Zrt v Erzsébet Sustikné Győrfi* [2009] ECR I-04713, Case C-168/05 *Elisa Maria Mostaza Claro v Centro Móvil Milenium SL* [2006] ECR I-10421, Joined Cases C-240/98 to C-244/98 *Océano Grupo Editorial SA v Roció Murciano Quintero and Others* [2000] ECR I-04941.
82. Joined Cases C-402/07 and C-432/07 *Sturgeon and Others* [2009] ECR I-10923.
83. Case C-489/07 *Pia Messner* v *Firma Stefan Krüger* [2009] ECR I-07315.
84. Case C-404/06 *Quelle AG v Bundesverband der Verbraucherzentralen und Verbraucherverbände* [2008] ECR I-02685.
85. Case C-412/06 *Annelore Hamilton* v *Volksbank Filder eG* [2008] ECR I-02383.
86. Case C-306/06 *01051 Telecom GmbH v Deutsche Telekom AG* [2008] ECR I-01923.
87. Case C-350/03 *Elisabeth Schulte and Wolfgang Schulte v Deutsche Bausparkasse Badenia AG* [2005] ECR I-09215.
88. Case C-168/00 *Simone Leitner v TUI Deutschland GmbH Co. KG* [2002] ECR I-02631.

purposes of the approximation of laws, the improvement of the internal market, and a high level of consumer protection, without asking oneself what might be a just and fair solution between typical parties to a contract of the kind at hand. How can one properly deal with such questions without invoking any contract law reasoning? It seems, therefore, that sooner or later the EU will have to develop its own general rules or principles of private law.[89]

It is in this context that the instrument could play an important (maybe its most important role). It could provide some guidance, some prima facie answers to the question what amounts to a high level of consumer protection and to more specific private law questions. Strictly speaking this would not be a case of teleological interpretation. Rather, it would be a solution for the mismatch between the vertical nature of directives with their public law aims, on the one hand, and the private law nature of the content of directives that deal with the rights and duties of private parties. In the absence of a European model or frame of reference, the interpreters of directives that aim at the harmonisation of private law simply remain without any substantive guidance in relation to the private law questions that come up when national courts perceive ambiguities and gaps in directives.

Comparative interpretation

In the case of comparative interpretation a court consults and compares solutions reached in other legal systems to the problem at hand. In the Member States this interpretation method is much more recent, much less generally accepted and much less widely used than the four more canonical methods discussed so far.[90]

Comparative interpretation is problematic in a number of ways, both theoretical and practical. The main theoretical difficulty is the methodological shift from the positive to the normative. How can any comparison of differences and similarities between a given number of legal systems ever per se contribute to interpreting rules of law? What does the state of the law in other

89. And the CJEU has started to do so. See above. In the same sense Weatherill, *An ever tighter grip*, op cit n 78.
90. In Germany, it is used by the German *Bundesverfassungsgericht* and *Bundesgerichtshof*, albeit only rarely. See S. Vogenauer *Die Auslegung von Gesetzen in England und auf dem Kontinent*, Vol. I (Tübingen: Mohr Siebeck, 2001), 43, who discusses comparative interpretation as a specific instance of systematic interpretation. For the Netherlands, see *Asser-Vranken***, 198. English judges regularly compare with other common law jurisdictions overseas. For a famous example of judicial comparison with civil law systems, see *White* v *Jones* [1995] 2 WLR 187 (per Lord Goff).

countries tell me about what the law is in my own country? And once we know that legal systems differ or are similar, what does that tell us about what is the better, more appropriate or otherwise preferred solution, without recourse to any additional normative criterion? The functional method of legal comparison has been suggested as a way out of this problem. Zweigert & Kötz have famously argued that the basic methodological principle of all comparative law is that of functionality. As they argue, this proposition 'rests on what every comparatist learns, namely that the legal system of every society faces essentially the same problems, and solves these problems by quite different means though very often with similar results.'[91] Clearly, if indeed we can compare legal rules and doctrines in terms of their functions, in particular their problem-solving function, then the observation that one system performs that function better than another system is hardly problematic. Thus, the problem seems to have evaporated. However, that impression is clearly based on an illusion. In functional legal comparison the normative question is only hidden. Everything depends on the function that is ascribed to a legal rule or doctrine. But is law, in particular private law, really best described (exclusively) in functional terms (as philosophical pragmatists have argued) or is it rather something that developed historically and is culturally imbedded?[92] And even if legal rules are best understood in terms of their function, who decides what the functions of our rules are? A rule may work perfectly well for one person or group but may be much less functional in the eyes of others also affected by it. In other words, functionalism does not solve the problem, it just postpones the question. Other types of normative legal comparison, e.g. counting the number of countries that have adopted a certain solution, seem to be even more problematic, indeed arbitrary.

The methodological difficulties in relation to normative legal comparison became especially clear in relation to the PECL and the DCFR. And that makes them relevant for the instrument on European contract law as well since the instrument will be based on the DCFR.[93] Both the PECL and the

91. K. Zweigert en H. Kötz, *Introduction to Comparative Law*, 3rd ed (Oxford: OUP, 1998), p. 34.
92. For the critique of functionalism, see especially G. Frankenberg, 'Critical Comparisons: Re-thinking Comparative Law', *Harvard International Law Journal* 26 (1985), 411 and P. Legrand, *Que sais-je? Le droit comparé* (Paris: PUF, 1999).
93. Art. 2, Commission Decision of 26 April 2010 Setting up the Expert Group on a Common Frame of Reference in the area of European contract law (2010/233/EU) *OJ* 27.4.2010, L105/109.

DCFR are claimed by their authors to be based on legal comparison.[94] However, the comparative basis of each has been severely challenged.[95] Of course, the use of the instrument as a toolbox can still be legitimised in other ways (e.g. simply because they are the 'best solutions' by some standard),[96] but that would then be a different, direct legitimation, not via comparative interpretation. Political legitimation will be discussed in the next section.

It is probably for the same reasons that in the national context the normative force of legal comparison is also not regarded as very strong. In the Netherlands, for example, Vranken, although considering comparative interpretation as one of the tools in the 'toolbox' (!) of a judge, immediately adds that its normative force is rather weak; at most it has 'persuasive authority'.[97] On the other hand, however, it has been pointed out that legal comparison may have a 'subversive effect'.[98] If all other Member States have adopted a rule or solution which is different from our own, should we not reconsider ours? This kind of reasoning may contribute, in spite of anti-functionalist critique, to legitimising comparative interpretation – or rather to comparative adjudication, which is a broader concept. As Ralf Michaels puts it, functional comparison 'emphasises differences within similarity'.[99] In this context clearly any common core research could play an important role. And within that context the instrument on European contract law, as a purported statement of the common core, with comparative notes in the DCFR which could support this, may be tempting. This role for the instrument is not exactly the same as the one via Europe-friendly interpretation discussed above. In prac-

94. See PECL, Introduction, xxvi; DCFR, Introduction, 63.
95. For the DCFR see, in particular, N. Jansen, 'The authority of the Academic 'Draft Common Frame of Reference',' H.-W. Micklitz & F. Cafaggi (eds.), European private law ofter the Common Frame of Reference (Cheltenham, UK: Edward Elgar, 2010), 147-172, 162. As to the PECL, the authors themselves acknowledge that '[s]ome of the provisions in the Principles reflect suggestions and ideas which have not yet materialised in the law of any State.' (Introduction, p. xxvi).
96. Cf. H.-W. Micklitz, 'Review of academic approaches to the European contract law codification project', in: M. Andenas et al (eds.), *Liber amicorum Guido Alpa: Private law beyond the national systems* (London: British Institute of International and Comparative Law, 2007), 699-728, at 726.
97. *Asser-Vranken***, 205.
98. G.P. Fletcher, 'Comparative Law as a Subversive Discipline', 46 *AJCL* (1998), p. 683 ff; H. Muir Watt, 'La fonction subversive du droit comparé', *RIDC* 3-2000, p. 503 ff.
99. Ralf Michaels, 'The functional method of comparative law', in: M. Reimann & R. Zimmermann (eds.), *The Oxford Handbook of Comparative Law* (Oxford: OUP, 2006), ch 10.

tice there will be a strong overlap, but the reasoning and the legitimation are somewhat different: here the argument is not so much 'more Europe' or 'an ever closer Union' or 'a level playing field'. The assumption is rather that one country could learn from the (collective) experience of others.[100]

Political legitimation

In addition to the new legal methods developed specifically in relation to EU law and the more traditional methods that have long belonged to the canons of interpretation in the Member States, but also applied today in relation to EU law, including European contract law, there is a third possible kind of legitimation of the use made by European courts of an instrument on European contract law as a source of inspiration, i.e. 'merely' political legitimation.

When such policy or political arguments can and should come in, is a vexed question. And this is certainly not the place to go deeply into these matters, let alone propose a novel theory. Suffice is to say that today it is quite broadly accepted that courts do more than merely interpret existing law. They also further develop it and create new rules. There is difference of opinion as to whether, even in hard cases, the law ever 'runs out' in the sense that judges then have discretion or that instead – from within: the internal perspective – there is always a right answer to every legal question (even though an external sceptic may point to all sorts of factors that actually strongly influence adjudication). However, it is generally acknowledged, also in Dworkin's right answer thesis, that finding the right answer is not merely a matter of 'fit' with the available legal materials but also of 'justification' in terms of political morality.[101]

So, what kind of policy considerations could justify the use of the instrument as a toolbox for judges? I will, discuss four possible types of justification: the endorsement by other political institutions, the substantive quality of the instrument, the prestige of its authors, good governance, and political philosophy. These are all instances of 'non legal' and 'merely political' legitimacy in the sense that they do not justify the use by the courts of the instrument because it somehow already is the law or because it can contribute to figuring out what already is the law, but rather because it should become the law in the (more or less strong) sense that it should obtain some legal authority.

100. See M.W. Hesselink, *The new European legal culture* (Deventer: Kluwer, 2001), 51.
101. Dworkin, *Law's Empire*, op cit n 48.

Political endorsement

Judges may want to rely on the instrument on European contract law because it enjoys strong political support. The DCFR has been drafted at the request of the Commission, with the backing of Parliament and Council and the instrument itself is currently being drafted for the Commission. As said, what steps exactly will follow the Green Paper consultation is still uncertain, but in any case there is broad political support for a legislator's toolbox function.[102] In spite of the separation of powers, according to which judges only have to apply the laws that the legislator has actually enacted, this political fact is likely to count for European judges.

Moreover, it is important to point out here that there is a difference, in this respect, (at least of degree) between criminal and administrative law, on the one hand, and much of private law on the other hand. Most of contract law and most of the rules in the DCFR can be set aside by the parties in their contract because they are only non-mandatory (or 'default') rules. In other words, rules of private law, although formally enacted as law, are in principle only binding on private parties when they want them to. Indeed, the notion of the rule of law in the sense of a government of laws and not of men (John Adams) or that no one is above the law (A.V. Dicey) does not apply to most of contract law, because the parties are actually above the main part of contract law.[103]

Having said that, there are different theories on the nature of non-mandatory rules. Legal economists tend to regard them as the 'hypothetical bargain', i.e. what typical contracting parties would have agreed but is now provided by the legislator in order to help them save transaction costs. However, in most European countries the idea is rather that non-mandatory rules have what the Germans call a 'Leitbildfunktion', i.e. they enshrine the legislator's view on what would be a fair and just solution. This idea plays a role, for example, in the context of determining the unfairness of contract terms. Whether a term is unfair depends, in part, on how much it deviates from the otherwise applicable (non-mandatory) rules.[104] This idea seems to have been implicitly accepted by the CJEU in *Freiburger Kommunalbauten* when it held that in determining whether a particular term in a contract is unfair the

102. This is, of course, general support for the instrument as whole, not for any specific rules contained in it.
103. But 'non-mandatory' rules often are de facto binding. See M.W. Hesselink, 'Non-Mandatory Rules in European Contract Law', 1 *ERCL* 2005, 43-84.
104. See § 307 BGB, para 2.

consequences of the term under the law applicable to the contract must also be taken into account.[105]

If the instrument is going to be adopted by the European Commission, the Council of the European Union and the European Parliament as a 'legislator's toolbox', will that be very different from a legislator's model (*Leitbild*) for just and fair solutions that the judge, for that reason alone, may want to follow? Therefore, especially for the non-mandatory rules in the instrument (i.e. the bulk of them), the line between a non-mandatory rule in actually enacted European legislation and the same rule contained legislator's toolbox which has become the object of a 'comply or explain' inter-institutional agreement is rather thin. This shows how hybrid the nature of the instrument will be. In different formal roles it is likely to give different degrees of formal effect to rules that do not change in substance. In such a context, a not so formalist judge is likely to take into account that, one way or the other, there is broad political support from the main political institutions for this particular set of rules.

Substantive quality

The instrument could obtain authority because of its substantive quality, i.e. simply because it contains rational solutions and quite apart from whether it would also be the binding law between the parties who have opted for it (optional instrument) or that it played a role in legislation (legislator's toolbox), or indeed that it may have played role (in other cases) within the context of one of the acknowledged methods of interpretation (see the previous two sections).[106] For example, in cases where a judge finds herself confronted with (what she regards as) a gap in the law.

A number of German scholars have argued that the Principles of European Contract Law today already enjoy such substantive authority.[107] However,

105. Case C-237/02 *Freiburger Kommunalbauten GmbH Baugesellschaft & Co. KG v Ludger Hofstetter and Ulrike Hofstetter* [2004] ECR I-03043, para 21.
106. Admittedly, this abstraction, although conceivable in theory, is somewhat hard to imagine in practice.
107. See C.-W. Canaris, 'Die Stellung der 'UNIDROIT Principles' und der 'Principles of European Contract Law' im System der Rechtsquellen', in: Jürgen Basedow (eds.), *Europäische Vertragsrechtsvereinheitlichung und deutsches Recht* (Tübingen: Mohr Siebeck 2000), 5-32, 28 ('Rechtsgewinningsquelle'); Jansen, *The authority of the academic 'DCFR'*, op cit n 95; H. Eidenmüller, F. Faust, H.C. Grigoleit, N. Jansen, G. Wagner and R. Zimmermann, 'The Common Frame of Reference for European Private Law – Policy Choices and Codification Problems', *Oxford J Legal*

some of the same authors are also argue, quite categorically, that the DCFR is not of sufficient quality for obtaining a similar authority.[108] This is somewhat surprising since the core of the DCFR, i.e. general contract, is strongly based on the PECL. Indeed, others have expressed a different view. For example, Lord Mance regards the DCFR as 'a wonderful piece of work'.[109] The explanation for the difference of opinion may lie in the fact that the German professors adopted 'academic quality' as their criterion.[110] In any case, the implication seems to be that, to the extent that the transformation of the DCFR into an instrument on European contract will bring a return to PECL (or to the Unidroit principles to which the same German scholars also attribute authority), as has been advocated,[111] the instrument could obtain substantive authority.

A similar, but somewhat different, possible reason for courts to rely on the instrument might be that it contains 'best solutions'. It was the Commission's explicit aim that the DCFR should contain best solutions[112] and be of high quality.[113] It is also what the drafters of both the PECL and the DCFR have claimed for their texts: insofar as they are not based on legal comparison, they purport to contain 'the best' or, more modestly, 'suitable' solutions.[114] This claim brings the legitimation close to functionalism in comparative law, which was discussed above in relation to comparative interpretation. And, of course, the same criticisms apply here as well: best solutions to what problem (and whose problem)? And who decides what the problems are? Both the concepts of 'legal quality' and 'best solutions' are clearly problematic.[115] Ex-

Studies (2008) 28 (4): 659-708 (previously published in German in 63 *JZ* (2008), 529-584).

108. See Jansen, *The authority of the academic 'DCFR'*, op cit n 95.
109. Lord J. Mance, 'The Common Frame of Reference', 18 *ZEuP* (2010), 457-462.
110. Eidenmüller et al, *Policy Choices and Codification Problems*, op cit n 107, 660.
111. O. Lando, 'The Structure and the Legal Values of the Common Frame of Reference', *ERCL* (2007), 245-256; R. Schulze & T. Wilhelmsson, 'From the Draft Common frame of Reference towards European Contract Law Rules', 4 *ERCL* (2008), 154; H. Collins, 'Review', *Modern Law Review* (2008), 840-844; Hesselink, *The CFR as a source of European private law*, op cit n 23.
112. Action Plan, loc cit n 3, 62.
113. The way forward, loc cit n 3, 10.
114. See DCFR, Introduction, 8.
115. See R. Sefton-Green, 'The DCFR: A Technical or Political Toolbox?' in A. Somma (ed), *The Politics of the Draft Common Frame of Reference* Alphen a/d Rijn: Kluwer Law International, 2009), 39-50; H. Schepel, 'The European Brotherhood of Lawyers: the Reinvention of Legal Science in the Making of European Private Law', 32 *Law & Social Inquiry* (2007), 183-199.

cept for contemporary believers in the law of reason (*Vernuftrecht*),[116] they require further evaluative criteria without which legitimation seems to remain rather weak (because largely idiosyncratic).[117]

Authorship

Another possible reason for courts to attribute authority to the instrument on European contract law could be its authorship. The DCFR was drafted by a 'network of excellence'.[118] And the instrument is being drafted by an 'expert group' whose members were appointed, according to the European Commission, 'from specialists with outstanding competence in the area of civil law, and in particular contract law.'[119] Could not then the instrument become a source of inspiration simply because of the reputation of its drafters? This seems very unlikely indeed. For whatever the current nature and scientific status of legal scholarship, the days of such a strongly scholastic attitude are long over.[120] Admittedly, the notion of *communis opinio doctorum* still play a role in legal discourse in many countries, in Germany a *herrschende Meinung* is still distinguished from a *Minderheitsansicht*,[121] while in France *la doctrine* is still regarded as a source of law,[122] and some have attributed authority to the Unidroit Principles and the Principles of European Contract law, in part, because of the 'very high professional qualifications' of their authors.[123] However, the selection by the Commission of its 'experts' has not been uncontroversial, to say the least. In Germany, a group of law professors challenged it in a letter to the editor in the *Frankfurter Allgemeine Zeitung*.[124]

116. On the historical law of reason, see F. Wieacker, *Privatrechtsgeschichte der Neuzeit unter besonderer Berücksichtigung der deutschen Entwicklung*, 2nd ed. [1967] (Göttingen: Vandenhoeck & Ruprecht, 1996), 249.
117. For an indication of what an analysis in terms of comprehensive theories of political philosophy might look like, see below.
118. Joint Network on European Private Law (CoPECL: Common Principles of European Contract Law), Network of Excellence under the 6th EU Framework Programme for Research and Technological Development, Priority 7 – FP6-2002-CITIZENS-3, Contract N° 513351.
119. Art. 4 para 2, Commission decision, loc cit n 6.
120. For a different view, see G. De Geest, 'Hoe maken we van de rechtswetenschap een volwaardige wetenschap?', *Nederlands Juristenblad* 2004, 58.
121. According to current practice in the German commentaries, like *Münchener Kommentar* and *Palandt*.
122. C. Jamin & P. Jestaz, *La doctrine* (Paris: Dalloz, 2004).
123. See Canaris, *Die Stellung der Principles*, op cit 107, 28.
124. J. Basedow, H. Eidenmüller, C. Grigoleit, S. Grundmann, N. Jansen, E.-M. Kieninger, H.-P. Mansel, W.-H. Roth, G. Wagner & R. Zimmermann, 'Ein europäisches

And in France the composition (through cooptation) of the Study Group on a European Civil Code, the main drafter of the DCFR, had already been under severe attack.[125] Therefore, it seems unlikely that any use made of the instrument on European contract law by judges as a toolbox can be legitimised by the purported reputation of its authors alone.

Good governance

Could a judges' toolbox function for the ECL instrument be justified in terms of good governance? As said, the idea of a common frame of reference was launched by the European Commission in its 2003 Action Plan and was presented there as a tool for making European contract law more coherent. In that plan the CFR was linked up explicitly to the Commission's more general policy towards improving European governance and reforming the regulatory environment in the EU,[126] which had been expressed in its 2001 White Paper on European Governance and its 2002 Better Regulation Action Plan,[127] where one of the five stated principles of good governance was coherence.[128] As we saw above, an instrument on European contract law as a toolbox, not only for legislators but also for judges, can certainly contribute to improving the coherence of European contract law.

However, there is more to good governance than coherence. The other four principles of good governance stated in the White Paper were: openness, participation, accountability and effectiveness.[129] Especially in relation to

Vertragsrecht kommt – aber zu welchem Preis?', *Frankfurter Allgemeine Zeitung*, 4 July 2010.

125. Y. Lequette, 'Quelques remarques à propos du projet de code civil européen de M. von Bar', *D.* 2002, 2202-2014, 2209: 'Quant au *choix des membres* de ces commissions. A ce que l'on sait, M. von Bar occupe le sommet de la pyramide et, sauf à respecter une certaine variété géographique, dispose d'une totale liberté pour choisir à sa seule convenance les membres de ce groupe. C'est là un pouvoir tellement exorbitant qu'il suscite immédiatement une autre question: d'où M. von Bar tient-il lui-même ses pouvoirs? Est-il l'oint du Seigneur? S'est-il auto-investi de la mission d'élaborer un code civil européen?' (emphasis in original).
126. Action Plan, loc cit n 3, 72.
127. See European Governance, a White Paper, COM(2001) 428 final, 25.7.2001; Communication from the Commission, Action plan 'Simplifying and improving the regulatory environment', COM(2002) 278 final, 5.6.2002.
128. White Paper, loc cit n 126, 10.
129. See also the Communication from the Commission, European Governance: Better law making, COM(2002), 275 final, 5.6.2002; 'promoting a culture of dialogue and participation' (p. 3). There is a reference to promoting good governance and ensuring the participation of civil society in Article 15 TFEU, para 1.

participation in the making of the CFR and the forthcoming instrument, doubts have been raised.[130] It is true that the Commission is currently undertaking its second broad consultation on European contract law in a decade and that, like the DCFR, also the current drafts for the instrument are being submitted to stakeholders.[131] However, the stakeholders have been selected by the Commission while the text potentially affects all citizens.[132] Moreover, the number of people having actual influence on the text is rather restricted.[133] Suggestions for a more inclusive process, like a convention or a Wiki-CFR, have not been followed.[134]

In the literature on European private law governance, much of the focus has been on the market regulatory functions played by private law and private actors,[135] although there are also broader and more inclusive perspectives.[136] Could an ECL toolbox for judges be relevant for private regulation? Only remotely, it seems. In a broad sense all contracts are examples of private regulation. Think only of the famous Art. 1134 Para 1 of the French Civil Code, according to which '[a]greements lawfully entered into take the place of the law for those who have made them.'[137] However, as the same provision underlines, in principle, such private regulations are only binding on the parties that made them. Indeed, it is a fundamental principle of contract law that parties can only bind themselves (privity or relativity of contract).[138]

130. Micklitz, *Review of academic approaches*, op cit n 96, draws an analogy to the so-called 'new approach' to technical standards.
131. See DG Justice, *Roadmap 2011*, August 2010, 4.
132. See M.W. Hesselink, 'Who has a stake in European contract law?' 3 *ERCL* (2005) 295-296.
133. As Micklitz, *Review of academic approaches*, op cit n 96, 728, points out with regard to the academic input into the DCFR, 'The network of excellence established by the European Commission excluded all academics who are not directly involved in the discussion.'
134. Hesselink, *The CFR as a source of European private law*, op cit n 23, 960.
135. See e.g. F. Cafaggi & H. Muir-Watt (eds.), *Making European Private Law Governance Design* (Cheltenham, UK: Edward Elgar, 2008); F. Cafaggi & H. Muir-Watt, *The Regulatory Function of European Private Law* (eds.) (Cheltenham, UK: Edward Elgar, 2009).
136. See especially H. Collins, *Regulating Contracts* (Oxford: OUP, 1999).
137. 'Les conventions légalement formées tiennent lieu de loi à ceux qui les ont faites.' For a political history of this provision, see C. Jamin, 'Une brève histoire politique des interprétations de l'article 1134 du code civil', 178 *Dalloz* (2002), 901-907.
138. H. Beale, B. Fauvarque-Cosson, J. Rutgers, D. Tallon and S. Vogenauer, *Contract Law; Ius Commune Casebooks for the Common Law of Europe* (Oxford: Hart Publishing, 2010), 1171.

Moreover, today even the strongest advocates of party autonomy acknowledge that contracts are not binding merely as a matter of natural law, but because private law enforces them.[139] So, how can private regulation ever become legally binding on individuals beyond the simple binding force of a contract between the parties? Well, to the extent that they are recognised by the law, i.e. through the civil code or statute, or via judicial recognition.[140] Private regulation can become legally relevant via the classical notion of custom or through open norms and standards such as good faith, good morals and diligence. In the same way, an optional instrument could also operate as an entrance door for private standards. The DCFR, especially Part IV, on specific contracts (e.g. service contracts and franchising), contains a great variety of potential openings, and also the non-conformity concept in art. IV.A.-2:301 could be coloured by acknowledged business standards. As to general contract law, the DCFR refers to usage in several provisions including art. II.-1:104. Think also of the duty of good faith and fair dealing (III.-1:103), the omnipresent standard of reasonableness and the notion of good commercial practice.[141] Similarly, in its role as a toolbox, be it for legislators or for judges, the instrument could contribute more softly to further legitimation as well. However, this is all about legitimation of private regulation through the ECL instrument. The question that really concerns us here is whether the idea of private regulation could somehow contribute to legitimating the use of the ECL instrument as a toolbox for judges. That could be the case if private regulation could be shown somehow to be intrinsically good, quite apart from any further normative standard. However, the legitimacy of private regulation rather seems to depend ultimately on either (individual or collective) private autonomy or on the general legitimation of private law that will be discussed in the next section.[142]

139. See e.g. W. Flume, *Allgemeiner Teil des Bürgerlichen Rechts*; Vol. II. *Das Rechtsgeschäft*, 4th ed. (Berlin/Heidelberg/New York: Springer, 1992), 1.
140. This is acknowledged by F. Cafaggi, 'Private Regulation in European Private Law', in: A.S. Hartkamp et al (eds), *Towards a European Civil Code*, 4th ed (Alphen a/d Rijn: Kluwer Law International, 2010), 91-126, 96.
141. See e.g. II.-9:405 (Meaning of 'unfair' in contracts between businesses).
142. Therefore, it seems doubtful that private regulation should be in need of any further legitimation, e.g. via public accountability. A given private standard is either not binding on a private party that did not agree to it, as a result of the privity principle (together with its corollary, the autonomy principle), or it is binding, via some broad standard of private law, such as reasonableness, but then the legitimation is the usual legitimation of (private) law. For an exploration of the public accountability path, see

Political philosophy

A final possibility would be purely normative legitimation. Sometimes theories of contemporary political philosophy (or more classical ones)[143] are explicitly invoked in order to justify a certain normative position in relation to European contract law.[144] More often, however, without any explicit claims being made by anyone, there often exist in fact structural similarities between discourses. For example, much of the law & economics contribution to the European private law debate is implicitly utilitarian, albeit sometimes combined – not wholly unproblematically – with some libertarian elements. Leading contemporary theories of social justice could be 'applied', as it were, to the grand questions of European contract law. This could lead to a rather comprehensive matrix of the main positions concerning the principal normative questions of European contract law. It is submitted that a political-philosophical analysis of European contract law along these lines would provide a fuller picture than one-dimensional schemes of left-versus-right,[145] or diachronic accounts featuring one leading idea at a time,[146] or spacetime

D. Curtin & L. Senden, 'Public Accountability of Transnational Private Regulation: Chimera or Reality?' (forthcoming, *Journal of Law and Society*).

143. Especially Kant is often invoked to explain the nature of contractual obligation, notably by German scholars. See recently e.g. H. Unberath, *Die Vertragsverletzung* (Tübingen: Mohr Siebeck, 2007) and J. Basedow, 'Freedom of Contract in the European Union', *ERPL* 16 (2008), 901-923.

144. For example, S. Grundmann, 'Consumer Law, Commercial Law, Private Law: How can the Sales Directive and the Sales Convention be so Similar?', *EBLR* (2003), 237-257 and J.M. Smits, 'European Private Law: a Plea for a Spontaneous Legal Order', in: Deirdre M. Curtin, Jan M. Smits, André Klip and Joseph McCahery, *European Integration and Law* (Antwerp and Oxford: Intersentia, 2006), 85, for F. von Hayek's libertarianism. Or S. Deakin, 'Capacitas: Contract Law, Capabilities and the Legal Foundations of the Market', in: Simon Deakin & Alain Supiot (eds.), *Capacitas: Contract Law, Capabilities and the Legal Foundations of the Market* (Oxford: Hart Publishing, 2009) pp. 1-30 for Amartya Sen's capabilities approach. Or R. Sefton-Green, 'Social Justice and European Identity in European Contract Law', 2 *ERCL* (2006), 275-286, 278, for Nancy Fraser's critical theory.

145. See D. Kennedy, 'The Political Stakes in 'Merely Technical' Issues of Contract Law', 10 *ERPL* (2002), 7-28. For European contract law see M.W. Hesselink, 'The Politics of a European Civil Code', 10 *European Law Journal* (2004), 675-697. For European sales law, see B. van Zelst, *The Politics of European Sales Law* (Alphen a/d Rijn: Kluwer Law International, 2008).

146. D. Kennedy, 'Three Globalizations of Legal Thought: 1850-2000', in: D. Trubek & A. Santos (eds) *The New Law and Economic Development. A Critical Appraisal* (Cambridge: CUP, 2006), 19-73.

analyses in terms of national political traditions.[147] What would contemporary theories of social justice have to say on the legitimacy of an instrument on European contract law as a toolbox for judges? What follows here are a few first impressions.[148]

For a utilitarian, what matters is social utility (or social welfare), often reduced in the law and economics literature to 'economic efficiency' and economic growth. On this view, the protection of rights, distributive justice and other values are not of direct importance; they should count at most indirectly, i.e. to the extent that individuals value them (which is an empirical matter) and maybe as proxies for variables that (so far) escape reliable measurement.[149] The 'economic argument' is quite prominently present in the European private law debate. It has been directed against the idea of a European civil code, on account of the claims (borrowed from the economics of federalism) that centralised and uniform law is bad, given (largely assumed) diverse preferences along Member States lines, and that competition between legal systems is more efficient.[150] The idea of an optional code has been sustained on the 'economic' grounds that more choice and competition are good,[151] although others have pointed out that competition is distorted by the endorsement of and subsidy to one of the models by the European legislator.[152] Finally, the content of the DCFR has been scrutinised in welfare economic terms.[153] This has led to severe criticism: many of the rules and doc-

147. See e.g. Micklitz, *Failure or Ideological Preconceptions*, op cit n 17.

148. In the selection of contemporary theories I essentially follow W. Kymlicka, *Contemporary Political Philosophy: An Introduction* (Oxford: OUP, 2002).

149. For a full statement of this idea, see L. Kaplow & S. Shavell, *Fairness versus Welfare* (Cambridge, Massachusetts: Harvard University Press, 2002).

150. See e.g. R. Van den Bergh, 'Forced Harmonization of Contract law in Europe: Not to be continued', in: S. Grundmann and J. Stuyck (eds.), *An Academic Green Paper on European Contract Law* (The Hague: Kluwer Law International, 2002), 249-268; A. Ogus, 'Competition between National Legal Systems: A Contribution of Economic Analysis to Comparative Law', 48 *International and Comparative Law Quarterly* (1999), 405-418.

151. See J.M. Smits, 'European Private Law and Democracy: a Misunderstood Relationship' in: M. Faure & F. Stephen (eds.), *Essays in the Law and Economics of Regulation in Honour of Anthony Ogus*, (Antwerp-Oxford: Intersentia, 2008), pp. 49-59.

152. S. Grundmann, 'The role of competition in the European codification process', in: H.-W. Micklitz & F. Cafaggi (eds.), *European private law ofter the Common Frame of Reference* (Cheltenham, UK: Edward Elgar, 2010), 36-55.

153. See, in particular, G. Wagner (ed), *The Common Frame of Reference: A View from Law & Economics* (Munich: Sellier, 2009); P. Larouche & F. Chirico (eds), *Economic Analysis of the DCFR* (Munich: Sellier, 2010).

trines have been rejected as 'inefficient'.[154] What are the implications for the legitimacy of the instrument as a toolbox for judges? Utilitarians would probably not mind the non-binding nature of it. On the other hand, they would probably be sceptical about its rather shadowy pedigree: the genesis of the instrument may give more an impression of privilege than of utility. More specifically, they would probably favour the use of the instrument as a toolbox to the extent (as exactly as possible) that the rules contained in it are efficient. This probably means that courts ideally would have to examine for each specific rule or doctrine whether it leads to efficient outcomes. And absent empirical data, they probably should take the available economic analyses in welfare economic terms into account.

What would be the view of a liberal egalitarian? For a Rawlsian the answer would crucially depend on whether contract law should be regarded as part of what Rawls called the 'basic structure' of society, which determines the distribution of the 'primary goods' that every one wishes to have, whatever their particular life plan or conception of the good.[155] For only if contract law is part of the basic structure are Rawls' two principles of justice (i.e. the 'equal basic liberties' and the 'difference' (or maximin) principle) applicable to contract law. Whether contract law is one of these basic institutions that provide the background justice against which individuals are free to make their own choices is controversial. Rawls himself probably did not regard contract law as part of the basic structure,[156] but others have argued that the two principles of justice should apply to contract law because of the important distributive role that contract law plays.[157] However, even if contract law, and thus probably an optional instrument,[158] were part of the basic structure, what

154. Ibidem.

155. See J. Rawls, *A Theory of Justice*, revised edition (Belknap Press, Cambridge, Massachusetts, 1999 [1971]). A. Sen, *The idea of justice* (London, Penguin, 2009), regards his own theory as Rawlsian even though he rejects the concept of a basic structure. Other prominent liberals, like R. Dworkin, *Sovereign Virtue; The Theory and Practice of Equality* (Cambridge Massachusetts: Belknap Press 2000), and I. Berlin, *Liberty* (Oxford: OUP, 2002) have never included such a concept in their theories.

156. See e.g. J. Rawls, *Political Liberalism*, expanded edition [first edition 1993] (New York: Columbia University Press 2005), 282-283.

157. See A.T. Kronman, 'Contract Law and Distributive Justice', 89 *Yale Law Journal* (1980) 472; K.A. Kordana & D.H. Tabachnick, 'Rawls and Contract Law', 73 *George Washington Law Review* (2005), pp. 598-632.

158. Although there might be further issues relating to the optional nature of the instrument. There is general agreement that even if contract law is part of the basic structure, contracts are not. It might be argued that, in this respect, an optional instrument is somewhere between a contract and contract law.

about the instrument on European contract law as a toolbox for judges? It seems rather farfetched to include that in the basic structure as well. The concept of a basic structure would risk becoming meaningless. Thus, the conclusion seems to be that from a Rawlsian liberal perspective it is indifferent whether or not an instrument on European contract law will become a toolbox for judges and, if so, what its content should be – with or without the toolbox (no matter what its content) a society would be equally just. Moreover, on trans- and post-national justice Rawls' theory is notoriously inadequate.[159] Therefore, Rawls' theory of justice seems to be blank on the question whether contract law (including a toolbox for judges) should be located on the European or national level of governance.

Like liberals, also libertarians come in different varieties. But what Nozick, Hayek, and Milton Friedman have in common is that they are all advocates of free markets and opponents of redistributive policies.[160] Therefore, a libertarian probably also would appreciate the non-binding nature of the toolbox idea. However, if the content of the instrument is going to be broadly similar to the DCFR, he or she would not be too pleased with it. In other words, she would find only few useful tools in it. The reason is, of course, that from their perspective the text gives insufficient prominence to formal party autonomy and to freedom of contract. It would probably be rejected as being socialist. Indeed, the DCFR has been criticised as being too much on the left.[161] However, unlike utilitarians a libertarian would not be per se sceptical about the European level as the right regulatory level for locating contract law: on this question Nozickian libertarians probably would be neutral whereas a Hayekian libertarian (because of its anti-nationalism) might even be favourable.[162] Therefore, the European character of the toolbox would probably not disturb a libertarian.

Also communitarianism is nothing like a single theory or school of thought. However, what such different philosophers as Sandel, MacIntyre

159. See M.C. Nussbaum, *Frontiers of Justice* (Harvard: Belknap, 2006), chapters 4 and 5.
160. F.A. Hayek, *Law, Legislation and Liberty; A new statement of the liberal principles of justice and political economy* (London and New York: Routledge, 2003); R. Nozick, *Anarchy, State and Utopia*, [first edition 1974] (Oxford: Blackwell Publishing 2006); M. Friedman & R. Friedman, *Free to choose: a personal statement* (New York: Harcourt: 1990 [1980]).
161. Eidenmüller et al, *Policy Choices and Codification Problems*, op cit n 107.
162. See M.W. Hesselink, 'A spontaneous order for Europe? Why Hayek's libertarianism is not the right way forward for European private law' in: H.-W. Micklitz & F. Cafaggi (eds.), *European private law ofter the Common Frame of Reference* (Cheltenham, UK: Edward Elgar, 2010), 123-172.

and Walzer have in common is an emphasis on community, traditions and the local, as opposed to the individual, rational and universal.[163] They would probably reject the toolbox idea to the extent that it is based on a rational design by experts for universal application across Europe which is meant to overcome the variety of legal traditions. At the most they would accept a much more gradual and 'natural' convergence: we should wait until a truly European tradition has developed, bottom up instead of any imposition top-down (even if only in the soft fashion of a toolbox for judges). Clearly, such ideas match very well with a number of evolutionary and organicist approaches to European private law, such as the neopandectism of Zimmermann (who explicitly invokes Savigny),[164] the emphasis on the historical development of tradition and authority by Nils Jansen,[165] the legal culturalism of Legrand[166] and, although less radical, Sefton-Green,[167] but also Teubner's theory of law as an autopoietic system.[168] However, to the extent that the instrument can be demonstrated to be, not a rationally designed instrument, but, on the contrary, merely a codification of an existing tradition, that would be more appealing in the eyes of a communitarian. This tradition could be either the by now almost a Century old international tradition, i.e. merely the next step in a historical line running from Rabel, via the Hague conventions LUF and LUVI, CISG, Unidroit Principles, PECL and the DCFR to the instrument on European contract law, where the same text has gradually developed further, from one version to the next. Or it could be a truly European tradition to the extent that the PECL, DCFR and the instrument can rightfully be claimed to represent the common core of contract law in Europe.[169] Having said that, the whole terminology of tools and problem fixing would probably just sound

163. M.J. Sandel, *Liberalism and the Limits of Justice*, 2nd ed (Cambridge: CUP, 1998); M. Walzer, *Spheres of Justice; A Defense of Pluralism and Equality* (Basic Books, 1983); A. MacIntyre, *After Virtue*, 3rd ed (London: Duckworth, 2007).
164. R. Zimmermann, 'Roman Law and the Harmonization of Private Law in Europe': in A.S. Hartkamp et al (eds), *Towards a European Civil Code*, 4th ed, (Alphen a/d Rijn: Kluwer Law International, 2010), 27-53.
165. Most recently, N. Jansen, *The Making of Legal Authority; Non-legislative Codifications in Historical and Comparative Perspective* (Oxford: OUP, 2010).
166. P. Legrand, 'Against a European Civil Code', 60 *MLR* (1997), 44-62.
167. R. Sefton-Green, 'Cultural diversity and the idea of a European civil code', in M.W. Hesselink (ed), *The Politics of A European Civil Code* (The Hague: Kluwer Law International, 2006).
168. G. Teubner, *Recht als autopoietisches System* (Frankfurt am Main: Suhrkamp, 1989).
169. On the problematic nature of this claim see above.

too pragmatic to anyone holding a more evolutionary understanding of the law.

As a final prominent group of theories in contemporary political philosophy, we can cite deliberative democracy and citizenship theories. These theories have in common that they are more process- than outcome-oriented. Unlike utilitarianism, communitarianism and liberal-egalitarianism, they focus on civic virtues and deliberation rather than on perfect or minimum outcomes. They are a response to 'passive' or 'private' citizenship. They emphasise that individuals and communities do not merely have rights, but also duties. There are different strands of citizenship theory. Some focus on the civic virtues of individuals. They aim at cultivating seedbeds of civic virtue. This approach is often referred to as 'civic republicanism'. Others focus more on a virtuous collective process. Advocates of deliberative democracy argue in favour of a shift from a vote-centric conception of democracy to a talk-centric conception of participation. Habermas underlines that there is no reason why there should be any difference, in this respect, between private law and public law: also in relation to private law citizens should be able to regard themselves not only as the addressees but also as the authors of the law.[170] Although any instrument on European contract law (be it as an optional instrument or a legislator's toolbox) will be the outcome of a public consultation, it is doubtful whether this consultation, or the stakeholder involvement during the drafting, will meet the requirements of an inclusive and deliberative process.[171] In earlier stages already the CFR process has been denounced as lacking legitimacy exactly in these terms,[172] whereas in the current stage there simply is not enough time for a meaningful public debate. And in any case, whatever the outcome, the consultation will never have included the question whether the instrument could also become a toolbox for judges. Therefore, there is little in terms of citizenship and deliberative democracy that a toolbox for judges could derive political legitimacy from. That might be different if, in the longer run, the instrument on European contract law as a source of inspiration were to become the object, maybe on a case to case basis, of a much broader and inclusive societal debate.

170. J. Habermas, *Faktizität und Geltung; Beiträge zur Diskurstheorie des Rechts und des demokratischen Rechtsstaats*, 5th ed. (Frankfurt: Suhrkamp, 1997), 52.
171. On some of the details, see above.
172. Study Group on Social Justice in European Private Law, 'Social Justice in European Contract Law: a Manifesto', 16 *European Law Journal* (2004), 653-674.

Conclusion

The forthcoming instrument on European contract law, be it in the shape of an optional code for cross-border contracts or as an official toolbox for the European legislator, is likely to have a spill-over effect on adjudication. Judges will have no great difficulty in finding model rules and definitions that might come in handy when dealing with gaps and ambiguities in European private law. However, the question is whether such a role as a toolbox for judges would be legitimate. I have discussed three types of possible legitimation strategies: new European methods (sincere cooperation and Europe-friendly interpretation, soft harmonious interpretation and general principles of EU law), traditional methods of legal interpretation (grammatical, historical, systematic, teleological and comparative), and merely political legitimation (in terms of political support, substantive quality, authorship, good governance, and political philosophy). It will often depend on the circumstances of the case at hand and the characteristics of the particular model rule or definition that is being borrowed what mode of legitimation will prove to be more convincing. However, generally speaking legitimation in terms of the general principles of civil law that the CJEU has recently been developing seems a particularly promising strategy. On the other hand, it seems unlikely that European courts could ever come under a duty, following e.g. from the principle of sincere cooperation, to use the instrument as a toolbox.

Methodology and Theoretical Disagreement

Dennis Patterson[1]

Introduction

Methodology matters. The ways in which it makes a difference are varied but, in law, methodology cannot be separated from one of the most fundamental questions: how do we decide what the law is? In this paper, I want to look at the problem of methodology from the point of view of philosophical questions about the nature of law and how we decide what the law is on any given question. To that end, I shall consider the problem of 'theoretical disagreement.' This topic is among the most contested in contemporary analytic jurisprudence. I believe that debate can tell us something about methodology, not only its importance but the importance of keeping the right perspective on the role of methodology in legal reasoning.

Is Law a Science?

The question of the scientific status of law has been the focus of sustained attention. One of the problems with these discussions is the fact that several different questions are conflated, leading to confusion and less-than-satisfactory answers. There is no doubt that there are genuine disputes and that these disputes will not be easily resolved. But the resolution of disputes requires clarity when it comes to the disputed questions. Thus, let us begin with the articulation of some of the questions implicated in these debates.

1. My thanks to Hans Micklitz for comments on a draft of this article and to my research assistant, Anna Södersten, for her assistance with this article. Finally, thanks to Alexander Somek for inspiring discussion of the issues raised in this paper.

First is the question of what we[2] mean by the word 'science'? Here, at least two distinctions need to be made. These distinctions flow from the demarcation of natural science from the human sciences (natur- versus geisteswissenschaften). There are at least two ways of drawing the distinction (i.e., this I will call 'The Demarcation Problem') between the natural and human sciences. The first is methodological and the second is one of focus. On the methodological dimension, natural science is the realm of what Carl Hempel labeled 'the hypothetico-deductive method.' In natural science, a hypothesis is formulated and then 'tested' by experiment. Experiment is the means by which a hypothesis is confirmed or, as we learned from Karl Popper, falsified. Questions of the relationship between truth, falsity and scientific method are important but they need not detain us here, for the basic point is that natural scientists are concerned with the question whether a given hypothesis can be confirmed or not. This process is often glossed as 'testing a conjecture against reality' but, as with truth and falsity, we need not take a position on this question, for our interest lies in articulating the methodological picture of natural scientific activity.

Next is the question of the object(s) of scientific activity. In an interesting and provocative essay, 'Texts and Lumps,'[3] the American philosopher Richard Rorty considers the demarcation question from the point of view of the objects of analysis. Some argue that the objects of science – that is, the things that interest scientists and form the scope of their work – are simply different from those of the social sciences. Natural scientists, it is argued, are concerned with things in the world, things that are in the realm of 'the natural world.' By contrast, human artifacts (e.g., texts, speech, human action) are the result of human purposes and intentions and, as such, their nature is different. In short, scientists are interested in 'lumps' and humanists are preoccupied with 'texts' (broadly understood).

Rorty disputes the distinction between the natural and the human sciences. He concedes that the objects of each are different, but those differences do not account for our strong intuition that the enterprises can be differentiated along the lines of the objects of investigation. Rorty is sensitive to the strong

2. I should, perhaps, say something about who 'we' are. From the Anglo-American point of view, Langdell is primary in the story of academic lawyers elevating law to the level of a 'science.' For Europeans, law can – and often is – understood as a 'Wissenschaft.' On this view, as Alexander Somek puts it, the law 'knows itself.' See Alexander Somek, 'The Indelible Science of Law.' I•CON 7, No. 3, (2009): 424-441.
3. Richard Rorty, *Philosophical Papers: Objectivity, Relativism, and Truth*, Volume 1, (Cambridge; New York: Cambridge University Press, 1991).

intuition that science is more exacting, objective and certain than literary criticism. Scientists cure diseases, explain gravity, and can account for why and how airplanes ascend and descend with ease. But if the differences between science and non-science are not to be explained along the lines of objectivity and its opposite, then in what does the difference consist?

Rorty sees the differences between science and non-science as best accounted for along broadly methodological lines, ones that could be characterized as 'cultural.' Here is what he says:

'[W]hen he is asked to interpret the felt difference between hard object and soft objects, the pragmatist says that the difference is between the rules of one institution (chemistry) and those of another (literary criticism). He thinks, with Stanley Fish, that 'all facts are institutional, are facts by virtue of the prior institution of some such [socially conceived dimensions of assessment].' The only way to get a noninstitutional fact would be to find a language for describing an object which was as little ours, and as much the object's own, as the object's causal powers. If one gives up that fantasy, no object will appear softer than any other. Rather, some institutions will appear more internally diverse, more complicated, more quarrelsome about ultimate desiderata than others.'[4]

Rejecting the notion that the objects of each enterprise are the ground of explanation for the felt sense that science is more 'hard' than literary criticism (or law?), Rorty explains that the felt sense of 'hardness' is best explained by the fact that, in science, participants agree at a deep level on the 'meta-rules' of the practice. That is, they agree on what constitutes 'confirmation' and 'non-confirmation' of a hypothesis. It is this agreement, not the object of analysis, that best explains why natural science looks and feels so much more determinate than literary criticism. As Rorty sees it, the meta-questions in natural science (e.g., what constitutes 'confirmation') are settled by agreement that can only be characterized as deep and abiding. In the human sciences, the participants not only contest claims about the meaning of their 'texts,' they contest the meta-questions regarding what will count as correct or incorrect characterization of a 'text.' It is only in virtue of the intersubjective consensus in science that scientists look like a community and unlike literary critics, who appear more contentious about fundamental questions (e.g., the value of a work of 'literature' or art).

4. Rorty, *Philosophical Papers: Objectivity, Relativism, and Truth*, 84, citing and quoting Stanley Fish, *Is There a Text in This Class? The Authority of Interpretive Communities* (Cambridge, Mass.: Harvard University Press, 1980), 198.

Let us now take up the question of the status of law. If law is a 'science,' it is not a natural science. Lawyers do not advance 'hypotheses' which are then confirmed or disconfirmed by legal materials. Another difference between the work of lawyers and that of natural scientists is that the 'truths' of law are specific to times and places and vary across jurisdictions. For example, it is 'true' in common law jurisdictions that consideration is a necessary predicate to creating an enforceable modification to a contract. But under the Uniform Commercial Code of the United States, it is possible to modify a contract without consideration. Legal truths are jurisdiction-specific and can and do change over time (think of the laws of slavery).

Now, to the second dimension of the demarcation question. In their work, are lawyers more like scientists or literary critics? Is there agreement on what constitutes 'legal method' or is it the case that lawyers are as quarrelsome about their 'texts' as literary critics are about theirs? While we will look at this question in more detail shortly, if Rorty is right, there is little point in answering this question in a direct way. The difference between science and law is not drawn by their objects of investigation. Rather, the differences lie in the particulars of scientific versus legal discourse. I want to be bold here and suggest that the ways in which scientists and lawyers appraise claims in their respective fields is different. There are no experiments in law. Likewise, no hypothesis about the natural world was ever confirmed by a statute, no matter how interpreted. What I am suggesting is that if we take Rorty seriously, the differences between natural science and law lie in the methods of appraisal in each discipline. The truth of a proposition of law is not determined by length, temperature, chemical composition, or any reasonably comparable characteristic. Likewise, scientific tribunals are not fora for justice. The aims and purposes of natural science and law are different. These differences are (perhaps, best) seen in the different questions each discipline asks and in the different methods used to appraise claims. These differences are (following Rorty) cultural. But there are differences. Is law a science? No more than science is literary criticism.

Producing Agreement

Rorty directs our attention to the particulars of practices as we try to discern how agreement is produced. Every practice has its own particular methodologies and means for achieving assent and mediating disagreement. As mentioned, the practice of natural science looks more objective and less contentious than literary criticism because scientists have managed to achieve deep consensus about what confirmation and verification look like. Rorty draws the contrast this way:

'In some Mayan ball game, perhaps, the team associated with a lunar deity automatically loses, and is executed, if the moon is eclipsed during play. In poker, you know you've won if you're dealt an ace-high straight flush. In the laboratory, a hypothesis may be discredited if the litmus paper turns blue, or the mercury fails to come up to a certain level. A hypothesis [in natural science] is agreed to have been 'verified by the real world' if a computer spits out a certain number. The hardness of fact in all these cases is simply the hardness of the previous agreements within the community about the consequences of a certain event.'[5]

Rorty is fighting the idea that natural science is about 'causal' explanation and explanation in the human sciences is about intentionality or some other 'soft' account of what happens. To start thinking about how explanation in law might work, we start with the observation that norms or rules are central to the legal enterprise. One of the features of law that must be accounted for is the fact that the participants seem to be referring to the same standards when they evaluate an action or event. Not everything in law is disputed all the time. In other words, it does appear to be the case that there is something of a continuum in law, running from cases no one would dispute to those that seem wholly irresolvable. How do we account for this? And in what terms should it be explained?

I want to use Wittgenstein's distinction between understanding and interpretation to explain the phenomenon of rule-following in law.[6] To put the matter slightly more broadly, our interest lies in explicating what Gerald Postema calls 'the common world.'[7] We can start to see the contours of this common world when we look at how we make meaning and, more importantly, how we create the basis for intersubjective normativity.

We begin with Wittgenstein, whose account of rule-following starts with this passage:

A rule stands there like a sign-post. ... Does the sign post leave no doubt open about the way I have to go? Does it shew which direction I am to take when I have passed it; whether along the road or the footpath or cross-country? But where is it said which way I am to follow it; whether in the direction of its finger or (e.g.) in the opposite one? ... And if there were, not a single sign-post, but a chain of adjacent ones or of chalk marks on the ground

5. Rorty, *Philosophical Papers: Objectivity, Relativism, and Truth*, 80.
6. Ludwig Wittgenstein, *Philosophical Investigations*, trans. G.E.M. Anscombe, (Oxford: Basil Blackwell, 1968), § 85.
7. Gerald J. Postema, ''Protestant' Interpretation and Social Practice,' *Law and Philosophy* 6, no. 3 (December 1987): 283.

... is there only one way of interpreting them? ... So I can say, the sign-post does after all leave no room for doubt. Or rather: it sometimes leaves room for doubt and sometimes not. And now this is no longer a philosophical proposition, but an empirical one.'[8]

How does a sign or a norm tell us what to do? How do we discern what it means to 'comply' with the norm? What does a rule require of us such that we might say what conformity consists in? These are the questions Wittgenstein takes up in his rule-following discussion. The point he is keen to make is that one idea that makes no sense at all is the notion that 'interpretation' is the key to understanding meaning and the ground of normativity. He writes: 'This was our paradox: no course of action could be determined by a rule, because every course of action can be made out to accord with the rule. The answer was: if everything can be made out to accord with the rule, then it can also be made out to conflict with it. And so there would be neither accord nor conflict here.'[9] Interpretation – the act of imposing meaning on a sign, text or norm statement – cannot explain meaning (nor normativity) because if anything can be made to 'fit' a rule then nothing fits. There has to be a way to decide among different construals of a rule or, and this is Wittgenstein's insight, the entire approach has to be rethought.

Wittgenstein opts for the latter view, the idea that interpretation is secondary to or dependent upon interpretation already being in place. The idea is that the meaning of signs and texts is a function of a practice, that is, a regular and shared way of construing objects. It is in the shared interaction of participants with the objects of the practice that meaning (e.g., how to read the arrow on a roadsign) arises. Rorty echoes Wittgenstein's emphasis on the particulars in practice when he stresses that understanding and interpretation occur within communities. One can see differences between communities by attending to the different ways in which communities constitute their cultural objects and how they manage disagreement.

But what about interpretation and disagreement? When does the need for interpretation arise? Wittgenstein argues that interpretation becomes necessary when we no longer agree on how to 'go on' with our practice. Disagreement may manifest itself in a host of ways but the important point is that interpretation arises from the failure of a shared background of understanding. When it comes to interpretation, we can see that interpretation depends

8. Wittgenstein, *Philosophical Investigations*, supra note 5, at § 85.
9. Id. at Sec 201.

upon understanding ... unreflective action ... already being in place.[10] We should, as Wittgenstein argues, 'restrict the term 'interpretation' to the substitution of one expression of the rule for another'.[11] Interpretation is an activity ... one that not only depends upon understanding already being in place, but an activity that is actuated by a breakdown or failure in understanding. In short, interpretation is a therapeutic, not foundational, activity.

Finding The Law: Methodology

The lesson of Wittgenstein's account of the distinction between understanding and interpretation is that understanding is grounded in repeated practice-based iterations. Time and repetition are fundamental to practice. More important than these is the role of judgment in the production of normativity. Normativity – the iterative judgments of norm application – require that participants in a practice employ the same modes of assessment for judging claims within the practice. It is through the process of judgment in accordance with shared criteria that understanding is engendered and the stage set for interpretation.

In the Anglo-American tradition of jurisprudence, H.L.A. Hart has provided the most perspicuous account of the framework for legal judgment. Legal judgment requires intersubjective agreement on criteria for legal sources. In addition, there must be agreement among participants in the practice of law as to how the agreed sources are to be construed in making normative assessments of compliance and divergence.[12] To understand this aspect of Hart's thought more thoroughly, let us quickly review the basics of his jurisprudence.

In the first six chapters of *The Concept of Law,*[13] Hart makes progress on two fronts. First, he shows that the Austinian picture of law fails to account for key features of the legal system. Hart replaces the Austinian 'command'

10. Wittgenstein, *Philosophical Investigations*, *supra* note 5, at § 219 ('When I obey a rule, I do not chose. I obey the rule blindly.').
11. Id. at § 201.
12. Hart did not speak to this latter aspect of legal judgment. I develop the idea in Dennis Patterson, 'From Conceptual Analysis to a Practice Theory of Law,' in *On Philosophy in American Law,* ed. Francis J. Mootz, (New York: Cambridge University Press, 2008).
13. H.L.A. Hart, *The Concept of Law* (Oxford: Clarendon Press, 1994).

theory of law with an account of law as a system of rules. It is with this second focus that Hart provides a new picture of law.

A central focus of Hart in *The Concept of Law* is with validity, specifically, legal validity. His central question is 'what is it that makes a rule a rule of law and not a rule of some other sort?' Rejecting Austin's answer of a habit of obedience to authorities, Hart introduced the master secondary rule, the Rule of Recognition.[14] The Rule of Recognition, Hart argued, was an intersubjective practice among legal officials, which practice certified the legal status of the work of legislatures, courts and other officials as 'valid.' It is the Rule of Recognition that provides what Hart described as a 'test' for law. The Rule of Recognition enables anyone (not only legal officials) to determine valid from invalid sources of law.

There are two important aspects of the Rule of Recognition that need to be highlighted in any discussion of the concept. First, the Rule of Recognition identifies valid sources of law. Although the Rule of Recognition tells us what counts as valid sources of law, it is itself neither valid nor invalid. On pain of infinite regress, the Rule of Recognition is a social, customary practice. In short, one consults the Rule of Recognition for criteria of validity for what may be called 'subordinate' legal rules. As an ultimate rule, the Rule of Recognition rests only on an intersubjective consensus manifest in the ongoing practice of officials.

The second point is more important and more controversial. In addition to identifying sources of law (e.g., statutes and precedents) the Rule of Recognition also identifies the customary ways of taking those sources and using them to decide cases. But the Rule of Recognition is not a complete guide to adjudication. The Rule identifies what counts as valid sources of law and it also contains the conventional ways of construing those sources to decide cases. But the rule of Recognition is not an algorithm: it is not a complete guide to adjudication.

The Rule of Recognition raises a number of problems, some of them epistemic and some metaphysical.[15] While it is clear that the Rule of Recognition

14. Id. at 94-95.
15. For a recent discussion of the conventional nature of the Rule of Recognition see Julie Dickson, 'Is the Rule of Recognition Really a Conventional Rule?', *Oxford Journal of Legal Studies* 27 (2007): 373-402 and Andrei Marmor, *Social Conventions: From Language to Law* (Princeton: Princeton University Press, 2009).

imposes a duty on judges to apply valid legal rules,[16] it is not always clear what 'correct application' consists in. Any account of the Rule of Recognition has to answer the question of the relationship between the validity-certifying aspect of the Rule and its role in adjudication. The reason for this is simply that a practice requires not only agreement on sources but also agreement in judgment.[17]

Do we have any reason to suspect agreement in judgment?[18] The question, I want to suggest, admits of an empirical answer. Consider the sum total of all legal questions, everything from the most pedestrian to the work of the ECJ. If we use the image of a pyramid,[19] the base of the pyramid would be all the mundane cases that traffic in lawyers' offices and in a host of everyday contexts. Bills for meals are paid on the spot, Forex transactions settled without question, property devolves from one person to another, and people are wed to and divorced from one another with punishing regularity. Making all these transactions possible is one thing: law. If the law for most questions were not settled, as it is, there would be no communal existence as we know it.

The only explanation for these facts is that there exists widespread, inter-subjective agreement on law. Contrary to the grandiose claims of some in the Critical Legal Studies Movement, law is not thoroughly indeterminate. In fact, law is largely determinate: its meaning, and its requirements, are readily available to all. Hart explains why the facts are as they are. The practice of legal officials (including lawyers) fixes the meaning of legal materials. There is convergence (i.e., agreement in judgment) about a wide range of legal materials and their significance. Most of the pyramid of law is settled. It is only the very top of the pyramid that requires elaborate explanation.

16. For Hart, the 'duty' to follow the Rule of Recognition is not a function of morality. Rather, it identifies the perception or attitude (Hart calls it the 'internal point of view') officials take to the Rule of Recognition.
17. See Wittgenstein, *Philosophical Investigations* supra note 5, at § 242. 'If language is to be a means of communication there must be agreement not only in definitions but also (queer as this may sound) in judgments. This seems to abolish all logic, but does not do so. – It is one thing to describe methods of measurement, and another to obtain and state results of measurement. But what we call 'measuring' is partly determined by a certain constancy in results of measurement.'
18. Frederick Schauer, 'Easy Cases,' *S. Cal. L. Rev.* 58 (1985): 399, 407. ('A theory, or at least a set of insights, about easy cases is the necessary first step toward development of a theory for dealing with hard cases.'). Postema, ''Protestant' Interpretation and Social Practice,' supra note 6 at 316 ('Disagreement, even substantial disagreement, then, has a place in a world of common meanings.').
19. The image is taken from Brian Leiter, 'Explaining Theoretical Disagreement,' *SSRN, U of Texas Law, Public Law Research Paper, no. 124* (August 2007), 14.

Theoretical Disagreement

Now we come to the cases and controversies represented at the top of the pyramid. These are cases that make their way to the highest courts in all jurisdictions. They represent a very small number of cases but they are significant, if for no other reason than they sometimes appear (correctly or incorrectly) to be outside the purview of normal legal argument. These cases are controversial for a variety of reasons, but there are three reasons consistent with the discussion thus far.

Three sorts of disagreements in law, disagreements that may properly be characterized as 'theoretical disagreements', are salient. First is a disagreement over sources of law. Lawyers may disagree that a certain statute or constitutional provision is salient for a dispute. Second, lawyers may disagree over how to construe a source. Some may take the position that a particular text should be read in a straightforward 'plain meaning' fashion, while another argues that the historical intent of the authors of the text is determinative of its meaning. Finally, lawyers and judges may disagree that a certain way of construing an agreed valid source is itself valid. For example, in the United States, some judges take the view that only the original meaning of a constitutional provision is valid. All other approaches to determining the content of constitutional law are invalid *ab initio.*

What do these three examples of disagreement tell us about theoretical disagreement? The first, and most important, point is that theoretical disagreement of any sort arises against the background of shared practice. For those in the hermeneutic tradition, particularly post-Heideggerians, all understanding is grounded in interpretation. Wittgenstein shows that this approach to meaning is a non-starter. But Wittgenstein tells us precious little about interpretation, even as understood as an activity that arises against a background of shared intersubjective practice (understanding).

Interpretation is an activity of repair. The need for interpretation arises when we no longer know our way about in our practice or we disagree about how to 'go on' with the practice. All interpretation must be judged by its ability to restore the quotidian character of practice. Like Quine's web of belief,[20] good interpretations repair the tear brought about by the need for interpretation.

Theoretical disagreement does not appear to be a pervasive feature of legal practice. Of course, there are disputes about norms, sources and interpretive

20. W.V.O. Quine, and J.S. Ullian *The Web of Belief* (New York: Random House, 1978).

methods, but these disputes are managed and resolved because the players in legal practice share a wide variety of background assumptions, beliefs and attitudes they bring to bear when they seek resolution of disagreements about how to go on with their joint practice.

What do these ideas of understanding, interpretation and theoretical disagreement tell us about the question of legal method, specifically a European legal method? In this context, I can easily imagine a criticism of the account of legal method I have just sketched. The criticism goes something like this. What I have described is accurate as far as national legal systems are concerned. But when it comes to European legal methodology, my account will not suffice for the simple reason that the background assumptions in place at the national level do not exist at the supra or post-national level. For this reason, debates about legal method are pointless because the values that those methods depend on are not in place. In short, as Martijn Hesselink puts it, the debates are about justice and not method.[21]

Understanding the methodology debate as a debate about justice obscures the nature of the debate. I rather think the debate presents a contrast between two different ways of conceiving the role of methodology in law or legal reasoning. As I see it, the proper contrast is between 'legalists' on the one hand and 'pragmatists' on the other. I will sketch these two positions and then demonstrate how we can make progress in this debate if we abandon the false premise of legalism and embrace the cold reality of pragmatism.

The premise of legalism, at least methodological legalism, is that by following a decisional path (i.e., utilizing a method to decide cases) a case will be 'correctly' decided. In the vast majority of cases, this is true. But let us not be fooled into thinking that deciding a case 'correctly' is anything more than affirming the sociology of the legal order. Objectivity, truth of legal propositions, and 'correctness' are different ways of expressing the fact that participants in a practice agree on ultimate desiderata. The 'fact' that a given legal question has a certain answer is, as Rorty notes about practices in general, a matter of antecedent choice about how we react to stimuli.[22]

21. Martijn Hesselink, 'A European Legal Method? On European Private Law and Scientific Method,' *European Law Journal* 15 (January 2009): 20-45.

22. See Rorty, *Philosophical Papers: Objectivity, Relativism, and Truth,* 81. The full passage reads: Facts are hybrid entities; that is, the causes of the assertibility of sentences include both physical stimuli and our antecedent choice of response to such stimuli. To say that we must have respect for facts is just to say that we must, if we are to play a certain language game, play by the rules. To say that we must have re-

I shall denominate a relaxed attitude about methodology as 'pragmatism.'[23] Of course, there are many meanings of 'pragmatism' and there is a particular history of pragmatist thought, starting with William James.[24] I do not wish to rehearse the history of pragmatism but rather to come to the point of saying something about pragmatism in the legal context, specifically the context in which we ask the question about a European method of legal methodology.

I start from the premise (a sociological observation) that many questions in both national legal systems and those of European law are amenable to identical treatment and disposition. Our interest lies in those cases at the top of the metaphorical pyramid, those that traverse the lines between national systems and European law. To be perfectly clear, I am not saying that law and legal method do not matter. They do. What I am saying is that as we move to the top of the pyramid, methodology becomes less important for determining outcomes because the intersubjective consensus reflected lower down in the pyramid is no longer present. In short, instead of consensus about desiderata there is debate. Now the question is the nature of that debate and what it tells us about the role of methodology in law.

In answering the question of how best to traverse the lines between European and national legal systems, a pragmatist attitude to the methodological issues is open not only to emendation and enhancement of legal (methodological) tools but to incorporation of the tools of social science (just to name one body of thought). Lest one think this choice is new, that is, something that interdisciplinary studies brings to law, let me disabuse you of that notion.

In virtually every area of law (and especially in matters methodological), the fundamental choice between legalism and pragmatism is, at bottom, a choice between Blackstone and Mansfield.[25] Blackstone's *Commentaries*[26] were meant to be the definitive statement of English common law. Of course, the law 'developed' as it was applied to new circumstances in decided cases, but the structure of the law was deemed to be akin to revealed truth, a truth

spect for unmediated causal forces is pointless. It is like saying that the blank must have respect for the impressed die. The blank has no choice, nor do we. Ibid.

23. For a recent pragmatist effort, see Richard A Posner, *How Judges Think* (Cambridge: Harvard University Press, 2008).
24. Of course, pragmatism proper starts with Peirce. What I have in mind in connection with James is his pragmatic approach to the question of truth.
25. This example is taken from Philip Bobbitt, *Terror and Consent: The Wars for the Twenty-First Century* (New York: A.A. Knopf, 2008), 460-462.
26. William Blackstone, *Commentaries on the Laws of England* (Oxford: Clarendon Press, 1765-1769).

dating back to King Alfred. As Grant Gilmore summed up the Blackstonian vision of the legal realm:

> 'Let us preserve, unchanged, the estate which we have been lucky enough to inherit. Let us avoid any attempt at reform – either legislative or judicial – since the attempt to make incremental changes in an already perfect system can lead only to harm in ways which will be beyond the comprehension of even the most well-meaning and far-sighted innovators.'[27]

The Blackstonian vision is as simple as it is attractive. Once the underlying architecture of law has been laid bare, no deviation from its path is to be tolerated. We must, if we are to do justice, adhere to the normative dictates of revealed truth. This is legalism at its finest.

The contrast I want to draw is with the great common law judge and commercial law innovator of the eighteenth century, Lord Mansfield. Mansfield is the first in a great line of commercial law thinkers that finds its summit in the person of Karl Llewllyn, the principal drafter of the American Uniform Commercial Code. To aid him in commercial law cases, Mansfield empaneled so-called 'Merchant Juries,' juries composed of members of the trade that was the subject of dispute. Mansfield pioneered the idea that the norms of actual commercial practice should inform judicial decision-making and be reflected in substantive law.

There is no better example of Mansfield's bold approach to the intersection of commercial life and law than his handling of sales of commercial paper and the common law rules of title. Under the common law rule of derivative title, the transferee of a chattel receives no greater title than that of the transferor. Mansfield contributed to the development of the doctrine of bona fide purchaser for value when he ruled that bona fide purchasers of bank notes took free of any underlying infirmities in the transferor's title, reasoning that, to hold otherwise, bills and notes would never be transferred freely and modern mercantile practices would never develop.[28]

Pragmatism means taking the world into account in fashioning rules of law. This is the lesson of Mansfield. For our methodological inquiry, the lesson is that we must deal with methodological questions on a basis that reflects the unique characteristics of each area of law. Thus, we would not expect

27. Grant Gilmore, *The Ages of American Law* (New Haven, Conn.: Yale University Press, 1977), 5.
28. For discussion, see Ronald J. Mann, 'Searching for Negotiability in Payment and Credit Systems,' *UCLA Law Review* 44 (April 1997): 956-62.

contract law problems to receive the same treatment we give to questions of choice of law or constitutional matters. Methodological rigidities are to be avoided at all costs, and openness to diverse solutions the proper attitude to managing methodological problems.

Conclusion

I began with the claim that methodology matters. Without methodology, there is no hope of giving an account of what it means to make, debate and appraise propositions of law. Methodology is the grammar of legal argument and the fabric of legal practice. Methodology is central to law. In a very real sense, debates about methodology implicate larger questions about the nature of law and legal practice. It is through these debates that we come to have a more perspicuous picture of law and legal practice.

Reference list

Blackstone, William. *Commentaries on the Laws of England*, Oxford: Clarendon Press, 1765-1769.

Bobbitt, Philip. *Terror and Consent: The Wars for the Twenty-First Century*. New York: A.A. Knopf, 2008.

Dickson, Julie. 'Is the Rule of Recognition Really a Conventional Rule?' *Oxford Journal of Legal Studies* 27, no. 3 (2007): 373-402.

Fish, Stanley. *Is There a Text in This Class? The Authority of Interpretive Communities*. Cambridge, Mass.: Harvard University Press, 1980.

Gilmore, Grant. *The Ages of American Law*. New Haven, Conn.: Yale University Press, 1977.

Hart, H.L.A. *The Concept of Law*. Oxford: Clarendon Press, 1994.

Hesselink, Martijn, 'A European Legal Method? On European Private Law and Scientific Method.' *European Law Journal* 15 (January 2009): 20-45.

Leiter, Brian, 'Explaining Theoretical Disagreement,' *SSRN, U of Texas Law, Public Law Research Paper* No. 124 (August 2007). http://papers.ssrn.com/sol3/papers.cfm?abstract_id=1004768.

Mann, Ronald J. 'Searching for Negotiability in Payment and Credit Systems.' *UCLA Law Review* 44 (April 1997): 956-1007.

Marmor, Andrei. *Social Conventions: From Language to Law*. Princeton: Princeton University Press, 2009.

Patterson, Dennis. 'From Conceptual Analysis to a Practice Theory of Law.' In *On Philosophy in American Law*, edited by Francis J Mootz, 223-231. New York: Cambridge University Press, 2008.

Posner, Richard A. *How Judges Think*. Cambridge: Harvard University Press, 2008.

Postema, Gerald J. ''Protestant' Interpretation and Social Practice.' *Law and Philosophy* 6, no. 3 (December 1987): 283-319.

Quine, W.V.O., and J.S. Ullian. *The Web of Belief.* New York: Random House, 1978.

Rorty, Richard. *Philosophical papers: Objectivity, relativism, and truth*, Volume 1, Cambridge; New York: Cambridge University Press, 1991.

Schauer, Frederick. 'Easy Cases.' *Southern California Law Review* 58, (1985): 399-440.

Somek, Alexander. 'The Indelible Science of Law.' I•CON 7, No. 3, (2009): 424-441.

Wittgenstein, Ludwig. *Philosophical Investigations.* Translated by G.E.M. Anscomb. Oxford: Basil Blackwell, 1968.

Part II
Comparative Perspective

European Legal Method from a Swedish Perspective – Rights, Compensation and the Role of the Courts

Jane Reichel[*]

The Swedish legal landscape has undergone significant changes in the past decades. From being largely self-reliant in the production of legal norms applicable within its borders, Swedish jurists today deal with internationally enacted norms from the EU, the Council of Europe and many other international organisations. The question addressed here is how this development has affected the traditional perception of the law, legal sources and their dignity within Swedish law. Consequently the object of this study is the phenomena of the Europeanized Swedish legal method from the perspective of Swedish legal actors. How are European sources dealt with by the Swedish courts and other legal actors, and does this differ from the 'traditional' Swedish solutions? As indicated by the title, specific focus is placed on the perception of individual rights, rights to compensation and how the Europeanized view of these matters has affected the role of the courts in Sweden.

The ambition here is to describe the Swedish legal method from a general perspective, and not from any particular field of substantive law. My own interest in constitutional and administrative law is, however, evident. Special attention is given to the recent amendments to the most central of Sweden's four constitutional acts, the Instrument of Government (IG),[1] effective as of 1

* I wish to express my gratitude to Carl-Fredrik Bergström and Joel Samuelsson at the Faculty of Law, Uppsala University and to Mauro Zamboni, Wiweka Warnling-Nerep and Laura Carlson at the Faculty of Law, Stockholm University for all their helpful comments to earlier drafts of this work. Any remaining errors are, however, my own.

1. SFS 1974:152. An English translation of the IG is available at the website of the Swedish Parliament, the Riksdag, www.riksdagen.se.

January 2011. To a certain extent these amendments add a European perspective to Swedish constitutional tradition, with a strengthening of the position of the courts as the most prominent example. Another, perhaps more symbolic, example is the inclusion of EU membership in the first chapter of the IG that sets out the basic principles of the form of Swedish government.[2]

The structure of this article is as follows. The first part describes and analyzes some basic features of the traditional Swedish view on law and legal sources, including Scandinavian legal realism, the doctrine of parliamentary sovereignty and the issue of judicial review. The effects of Europeanization, namely the emphasis on individual rights, the juridification of politics and the importance attributed to the possibility of receiving compensation from the state when rights are not duly upheld are addressed in part two. The effects of pluralisation are discussed in part three, regarding both the content of the legal sources and their hierarchies. An attempt to assess the effects of Europeanization on Swedish legal method is made in part four. Some conclusive remarks are given in the final part five.

1 Traditional Swedish Legal Method

Certain basic features of the Swedish legal system are described and analyzed in this first part, namely those identified as being relevant for the development of the Swedish legal method. One general point of departure may already be underlined here. This section describes Swedish legal method from a national, pre-EU, pre-globalisation perspective, in the sense that the relevant legal sources are to a very high extent solely Swedish.

1.1 Scandinavian Legal Realism

Scandinavian legal realism has its roots in the works of the philosopher Axel Hägerström and was introduced into legal theory by his followers Vilhelm Lundstedt and Karl Olivecrona. Another representative of this school is Danish legal theorist Alf Ross.[3] Scandinavian legal realism has been very influen-

2. Article 1:10 IG.
3. The school of the Scandinavian legal realism is presented here in an overall perspective. For a more detailed account of differences between the representatives, see Strang, Johan *'Two Generations of Scandinavian Legal Realism'*, Retfaerd 2009 nr 1/124, pp. 62-82.

tial in Sweden, even though few jurists, even in academia, today study the basic texts of these authors.[4]

The core of Scandinavian legal realism is its objective of a 'scientific' approach to the law. In essence, this means that the law should be understood as separate from metaphysic elements. Legal concepts and categories are *per se* conceived of as being detached from any system of moral, religious or political values.[5] Ross held that legal concepts, such as the concept of ownership, in reality are meaningless words (just like 'tû-tû'), without any semantic reference, serving solely as tools for representation.[6] To be able to reach any knowledge of the content of legal concepts, lawyers must search in the legal sources that are part of the valid law.[7] Even though, for example, the concept of ownership does not have any content in itself, the surrounding world, the 'real' world, provides content through legally relevant procedures. The source of validity has to be found outside the law, namely within the space-time coordinates of the empirical reality.[8] The legal phenomenon is compared to a machine, treating the legal material completely neutrally, irrespective of which direction in terms of political choices the law takes.[9] In order to correctly interpret legal concepts, lawyers must take into account the world outside the legal sphere, but the interpretation must be channelled through the doctrine of sources of law.[10] Scandinavian legal realism has been described as having a flexible approach to the selection of law-defining actors, and fur-

4. Samuelsson, Joel, *Bulleri buller bock. Hur många horn står opp? Kommentar till Johan Strangs 'Two Generations of Scandinavian Legal Realism'*, Retfaerd 2009 nr 1/124, pp. 83-88 at 87.
5. Zamboni, Mauro, *Law and Politics: a Dilemma for Contemporary Legal Theory*, Springer, Berlin, 2008, p. 96.
6. Ross, Alf, *Tû-tû,* Harvard Law Review 70:812-825, p. 820 and Lundstedt, Vilhelm, *Legal Thinking Revised: my Views on Law*, Almqvist & Wiksell, Stockholm, 1956, p 301. See further, Nielsen, Ruth, *Scandinavian Legal Realism and EU Law*, Neergaard, Ulla B., Nielsen, Ruth & Roseberry, Lynn M. (ed.), The Role of Courts in Developing a European Social Model – Theoretical and Methodological Perspectives, DJØF Publishing, Copenhagen, 2010, p. 240.
7. Ross, Alf, *On Law and Justice*, Stevens, London, 1958, p. 29.
8. Olivecrona, Karl, *Law as fact*, 2 ed, Stevens, London, 1971, pp. 4 and 110. See also Zamboni, Law and Politics: a Dilemma for Contemporary Legal Theory, *op cit* note 5, p. 98.
9. Zamboni, Law and Politics: a Dilemma for Contemporary Legal Theory, *op cit* note 5, p. 97.
10. Ross, On Law and Justice, *op cit* note 7, p. 75 and Lundstedt, Legal Thinking Revised: my Views on Law, *op cit* note 6, p. 309. See also Nielsen, Scandinavian Legal Realism and EU law, *op cit* note 6, p. 237.

thermore, understanding the law as partially open to the political world outside.[11]

Two features of Scandinavian legal realism may be considered especially relevant when analyzing Swedish legal method from a European perspective. Firstly, as seen above, this understanding of the law by Scandinavian realists opens up for a pragmatic and informal attitude to legal sources. Legislation is often vague and lawyers need to find guidance in the process of determining its content from other sources. The legal text is but one of several factors, albeit the most important, that must be taken into consideration in the application of a norm.[12] Law-defining actors, such as courts and judges, play a central part in Scandinavian realism, since their task is to define the content of the law by reference to valid legal sources.[13] The method by which judges and other lawyers treat the legal sources thus becomes all important. Consequently, Ross holds that the doctrine of legal sources is normative, not descriptive.[14] On the other hand, since the doctrine of legal sources is a part of the legal system itself, it is natural that the method applied will vary between various legal systems.[15]

Correspondingly, Scandinavian legal realists consider law to be partially open to the political world in that the law-making process allows for the inclusion of non-legal elements, political elements, into the legal world.[16] In Sweden, however, the centrality of the Swedish Parliament (Riksdag) in the law-making process, together with the weak position held by the Swedish courts,[17] has contributed to narrowing the Scandinavian realists' spectrum of theoretical solutions to the issue of how the law-making process relates to the

11. Nielsen, Scandinavian Legal Realism and EU law, *op cit* note 6, p. 236 and Zamboni, Law and Politics: a Dilemma for Contemporary Legal Theory, *op cit* note 5, p. 95.
12. Lyles, Max, *A Call for Scientific Purity: Axel Hägerström's Critique of Legal Science*, Institutet för rättshistorisk forskning, Stockholm, 2006, pp. 527 and 531, and Zamboni, Law and Politics: a Dilemma for Contemporary Legal Theory, *op cit* note 5, p. 120.
13. Ross especially emphasized the predictive nature of the work of lawyers, Ross, On Law and Justice, *op cit* note 7, p. 42. See also Nielsen, Scandinavian Legal Realism and EU law, *op cit* note 6, p. 237.
14. Ross, On Law and Justice, *op cit* note 7, p. 104.
15. *Ibid.* at 110.
16. Lundstedt, Legal Thinking Revised: my Views on Law, *op cit* note 6, p. 171 and Olivecrona, Law as Facts, *op cit* note 8, p. 86. See also Zamboni, Law and Politics: a Dilemma for Contemporary Legal Theory, *op cit* note 5, p. 110.
17. Nergelius, Joakim, *Konstitutionellt rättighetsskydd: svensk rätt i ett komparativt perspektiv*, Fritze, Stockholm, 1996, p. 611. See further Sections 1.2 and 1.3 *infra*.

political world.[18] On a more practical level, the historically close ties between Scandinavian legal realism and the Social Democratic Party, holding government in Sweden for the major part of the 20th century, may also be relevant.[19] The understanding of legal concepts as not having specific meanings in themselves, but rather as vessels that may be filled by the legal process, thereby worked as a tool for realizing the ideals of the welfare state.[20]

Secondly, the understanding of legal concepts as empty vessels leads to the denial of the existence of legal rights *per se*. According to Lundstedt, legal rights and duties can have no meaning other than that which follows from the valid law.[21] Legal rights and duties therefore can only exist within a legal order and do not have any meaning unless connected to the possibility of having procedural and executive consequences.[22] Olivecrona emphasizes the functions of words in the description of legal concepts, such as 'rights', namely as tools that can describe legal transactions by using certain forms of language.[23] This understanding of rights was to become relevant in the Swedish debate for decades, where the word 'right' was to be avoided and rephrased by using a more explicit language.[24] When this tradition meets EU

18. Zamboni, Law and Politics: a Dilemma for Contemporary Legal Theory, *op cit* note 5, p. 106.
19. Two professors of law active in the field of Scandinavian legal realism were also active within the Social Democratic Party, as members of the Riksdag, Vilhelm Lundstedt, and in the government itself, Östen Undén. See further Wiklund, Ola, *Juristokratin och den skandinaviska rättsrealismens uppgång och fall*, Lundin, Anna-Karin (ed), Regeringsrätten 100 år, Iustus, Uppsala, 2009, p. 88.
20. *Ibid.* at 86.
21. Lundstedt, Legal Thinking Revised: my Views on Law, *op cit* note 6, pp. 77, especially p. 114. Lundstedt, in an often quoted statement, maintained that 'any talk of a new law being able to violate property rights is as meaningless as a parrot's blather'. Lundstedt, Vilhelm, Socialdemokraten, 10 September 1928, quoted in Sundberg, Jacob W. F., *Fr. Eddan t. Ekelöf: repetitorium om rättskällor i Norden*, 2 ed., Juristförlaget, Stockholm, 1990, p. 193. See further Ross, Tû-tû, *op cit* note 6, p. 821.
22. Lyles, A Call for Scientific Purity: Axel Hägerström's Critique of Legal Science, *op cit* note 12, p. 353. For a comparison between the Swedish and EU understandings of enforceable rights, see Andersson, Torbjörn, *Rättsskyddsprincipen: EG-rätt och nationell sanktions- och processrätt ur ett svenskt civilprocessuellt perspektiv*, Iustus, Uppsala, 1997, p. 150.
23. Olivecrona, Law as fact, p. 245. See also Samuelsson, Joel, *Tolkning och utfyllning: undersökningar kring ett förmögenhetsrättsteoretiskt tema*, Iustus, Uppsala, 2008, p. 349.
24. Samuelsson, Tolkning och utfyllning: undersökningar kring ett förmögenhetsrättsteoretiskt tema, *op cit* note 23, p. 360 and Andersson, Rättsskyddsprincipen, *op cit* note 22, p. 162.

law, with its instrumental use of individual rights particularly in the doctrines of direct effect and supremacy,[25] the Swedish legal vocabulary does not correspond with its European equivalent. As Andersson has put it, while according to the common Swedish perception, the existence of a legal right is conditioned on its capability of producing procedural and executive consequences, the point of departure in EU law is the opposite; a legal right must be protected (by national courts) because it exists.[26]

1.2 The Doctrine of Parliamentary Sovereignty

The role of the Parliament is central in the Swedish constitutional system. The Swedish constitution, and in particular the Instrument of Government (IG), identifies the principle of the sovereignty of the people as the governing principle for the organization of the state, with the Riksdag being the people's foremost representative.[27] The understanding of democracy as guided primarily by the majoritarian principle has been prevailing in Nordic states and Sweden, with both Ross and the influential Swedish political scientist and publicist Tingsten as spokesmen.[28] In this aspect, the Nordic states, including Sweden, have been described as majoritarian rather than constitutional.[29] The Nordic countries allocate the task of choosing what role fundamental rights should play in the domestic legal system to the parliament, whereas in the constitutional model this task is given to the courts, which assume the task of reviewing legislation in view of its compliance to fundamental rights.[30] The Riksdag in fact operated for a long period quite independent of the Swedish

25. As put by the Court of Justice, EU law can produce direct effects and create individual rights which national courts must protect, case 26/62 *Van Gend en Loos mot Nederlandse Administraie der Belastingen* ECR [1963], English special edition, p. 1. See further Section 2.1 *infra.*
26. Andersson, Rättsskyddsprincipen, *op cit* note 22, p. 170.
27. Articles 1:1 and 1:4 IG.
28. Ross, Alf, *Varför demokrati? Med efterskrift av Karl-Göran Algotsson*, Santérus förlag, Stockholm, 2003, p. 89 and Tingsten, Herbert, *Demokratins problem*, Norstedt, Stockholm, 1945, p. 102. See also Nergelius, Konstitutionellt rättighetsskydd, *op cit* note 17, p. 133.
29. Wind, Marlene, Martinsen, Dorte Sindbjerg & Rotger, Gabriel Pons, *The Uneven Legal Push for Europe: Questioning Variation when National Courts go to Europe* European Union Politics March 2009 vol. 10 no. 163-88, p. 71 and Nielsen, Scandinavian Legal Realism and EU law, *op cit* note 6, pp. 238 and 261.
30. Nielsen, Scandinavian Legal Realism and EU law, *op cit* note 6, p. 261. See regarding Finnish traditions Ojanen, Toumas, *From Constitutional Periphery toward the Center – Transformation of Judicial Review in Finland*, Nordisk tidsskrift for menneskerettigheter, 2009, nr 2, s. 194-207, p. 197.

constitution altogether. The 1809 IG, predecessor to the current 1974 IG, was based on a constitutional system resting on separation of powers. Parliamentarism was introduced in Sweden in the beginning of the 20th century, but without any formal changes to the IG. Not until the late 1960's, and more thoroughly with enactment of the new 1974 IG, did the written constitution correspond to the actual functioning of the Riksdag.[31] This period in time has been characterized as a 'constitution-less half-century', i.e. the constitution was not considered to be part of positive, valid law, but rather a political document not even giving an adequate picture of political life.[32] Even though the situation is different today, the Swedish constitution continues to play a lesser role in Swedish case law than in other democracies, mainly because of the limited form of judicial review.[33]

The introduction of rules protecting fundamental rights in the 1974 IG was in itself controversial.[34] A separate chapter, including a list of fundamental rights to be protected, was introduced first in the IG in 1980, and later strengthened in connection to the Swedish accession to the EU and the incorporation of the European Convention of Human Rights in Swedish law and more thoroughly in the present revision of the IG.[35] The idea of limiting the legislative powers of the Riksdag, the representative of the sovereign people, by permitting the courts to review the conformity of the laws vis-à-vis a 'higher' law, would entail an at least potential risk of transferring political powers to the courts, which was considered foreign to the Swedish tradition. Even today, it is not entirely clear whether the catalogue of rights in chapter two of the IG actually contains judicially invocable rights conferred on individuals, or whether it is to be understood as an instruction to the legislator of what rights listed in the chapter may be limited through legislation and if so,

31. Enzell, Magnus, *Requiem for a Constitution: Constitutionalism and Political Culture in early 20th Century Sweden*, Stockholm University, 2002, p. 123.
32. Sterzel, Fredrik, *Författning i utveckling: tjugo studier kring Sveriges författning*, Iustus, Uppsala, 2009, p. 13 and Taube, Caroline, *Regeringsformen: positiv rätt eller redskap för rättshaverister?*, Smith, Eivind & Petersson, Olof (ed), Konstitutionell demokrati1, SNS förlag, Stockholm, 2004.
33. Peczenik, Aleksander, *Principer i det svenska statsskicket*, Berggren, Niclas, Karlson, Nils & Nergelius, Joakim (ed), Makt utan motvikt: om demokrati och konstitutionalism, City Univ. Press, Stockholm, 1999, p. 110. See further Section 1.3 *infra*.
34. Bull, Thomas & Sterzel, Fredrik, *Regeringsformen: en kommentar*, SNS förlag, Stockholm, 2010, p. 61 and Nergelius, Konstitutionellt rättighetsskydd, *op cit* note 17, p. 605.
35. Sterzel, Författning i utveckling: tjugo studier kring Sveriges författning, *op cit* note 32, p. 23 and Bull & Sterzel, Regeringsformen: en kommentar, *op cit* note 34, p. 61.

how.[36] This technique has not been changed in the current revision of the IG.[37]

The strong position of the Riksdag as the representative of the people is also reflected in how legal rules and provisions are interpreted in adjudication; that is, in legal method. The interpretation of the legal text in light of the legislative preparatory works, *travaux préparatiore,* has held a very strong position in the Swedish hierarchy of legal sources.[38] A well-known case from 1985 concerned the conviction of a Swedish heavy weight boxing champion, Anders 'Lillen' Eklund, for violating the Swedish criminal prohibition as to professional boxing.[39] The Supreme Court interpreted the concept of 'training match' in light of the legislative preparatory works, finding that the concept included 'sparring', even though in the boxing world, the two are understood as separate.[40] Even though this particular case has been criticized on goods grounds in the legal scholarship,[41] the technique in itself, filling out statutory provisions with instructions by way of legislative preparatory works, is still practised. Furthermore, this method has been accepted by the Court of Justice as a permissible way of implementing an annex to an EU directive.[42] On the other hand, it seems clear that the Europeanization of Swedish law has brought about a diminished role for legislative preparatory works, not merely in fields where Swedish law has been enacted in order to implement EU law, but also in other areas.

36. Sterzel, Författning i utveckling: tjugo studier kring Sveriges författning, *op cit* note 32, p. 41 and Peczenik, Principer i det svenska statsskicket, *op cit* note 33, p. 112. Further, contrary to that which is the case regarding breaches of individual rights in EU law or the European Convention of Human Rights, Swedish courts have not developed a right to damages on grounds of breaches of the provisions in chapter two of the IG. See Section 2.3 *infra* and Crafoord, Clarence & Strömmer, Gunnar, *Är Regeringsrätten en fullvärdig garant för fri- och rättigheter?*, Lundin, Anna-Karin (ed), Regeringsrätten 100 år, Iustus, Uppsala, 2009, p. 83.
37. Bull & Sterzel, Regeringsformen: en kommentar, *op cit* note 34, p. 63.
38. Ekelöf, Per Olof, *Teleological Construction of Statutes,* Scandinavian Studies in Law 1958, pp. 75-117 and 93, Peczenik, Principer i det svenska statsskicket, *op cit* note 33, p. 123 and Zamboni, Law and Politics: a Dilemma for Contemporary Legal Theory, *op cit* note 5, p. 120.
39. Article 1 of the Professional Boxing Act (1969:612), no longer in force.
40. NJA 1985 p. 788
41. Spaak, Torben, *Guidance and Constraint: the Action-guiding Capacity of Neil MacCormick's Theory,* Law and Philosophy (2007) 26:343-376 and 365.
42. Case C-478/99 Commission v. Sweden ECR [2002], p. I-4147 and Nielsen, Scandinavian Legal Realism and EU law, *op cit* note 6, p. 251.

1.3 A Sceptical Attitude towards Judicial Control

With the strong emphasis on the doctrine of parliamentary sovereignty, the role of Swedish courts in the Swedish constitutional system has, in an international comparison, been rather modest.[43] The political powers of the state are to be restricted to organs that directly or indirectly answer to the Riksdag and not to the courts. The state can therefore be described as identifying itself with majoritarian or paternalistic policies,[44] giving preference to institutional or public enforcement models through public authority, rather than private enforcement models through courts.[45] It is the responsibility of the state to insure that its subjects, citizens, enjoy the fruits of enacted politics, such as different aspects of the welfare state.[46] One example may be given from general administrative law. In the Swedish interpretation of what may be referred to as good administration, emphasis is placed on the obligation for authorities to help and guide individuals in the administrative legal jungle. Legal certainty is to be gained by the authorities 'lending the individuals a helping hand', rather than strict observance of procedural safeguards.[47] An exception to this tradition is the organization of the Swedish labour market, where rulemaking to a large extent has been entrusted the social partners of the labour market.[48]

43. Nergelius, Konstitutionellt rättighetsskydd, op cit note 17, p. 660. See further Reichel, Jane, *Ansvarsutkrävande – svensk förvaltning i EU*, Jure, Stockholm, 2010, p. 97 and Warnling-Nerep, Wiweka, *Rätten till domstolsprövning & rättsprövning*, 3 ed., Jure, Stockholm, 2008, p. 29. See regarding Finnish law, Ojanen, From Constitutional Periphery toward the Center – Transformation of Judicial Review in Finland, *op cit* note 30, p. 195.
44. Bakardjieva Engelbrekt, Antonina *Institutional Theories, EU Law and the Role of Courts for Developing a European Social Model*, Neergaard, Ulla B., Nielsen, Ruth & Roseberry, Lynn M. (ed.), The Role of Courts in Developing a European Social Model – Theoretical and Methodological Perspectives, DJØF Publishing, Copenhagen, 2010, p. 339.
45. Reichel, Jane, *Judicial Control in a Globalized legal Order – A One Way Track? An analysis of the case C-263/08 Djurgården-Lilla Värtan,* Review of European and Administrative Law, Vol. 3, No. 2, pp. 69-87, 2010.
46. Wiklund, Juristokratin och den skandinaviska rättsrealismens uppgång och fall, *op cit* note 19, p. 86.
47. Reichel, Jane, *God förvaltning i EU och i Sverige*, Jure, Stockholm, 2006. p. 314 and Hellners, Trygve & Malmqvist, Bo, *Förvaltningslagen med kommentarer*, 2 ed., Norstedts juridik, Stockholm, 2007, p. 11, Strömberg, Håkan under medverkan av Lundell, Bengt, *Allmän förvaltningsrätt*, 22 ed., Liber ekonomi, Malmö, 2003, p. 166.
48. Carlson, Laura, *The Fundamentals of Swedish Law: a Guide for Foreign Lawyers and Students* Studentlitteratur, Lund, 2009, p. 361.

The question of a judicial review of legislation has been controversial in Sweden. Judicial review was first introduced by the courts in the 1920s and 30s, and for a long time, was carried out only to a limited extent.[49] This case law was officially recognized in the preparatory works of the 1974 IG[50] and introduced in Article 11:14 of the IG in 1980. Under that provision, the courts have the mandate to set aside statutory acts only in the case at hand, if the act is not in conformity with higher ranking law or if an important procedural error has been committed in the enactment of the act. Even though Swedish constitutional law does not contain any actual prohibition on abstract forms of judicial review, Swedish law does not provide for any remedy with respect to an application for a declaratory judgment by a party.[51]

The Swedish interpretation of judicial review has two traits worth mentioning here. In one sense, judicial review is wider than is customary in most western democracies, in that it allows all public bodies, in addition to the courts, to perform a review of whether laws and other statutes in the matter presented are in compliance with higher ranking law.[52] In reality, however, it never has even been suggested that this review would have any practical importance. In another sense, the review is narrower. In the review of statutory acts enacted by Riksdag or the government, up until the 2010 amendments of the IG, Article 11:14 IG stated that courts (and public bodies) could only set aside the act only if the error found is manifest.[53] The court therefore had to leave some margin to the Riksdag (or the government) to resolve matters of controversy between acts of different hierarchical value within political sphere.[54] In regard to EU law, it is clear that whatever margin the Riksdag has when implementing EU law, this margin cannot be solely decided by the Riksdag, but has to be adjusted to the doctrine of direct effect and supremacy.

49. For a historic background, see SOU 2008:125 Grundlagsutredningens betänkande En reformerad grundlag, p. 365 and Lagerqvist Veloz Roca, Annika, *Föreskrift och föreskriftsprövning enligt 1974 års regeringsform*, Jure, Stockholm, 1999.
50. Legislative Bill 1973:90 med förslag till ny grundlag.
51. Andersson, Torbjörn, *Abstrakt lagprövning – en aspekt på Unibetmålet*, Heckscher, Sten & Eka, Anders (ed.), Festskrift till Johan Hirschfeldt, Iustus, Uppsala, 2008, p. 22. The question whether EU law required Sweden to provide for such remedy was referred to the Court of Justice in case C-432/05 *Unibet v. Justitiekanslern* ECR [2007], p. I-2271. See further Section 2.3 *infra*.
52. After the 2010 amendments to the IG, the right of public bodies to perform a review as to legality/constitutionality is found in a separate provision, Article 12:10.
53. Bull & Sterzel, Regeringsformen: en kommentar, *op cit* note 34, p. 271.
54. Sterzel, Författning i utveckling: tjugo studier kring Sveriges författning, *op cit* note 32, p. 48.

This notion was recognized in the legislative preparatory works to the Swedish accession,[55] and consequently, Swedish courts have not applied Article 11:14 IG in this context.[56]

This sceptical attitude towards judicial review mirrors the position the courts have held in Swedish society at large. Swedish constitutional tradition has not upheld a strict division between courts and public authorities, mainly due to the strong and at least partially independent position of the public authorities.[57] In the recent amendments to the IG, however, the role of the courts was enhanced, both in general and in judicial review in particular. The general strengthening of the courts is manifested foremost in the structural amendments to the IG, separating Chapter 11 that until now has contained rules on both courts and public authorities, into two chapters.[58] The grounds given in the preparatory works for this separation was the need to emphasize the independence of the courts, especially in light of the new role Europeanization has brought to the Swedish Courts, both the European Convention of Human Rights and the EU.[59]

The courts' role as to a review of legality of acts of law was also strengthened. The Swedish constitution provides for the involvement of the courts both before and after enactment, beforehand through a specific council made up of judges from the two high courts, the Supreme Court and the Supreme Administrative Court, the Council on Legislation, *Lagrådet*, and the abovementioned review in Article 11:14 and 12:10 IG. In the current IG, it is mandatory for the legislator to hear the Council on Legislation within certain areas. Further, the criteria of manifest error are removed from Article 11:14 and 12:10 IG. These changes, however, are not intended to entail any diminishing of the role of the

55. Legislative Bill 1993/94:114 Grundlagsändringar inför ett svenskt medlemskap i Europeiska unionen, p. 27.
56. SOU 2008:43 Tre rapporter till Grundlagsutredningen, p. 26.
57. Bull & Sterzel, Regeringsformen: en kommentar, *op cit* note 34, pp.259 and 275 ff.
58. The procedure for appointing permanent judges has also been reinforced, Article 11:6 IG and Bull & Sterzel, Regeringsformen: en kommentar, *op cit* note 34, at 265.
59. Legislative Bill 2009/10:80 En reformerad grundlag, p. 119. The independence of the courts is further strengthened through new provisions on the appointment of judges, p. 133.

Riksdag, which is to remain the foremost representative of the people.[60] A new second paragraph is therefore introduced in Article 11:14 IG:[61]

> 'When reviewing acts of laws as set out in para. 1, the courts must in particular observe that the Riksdag is the foremost representative of the people and the fact that the constitution takes precedence over acts of law.'

On the other hand, the new role of courts in the Europeanized areas of Swedish law has evidently affected the relationship between the courts and the legislator.[62] Even though there is a tendency not to acknowledge this development too openly, there are definitely signs even in the legislative preparatory works of an awareness of this changing scenery. The Swedish Government Official Reports on the revision of the IG, *Grundlagsutredningens betänkande*, a preparatory work from an earlier stage of the legislative chain, contained interesting wordings regarding the interpretative value of previous statements in preparatory works to the IG.[63] The earlier statement contained an interpretation of the margin for Swedish courts to perform an *ultra vires* review of EU acts in relation to the IG provisions on transferral of power to the EU, Article 10.5 IG. Quite representative for the Swedish view on judicial review, it stated that this question should be dealt with by the Riksdag itself and not the courts.[64] In the official report to the latest revision of the IG, this view is questioned. The report states that the mandate of the courts to review the legality of acts in Sweden cannot be limited simply through legislative preparatory works, without a clear statement in the actual provision of the IG that the usual competence for judicial review is not available.[65] It seems as if this statement in the official report actually aims at diminishing the role of preparatory works and increasing the role of judicial review. It must be seen as rather typical for Swedish legal tradition that this interpretation is found in a type of legislative preparatory work, rather than in the case law.

60. *Ibid.* at 146.
61. Original text: Vid prövning enligt första stycket av en lag ska det särskilt beaktas att riksdagen är folkets främsta företrädare och att grundlag går före lag. Translation by the author.
62. See further Sections 2.1-2.3 *infra.*
63. Legislative Bill 2001/2002:72 Ändringar i regeringsformen – samarbetet med EU m.m.
64. *Ibid.* at 35.
65. SOU 2008:125 Grundlagsutredningens betänkande., p. 500.

2 The Effects of Europeanization

Certain basic features of EU law identified as relevant for the development of a Swedish Europeanized legal method are presented in this part. The focus is therefore its effects on the Swedish legal method, rather than on the legal method of EU law in itself. The main question is how the continual search for an effective and uniform application of EU law in all the Member States has affected Swedish law.

2.1 Individualisation and Private Enforcement

In the very early development of the doctrine of direct effect and supremacy, the Court of Justice made a close connection between the individual rights which the EU confers on the nationals of the Member States and the obligation of the Members States, especially the national courts, to give effect to the EU law. As famously put by the Court of Justice in the *Van Gend en Loos*-case, EU law can produce direct effects and create individual rights, which national courts must protect.[66] This interpretation of individuals as the recipients of EU law and the obligation laid on national court to protect these rights has in turn led to the emphasizing of private enforcement models of EU law in the Member States. The Court of Justice in the *Van Gend en Loos*-case was quite clear on why this is a beneficial model for EU law:

> The vigilance of individuals concerned to protect their rights amounts to an effective supervision in addition to the supervision entrusted by articles 169 and 170 [today 267 and 268 FEUF, the infringement proceedings] to the diligence of the Commission and of the Member States.

In order to safeguard an effective enforcement model for EU law, the Court of Justice directed its attention to individual litigants in the Member States already from the beginning, turning them into advocate generals of EU law in their respective states.[67]

This perception of individual rights as bearing components of the law differs from the Swedish majoritarian perception of the law,[68] where the will of

66. Case 26/62 Van Gend en Loos, *op cit* note 25. See further Roth, Wulf-Henning, *The Importance of the Instruments Provided for in the Treaties for Developing a European Legal Method*, in this volume.
67. Kilpatrick, Claire, *The future of remedies in Europe*, Kilpatrick, Claire, Novitz, Tonia & Skidmore, Paul (ed), The future of remedies in Europe, Hart, Oxford, 2000, p. 2.
68. Sections 1.2 and 1.3 *supra*.

the people is expressed through the legislator, whose production, legislation, is generally speaking considered to be best transmitted to the public through an institutional enforcement model. The difference in these two models became apparent in the recent *Djurgården-Lilla Värtan*-case, where the Court of Justice found that the Swedish implementation of the Aarhus Convention via different EU Directives was incorrect.[69] The Court of Justice did not accept the restrictive Swedish requirements on access to the courts for environmental non-governmental organizations, enacted in order allow the public authority in the field to continue to uphold the role as the sole representative of the will and interest of the public within environmental law.[70]

2.2 The Juridification of Politics and the Importance of General Principle of Law

EU law displays two basic features that clearly distinguish it from traditional Swedish law. Firstly, general principles of law are used in a far more practical and apparent way than in Swedish law. Secondly, the application of Treaty-based rules, especially the rules of free movement of goods, services, workers and capital, have brought about a new category of politically highly sensitive cases to the Swedish courts, where the courts are asked to balance EU rights against national policies intended to protect, at least allegedly, public health, the environment, consumer protection, etc. *Franzén*, *Gourmet*, *Hanner* and *Laval* are all Swedish cases where national policies of different kinds have been challenged by way of litigation before Swedish courts, which to different degrees, after having asked the Court of Justice for guidance,[71] have set aside Swedish law. This juridification of politics has been subject to heavy criticism by Swedish politicians and others, who complain that it is courts and lawyers that ultimately decide questions that should be matters for politicians.[72]

69. Case C-263/08 Djurgården-Lilla Värtans Miljöskyddsförening v. Stockholms kommun genom dess marknämnd ECR [2009], nyr.
70. Reichel, Judicial Control in a Globalized legal Order – A One Way Track?, *op cit* note 45, p. 73.
71. Case C-189/95 *Criminal proceedings against Franzén* ECR [1997], p. I-5909, case C-405/98 *KO v. Gourmet International Products* ECR [2001], p. I-01795, case C-438/02 *Criminal proceedings against Hanner* ECR [2005], p. I-4551 and case C-341/05 *Laval un Partneri v. Svenska Byggnadsarbetareförbundet* ECR [2007], p. I-11767.
72. Wiklund, Ola, *Merging law and politics*, From Embracing Globalisation to the Limits of Tolerance – Themes from Axess magasin 2006, Axel and Margaret Ax:son Johnson Foundation Danmark 2007. For criticism from an academic point of view,

Returning to the first feature, it must be underlined that general principles of law exist in every legal system, but in EU law, they often play a more visible and prominent role than in more mature legal orders.[73] EU law is a comparatively new legal order with, at least initially, rather large lacunas. It is further built on the basis of the principle of transferred powers from its Member States, with its competence to decide limited to certain predestined areas of law. Last but not least, the implementation of EU law is to a large extent dependent on the legal orders of the Member States. On many occasions the Court of Justice has considered its task to work around these inherent limitations of the applicability of EU law by way of developing general principles of law.[74] This approach has allowed the Court of Justice to find, according to its own perception, appropriate solutions for legal problems that the legislature has not – yet – provided any answers to.[75] This has resulted in the allocation of the task to develop a functional legal system to the Court of Justice, rather than to the legislature. Further, by defining general principles as being on the same level in the hierarchy of norms as the Treaties, and by interpreting secondary legislation in light of general principles, with the *Mangold* and the *Kücükdeveci*-cases[76] as recent examples, the Court of Justice has been able to develop a rather large room for manoeuvrability in its legal adjudication.[77]

When the Swedish courts act within the sphere of Union law, in their role as protectors of EU law, this room for manoeuvrability to a certain extent is also transferred to them. In the abovementioned cases of free movement, Swedish courts have responded loyally to the preliminary rulings given by the Court of Justice by evaluating Swedish laws on alcohol or labour law through the lenses of EU law, including the application of broad principles,

see Scharpf, Fritz W., *Legitimacy in the Multilevel European Polity,* European Political Science Review (2009), 1:2, pp. 173-204.

73. Tridimas, Takis, *The General Principles of EU Law*, 2 ed., Oxford University Press, Oxford, 2006, p. 17.
74. See for example case 222/86 *Unectef v. Heylens* ECR [1987], p. 4097, case C-6/90 and C-9/90 *Francovich v. Italien* ECR [1991], p. I-5357 and case C-105/03 *Criminal proceedings against Pupino* ECR [2005], p. I-5285. See also Groussot, Xavier, *General Principles of Community Law*, Europa Law Publishing, 2006, p. 10.
75. See further Section 3.1 *infra*.
76. Case C-144/04 *Mangold v Rüdiger Helm* ECR [2005], p. I-9981 and case C-555/07 *Kücükdeveci v. Swedex* ECR [2010], nyr.
77. Herdegen, Matthias, *General Principles of EU Law – the Methodological Challenge*, Bernitz, Ulf, Nergelius, Joakim & Cardner, Cecilia (ed), General Principles of European Community. Law in a Process of Development, 2 ed, Kluwer, 2008.

such as the principle of proportionality.[78] Clear signs of a Europeanized approach to general principles can also be traced in other case, for example two cases from the Supreme Administrative Court, the *Lassagård* case on the principle on the right to an effective remedy[79] and the *Barsebäck* case, again on the principles of proportionality.[80] However, as discussed below,[81] the application of general principles of EU law still constitutes a foreign enterprise for many Swedish judges.

2.3 Compensation as a Tool for Enforcement

The *Francovich* case[82] has had a tremendous impact on the enforcement powers of EU law, with important repercussions on the legal orders of the Member States.[83] Again, there is a focus on individual rights. According to the requirements set out by the Court in the *Brasserie du Pêcheur* case, only legal rules intended to give rise to individual rights may ground a right to compensation from the state, not other categories of rules that may cause harm to individuals.[84] In critical terms, Harlow has described the influence of supranational law, with its emphasis on conferring rights to individuals, as building up a compensation culture, based on an 'I-want-one-too' consumer mentality.[85]

As made clear by the *Unibet* case, there is also a close connection between the right to an efficient remedy under EU law and the possibility for an indi-

78. For example case Marknadsdomstolens avgörande den 5 februari 2003 i mål nr T 8-1111-97, and Eriksson, Ida Otken, *Marknadsdomstolens dom i Gourmet-målet: Resonemang kring proportionalitet,* Europarättslig tidskrift 2003, pp. 585-598, regarding the Gourmet case, and Arbetsdomstolens dom den 2 december 2009 i mål nr A 268/04 and Bernitz, Ulf, *Europarättens genomslag i svensk rätt – var står vi idag?,* Juridisk Tidskrift Nr 3 2009/10, pp. 477-501, p 490, regarding the Laval case.
79. Case RÅ 1997 ref. 65.
80. Case RÅ 1999 ref. 76. See further Groussot, General Principles of Community Law, pp. 410 and 402 respectively.
81. See Section 4 *infra.*
82. Case C-6/90 and C-9/90 Francovich, *op cit* note 74.
83. Tridimas, The General Principles of EU Law, *op cit* note 73, p. 498, Biondi, Andrea & Farley, Martin, *The Right to Damages in European Law*, Wolters Kluwer, Alphen aan den Rijn, 2009, p. 26 and Harlow, Carol, *State Liability: Tort Law and Beyond*, Oxford University Press, Oxford, 2004, p. 61.
84. Case C-46/93 and C-48/93 *Brasserie du Pêcheur v. Germany and The Queen v. Secretary of State for Transport, ex parte: Factortame Ltd* ECR [1996], p. I-1029, para 51 and case C-222/02 *Peter Paul v Bundesrepublik Deutschland* ECR [2004], p. I-9425, para 47.
85. Harlow, State Liability: Tort Law and Beyond, *op cit* note 83, p. 6.

vidual to receive damages from the state for not having their rights met through national law.[86] The international gambling company, Unibet, brought the case wishing to have the Swedish legislation on gambling assessed against EU law, as Unibet interpreted it as being contrary to the right to free movement of services, hindering Unibet from marketing their Internet gaming services in Sweden. Their first claim therefore was that the EU principle of a right to an effective remedy also included a right to an application for a declaratory judgment, which Swedish law does not provide.[87] The Court of Justice, however, accepted the restrictive stance in Swedish law, content with declaring that as long as there were alternative ways to gain access to court, which in this case effectively meant through a proceeding for damages, the right to an effective remedy was fulfilled.[88]

Characteristic for the sceptical Swedish attitude to judicial control over the legislature,[89] the possibility of holding the state liable for its illegal or otherwise incorrect conduct has been significantly limited, all though not non-existent, in Sweden. It is now apparent that Sweden must be able to provide for effective remedies in this field within the field of application of EU law, even in cases where the purpose of the proceedings is not in the first hand to receive pecuniary compensation from the state, but rather to initiate the review of whether Swedish law is in conformity with EU law, as in the *Unibet* case.[90] Furthermore, the Swedish Supreme court has on its own initiative introduced a right to damages from the Swedish state for transgressions of individual rights based on the European Convention on Human Rights.[91] Europeanization in this area has therefore led to two separate levels of protection within the Swedish legal system: one based on European sources and one on Swedish sources, where individuals who base their right on European sources have a more extended right to damages than those with claims based on Swedish law.[92]

86. Case C-432/05 Unibet, *op cit* note 51.
87. See Section 1.3 *supra*.
88. Case C-432/05 Unibet., *op cit* note 51, para 65.
89. See Section 1.3 *supra*.
90. Andersson, Abstrakt lagprövning – en aspekt på Unibetmålet, *op cit* note 51, p. 25.
91. Case NJA 2005 p. 462, case NJA 2007 p. 295, case NJA 2007 p. 540 and case NJA 2007 p. 584. See also Åhman, Karin, *Skadestånd på grund av konventionsbrott – eller har HD blivit naturrättare?,* Juridisk tidskrift 2005/06 pp. 424-430.
92. The European forms of rights to damages must, however, also be kept separate: see further Section 3.1 *infra*.

3 Effects of Pluralisation

If twenty or thirty years ago Swedish law could be described as generally based on legal sources from one single legal order, the Swedish one, the situation is quite different today.[93] Globalization in general and Europeanization specifically has brought about a legal landscape with a multitude of legal sources with at times unclear positions in the formerly ordered hierarchy of legal sources.[94]

3.1 A Pluralistic Approach to the Sources of Law

Legal sources in EU law can be described as having pluralistic traits in several ways. The legal sources in EU law are often developed on the basis of legal materials from the Member States, in the forms of concepts and categories, before being moulded and transformed into autonomous, independent EU sources. Even though the legal sources of EU law may only be interpreted and reviewed in the light of EU law itself,[95] their multinational background is nonetheless of importance in adjudication.

The general principles of law are in themselves often the result of comparative studies of the Member States' different legal situations as to a common problem. In the classic *Algera* case, the Court of Justice holds that solutions to legal problems in EU law, for which the treaties does not contain an answer, are to be found by reference to the rules acknowledged by the legislation in the scholarship and case law of the Member States.[96]

93. Rosas, Allan, *Tolknings- och tillämpningsproblem i mötet mellan nordisk och internationell juridisk metod,* Forhandlingerne ved det 37. nordiske juristmøde i Reykavik 18.-20. august 2005, p. 319.
94. See for example Walker, Neil, *Beyond Boundary Disputes and Basic Grids: Mapping the Global Disorder of Normative Orders,* International Journal of Constitutional Law, 2008 vol. 6 nr 3-4, pp. 373-396, Barber, N.W., *Legal Pluralism and the European Union,* European Law Journal, Vol. 12, No. 3, 2006, pp. 306-329, Maduro, Miguel Poiares *Interpreting European Law – Judicial Adjudication in a Context of Constitutional Pluralism,* Working Paper IE Law School WPLS08-02 05-02-2008 and Wennström, Bo, *EU-rätt, osäkerhet och rättens nya landskap,* Juridisk tidskrift nr 2 2009/10, pp. 444-473.
95. Case 11/70 *Internationale Handelsgesellschaft v. Einfuhr- und Vorratsstelle für Getreide und Futtermittel* ECR 1970, p. 1125, para 3.
96. Case 7/56 and 3-7/57 *Algera v. Common Assembly of the European Coal and Steel Community* ECR English special edition 1957-1958, p. 39.

The legislative procedure is also to a large extent carried out in the form of negotiations between Member States.[97] From the outside, the result can appear to have drawn inspiration from different national traditions on an *ad hoc* basis. An example may be taken from administrative law. In the Services Directive, a form of administrative decision making commonly found in French and Spanish administrative law is introduced, the tacit authorization scheme, meaning that a public authority has a certain time limit to reach its decision, and if this limit is exceeded, the authority is obliged to give an individual applicant an automatic approval.[98] The Regulation on mutual recognition of goods contains something similar, but here connected to the right to be heard in an administrative procedure.[99] These administrative solutions are quite foreign to the Swedish administrative tradition.[100] In the future, when national courts begin to refer questions for preliminary rulings on these administrative procedures, the question, and to some extent also the answer by the Court of Justice, will be tinged by the context of the national courts having to interpret the EU source within a national legal system. This may in itself be a reason for national courts to refer questions to the Court of Justice, since it is an opportunity for these courts to engage in a constructive dialogue with the Court of Justice on the interpretation of EU law, thereby ascertaining that the legal traditions of the national court's own state will be taken into account in the process.[101]

Further, when interpreting EU sources in the Member States, national courts may not limit themselves to the bilateral relationship between EU law and the national law. According to the conditions set out in the *CILFIT* case, all national courts must, in order to determine whether the legal question ought to be referred for a preliminary ruling, take into account how the act is interpreted in all other Member States.[102] Even if an EU rule may easily fit

97. Curtin, Deirdre, *Executive power of the European Union: law, practices, and the living constitution*, Oxford University Press, Oxford, 2009, p. 59.
98. Article 13.4 of the Directive 2006/123/EC of the European Parliament and of the Council of 12 December 2006 on services in the internal market.
99. Article 6.4 of the Regulation (EC) No 764/2008 of the European Parliament and of the Council of 9 July 2008 laying down procedures relating to the application of certain national technical rules to products lawfully marketed in another Member State.
100. Reichel, Jane, *A New Proposal for a Regulation on Mutual Recognition of Goods – Towards a Harmonized Administrative Order?* Sieps, European Policy Analysis Issue 3-2007.
101. Groussot, Xavier, *Spirit, Are You There? – Reinforced Judicial Dialog and Preliminary Ruling Procedure,* Europarättslig tidskrift 2008 pp. 934-966.
102. Case 283/81 *CILFIT mot Ministero della santà* ECR [1982], p. 3415, para 16.

into the legal culture of one Member State, as for example the abovementioned tacit authorization scheme in the Services Directive in French law, French courts must, at least in theory, take into account the problems Swedish courts may have in applying the rules. Even though French administrative law might have been used as model for the Services Directive, the Directive itself is no more French law than Swedish law.

Another aspect is that EU law can intermingle with national law in a way that makes it difficult to distinguish where the field of application of EU law ends and the national law begins. In the both the *Courage* case[103] and the *Wells* case,[104] the Court of Justice refers to the possibility for individuals to receive damages for breaches of Union law without making clear whether this follows from an extensive interpretation of the *Francovich* line of cases, or whether it is a reference to the general obligation on the Member States, following the principle of loyal cooperation, to take any measure in their own power to nullify the unlawful consequences of a breach of Union law. In the same manner, the Swedish Labour Court in its *Laval* judgment is not quite clear whether the damages it awards the Estonian company is based on EU law or Swedish law.[105]

On the other hand, it is also evident that courts in different legal systems may draw inspiration from each other when developing their own case law.[106] When the Swedish Supreme Court developed the right to damages for breaches of the European Convention on Human Rights in Sweden, the court referred to the case law of both the European Court of Human Rights and the European Court of Justice as a ground for introducing an equivalent protection in regard to the Convention.[107] The Supreme Court thus stated that the European Court of Justice in its case law[108] had explicitly referred to the very same conditions for assuring just satisfaction to the injured party as the European Court of Human Rights had. When applying these two sets of European rights to damages in Sweden, it is important to appreciate that the effects of Europeanization differ between them. The EU right to damages is an EU

103. Case C-453/99 *Courage v. Crehan* ECR [2001], p. I-6297.

104. Case C-201/02 *The Queen, on the application of Delena Wells v. Secretary of State for Transport, Local Government and the Regions* ECR [2004], p. I-723.

105. Arbetsdomstolens dom den 2 december 2009 i mål nr A 268/04.

106. Garlicki, Lech, *Cooperation of courts: The role of supranational jurisdictions in Europe,* International Journal of Constitutional Law, 2008 vol. 6 nr 3-4, pp. 509-530 at 512.

107. Case NJA 2005 p. 462.

108. The Supreme Court referred to the case C-185/95 P *Baustahlgewebe v. Commission* ECR [1998], p. I-8417.

right entirely based on EU law, which in effect hinders the Member States from singlehandedly disposing of the rights at the national level. When the Swedish legislature wanted to start an inquiry on the possibility of introducing European rules in the Swedish Liability for Damages Act,[109] it therefore found it best to leave out all EU-based rights to damages.[110]

3.2 A Pluralistic Theory of Hierarchy of Law?

A consequence of the globalized and Europeanized legal context that Sweden and other states now live in is the phenomena of non-linear legislative procedures. Simply put, legislation within a single nation state can be described as a procedure with a beginning and an end, where organs organized in a hierarchal structure have demarcated tasks. A globalized law-making procedure can on the other hand be described as circular, involving organs from the same level of hierarchy collaborating within an international organisation, or several international organisations collaborating with each other, with the outcome of the negotiations being implemented individually by the each state.[111]

In interpreting these legislative products, it is not always clear what organ, at what level, may assume the role as the final arbitrator of the enacted acts, and which court's decisions will be accepted as judicial precedents. Within EU law, the Court of Justice has, through the doctrine of direct effect and supremacy, appointed itself as the sole legitimate interpreter of all EU acts.[112] When the EU represents the Member States at the international level, as in the UN, the scene is different. In the *Kadi and Al Barakaat* case,[113] admit-

109. SFS 1972:207.
110. Dir. 2009:40 Statens skadeståndsansvar vid överträdelser av Europakonventionen. See further Åhman, Skadestånd på grund av konventionsbrott – eller har HD blivit naturrättare?, *op cit* note 91, Kleineman, Jan, *Europakonventionen och den svenska skadeståndsrättens utveckling,* Juridisk tidskrift 2008/09, pp. 546-563, Schultz, Mårten, *Skadeståndsrätten i de mänskliga rättigheternas tjänst,* Juridisk tidskrift 2007/08, pp. 140-147, and Andersson, Håkan, *Problematiska forumfrågor vid EKMR-talan,* Infotorg Juridik, January 2010.
111. Zamboni, Mauro, *Globalization and Law-making: Time to Shift a Legal Theory's Paradigm,* Legisprudence. International Journal for the Study of Legislation 1/1, pp. 125-153 (2007). Regarding the rule-making within the European integrated administration, see further Reichel, Ansvarsutkrävande – svensk förvaltning i EU, *op cit* note 43, p. 85.
112. Case 11/70 Internationale Handelsgesellschaft., *op cit* note 91 and case 314/85 *Foto-Frost v. Hauptzollamt Lübeck-Ost* ECR [1987], p. 4199.
113. Case C-402/05 P *Kadi and Al Barakaat International Foundation v. Council and Commission* ECR [2008], p. I-6351.

tedly an extraordinary example, the European Court of Justice still found itself competent to review an EU regulation enacted in order to implement resolutions from the UN Security Council. In a less unusual example, the Court of Justice in the *Djurgården-Lilla Värtan* case could make good use of the preliminary ruling procedure and the EU principle of effectiveness when reviewing the implementation of the Aarhus Convention, a UN/ECE Convention, in Sweden via EU directives.[114]

A comparison can be made to a remarkable line of cases from Swedish courts regarding the procedural principle of *Ne bis in idem.* Since the Grand Chamber of the European Court of Human Rights in February 2009 revised its interpretation of the principle of double jeopardy, as set out in Article 4 of Protocol 7 to the European Convention on Human Rights,[115] the much debated question whether the Swedish tax system could be considered to be in conformity with the principle arose again.[116] The Swedish system allows both a criminal and an administrative sanction (*skattetillägg*) for the same tax offence. The fact that both the Supreme Administrative Court[117] and the Supreme Court[118] has found that Swedish law was acceptable in light of the Convention has not been deemed sufficient to settle the issue. The Supreme Court, which was more elaborate in its verdict, found that there was not sufficient support in the case law of the European Court of Human Rights to come to conclusion that the Swedish legislation was in breach of the *Ne bis in idem* principle.[119] The Supreme Court was not unanimous in its verdict. Two Justices delivered a joint dissenting opinion, with one of them adding a further

114. Case C-263/08 Djurgården-Lilla Värtan, *op cit* note 69.

115. Zolotukhin v. Russia, European Court of Human Rights judgement of the 10 February 2009 Application No. 14939/03, 2009.

116. The question has been vastly commented upon; Åhman, Karin, *Europakonventionen och förbudet mot dubbelbestraffning,* Svensk Skattetidning 2010, p. 104, Simon Almendal, Teresa, *Ne bis in idem – ett nytt rättsläge?,* Juridisk tidskrift 2009/10, pp. 549-570, Gulliksson, Magnus, *Regeringsrätten, skattetilläggen och Zolotukhin-avgörandet,* Juridisk tidskrift 2009/10, pp. 653-665, Zetterquist, Ola, *Högsta domstolens och Regeringsrättens bedömning av förenligheten av det svenska skattetillägget/skattebrottet med dubbelbestraffningsförbudet i Europakonventionen,* Europarättslig tidskrift 2010, pp. 592-599, Asp, Petter, *Inte bis in idem?,* Juridisk tidskrift 2010/11, pp. 102-110, Bylander, Eric, *Högsta domstolens dubbelbestraffningsbeslut som bidrag till ledning av rättstillämpningen,* Juridisk tidskrift 2010/11, pp. 111-116 and Cameron, Ian, *Högsta domstolens beslut om dubbelbestraffning ur konstitutionellt perspektiv,* Juridisk tidskrift 2010/11, pp. 117-123.

117. Case RÅ 2009 ref. 94.

118. Case NJA 2010 p. 168 I och II.

119. *Ibid.*, paras. 35-38.

remark, and two other Justices from the majority also came forward with concurring opinions.

Since then, several District Courts[120] and the Court of Appeal for Western Sweden,[121] have defied the judgments of the two high courts and acquitted suspected tax criminals, on the grounds that the Swedish system is contrary to prohibition against double jeopardy, the *Ne bis in idem* principle, as found in the European Convention. The Court of Appeal held that even though it normally considered the judgments of the Supreme Court as sources of law carrying great weight, it was clear that in a conflict between the Supreme Court and the European Court of Human Rights, the latter would carry an even greater weight in questions of law regarding the Convention.

Further, Judge Hans Sundberg in the Court of Appeal for Northern Norrland argued in a dissenting opinion that the issue would have to be resolved differently if EU law was to be taken into account.[122] He held that since the Court of Justice in its case law has interpreted the *Ne bis in idem* principle in a way that would target the Swedish system, and that the principle is included in Article 50 of the EU Charter of Fundamental Rights which today has binding force, EU law would hinder an application of Swedish tax law, at least within the sphere of application of EU law. Since it would not be in conformity with the principle of equal treatment, especially important in penal law, to allow the interpretation of the *Ne bis in idem* principle to vary according to what European sources of law were applicable in the actual case, he argued that the EU version should be applied in all cases. In December 2010, a district court followed this line of reasoning and referred a question to the European Court of Justice, asking for an interpretation of the *Ne bis in idem* principle even though the situation in the case at hand did not seem to fall within the sphere of application of EU law.[123]

The difficulty for Swedish judges to determine what court can be considered to be the final arbitrator of law in Sweden when it comes to applying European sources may be considered illustrative of the legal landscape that

120. Solna tingsrätts dom den 14 april 2010 i mål nr B 8288-09, Stockholms tingsrätt dom den 14 september 2010 i mål nr B 12196-09,Varbergs tingsrätt beslut den 26 oktober 2010 i mål nr B 2501-09, Värmlands tingsrätt beslut den 23 november 2010 i mål nr B 2159-09.

121. Hovrättens för Västra Sverige dom den 23 juni 2010 i mål nr B 2432-09.

122. Dissenting opinion by Judge Sundberg in Hovrättens för övre Norrland dom den 8 september 2010 i mål nr B 801-09.

123. Haparanda tingsrätts beslut den 23 december 2010 i mål nr B 550-09, paras 14-15.

has developed over recent decades.[124] National courts will have to apply different hierarchies of norms depending on what sources of law are applicable in the case, and the courts above in the hierarchal chain of the national court system may not always be the court whose judgment should be followed. At least when it comes to EU law, the Court of Justice has made it clear that lower level courts are under the obligation to give effect to a correct interpretation of EU law, even if this goes against findings made by a higher court in the same case:[125]

> European Union law precludes a national court which is called upon to decide a case referred back to it by a higher court hearing an appeal from being bound, in accordance with national procedural law, by legal rulings of the higher court, if it considers, having regard to the interpretation which it has sought from the Court, that those rulings are inconsistent with European Union law.

It seems that globalization and the Europeanization of national law have opened up the well-known and familiar hierarchies of norms that the lawyers acting within one legal order are so accustomed to, that they are used completely automatic and without much consideration.[126] As it is difficult to perceive that an equivalent hierarchy could find uniform acceptance in the globalized legal world, Delmas-Marty argues that the role of the courts has become central:[127]

> 'To summarize, a stringent hierarchy is a guarantee of legal certainty (foreseeability), but one acknowledged only with difficulty worldwide because of the uniformity it imposes; conversely, a relaxed hierarchy, albeit more readily embraced because it allows of a certain pluralism, entails a

124. The issue is naturally not limited to the *Ne bis in idem* principle and tax law. Regarding the relationship between administrative charges and the European Convention on Human Rights in general, see Warnling-Nerep, Wiweka, *Sanktionsavgifter – särskilt i näringsverksamhet* Norstedts Juridik, Stockholm, 2010, p. 143. See further Section 4 *infra*.
125. Case C-173/09 *Ivanov Elchinov v. Natsionalna zdravnoosiguritelna kasa* ECR [2010], nyr., para 32.
126. Walker, Neil, Beyond boundary disputes and basic grids: Mapping the global disorder of normative orders, *op cit* note 94, p. 375.
127. Delmas-Marty, Mireille, *The great legal complexity of the world*, From Embracing Globalisation to the Limits of Tolerance – Themes from Axess magasin 2006, Axel and Margaret Ax:son Johnson Foundation Danmark 2007, p. 188.

transfer of power to the judge, and hence a risk of subjectivity and arbitrariness. This risk can be lessened by an overly generous measure of transparency and stringency.'

Delmas-Marty thus points to transparency and stringency as measures that may counter the risk of shaky and individually tainted judgments. The reception of EU law in the Swedish courts and legal method are analyzed in the final part below.

4 Is There a Europeanized Version of Swedish Legal Method?

The strong emphasis on the private enforcement of individual rights in EU law, coupled with a pluralistic approach to both legal sources and hierarchies of legal norms, has directed attention to national courts instead of national legislatures. It is for the national courts to protect EU law within their own legal order, and the opening up of available sources and hierarchies may put the courts in a position where they may pick and chose between legal norms.[128]

4.1 The Reception of European Sources in Sweden

How have Swedish courts responded to this and how has this affected Swedish legal method? As described above, Scandinavian legal realism shows an open and pragmatic attitude to legal sources.[129] The key question, however, is who may legitimately define what the valid law is. If the legal machinery is to be neutral to all non-legal elements[130] and legal concepts are perceived as empty vessels whose content is to be decided through a normative doctrine of legal sources,[131] there seems to be a need for a high degree of uniformity in the perception of how to apply the doctrine of legal sources among law-defining actors. On the other hand, Ross accepts that the doctrine of legal sources may vary between different legal systems.[132] Naturally, the followers

128. von Bogdandy, Armin, *Pluralism, direct effect, and the ultimate say. On the relationship between international and domestic constitutional law,* International Journal of Constitutional Law, 2008 vol. 6 nr 3-4, pp. 397-413.
129. See Section 1.1 *supra*.
130. Zamboni, Law and Politics: a Dilemma for Contemporary Legal Theory, *op cit* note 5, p. 97.
131. Ross, On Law and Justice, *op cit* note 7, p. 104.
132. *Ibid.* at 110.

of the Scandinavian legal realism did not take into account in their analysis the Europeanized and globalized legal order of today, where several legal systems are to co-exist within a geographical area, and within the jurisdiction of the courts of that area.[133] The remaining influence of the Scandinavian legal realism on the legal thinking in Sweden today, with a stripped down, minimalistic perception of the law, seem however to have left the law-defining actors without much guidance in their tasks of evaluating and balancing legal sources emanating from different legal systems against each other.

Even if the Swedish tradition has shown an open attitude to legal sources, Swedish lawyers and courts have traditionally been loyal to the Swedish legislature.[134] In line with the majoritarian democratic model,[135] courts in general have been reluctant to review acts of law, insofar as it has entailed setting aside legislation, in order to uphold general principles of constitutional law or human rights. On this last point, Swedish law has undergone important changes during recent decades. Swedish courts have not hesitated to set aside acts of law on the basis of their being contrary to European legal sources on human rights, as well as broad principle-oriented provisions with strong economic and political connotations as the Treaty-based EU rules on free movement. The importance of general principles of law, court-based legal instruments, has increased, whereas legislative preparatory works, emanating from the legislator, have undergone a decrease in importance.[136] Wiklund goes as far as to call this development a constitutional revolution, including the abandoning of the principle of the sovereignty of the people.[137]

Certain tendencies in Swedish legal method will now be pinpointed as decisive for understanding the Swedish reception of European legal sources, in the first hand, EU law. There is always a question of how much the internal

133. This does not mean that the analysis of the Scandinavian legal realism could not be made relevant to legal problems of today; see Nielsen, Scandinavian Legal Realism and EU law, *op cit* note 6, p. 249, with further references.

134. Joakim Nergelius, *North and South: Can the Nordic States and the European Continent Find each other in the Constitutional Arena – or Are They too Different?*, Scheinin, Martin (ed), Welfare state and constitutionalism: Nordic perspectives, Nordic Council of Ministers, Copenhagen, 2001, p. 88 and Wind, Martinsen & Rotger, The Uneven Legal Push for Europe: Questioning Variation when National Courts go to Europe, *op cit* note 29, p. 72.

135. See Section 1.2 *supra*.

136. Nielsen, Scandinavian Legal Realism and EU law, *op cit* note 6, p. 250.

137. Wiklund, Juristokratin och Den Skandinaviska rättsrealismens uppgång och fall, *op cit* note 19, p. 86.

system should open up to the surrounding world, and how much it should strive to retain the internal consistency of the legal system. In order to follow the suggestion put forward by Delmas-Marty, to use transparency and stringency as measures to counter the risk of legal uncertainty in a world of dissolving legal hierarchies and structures, the effects of Europeanization on Swedish legal method will be assessed through these two principles.

4.2 A Hidden Development

First, it should again be highlighted that in general Swedish courts have not been reluctant to assume the task of protecting EU law in Sweden. This means that there is some sort of realization among the courts that there is a need for a Europeanized version of the Swedish legal method, different from the method usually applied in cases concerning solely Swedish legal sources.[138] Quite often, however, the methodological choices are not made explicit, with the legal handiwork performed in a more cautious and subtle manner. Bernitz has coined it as an indirect adjustment of Swedish law to EU law, in that the Swedish courts choose to apply Swedish sources in accordance to European sources, without actually mentioning EU law.[139] For example, Swedish courts have step-by-step expanded access to the courts for the review of administrative decisions, abandoning the traditional Swedish right to turn to the highest representatives of the administration, initially the King and later on the government.[140] The leading case in this area, the *Lassagård* case,[141] is an exception to this since the Supreme Administrative Court there openly set aside the relevant Swedish statutory law and based its judgment on the EU general principle of a right to an effective remedy instead.[142] Other cases are more representative, such as the *Olive oil* case[143] and

138. Ragnemalm, Hans, *EG-rätten i Regeringsrätten* Eliason, Marianne, Regner, Göran & Vogel, Hans-Heinrich (ed), Festskrift till Rune Lavin, Juristförlaget, Lund 2006.
139. Bernitz, Europarättens genomslag i svensk rätt – var står vi idag?, *op cit* note 78, p. 486. The situation seems to be similar in other Nordic countries, see regarding Finland, Ojanen, From Constitutional Periphery Toward the Center – Transformation of Judicial Review in Finland, *op cit* note 30, p. 201 and Denmark, Wind, Martinsen & Rotger, The Uneven Legal Push for Europe: Questioning Variation when National Courts go to Europe, *op cit* note 29, p. 75.
140. Warnling-Nerep, Rätten till domstolsprövning & rättsprövning, *op cit* note 43, pp. 30.
141. Case RÅ 1997 ref. 65.
142. Nergelius, Joakim, *Förvaltningsprocess, normgivning och Europarätt*, Norstedts juridik, Stockholm, 2000, p. 77.
143. Case RÅ 2004 ref. 8.

Pfizer case,[144] where the Supreme Administrative Court did not refer to European sources at all, even though it seems clear that EU law had a strong influence on the outcome. A more transparent approach to the influence of EU law in the development of general principles of Swedish administrative law would have been more than welcomed, not in the least by the interest of developing a Europeanized Swedish method.[145]

4.3 A Remaining Uncertainty in Applying Vague but High-ranking Principles

The next aspect to address is of a slightly different character, namely the remaining uncertainty of the Swedish courts as to how to handle vague and goal-oriented, yet high-ranking sources of law, general principles of EU law and the European Convention of Human Rights. There are examples of Swedish courts facilitating a very wide impact of EU law, by interpreting the doctrine of direct effect,[146] or, as in the previously discussed *Laval* case,[147] the principle of Member State liability in a manner that probably exceeds that requested of the Swedish courts in regards to the principle of loyal cooperation. On the other hand, the opposite is probably more common. Warnling-Nerep has in a recent article analyzed a judgment of the Environmental Appeal Chamber of the Svea Court of Appeal,[148] criticizing the court for not applying the principle of proportionality correctly, due to the fact that the court had evidently not found that Swedish law gave sufficient room for such assessment.[149] EU law is still a foreign material for many judges, and the uncertainty as to how to handle it remains.

Also in regard to this aspect, the higher courts are unfortunately not always as clear in their adjudication as one could hope for in order to set precedents in questions of methodological character. This may be a reason why the judgments of the Supreme Court in the abovementioned *Ne bis in idem* cases

144. Case RÅ 2006 ref 9.
145. Engström, Johanna, *The Europeanisation of Remedies and Procedures through Judge-made Law – Can a Trojan Horse Achieve Effectiveness? Experiences of the Swedish Judiciary*, Departement of Law, European University Institute, Florence, 2009, p. 579 and Reichel, God förvaltning I EU och i Sverige, p. 580.
146. Migrationsdomstolen i Stockholm dom den 5 december 2008 i mål UM 3231-08.
147. Arbetsdomstolens dom den 2 december 2009 i mål nr A 268/04.
148. Miljööverdomstolens dom den 14 sept. 2010 mål 7801-09.
149. Warnling-Nerep, Wiweka, *Hur tillämpas europarättsliga principer i våra myndigheter? En kommentar av en ny dom från Miljööverdomstolen,* Juridisk tidskrift 2011, forthcoming.

have not been fully accepted by the lower courts.[150] The Supreme Court found that the Swedish system for allowing both a criminal and an administrative sanction for the same tax offence did not transgress the prohibition of *Ne bis in idem* as found in the European Convention on Human rights, since there was not 'sufficient support' in the case law of the European Court of Human Rights to come to any other conclusion. The Supreme Court is not quite clear on what is meant by 'sufficient support', but in the legal scholarship,[151] as well as in the dissenting opinion of Judge Hans Sundberg in the Court of Appeal for Northern Norrland,[152] it has been discussed whether the expression was used as measure to externalize the Convention and thereby diminish its importance. The lasting impression is that the Supreme Court did not want to take responsibility for declaring the entire system contrary to the European Convention and therefore buried the question in unclear vocabulary. For a better understanding of the new legal landscape Europeanization has brought about, and not least for a more stringent approach to the new hierarchies of legal sources this has entailed, regret can be once again be expressed for the situation that the Swedish courts are not more explicit as to how different legal sources should be weighed against each other. The Swedish courts have a fundamental task to ensure that these constitutional questions are discussed openly.[153]

Perhaps not surprisingly, a driving force in the Europeanization of Swedish law seems to come from the legislator. The changes in the Instrument of Government, where the task of the Swedish courts to protect European law in Sweden is emphasized, have already been discussed above in Section 1.3. Another example is the ongoing legislative work on the Swedish General Administrative Act, where suggestions have been brought forward to include typical European features in the act, for example codifying basic general principles on good administration in one of the introductory paragraphs of the act and to introduce a failure to act procedure.[154] This is in line with the majoritarian view of the Swedish legal system, where the legislature is the en-

150. Case NJA 2010 p. 168 I och II. See Section 3.2 *supra*.
151. Zetterquist, Högsta domstolens och Regeringsrättens bedömning av förenligheten av det svenska skattetillägget/skattebrottet med dubbelbestraffningsförbudet i Europakonventionen. and Bylander, Högsta domstolens dubbelbestraffningsbeslut som bidrag till ledning av rättstillämpningen., p. 113, both *op cit* note 116.
152. Dissenting opinion by Judge Sundberg in Hovrättens för övre Norrland dom den 8 september 2010 i mål nr B 801-09.
153. Reichel, Jane, *Lojalitet, legalitet och legitimitet – nya utmaningar i EU:s integrerade förvaltning,* Europarättslig tidskrift 2009, pp. 607-614, at 614.
154. SOU 2010:29 En ny förvaltningslag.

gine of legal development and directs other actors within the Swedish legal system towards a certain goal.

5 Conclusive Remarks

European legal sources are not avoided by Swedish courts and other legal actors, but they are still treated, at least to some extent, as foreign objects in Swedish law. The further European integration proceeds, the greater the number of substantive legal areas directly affected by EU secondary legislation, either by harmonization through directives, or by directly applicable regulations. As seen above, there are also tendencies by the Swedish legislator to adopt a Europeanized perspective even in areas not strictly covered by EU law. Even if these legislative initiatives may be welcomed as a way of bringing together the Swedish traditional legal perception of the law with a European view, this may also have as an effect increasing the complexity of the relationship between the European and national, Swedish legal order. The key question of who may legitimately define what valid law is in the Europeanized area of Swedish law cannot be answered solely by the Riksdag, through Swedish acts of law or in legislative preparatory works. Swedish courts cannot escape the responsibility of answering the questions put before them, including the question of when and why different legal sources are to be applied and if there is any reason to use different legal methods in the different situations.

The task Swedish courts face is therefore twofold: to develop a stringent and transparent method for the Europeanized area of Swedish law and to make sure that its compatibility with the method applied in original Swedish cases also, as far as possible, is stringent and transparent. The goal is not to Europeanize the entire body of Swedish law, but to bring some light to the legal cultural differences and how they can be addressed. In the interest of legal certainty, equal treatment and foreseeability, different outcomes to the application of similar, or even the very same, legal provisions depending on whether the situation at hand is within the sphere of application of international, European or Swedish legal sources, ought to be avoided as far as possible. The first task, to develop a method for the Europeanized area, can preferably be carried out in collaboration and mutual understanding with other courts, both on the European and national levels. Twenty-seven Member States of the EU, facing if not the same, at least similar challenges in remoulding the national legal cultures to an Europeanized and globalized legal reality, must have something to learn from each other. Legal scholarship can assist in this development by identifying the challenges in the respective legal systems and by uncovering possible avenues ahead.

Bibliography

Andersson, Håkan, *Problematiska forumfrågor vid EKMR-talan,* Infotorg Juridik, januari 2010.

Andersson, Torbjörn, *Rättsskyddsprincipen: EG-rätt och nationell sanktions- och processrätt ur ett svenskt civilprocessuellt perspektiv*, Iustus, Uppsala, 1997.

– *Abstrakt lagprövning – en aspekt på Unibetmålet*, Heckscher, Sten & Eka, Anders (ed), Festskrift till Johan Hirschfeldt, Iustus, Uppsala, 2008.

Asp, Petter, *Inte bis in idem?,* Juridisk tidskrift 2010/11, pp. 102-110.

Bakardjieva Engelbrekt, Antonina *Institutional Theories, EU Law and the Role of Courts for Developing a European Social Model*, Neergaard, Ulla B., Nielsen, Ruth & Roseberry, Lynn M. (ed), The Role of Courts in Developing a European Social Model – Theoretical and Methodological Perspectives1576, DJØF Publishing, Copenhagen, 2010.

Barber, N. W., *Legal Pluralism and the European Union,* European Law Journal, Vol. 12, No. 3, 2006, pp. 306-329.

Bernitz, Ulf, *Europarättens genomslag i svensk rätt – var står vi idag?,* Juridisk Tidskrift Nr 3 2009/10, pp. 477-501.

Biondi, Andrea & Farley, Martin, *The Right to Damages in European Law*, Wolters Kluwer, Alphen aan den Rijn, 2009.

Bylander, Eric, *Högsta domstolens dubbelbestraffningsbeslut som bidrag till ledning av rättstillämpningen,* Juridisk tidskrift 2010/11, pp. 111-116.

Bull, Thomas & Sterzel, Fredrik, *Regeringsformen: en kommentar*, SNS förlag, Stockholm, 2010.

Cameron, Ian, *Högsta domstolens beslut om dubbelbestraffning ur konstitutionellt perspektiv,* Juridisk tidskrift 2010/11, pp. 117-123.

Delmas-Marty, Mireille, *The great legal complexity of the world*, From Embracing Globalisation to the Limits of Tolerance – Themes from Axess magasin 20061597, Axel and Margaret Ax:son Johnson Foundation Danmark 2007.

Carlson, Laura, *The Fundamentals of Swedish Law: a Guide for Foreign Lawyers and Students* Studentlitteratur, Lund, 2009.

Curtin, Deirdre, *Executive power of the European Union: law, practices, and the living constitution,* Oxford University Press, Oxford, 2009.

Ekelöf, Per Olof, *Teleological Construction of Statutes,* Scandinavian Studies in Law 1958, pp. 75-117.

Engström, Johanna, The Europeanisation of Remedies and Procedures through Judgemade Law – Can a Trojan Horse Acheive Effectiveness? Experiences of the Swedish Judiciary, Departement of Law, European University Institute, Florence, 2009.

Enzell, Magnus, *Requiem for a constitution: constitutionalism and political culture in early 20th century Sweden*, Stockholm Studies in Politics, Department of Political Science, Stockholm University, Stockholm, 2002.

Eriksson, Ida Otken, *Marknadsdomstolens dom i Gourmet-målet: Resonemang kring proportionalitet,* Europarättslig tidskrift 2003, pp. 585-598.

Garlicki, Lech, *Cooperation of courts: The role of supranational jurisdictions in Europe,* International Journal of Constitutional Law, 2008 vol. 6 nr 3-4, pp. 509-530.

Groussot, Xavier, *Spirit, Are You There? – Reinforced Judicial Dialog and Preliminary Ruling Procedure,* Europarättslig tidskrift 2008 pp. 934-966.

– *General Principles of Community Law*, Europa Law Publishing, 2006.

Gulliksson, Magnus, *Regeringsrätten, skattetilläggen och Zolotukhin-avgörandet,* JT 2009/10, pp. 653-665.

Harlow, Carol, *State Liability: Tort Law and Beyond*, Oxford University Press, Oxford, 2004.

Hellners, Trygve & Malmqvist, Bo, *Förvaltningslagen med kommentarer*, 2 ed., Norstedts juridik, Stockholm, 2007.

Herdegen, Matthias, *General Principles of EU Law – the Methodological Challenge*, Bernitz, Ulf, Nergelius, Joakim & Cardner, Cecilia (eds.), General Principles of European Community. Law in a Process of Development 1298, 2 ed, Kluwer, 2008.

Kilpatrick, Claire, *The future of remedies in Europe*, Kilpatrick, Claire, Novitz, Tonia & Skidmore, Paul (eds.), The future of remedies in Europe, Hart, Oxford, 2000.

Kleineman, Jan, *Europakonventionen och den svenska skadeståndsrättens utveckling,* Juridisk tidskrift 2008/09, pp. 546-563.

Lagerqvist Veloz Roca, Annika, *Föreskrift och föreskriftsprövning enligt 1974 års regeringsform*, Jure, Stockholm, 1999.

Lundstedt, Vilhelm, *Legal Thinking Revised: my Views on Law*, Almqvist & Wiksell, Stockholm, 1956.

Lyles, Max, *A Call for Scientific Purity: Axel Hägerström's Critique of Legal Science*, Institutet för rättshistorisk forskning, Stockholm, 2006.

Nergelius, Joakim, *North and South: Can the Nordic States and the European Continent Find each other in the Constitutional Arena – or Are They to Different?*, Scheinin, Martin (ed), Welfare state and constitutionalism: Nordic perspectives, Nordic Council of Ministers, Copenhagen, 2001.

– *Förvaltningsprocess, normgivning och Europarätt*, Norstedts juridik, Stockholm, 2000

– *Konstitutionellt rättighetsskydd: svensk rätt i ett komparativt perspektiv*, Fritze, Stockholm, 1996.

Nielsen, Ruth, *Scandinavian Legal Realism and EU law*, Neergaard, Ulla B., Nielsen, Ruth & Roseberry, Lynn M. (eds.), The Role of Courts in Developing a European Social Model – Theoretical and Methodological Perspectives, DJØF Publishing, Copenhagen, 2010.

Maduro, Miguel Poiares *Interpreting European Law – Judicial Adjudication in a Context of Constitutional Pluralism,* Working Paper IE Law School WPLS08-02 05-02-2008

Ojanen, Toumas, *From Constitutional Periphery toward the Center – Transformation of Judicial Review in Finland,* Nordisk tidsskrift for menneskerettigheter, 2009, nr 2, pp. 194-207.

Olivecrona, Karl, *Law as fact*, 2 ed, Stevens, London, 1971.

Peczenik, Aleksander, *Principer i det svenska statsskicket*, Berggren, Niclas, Karlson, Nils & Nergelius, Joakim (eds.), Makt utan motvikt: om demokrati och konstitutionalism, City Univ. Press, Stockholm, 1999.

Ragnemalm, Hans, *EG-rätten i Regeringsrätten*, Eliason, Marianne, Regner, Göran & Vogel, Hans-Heinrich (eds.), Festskrift till Rune Lavin, Juristförlaget, Lund 2006.

Reichel, Jane, *Ansvarsutkrävande – svensk förvaltning i EU*, Jure, Stockholm, 2010.
- *Judicial Control in a Globalized legal Order – A One Way Track? An analysis of the case C-263/08 Djurgården-Lilla Värtan,* Review of European Administrative Law, Vol. 3, No. 2, pp. 69-87, 2010.
- *Lojalitet, legalitet och legitimitet – nya utmaningar i EU:s integrerade förvaltning,* Europarättslig tidskrift 2009, pp. 607-614.
- Reichel, Jane, *A New Proposal for a Regulation on Mutual Recognition of Goods – Towards a Harmonized Administrative Order?,* Sieps, European Policy Analysis Issue 3-2007.
- *God förvaltning i EU och i Sverige*, Jure, Stockholm, 2006.

Rosas, Allan, *Tolknings- och tillämpningsproblem i mötet mellan nordisk och internationell juridisk metod,* Forhandlingerne ved det 37. nordiske juristmøde i Reykavik 18.-20. august 2005.

Ross, Alf, *Varför demokrati? Med efterskrift av Karl-Göran Algotsson*, Santérus förlag, Stockholm, 2003.
- *On Law and Justice*, Stevens, London, 1958.
- *Tû-tû,* Harward Law Review 70:812-825.

Roth, Wulf-Henning, *The Importance of the Instruments Provided for in the Treaties for Developing a European Legal Method*, Nielsen, Ruth, Neergaard, Ulla & Roseberry, Lyne (eds.), forthcoming April 2011.

Samuelsson, Joel, *Bulleri buller bock. Hur många horn står opp? Kommentar till Johan Strangs 'Two Generations of Scandinavian Legal Realism',* Retfaerd 2009 nr 1/124, pp. 83-88.
- *Tolkning och utfyllning: undersökningar kring ett förmögenhetsrättsteoretiskt tema*, Iustus, Uppsala, 2008.

Scharpf, Fritz W., *Legitimacy in the Multilevel European Polity,* European Political Science Review (2009), 1:2, pp. 173-204.

Schultz, Mårten, *Skadeståndsrätten i de mänskliga rättigheternas tjänst,* Juridisk tidskrift 2007/08 pp. 140-147.

Simon Almendal, Teresa, *Ne bis in idem – ett nytt rättsläge?,* Juridisk tidskrift 2009/10, pp. 549-570.

Spaak, Torben, *Guidance and Constraint: the Action-guiding Capacity of Neil MacCormick's Theory,* Law and Philosophy (2007) 26:343-376.

Sterzel, Fredrik, *Författning i utveckling: tjugo studier kring Sveriges författning*, Iustus, Uppsala, 2009

Strang, Johan 'Two Generations of Scandinavian Legal Realism', Retfaerd 2009 nr 1/124, pp. 62-82

Strömberg, Håkan under medverkan av Lundell, Bengt, *Allmän förvaltningsrätt,* 22 ed., Liber ekonomi, Malmö, 2003.

Sundberg, Jacob W. F., *Fr. Eddan t. Ekelöf: repetitorium om rättskällor i Norden,* 2 ed., Juristförlaget, Stockholm, 1990.

Taube, Caroline, *Regeringsformen: positiv rätt eller redskap för rättshaverister?*, Smith, Eivind & Petersson, Olof (eds.), Konstitutionell demokrati, SNS förlag, Stockholm, 2004

Tingsten, Herbert, *Demokratins problem*, Norstedt, Stockholm, 1945.

Tridimas, Takis, *The General Principles of EU Law*, 2 ed., Oxford University Press, Oxford, 2006.

Walker, Neil, *Beyond boundary disputes and basic grids: Mapping the global disorder of normative orders,* International Journal of Constitutional Law, 2008 vol. 6 nr 3-4, pp. 373-396.

Warnling-Nerep, Wiweka, *Sanktionsavgifter – särskilt i näringsverksamhet* Norstedts Juridik, Stockholm, 2010.

– *Rätten till domstolsprövning & rättsprövning*, 3 ed., Jure, Stockholm, 2008.

– *Hur tillämpas europarättsliga principer i våra myndigheter? En kommentar av en ny dom från Miljööverdomstolen,* Juridisk tidskrift 2011, forthcoming.

Wennström, Bo, *EU-rätt, osäkerhet och rättens nya landskap,* Juridisk tidskrift nr 2 2009/10, pp. 444-473.

Wiklund, Ola, *Merging law and politics*, From Embracing Globalisation to the Limits of Tolerance – Themes from Axess magasin 2006, Axel and Margaret Ax:son Johnson Foundation Danmark 2007.

– *Juristokratin och den skandinaviska rättsrealismens uppgång och fall*, Lundin, Anna-Karin (eds.), Regeringsrätten 100 år, Iustus, Uppsala, 2009.

Wind, Marlene, Martinsen, Dorte Sindbjerg & Rotger, Gabriel Pons, *The Uneven Legal Push for Europe: Questioning Variation when National Courts go to Europe* European Union Politics March 2009 vol. 10 no. 163-88.

von Bogdandy, Armin, *Pluralism, direct efffect, and the ultimate say. On the relationship between international and domestic constituional law,* International Journal of Constitutional Law, 2008 vol. 6 nr 3-4, pp. 397-413.

Zamboni, Mauro, *Law and Politics: a Dilemma for Contemporary Legal Theory*, Springer, Berlin, 2008.

– *Globalization and Law-making: Time to Shift a Legal Theory's Paradigm,* Legisprudence. International Journal for the Study of Legislation 1/1, pp. 125-153 (2007).

Zetterquist, Ola, *Högsta domstolens och Regeringsrättens bedömning av förenligheten av det svenska skattetillägget/skattebrottet med dubbelbestraffningsförbudet i Europakonventionen,* Europarättslig tidskrift 2010, pp. 592-599.

Åhman, Karin, *Europakonventionen och förbudet mot dubbelbestraffning,* Svensk Skattetidning 2010, p. 104.

– *Skadestånd på grund av konventionsbrott – eller har HD blivit naturrättare?,* Juridisk tidskrift 2005/06 pp. 424-430.

EU-compatible Interpretation of the National Law with some Constitutional Reservations – Case of the Czech Republic

Kristina Koldinská

Introduction

When the Czech Republic, along with nine other countries, joined the European Union, it was not expected that at any point in the future such a small country would cause the Union as a whole any trouble, as happened, for example, when approving the Treaty of Lisbon in 2009. Participation in the referendum on accession to the European Union was high, and the citizens of the Czech Republic voted with a relatively powerful voice to join the Community.[1]

Along with the other post-communist countries, from the time it applied for EU membership, the Czech Republic faced a difficult task. The democratisation of society begun early in 1990 needed to be completed, and at the same time many areas of law had to be adapted to the law of the European Community (today called EU law, which we will use hereinafter). In order to be effective and fair, the harmonisation of national legislation with EU law necessarily entailed an interpretation of national law that was EU-compatible, meaning such an interpretation as would correspond to the meaning of EU

1. 77 percent of the people supported a referendum on the Czech Republic joining the European Union. In a referendum, held June 13 to 14, 2003, citizens had to answer this question: Do you agree that the Czech Republic should become a member of the European Union in accordance with the Treaty of Accession of the Czech Republic to the European Union? Turnout was 55 percent. The results of the referendum are available at http://www.euroskop.cz/187/sekce/referendum/ (visited October 11, 2010).

law, while respecting the interpretation contained in the jurisprudence of the European Court of Justice, in accordance with Article 267 of the Treaty on the Functioning of the European Union (formerly Article 234 of the EC Treaty).

The main focus of this paper will be an analysis of national jurisprudence, i.e. above all the jurisprudence of the Czech Constitutional Court and Supreme Administrative Court,[2] and even then primarily in relation to EU law. We will discuss how EU law and the jurisprudence of the European Court of Justice are reflected in the decision making of these two national courts. Particular attention will be devoted to questions of the relationship between national laws and EU law, concerning which the Czech national courts have already expressed themselves several times.

Analysis of some selected rulings will demonstrate how Czech law works with EU law, as well as with the case law of the European Court of Justice. Given that the Czech Republic, through its President, was the last Member State to approve the Lisbon Treaty, this aspect will also be discussed in this paper, especially in light of two findings of the Constitutional Court relating directly to the Lisbon Treaty.

Last but not least, we will discuss some interesting preliminary questions that the Czech courts have already submitted to the European Court of Justice (or, if you like, the EU Court of Justice).

In conclusion, the author then argues that, based on the existing case law of national courts in the Czech Republic, as well as on the literature reflecting current discussions among Czech legal scholars, it can be concluded that, in its consistent attitude towards the duty to adhere to the European Court of Justice's interpretation of EU law, as well as in its critical study of some aspects of EU law or European Court of Justice case law, Czech legal theory and judicial practice may be contributing significantly to the consolidation of a European Legal Method.

2. The Supreme Administrative Court is a judicial institution that oversees the quality of administrative decision making after more than 50 years of non-existence. It existed during the First Republic, then was cancelled during the communist era and was reestablished in January, 2003. The task of the administrative justice is to provide protection to the individual (subjective) public rights of natural and legal persons. It is performed by administrative courts, specialised chambers within regional courts acting as Administrative Courts of first instance, and the Supreme Administrative Court as the court of last instance. See www.nssoud.cz.

Historical Conditionality

It is true that more than 20 years have already passed since the collapse of communism in Central and Eastern Europe. It may therefore seem that sufficient time has already lapsed to ensure that there is no longer any need for this time period to be mentioned in reflections and analysis related to the present. On the contrary; without an understanding of the history that still conditions much of contemporary social trends and thinking, it would be difficult to perceive contemporary reality or estimate future developments correctly.

It is worth emphasising Havelková's assertion that, throughout the entire Communist era, no judicial authority was empowered to review complaints of violations of the fundamental rights guaranteed by the Constitution – for most of this period there was no mechanism that would allow for the establishment of a Constitutional Court, and even when the law did allow one to be established, this step was avoided.[3] Furthermore, litigation was also inhibited by the fact that the courts were not regarded as an impartial body, as documented by Motejl.[4] Kühn,[5] on the subject of the justice of that time, adds that 'the socialist case indeed often did not require a complicated legal structure; the permanent threat of abuse of the law by the communist regime made any ideology tied to strict application of the law the least of all possible evils. Only the situation after 1989 and a fundamental change in the cases arbitrated by the justice system brought about radical change in Central Europe.'

The complicity with the communist establishment referred to above, therefore, undoubtedly permeated the Czech justice system. As pointed out by Wagnerová, for example, it is particularly so because 'the institution of the

3. Cf. in more detail Havelková, B. *Kontinuita a změny sociálního postavení žen a mužů – období socialismu a transformace* (Continuity and change in the social status of women and men – and the transformation of socialism). In Koldinská, K., Štefko, M. *Sociální reformy ve střední Evropě* (Social Reform in Central Europe). Auditorium. Prague, 2010.
4. Motejl, O. 'Soudnictví a jeho správa' (The Judiciary and its Management) In: Bobek, M., Molek, P., and Šimíček, V. (eds.) *Komunistické právo v Československu – Kapitoly z dějin bezpráví* (Communist Law in Czechoslovakia – Chapters from the history of injustice). International Institute of Political Science of Masaryk University. Brno, 2009.
5. Kühn, Z. *Ideologie aplikace práva v době reálného socialismu* (Ideology of the Application of Law in the Time of Real Socialism). In: Bobek, M., Molek, P., and Šimíček, V. (eds.) *Komunistické právo v Československu – Kapitoly z dějin bezpráví* (Communist Law in Czechoslovakia – Chapters from the history of injustice). International Institute of Political Science of Masaryk University. Brno, 2009, p. 92.

judiciary, by its very nature, serves as a stabilising and preservative factor. Judges, starting from verdicts given by their predecessors, build on the inherited doctrines of legal institutions.' Judges are often affected by the socio-political reality of which they are contemporaries, and even more so by genuine change in the political system.[6] Moreover, given that no real replacement of personnel in the judiciary took place after the fall of communism, it is clear that a relatively large number of the judges who were to begin to comment on European law were influenced by their practices prior to this major social change.

In this connection Kühn points out the legal formalism of the general courts and provides a reflection on the application of law during the 1990s in the light of upcoming entry of post-communist countries in the EU.[7]

The same, however, cannot be said of the Constitutional Court and the Supreme Administrative Court, for one simple reason, which lies in the fact that neither of these courts existed during the period of socialism. Both courts were established after 1989 (the Supreme Administrative Court even very late in 2003), and it was therefore possible to fill their chambers with judges who were not strongly marked by socialist legal practice.

This fundamental change in the cases decided by the law epitomises not only the transition to democracy in the early '90s, but also the subsequent entry of the Czech Republic into the European Union, which brought about the need for decisions to be taken in the light of EU law, or more precisely, in accordance with it. The following passages shed light on this requirement of the current legal system and how Czech jurisprudence is reacting to its judgments. This paper will stick to the jurisprudence of Czech courts, as the EU legal method is hardly a subject of analysis or deeper discussion in the Czech legal scholarship. If there is any discourse on the EU law, it is more focused on some particular problems and questions on the harmony of the Czech legal system with EU law.[8] There are no real in-depth theoretical works which discuss the EU legal method in a theoretical way.

6. Wagnerová, E. *Základní práva* (Fundamental Rights). In: Bobek, M., Molek, P., and Šimíček, V. (eds.) *Komunistické právo v Československu – Kapitoly z dějin bezpráví* (Communist Law in Czechoslovakia – Chapters from the history of injustice). International Institute of Political Science of Masaryk University. Brno, 2009, p. 357.
7. Kühn, Z. *Aplikace práva soudcem v éře středoevropského komunismu a transformace.* C.H.Beck. Praha, 2005, pp. 117-149.
8. Bobek, M. *Předběžná otázka v komunitárním právu.* Linde. Praha, 2005, Bobek, M. *Porušení povinnosti zahájit řízení o předběžné otázce.* C.H.Beck. Praha, 2004,

EU Law in the Judicial Decisions of the Czech Courts

At the present time it is perhaps still too early for a more detailed assessment of the question of whether Czech jurisprudence and legal science are influencing EU legal method to any marked extent. With respect to the country itself, which has been an EU Member State since 2004, it is perhaps more interesting and more rewarding to give a picture of how Czech jurisprudence and, to some extent, Czech academics and occasionally their connections (Czech courts cite the academic literature quite frequently in their decisions, and the Czech literature is not excluded), contend with the interpretation of national law in the light of EU law. In the following lines it will be showed that in the decision making of Czech higher courts there is a strong connection between the EU and national legal method in a sense that the decision making of the Czech courts is very strongly influenced by the EU legal method. In legal questions regarding EU law the Czech courts always try to explain Czech law in the light of EU law and ECJ decision making.

In the following, we will focus on main areas of decision making, related to EU law. First, we will talk about timing issues connected with the entry of the Czech Republic in the EU. Subsequently, certain decisions where the Czech courts have defined the relationship of national law to EU law and have repeatedly stated their duty to provide a harmonious EU-compatible interpretation of the national law will be discussed. It will be showed, however, in some discrimination cases that the secondary EU law is sometimes not taken sufficiently into account. In the last part of this paper, attention will be drawn to some fundamental issues of the relationship between national and EU law, or better said between the Czech Constitution and EU law. In the very end, we will briefly mention the judgments of the Constitutional Court in relation to the Treaty of Lisbon.

Timing issues arising from EU law in relation to national law

On May 1, 2004, the Czech Republic became a member of the European Union and at that moment the law of the European Union, the *acquis communautaire* to be precise, began to apply in the Czech Republic. As with any other Member State joining the Community, the Czech courts had to address the question of the temporal effects of EU law, particularly in cases where

Štefko, M. *Vysílání zaměstnanců.* C.H.Beck. Praha, 2009, Pichrt, J. *Právo zaměstnanců na nadnárodní informace a projednání.* C.H.Beck. Praha, 2010.

certain legal situations actually occurred before accession, but had legal effect only after the date of the Czech Republic's entry into the EU.

It should be pointed out that, even prior to that moment, the Czech courts had had a tendency to interpret national law in an EU-compatible way, especially if there were legal rules adopted into Czech law as the implementation of EU law. The Supreme Administrative Court adds: 'As regards the legal assessment of the facts of a situation occurring before the Czech Republic's accession to the European Union ... the Community's legal directives and the jurisprudence of the EC Court of Justice serve as appropriate interpretative guidance in the interpretation of Czech law, even when the facts considered occurred before the Czech Republic's accession into the European Union. A prerequisite of this 'inspiration by European Community law and the jurisprudence of the Court of Justice' is the reality that provisions of Czech legislation had already been construed and adopted with a view to approximation of Czech law to the law of the European Community, and Czech lawmakers had expressed no intention of departing from the rules of Community law.'[9]

It is obvious that this explanatory 'instruction' of the Supreme Administrative Court is not directly related to the timing issues arising from EU law. However, it is an important sign of the readiness of the Czech judiciary to interpret their law in harmony with EU law at a time when the Czech courts were not bound by such an interpretation. This attitude, which is evident from subsequent decisions of the Czech courts, can be seen as an expression of the pro-European character of the interpretation of national law that pervades recent cases in the Czech courts, particularly those at higher levels.[10]

The Supreme Administrative Court, using the arguments of the European Court of Justice judicature,[11] in one of its judgments in a case touching on

9. Judgment of the Supreme Administrative Court of 29/9/2005, No. 2 Afs 92/2005 – 45, judgment of the Supreme Administrative Court of 22/3/2007, No. 9 Afs 5/2007 – 70, judgment of the Supreme Administrative Court of 16/6/2008 File No. 5 As 25/2007 – 96.
10. Cf. in more detail Bříza, P. The Czech Republic. The Constitutional Court on the Lisbon Treaty Decision of 26 November, 2008. *European Constitutional Law Review.* No. 5. 2009, pp. 143-164, Albi, A. Ironies in Human Rights Protection in the EU: Pre-Accession Conditionality, and Post-Accession Conundrums. *European Law Journal.* No. 1. 2009. pp. 46-69.
11. In its decision, the Supreme Administrative Court quoted, for example, the judgment of the EC Court of Justice in cases C – 28/00, Liselotte Kauer v. Pensionversicherungsanstalt der Angestellten, paragraph 21, and C – 290/00, Johann Franz Duchon v. Pensionversicherungsanstalt der Angestellten, paragraph 22, therefore those decisions

'Czechoslovak' pensions, stated that the timing issues of European Community law (especially in relation to the legal environment of the newly acceded members) are generally characterised by a prohibition of direct retroactivity, yet allow for indirect retroactivity, i.e. the possibility of the application of 'new' laws to existing or future effects or consequences of situations occurring in the lifetime of the 'old' laws. The Supreme Court also stated that 'no regulation (in this case it was EC Council Regulation 1408/71 of June 14, 1971) establishes a claim for the period prior to the date of its entry into force (Article 94, Paragraph 1). By date of entry into force of a regulation is understood the day of its entry into force in the territory of the member nation.'[12]

The above example, or more precisely, cases of this type, not only concern issues arising from the timing of the introduction of EU law, but also the effects of the bilateral social security agreements negotiated between the Czech Republic and the Slovak Republic at the time of the break-up of Czechoslovakia. The subject of a dispute that has been going on for several years now is Article 20 of this bilateral Treaty, under which 'the period of provision completed before the separation of the Czech and Slovak Federal Republics shall be considered as time insured in the contracting State in whose territory the employer of the citizen had a residence up until the day of the separation of the Czech and Slovak Federal Republics or the last period before that date.' The quoted provision was added to Annex III to Regulation 1408/71, saying that it is to be applied in the cases mentioned therein.

The Supreme Administrative Court in this case has long argued with the Constitutional Court,[13] and the legal opinions of these two benches are so contradictory that the Supreme Administrative Court decided to submit a preliminary question to the Court of Justice of the EU. In a preliminary question dated October 16, 2009, the Supreme Administrative Court essentially asks

where the ECJ dealt with the temporal effects of EU law for Austria, in relation to the coordination of social security, specifically the coordination of pension insurance.

12. Judgment of the Supreme Administrative Court, dated February 23, 2005, File No. 6 Ads 62/2003-31.
13. Viz. e.g. Constitutional Court II.ÚS 405/02, dated 3/6/2003, in which the Constitutional Court dealt only with the international agreement without addressing the fact that this, after having been inserted in Annex III to Reg. 1408/71, became part of EC law. The Constitutional Court also expressed itself on Article 20 in its other decisions (viz. Files No. II. ÚS 405/02, III. ÚS 252/04, IV. ÚS 158/04, IV. ÚS 301/05, IV. ÚS 298/06, I. ÚS 365/05, II. ÚS 156/06, IV. ÚS 228/06, I. ÚS 366/05, I ÚS 257/06, I. ÚS 1375/07 and Pl. ÚS 4/06) and, in conflict with the Supreme Administrative Court, expressed its binding legal opinion in relation to decisions of the Supreme Administrative Court.

the European Court of Justice whether EU law precludes the application of national laws according to which a Czech institution fully assesses entitlement to benefits and determines the amount of insurance completed in the former Czechoslovakia, even though its value has implications relevant to the Slovak social security system. Further, the Supreme Administrative Court asks whether EU law precludes time of insurance obtained in the social security system during the existence of Czechoslovakia from being fully evaluated for eligibility for claiming old-age benefit and its amount determined, solely for nationals of the Czech Republic resident in its territory.[14]

There is insufficient space in this paper for a more detailed analysis of this complex case. It is perhaps possible, however, just to state that it can be assumed that the arguments of the Supreme Administrative Court are highly persuasive and well worked out, which unfortunately cannot be said of those of the Constitutional Court.

In connection with the timing issues arising from EU law, it is perhaps interesting to note the preliminary question dated January, 2010, put to the European Court of Justice by the Regional Court in Brno. This raises the question of whether competition rules laid down in EU law should be applied to the entire lifetime of a cartel formed in the Czech Republic before its accession into the EU, which continued and was terminated after accession to the EU. At the same time, the referring court also asked whether the competition authorities of Member States lose the right to deal with the same act once and for all without anything further, and to apply the provisions of national law which contain similar legislation to the EU law for the same conduct.[15]

EU-Compatible Interpretation

After accession of the Czech Republic to the EU, the Czech courts promulgated several important judgments in which, among other things, they demonstrated their consciousness of a duty to produce EU-compatible interpreta-

14. C-399/09 Marie Landtová v. Czech Social Security Administration – Preliminary question filed on October 16, 2009.
15. C-17/10 Toshiba Corporation, Areva T & D Holding SA, Areva T&D SA, Areva T&D AG, Mitsubishi Electric Corp., Alstom, Fuji Electric Holdings Co. Ltd., Fuji Electric Systems Co. Ltd., Siemens Transmission & Distribution SA, Siemens AG Österreich, VA TECH Transmission & Distribution GmbH & Co. KEG, Siemens AG, Hitachi Ltd., Hitachi Europe Ltd., Japan AE Power Systems Corp., Nuova Magrini Galileo SpA v. Office for the Protection of Competition – preliminary question filed on January 11, 2010.

tions of laws, as well as their competence to use EU law, including the jurisprudence of the European Court of Justice, in their arguments.

The Constitutional Court, for example, expressed its belief that since the Czech Republic became a fully fledged member of the EC, or more precisely, the EU, it has not been possible to conduct constitutional legal reviews in this area in isolation, regardless of the criteria and regulatory limits set by Community law and refined in the past by judgments of the ECJ.

This opinion was expressed by the Constitutional Court in one of its key recent decisions, namely, in the decision known as Sugar Quota III,[16] in which the Constitutional Court continues: '... when assessing compliance of a selected key with the constitutional order of the Czech Republic, how the issues of quotas and the ways of their distribution are handled by European law and the European Court of Justice cannot be completely ignored. At the same time, unlike previous decisions of the Constitutional Court, it is not possible to approach Community law merely as an object of comparison, which would give rise to indirect arguments in relation to domestic adaptation because Community law nowadays permeates through to the constitutional order of the Czech Republic when it is to be applied in areas of legal regulation connected with Community law.' This doctrine of pervading different levels of the law was referred to still further by the Constitutional Court in its next decision.[17] In its judgment, the Constitutional Court explains: 'Although the frame of reference for review by the Constitutional Court remains the rules of the constitutional order of the Czech Republic even after May 1, 2004, the Constitutional Court cannot entirely overlook the impact of Community law on the creation, application and interpretation of national law, especially in the area of adaptation of the law, the genesis, operation and purpose of which is directly linked to Community law. The Constitutional Court in this case interprets constitutional law while taking into account the principles arising out of Community law ...'

The Constitutional Court's ruling on the nature of sugar quotas concluded that it must examine the extent to which it is not authorised to assess the constitutionality of laws that are based on Community law. In relation to the adjustment of sugar quotas, the Constitutional Court stated that this is 'a sphere in which domestic regulation merges into regulation contained in the *acquis communautaire.*' At the same time, the objectives and purposes of this regulation, which is one of the instruments of the Common Agricultural Policy,

16. Constitutional Court judgment File No. Pl. ÚS 50/04 dated March 8, 2006.
17. IV. ÚS 27/09, dated September 11, 2009, Pl. ÚS 34/09, dated September 7, 2010, I. ÚS 1357/10, dated July 9, 2010.

are covered by the rules of European law, and under those rules the identification and selection of related means by which the objectives are to be achieved are left to the Member States.

The Constitutional Court, when answering the question of its competence to judge the constitutional conformity of EU legal regulations, ruled that 'it is not competent to judge questions of the validity of Community laws. Such matters fall within the exclusive competence of the European Court of Justice. From the perspective of Community law, as previously interpreted by the European Court of Justice, Community laws enjoy priority application over the laws of the Member States of the European Community. According to the ECJ, where Community law has exclusive authority, this law has priority and cannot be denied by criteria laid down by national law, including criteria applied at the constitutional level.' This conclusion was reached by the Constitutional Court notwithstanding the fact that the highest courts of some Member States such as Italy[18] and Germany,[19] or Ireland[20] and Denmark,[21] have never fully conformed to the doctrine of absolute primacy of Community law over all constitutional law, especially leaving themselves a certain leeway in the interpretation of such principles as the principle of democratic rule of law and the area of the protection of fundamental rights and freedoms. Nevertheless, the Constitutional Court did not, by its decision, deny its right to judge in the above sense, i.e. to interpret the basic principles on which the entire legal structure of the Czech Republic is founded, such as the principle of a democratic legal state and the defence of basic human rights and freedoms. In the end this principle was also deduced by the Constitutional Court from the jurisprudence of the European Court of Justice in which one of the general principles of Community law refers to the postulate of protection of fundamental rights.[22]

18. Judgment dated 27/12/1973, No. 183/73 Frontini v. Ministero delle Finanza, Constitutional Court; judgment dated 21/4/1989 No. 232/1989 Fragd v. Amministrazione delle Finanze dello Stato, Constitutional Court.
19. Judgment dated 22/10/1986 No. 2 BvR 197/83 Wuensche Handelsgesellschaft, Solange II; judgment dated 12/10/1993 No. 2 BvR 2134 and 2159/92 zum Vertrag über die Europäische Union.
20. Supreme Court judgment dated 19/12/1989 Society for the Protection of Unborn Children (Ireland) Ltd. v. Grogan and dated 5/3/1992 Attorney General v. X.
21. Supreme Court judgments dated 6/4/1998 No. I-361/1997 Carlsen and Others v. Rasmussen.
22. Case 5/88 – Hubert Wachauf v. Bundesamt für Ernährung und Forstwirtschaft. (1989) ECR 2609; Case C-459/02, Willy Gerekens and the Association pour la Promotion Agricole de la Commercialization Laitière Procola v. Etat du grand-duché de

In the decision of the Czech Constitutional Court cited above, for example, Albi sees some signs of an amicable relationship with EU law when stating: 'As regards the Czech Constitutional Court, it will be recalled that the sugar quota case subjected EU-friendly interpretation to the condition that respect for democracy, rule of law and fundamental rights are not jeopardised.'[23]

In some of its decisions the Supreme Administrative Court also pointed out that it is aware of its obligation to interpret national law in an EU-compatible way, especially where it would be possible to use the doctrine of the regulations' indirect effect. Such was used in a case concerning Value Added Tax, where at the time of the Czech Republic's accession to the EU, the introduction of EU law created timing conflicts which also carried an obligation of EU-compatible interpretation. The Supreme Administrative Court in its decision, among others, stated, inter alia, that 'the greater the power of national courts to formulate their own law, the greater their obligation to interpret it in an EU-compatible way. The Supreme Administrative Court concluded that, in this case, it was right to interpret the relevant VAT provisions in this way, and so decided to apply the doctrine of indirect effect of the directive.'[24] The Court did so in the knowledge that the indirect effect of Community law cannot be *contra legem*, but may yet go against the taxpayer, as actually occurred in the above case.

The obligation to interpret national law in an EU-compatible way has also been emphasised by the Supreme Administrative Court in other cases. The Supreme Administrative Court ruled that: 'EC law would have to be taken into account or, more precisely, applied, even without any objection by a participant, if its violation resulted in the defects mentioned in Administrative §109, paragraph 2, 3 of the Civil Procedure Code, or if it was a breach of a regulation of comparable significance, for example, to the provisions for protection of fundamental human rights, whose obligatory application is derived from the jurisprudence of the Supreme Administrative Court. This restriction does not preclude the obligation of the Supreme Administrative Court, in its decisions in the context of a plaintiff's objection, to interpret national legal

Luxembourg, paragraph 21. The Supreme Administrative Court is working extensively with ECJ case law and as well in its Supreme Administrative Court judgment dated June 16, 2008 File No. 5 As 25/2007 – 96.

23. Albi, A. Ironies in Human Rights Protection in the EU: Pre-Accession Conditionality, and Post-Accession Conundrums. *European Law Journal.* No. 1. 2009, p. 66
24. Cf. judgment of the Supreme Administrative Court dated February 1, 2010, File 5 Afs 68/2009-113.

rules in an EU-compatible manner, and in its conclusions or in the case of an appeal to the Court, to require an EU-compatible interpretation.'[25]

The lower courts are also aware of the obligation of EU-compatible interpretation. This follows from the findings of the Constitutional Court in which it gives the general courts guidance on how to proceed with European Community law when examining conflicts concerning the legal statute the court ought to apply. According to the Constitutional Court, where the general court will primarily focus on the examination of compliance with European Community law, arguing that a provision is in contradiction with EU law, it must draw the conclusion from this belief, in accordance with the requirements of the jurisprudence of the Court of Justice, not to apply the contested provision. The Constitutional Court referred to the ECJ's key decision in this matter, and stated that: 'If the general court, turning to the Constitutional Court for annulment of a law or its individual provisions, states that the contested provisions of the law (in addition to violation of the Constitutional Order) is also contrary to European Community law, irrespective of whether there are arguments for this conclusion, such a situation must be decided in the first place on the basis of the requirements stipulated in the judgment of the Court of Justice of the European Community in Simmenthal II[26] concerning the inapplicability of a ruling attacked for its conflict with European Community law.[27] In connection with the above judgments, Simmenthal has also emphasised the primacy of EC law over the national legislative version, and even over the decisions of the Supreme Administrative Court.'[28]

The Czech courts have recently dealt with cases where the legal question was about the possibility to apply the EU law. In one of recent cases, counsel of one party to the dispute was referred to the Charter of Fundamental Rights of the European Union about the legal arguments. According to the Czech courts, this was not applicable in a given case because the national law of the Czech Republic was being applied, not the law of the European Union. The Regional Court referred to the first sentence of paragraph 1 of Article 51 of

25. Judgment of the Supreme Administrative Court, dated June 18, 2009, File No. 8 As 33/2009-56. The Supreme Administrative Court judgments dated 29/8/2007, File No. 1 As 3/2007-83, No. 1401/2007 Coll. NSS dated 29/4/2008, File As 69/2006-92, and, for example, dated 23/4/2009, File Afs 93/2008-43 equally came to similar conclusions.
26. Amministrazione delle Finanze dello Stato v. Simmenthal SpA dated March 9, 1978, 106/77.
27. The ÚS finding dated February 12, 2008, File No. Pl. ÚS12/08.
28. Judgment of the Supreme Administrative Court dated February 23, 2005, File No. 6 Ads 62/2003-31.

the Charter of Fundamental Rights of the EU, which states that the provisions of this Charter are addressed to the institutions and bodies of the Union, with due regard for the principle of subsidiarity, and to the Member States only when they are implementing EU law.[29] The Supreme Court in the above case also decided whether the dispute in question is even covered by EU law. Since it concerned a special contribution to a pension, which is of a compensatory or rehabilitative character, specifically settlement benefits in satisfaction, and is not a social security benefit and does not fall into any other areas regulated by European law, the Supreme Administrative Court stated that European Union law will not apply to it. From this the court subsequently concluded that, in connection with such contributions, the prohibition of discrimination according to nationality or citizenship cannot be taken into account, as it derives from Article 21, paragraph 1 of the Charter of Fundamental Rights of the European Union.[30]

The Supreme Administrative Court also addressed the question of whether concurrence of Community and national legal offences is possible in a single action, specifically whether it is possible to apply Community and national law in parallel and simultaneously to a specific legal infraction in the area of protection of economic competition. After analysis of Czech legislation and Community Regulation 1/2003, the Supreme Administrative Court concluded that 'such overlapping is possible, because the interests protected by the factual basis of legal offences under the EC Treaty and the factual basis in compliance with Act No. 143/2001 Coll. on the protection of competition, are different.'[31] In its decision, the Supreme Administrative Court also noted that: 'Community law in its current form does not mandate nor, under certain conditions, does it preclude the simultaneous application of national competition law.' According to the opinion of the Supreme Administrative Court, it is impossible to agree with any interpretation according to which this provision would imply generally and for all Member States that the simultaneous application of Community law and national law applies only in the first stage of the investigation of anticompetitive conduct, but that after finding the com-

29. At that time the District Court also noted that the Charter of Fundamental Rights of the European Union is not a formally binding source of law of the European Union, as it had not yet come into force.
30. Judgment of the Supreme Administrative Court dated June 24, 2010, File No. 6 Ads 170/2009-46. Similarly, the ruling of the Supreme Administrative Court dated June 16, 2010, File No. 6 Ads 155/2009-42.
31. Jjudgment of the Supreme Administrative Court dated 31/10/2008, File 5 Afs 9/2008-328.

munity element in the case, it is then only possible to conduct proceedings for infringement of Community law.

Czech Jurisprudence in the Area of Discrimination

While the above overview shows that the Czech courts place great emphasis on the EU-compatible interpretation of Czech law, and that if EU law has a role to play in a case they always try to define the relationship of the applicable regulation to the national legal rule properly, it is perhaps useful to note in this connection the legal practice of Czech courts in cases of discrimination, particularly discrimination on the basis of sex, which appears to be somewhat inconsistent with that stated above. As we will demonstrate in the following, when it comes to cases of discrimination, the Czech courts sometimes do not work enough with EU law, not even where the EU law is argued in filings of the individual submission, usually the plaintiff's. To a great extent this deficiency is not compensated for until the higher courts are involved.

It is interesting that, in the Czech courts, recent case law on discrimination has been determined purely on the basis of whether both sides have carried out their duty to claim and assignment of burden of proof. The Courts have thus largely focused on the procedural aspects of the discriminatory causes dealt with, while currently there is no major national case law available that would clearly refer to the case law of the European Court of Justice, or at least some doctrine to have emerged around issues of discrimination.[32]

In the area of equal pay, for example, it is worth mentioning a Czech court's decision in a case where the plaintiff claimed financial discrimination, since it emerged that she was treated less favourably than her male predecessor in the same position. In this situation the burden of proof should have been shifted at the point where the plaintiff had demonstrated the difference in treatment. The burden of proof actually was shifted, but the plaintiff did not succeed with her complaints of discrimination, not even in the Constitutional Court, because, according to the Court, her employers were able to demonstrate that they did not discriminate against the plaintiff.[33, 34]

32. On the Czech case law regarding gender equality and discrimination issues, see also Koldinská, K. *Gender a sociální právo*. C.H.Beck. Praha, 2010.
33. Resolution of the Supreme Court of 6/11/2007 File No. 21 Cdo 3069/2006, resolution of the Constitutional Court File No. IV. ÚS 184/08 dated June 2, 2009.
34. The issue of equal pay is also addressed in detail in the publication Havelková, B. *Rovnost v odměňování žen a mužů* (Equality of pay for women and men). New York: Auditorium, 2007.

In connection with provisions governing retirement age, specifically different conditions for pensions for men and women, it is appropriate to point out two interesting findings of the Constitutional Court of the Czech Republic.

In the first of the cases treated,[35] the complaint was against the provisions of the Act on Pension Insurance, according to which childcare time was taken into account for the insurance for men, but only if they had applied to participate in the pension scheme within two years after the end of the childcare. That period was preclusive. For women, mothers, no such rule has been established as an administrative requirement. The Constitutional Court declared this provision unconstitutional and cancelled it. In its ruling, the Court, among other things, pointed to its earlier ruling, according to which: 'It is up to the State, in the interest of securing its functions, to decide that certain groups will have fewer benefits than others. Even here, however, it cannot proceed entirely freely ... If the law specifies a benefit for one group and at the same time places disproportionate obligations on others, it can only be done with reference to the public interest.'

In this context it should also be noted that the Constitutional Court in its judgment rejected an absolute understanding of the principle of equality, and conceived equality as a relative category, which in particular requires the removal of unjustified disparities and the elimination of arbitrariness. According to the Constitutional court: 'Legal discrimination in the access to certain rights shall not therefore be a manifestation of arbitrariness, but the categorical conclusion that everyone would have to be granted any right whatsoever does not follow.'[36]

Nonetheless, it is surprising that the Constitutional Court did not reach a similar conclusion in another, equally important issue, in which the provisions of the same Pension Insurance Act regulating the retirement age for old age retirement have been challenged as unconstitutional. This provision is problematic in terms of gender equality; not because of different retirement ages for men and women,[37] but because it lowers the retirement age for women depending on the number of children they have brought up, while the law does not envisage any such process for men. The Constitutional Court in

35. Finding File No. Pl. ÚS 42/04 dated June 6, 2006, published under No. 405/2006 Coll.
36. Cf. Point 25 of Finding, File No Pl. ÚS 42/04 dated June 6, 2006.
37. The relevant EC Directive allows different retirement ages for men and women that appear in Czech legislation not only in relation to retirement benefits, but also widow and widower pensions to be paid more than one year after the death of the husband.

its judgment[38] stated that: 'if there were to be an annulment of the contested provision, it would have taken some advantage from women – mothers – without the 'equal rights' to those advantages going to men – fathers – as the women – mothers.'[39]

Although ECJ case law has found an argument similar to the one raised by the Constitutional Court, namely that the abolition of graduated retirement age for women according to the number of children would only remove the benefits for women without men having acquired other benefits, it does not appear too suitable in this case and in this context.

Nowhere in the decision cited do the Czech courts manage to work with the relevant case law to deal with the European context of the contested provisions and negotiations; in some cases, they did not even confront arguments based just on EU law, specifically the relevant anti-discrimination directives.

A sort of exception to the above is the issue of shifting the burden of proof. In its finding Pl. ÚS 37/04,[40] the Constitutional Court ruled on the proposal of a general court for the annulment of a provision of the Civil Procedure Code which regulates the transfer of the burden of proof. In this particular case it was a question as to whether the provisions of §133a, paragraph 2 of the Civil Procedure Code are already unconstitutional, and thus the implementation of Directive 2000/43 is unconstitutional, or whether the directive quoted is unconstitutional as such. Ultimately, the Constitutional Court interpreted the contested provisions as being consistent with the Constitution. The Constitutional Court stated in its decision that the transfer of the burden of proof is neither absolute nor automatic. Among other things, it stated that 'a person who claims to be a victim of discrimination must have first submitted evidence to the court sufficient to justify a conclusion on the possible existence of discrimination, even if it is not sufficiently clear from the wording of §133a, paragraph 2 of the Civil Procedure Code.'

The finding of the Constitutional Court, however, also showed that the implementation of the EC directive had not taken place entirely correctly, because under the literal wording of the contested provisions to implement the Directive, the plaintiff was placed in a more difficult position than the Direc-

38. Finding File No. Pl. ÚS 53/04 dated October 16, 2007, published under No. 341/2007 Coll.
39. Cf. points 33 and 36 of finding File No.Pl. ÚS 53/04 dated October 16, 2007.
40. Finding File No. Pl. ÚS 37/04 dated April 26, 2006, published in the Collection of Laws under No. 419/2006 Coll.

tive had anticipated.[41] Further legislative developments corrected the anti-discriminatory legal situation surrounding the provisions of §133a Code of Civil Procedure as adopted. In this finding of the Constitutional Court, B. Havelková[42] actually sees some expression of the Constitutional Court's euro-optimism.

The Power to Decide the Constitutionality of the EU Rule of Law

With the above decision of the Czech courts in relation to EU law, the decision-making activity with which the Czech courts, specifically the Constitutional Court, have confronted the question of the relationship of Czech constitutional law to EU law should also be specifically mentioned. In recent years, on several occasions the problem of the relationship between EU law and the constitutional order of the Czech Republic has come up, concerning the powers of the Constitutional Court to rule on the constitutionality of the European Rule of Law.

We have come across two decisions of the Constitutional Court in this area in both of which cases the question of this relationship was raised. In both cases the Constitutional Court came to the same conclusion, but one of these findings has been criticised, directly in the context of the decision, in the dissenting opinion of two district judges. The issue to be addressed by the Constitutional Court was indeed similar in both cases, namely, to what extent has the Constitutional Court the right to review whether a European regulation is in line with the Czech Constitutional Order. In its decisions the Constitutional Court kept to the principle that EU law takes precedence over national law. But its decision has failed to adapt to the fact that in one case it was an EU legal rule, which was part of the *acquis*, whereas in the second case it was merely a framework decision, which does not fall into the *acquis* and is only part of the third pillar of EC law. This was indeed the essence of the above-mentioned dissenting opinion.

We have already cited above the sugar quota judgment, which should, to some extent, have become an inspirational basis for further decisions of the Constitutional Court promulgated in the case of the European Arrest Warrant.

In its findings on sugar quotas, the Constitutional Court also outlined the opinion that it does have jurisdiction to review the constitutionality of Czech

41. The same is true of Directive 97/80, which provided for transferring the burden of proof in cases of discrimination based on sex.
42. Havelková, B. Burden of Proof and positive action in the United and Slovak Constitutional Courts – Milestones or Millstones in Implementing EC equality law. In European Law Review, 2007, No. 32 sv. 5 No. 32.

Republic legislation adopted as the transposition or implementation of European law. It is a particularly relevant question whether Czech constitutional law, particularly the essential requirement of a democratic state governed by the rule of law within the meaning of Article 9, paragraph 2 of the Constitution, allows an international organisation to which the Czech Republic has transferred part of its sovereignty, to have the power in those areas in which such a transfer has occurred to create a law applicable in preference to the entire Czech constitutional order.

In a situation where Member States implement EU law, and the rules of implementation leave the Member State discretion as regards the choice of means for achieving the objective set out in the European legal rule, the Member State may examine the result in terms of compliance with its own constitution. Member States are therefore free to choose the instruments provided by Community law to ensure these goals by selecting those resources that are in accordance with their Constitution and eliminate those that are in conflict with it. In Finding File No. Pl. ÚS. 50/04 (Sugar Quota II), therefore, the Constitutional Court followed the doctrine according to which the delegation of powers to the Member State does not have any discretion regarding the choice of means. According to the Constitutional Court, it is where the Czech law reflects a binding rule of European law, the doctrine of primacy of Community law applies. In principle the Constitutional Court does not allow consideration of such Czech rules in terms of their conformity with the constitutional order of the Czech Republic, of course with the exception already mentioned above, i.e. that if it does not concern absolutely fundamental principles underlying the state as such, namely the principle of democratic rule of law and principles of basic rights.

The Constitutional Court also stated that, in the re-delegation of powers from EU institutions to the institutions of the Czech Republic, the Constitutional Court will examine any resulting regulations from the point of view of the constitutional order of the Czech Republic, which of course for this case should be read in light of ECJ jurisprudence on those principles that are identical to the principles contained in the constitutional order of the Czech Republic.

In the decision on the European Arrest Warrant, however, the Constitutional Court pointed out that ECJ case law is not uniform in either its relation to the framework decisions or their relationship to the legal order of the Member States. The ECJ found that the EU Treaty contains a principle of loyal cooperation, analogous to that which is laid down in Article 10 of the

EC Treaty. In consequence of this principle, framework decisions have an indirect effect.[43] The Constitutional Court also stated that it is clear that the jurisprudence of the ECJ concerning the exact nature of Union law, for example the framework decisions, is still in development, since the ECJ in its decision making has not yet touched on the issue of primacy, i.e. whether, as in the case of Community law, framework decisions have precedence over national law; in other words, are the national courts obliged to push the national law to the sidelines if it runs counter to the framework decision.[44]

In this context, even the Constitutional Court stated that the obvious thing would be to put it to the European Court of Justice as a preliminary question concerning this obligation, specifically the primacy of the framework decision over national law. This step, however, was not taken because it had already been done by the Belgian Cour d'arbitrage when the ECJ was asked a question pertaining to the validity of framework decisions. The Constitutional Court did not consider it necessary or advisable to wait for the ECJ's decision, and proceeded to assess whether the fundamental rights of those subjected to a European Arrest Warrant are threatened or not. In an effort to resolve this dilemma, the Constitutional Court decided to consider whether the provisions implementing the framework decision may be interpreted in accordance with the Czech constitutional order.

The Constitutional Court therefore did not wait for the ECJ, and moved towards a teleological interpretation in this matter, holding that it 'is not consistent with the principle of an objective teleological interpretation, reflecting the reality of the current EU and based on the high mobility of citizens within the EU area, for Article 14, paragraph 4 of the Charter to be interpreted in such a way as not to allow for even time-limited transfer of a citizen to another Member State for the purpose of prosecution for a crime committed by that citizen in that country if it is guaranteed that after criminal proceedings he shall, on request, be returned to the Czech Republic for the eventual serving of his sentence. A time-limited handing over of a citizen for criminal proceedings in process in another EU Member State conditional on his subsequent transfer back to his own country is not and cannot therefore be considered compulsory exile from his homeland in the sense of Article 14, paragraph 4 of the Charter. From this it follows that nobody is to be sent abroad to be imprisoned without their consent.' Moreover, the Constitutional Court also expressed its belief that the current standard of protection of fundamental

43. Cf. Case C-105/03 Maria Pupino dated 16/6/2005, paragraphs 42-43 quoted in finding on the European Arrest Warrant.
44. Paragraph 58 of the Finding File No. Pl. ÚS. 66/04 dated May 3, 2006.

rights within the European Union gives the Constitutional Court no reason to believe that the standard of protection of fundamental rights through the application of principles stemming from them is of a lower quality than that provided in the Czech Republic. The Constitutional Court, therefore, approved implementation of the rules on issuing a European Arrest Warrant as possible and in accordance with the Czech constitutional order. Another argument of the Constitutional Court also heard was that if the Czech people are beneficiaries of the benefits associated with the status of EU citizenship, in this context it is natural that, along with these advantages, they must also accept some degree of responsibility.

Some judges of the Constitutional Court, however, took a different position on this decision, which mainly referred to the one mentioned above, namely that in its legal arguments the Constitutional Court misapplied the ruling in sugar quotas.[45]

The dissenting opinion is so succinctly worded that it deserves that we stop at it. In one of its parts it states:

> 'The justification of the majority is based on application of the doctrine formulated by the Constitutional Court in its judgment File No. Pl. ÚS 50/04, which was concerned, however, with Community law, i.e. rules which are part of the *acquis communautaire* and the first pillar of the EU. In this judgment the Constitutional Court formulated the doctrine according to which, in relation to Article 10a of the Constitution, it was made possible for the Czech Republic to be able to transfer certain powers from its institutions to the institutions of the EC (EU). ... the Constitutional Court did not find reasons for application of Community law in the Czech environment directly in the Constitution, but in it, it found a threshold for such procedures. This doctrine formulated by the Constitutional Court less than two months ago is altered by today's majority opinion, which claims that the Czech Republic's accession to the EU brought about a 'certain reduction in the powers of the Constitutional Court' and 'where Czech law reflects a mandatory rule of European law, the doctrine of primacy of Community Constitutional law does not permit the court to review Czech regulations from the point of view of its conformity with the constitutional order of the Czech Republic.'

45. Dissenting Opinion of Judge Eliška Wagnerová, with which Judge Vlasta Formánková concurred.

The dissenting opinion is questioning the very idea of whether, in the case of the European Arrest Warrant, it is a mandatory rule of European law to which the doctrine of primacy of Community law should apply. The judge cautioned that the framework decision that governs the European Arrest Warrant falls under the third pillar of the EU, in which the Czech authorities' powers did not and could not pass on to EU institutions under Article 10a of the Constitution. If they do so, it would be basically issuing a 'blank cheque' for EU institutions in a vague, quite loosely defined area, such as, in this case, criminal proceedings connected to the judiciary and the police. Such a standard 'flat' transfer of powers to EU institutions under Article 10a of the Constitution would seem contrary to the essential requirements of a democratic rule of law. Moreover, according to the dissenting opinion, the Czech Republic can only with great difficulty give up control over criminal matters and the ability of the Constitutional Court to intervene in the event that this power be exercised at EU level, in contradiction with the principle of democratic rule of law enshrined in Article 9, paragraph 2 of the Constitution.'[46]

It is possible to agree with the dissenting opinion quoted here while also taking into consideration the existing practice of the Constitutional Court, which has already been quoted. Although the Constitutional Court held that the jurisprudence of the ECJ, which was what was intended to be taken into account, was not yet stabilised in the framework opinions, its interpretation given in the case cited above is still not entirely in line with considerations related to the transfer of powers to EU institutions which it had in its earlier jurisprudence. Moreover, in criminal matters we can really count on the fact that the Constitutional Court will protect the constitutionality of intervention in the fundamental rights of individuals, and will monitor compliance with the constitutional order, even though it would have come to the conclusion that the European Arrest Warrant is in line with the constitutional order.

The Constitutional Court has used the EU-compatible interpretation, but not only to justify its findings in those cases it is deciding. The Constitutional Court has also recently used an argument from ECJ case law to support the fact that it has departed from its previous conclusions. The Constitutional Court decided on this step at the moment it acknowledged that it is clear from ECJ jurisprudence that, in relation to measures that are a part of the Common Agricultural Policy, this Court does not feel entitled to evaluate substantive aspects of these measures. The Constitutional Court refused to review these conclusions, while it described taking such a step as a certain principle of

46. Finding of Constitutional Court dated May 3, 2006 File No. Pl. ÚS 66/04.

constitutional self-restraint as far as measures of an economic nature in pursuit of goals resulting from European Community policy. The Constitutional Court was indeed aware of that when it issued judgment File No. Pl. ÚS 39/01, which stated in its reasoning that it is impossible to accept such conclusions regarding whether it concerns the extent of review activity that would ultimately hinder the Czech Republic's membership in the European Union, despite its conclusion that to some extent it denied this self-restraint. The Constitutional Court, in its deviation from its own finding above, therefore found that it no longer feels competent to subject such a key to constitutional review on the abstract level in the way it did File No. Pl. ÚS 39/01.[47]

From the above stated it appears that the Czech courts, especially the Czech Constitutional Court, apply the EU law as far as possible, however, with a reservation of the basic principles of the Czech Constitution. Still, some inconsistencies may be observed, which is to be understood as a sign of a dynamic development of the Czech case law in relation to the EU law. The discourse about the relationship between the Czech Constitution and the EU law continued in a specific and intense way when the constitutionality of the Lisbon Treaty has been twice questioned before the Constitutional Court.

The Treaty of Lisbon and its relationship to the Czech constitutional order

As is well known, the Czech Republic was the last country to complete ratification of the Treaty of Lisbon. This fact was preceded by a lively debate at both the national and international policy level, as well as several submissions to the Constitutional Court which challenged the constitutionality of the Treaty of Lisbon, specifically some of its provisions.

The Constitutional Court was asked to rule on the Treaty of Lisbon not only *qua* international treaty, but also to analyse the position of EU law in relation to the national legal order in light of certain selected provisions of the Treaty of Lisbon that were attacked and labelled unconstitutional.

According to the Constitutional Court, the purpose of the proceedings concerning compliance of the international agreement with the constitutional order is preventive, eliminating the risk that the Czech Republic will take on an international commitment which would conflict with its own constitutional order. In this context, it is clear that the reasoning of the Constitutional Court had to be conducted differently from the way it was in the case, when considering the constitutionality of some of the parts of EU law already in force and

47. Finding of Constitutional Court File No. Pl. ÚS. 50/04 dated March 8, 2006.

therefore binding for the Czech Republic. The constitutionality of the *acquis communautaire* could only be tested, as stated above, if there was some doubt about whether this or some other rule of EU law conflicts with the fundamental principles underlying the Czech Constitution, i.e. the principles of the democratic rule of law and respect for human rights and fundamental freedoms. In relation to the Treaty of Lisbon, however, it was necessary to address other legal issues, as it concerned an international treaty which had to represent certain obligations for the Czech Republic in relation to EU law.

The first finding of the Constitutional Court that this bench has issued with regard to the Treaty of Lisbon was a reaction to a submission from a group of Senators. They argued in their proposal that the Treaty of Lisbon brings about fundamental changes which affect substantive elements of the nationhood and constitutional characteristics of the Czech Republic as a sovereign, unified and democratic legal state. According to the Senate, the Treaty on the Functioning of the EU creates a classification of legal powers more characteristic of federal states by introducing a category of exclusive EU powers into which complex areas of legal regulation fall. The Senate asked for a review of Article 352, paragraph 1, Article 216 and Article 48, paragraphs 6 and 7 of the Treaty on the Functioning of the European Union. It also questioned the compatibility of Article 2 of the Treaty on European Union and an oblique allusion to the Charter of Fundamental Rights together with the forthcoming EU accession to the European Convention on Human Rights and Fundamental Freedoms. In its submission, the Senate also stated, among other things, that it is not clear whether this structure will enhance or impair standards of internal protection of human rights enshrined in the Czech Charter of Fundamental Rights and Freedoms.

One of the essential characteristics of the filed proposal was a concern about the sovereignty of the Czech Republic as an independent state. In reply the Constitutional Court has said that nowadays sovereignty cannot be understood absolutely, but rather in the sense of practical sovereignty. In this sense, a transfer of certain competencies of the state that emanates from the free will of the Sovereign, and will continue to be exercised with his participation in a pre-agreed and controlled manner, is not a conceptual weakening of state sovereignty, but instead may in effect lead to its strengthening in the common approach of an integrated whole.

To the objections of the Senate touching on the Charter of Fundamental Rights of the EU, the Constitutional Court expressed its opinion that the Charter does not extend the application of Union law over and beyond the powers of the Union, and also as a result of EU accession to the European Convention on Human Rights and Fundamental Freedoms, including the

Court of Justice, it will become subject to control on the part of the European Court of Human Rights, which will strengthen the mutual conformity of both systems of protection of fundamental rights and freedoms.

At this point it is perhaps worth noting that the rules of the Court of Justice of the European Union and the European Court of Human Rights can be also expected to be fully compatible, since their competences are different. The European Court of Human Rights in no way substitutes for the activities of the Court of Justice of the European Union, which decides how to interpret EU primary law in relation to secondary law. On the other hand, the European Court of Human Rights will henceforth decide whether institutions of the European Union have harmed the individual's rights through violation of any of the rights guaranteed by the Convention. Similarly, the European Court of Human Rights is likely to have the authority to evaluate EU legal documents in light of the provisions of the Convention. If a discrepancy is found between any of the provisions of EU law and the Convention, it would mean that the Union's institutions responsible for implementation of any such document would have to take appropriate measures to ensure that EU law is in accordance with the provisions of the Convention and the Convention as a whole. In this way a coherent system of protection of fundamental rights on the entire European continent should be created, which will enable Europe to appear from the outside to act as a single entity, effectively united by law and proclaimed values. It will allow the European Court of Human Rights to continue to ascribe the acts of organs or institutions of the EU directly to the body concerned, rather than to the 27 Member States as a whole.[48]

Just as in the decision on the Treaty of Lisbon, as well as in its other decisions, the Constitutional Court has repeatedly stressed that the transfer of powers of the Czech Republic to the international organisation under Article 10a of the Constitution of the Czech Republic cannot go so far as to destroy the very essence of the Republic as a sovereign state based on the democratic rule of law and respect for the human rights and freedoms of individuals and citizens, and to establish a change in the basic elements of the democratic requirements of a democratic legal state. Otherwise, according to the Constitutional Court, the extent of devolution of power becomes a question of political sovereignty. This is so for the simple reason that it would be in conflict with the Constitution if, based on the transfer of powers, an international or-

48. On this, cf. further e.g. Besson, S. Gender Discrimination under EU and ECHR Law: Never Shall the Twain Meet? Human Rights Law Review (2008) Vol. 8 No. 4: pp. 647-682, Koldinská, K. *Gender a sociální právo* (Gender and Social Rights). C.H. Beck. Prague 2010, pp. 78-81.

ganisation could continue to alter its hegemony arbitrarily and independently of its members, meaning it would have transferred to itself constitutional jurisdictional competence. The Treaty of Lisbon certainly does not aspire to such a transfer of competences.[49]

In the context of this decision, Bříza praises the Constitutional Court for also using foreign sources in its decision, above all, being strongly influenced by the conclusions of the German Federal Constitutional Court. At the same time, the Constitutional Court sent a clear signal to Luxembourg that it intends to remain the ultimate guardian of the Constitution of the Czech Republic, and in this characterisation it is nothing less than an equal partner of the European Court of Justice.[50]

In the second decision on the Treaty of Lisbon, which was again initiated by a group of senators, the Constitutional Court also considered, inter alia, a proposal to review the Treaty on the Functioning of the European Union and the Treaty on European Union as a whole. In its ruling the Constitutional Court stated that it is possible to accept the review of an international treaty as a whole if, of course, in this respect the petitioner raised the relevant constitutional arguments and respected the limits that arose from the standing of the Constitutional Court in the context of the constitutional system of the Czech Republic. The Constitutional Court in this regard noted that many of the arguments of the petitioners in fact sought only to oppose selected provisions of the Treaty of Lisbon, so it dealt with them in the appropriate way. The Constitutional Court essentially rejected the proposal for a holistic review of the Treaty of Lisbon, although it has not entirely satisfactorily explained why.[51]

In the Lisbon II judgment, the Constitutional Court should have also addressed the question of the authority of the EU Court of Justice as laid down in the Treaty of Lisbon. The Senators argued that the adoption of Article 19, paragraph 1 of the Treaty on the European Union would make it impossible to get the Constitutional Court to make an independent decision pertaining to an interpretation of the international agreement pursuant to Article 10A if it will be deciding on its compliance with the constitutional order of the Czech Republic. In the opinion of the petitioners, the EU Court is in the superior position during the interpretation of primary law, even in the event that it is interpreted by the constitutional court of a Member State. The Constitutional

49. Finding of the Constitutional Court dated November 26, 2008 Pl. ÚS 19/08.
50. Bříza, P. *The Constitutional Court on the Lisbon Treaty Decision of 26 November 2008*. Constitutional European Law Review. No. 5. 2009, p. 164.
51. Finding of the Constitutional Court dated November 3, 2009 Pl. ÚS 29/09.

Court also dismissed this petition with reference to its previous jurisprudence which, among other things, allowed for the application of EU legal primacy if that would not conflict with the substantive focus of the Constitution.

The Constitutional Court in its decision concerning the constitutionality of the Treaty of Lisbon rejected the arguments of the group of senators in most cases, and maintained its position that the Treaty of Lisbon is not in conflict with the constitutional order of the Czech Republic.

Despite some shortcomings of the decision of the Constitutional Court in the case of the Treaty of Lisbon, it should be noted that the Constitutional Court of the Czech Republic essentially justified its decision sufficiently, and although these are not decisions that would constitute part of the jurisprudence concerning the applicability of EU law in the legal order of the Czech Republic (as we have shown above), it is possible to identify these decisions as important if only because they reply to fundamental questions closely related to the Czech Republic's membership in the EU, and these issues of sovereignty imply a possible violation of the Constitutional material core by accepting the Treaty of Lisbon, the position of the Charter of Fundamental Rights, etc.

Conclusions

The above may be a source of some conclusions which may underscore the claim that Czech jurisprudence is still somewhat fragmented, not always consistent, and sometimes its conclusions may also be problematic.

On the other hand, Czech courts in most cases cannot be denied the desire to work actively with EU law and to apply national laws in an EU-compatible way. The Czech courts are also aware that, in relation to the European Court of Justice, they cannot – nor do they intend to – exceed their powers, and they leave revision of EU law entirely to the European Court of Justice. In fact, some preliminary questions have been already referred to the ECJ. The Czech courts indeed do respect their duty to interpret national law in conformity with EU law.

The Constitutional Court, however, has retained, and in its findings also confirmed, the position of last resort if it comes to assessing the relationship of legal rules with the Constitution of the Czech Republic. This has been argued especially in connection with the Lisbon Treaty, where its constitutionality has been questioned.

Of course the relatively recent entry of the Czech Republic in the EU also brought big changes in the national legal method, which had to change already during the pre-accession preparative works, especially in the field of legislative work on the harmonisation of the national law with the EU law. The other big change was brought right after the accession, when the Czech courts had to accept another legal system and take it into account in their decision-making. This has been a case especially of higher courts, whereas some regional courts are still facing difficulties when having to interpret the national law in accordance with the EU law. It could be argued that the national legal method has been extended because of the duty of Czech courts to provide EU law-compatible decision-making.

Especially the above-mentioned EU-compatible position of the Constitutional Court, a position that can be termed euro-optimistic, can be seen as a sign that in future it will possible to count on the Czech courts in the future development of the EU legal method.

European Legal Method from a French Perspective. The Magic of Combination: Uses and Abuses of the Globalisation of Sources by European Courts

Sophie Robin-Olivier

Introduction

In a case decided on April 14, 2010 by the French highest court for civil matters (*Cour de cassation*),[1] French judges founded their decision (about Union's rights and the right to collective bargaining) on a series of sources of International and European law. Although referring to the International Labor Organization (ILO) conventions is not unusual for French Courts, other recent cases decided by the *Cour de cassation* had already raised debate about the legitimacy of the use of non-domestic sources by the judiciary.[2] In the case decided in April 2010, it is not only the interpretation of an ILO convention by national judges to decide on the validity of national law that causes unrest but also the reference to European law. Indeed, the Court does not resort to European legal instruments that are obviously binding in the case, but applies the European Social Charter adopted in 1961 and the Charter for the protection of fundamental rights of the European Union.

1. Cour de cassation, Chambre sociale, n° 09-60.426. On that decision, see namely: J.-F. Akandji-Kombé, Revue de Droit du Travail, 2010, pp. 374-376.
2. See, in particular, Cass. Soc. 1 July 2008, no 07-44.124, applying directly the ILO convention 158 to set aside a French Statute establishing a *contrat nouvelles embauches* (allowing dismissal at will during the first two years of employment). See also, more recently, Cass Soc 16 Dec 2008, no 05-40876, applying the International Covenant on Economic, Social and Cultural rights to set aside a provision of domestic law.

Beyond the use of international law in courts, which largely depends on constitutional traditions, the most interesting phenomenon, from a French point of view, is the use of a combination of sources, which stem from different legal systems, and are not necessarily binding, to decide cases. In systems, such as French law, in which judges are supposed to be '*la bouche qui prononce les paroles de la loi'* (Montesquieu),[3] and courts mere interpreters of the language of codes, the stance taken by the highest court deserves particular attention.

Looking at what is happening in French courts, even if it concerns only a limited number of cases, one cannot avoid comparing with the recent case law developed by European Courts, and wonder how much the French experience is the result of contamination. Indeed, European courts have not hesitated, in recent times, to combine sources of diverse origins in order to work out solutions for the case before them.

The hypothesis can be made that this tendency to refer to a mix of sources from different systems of law (or different levels of a system of law) is an aspect of the 'globalization' of law: in a legal world without borders, sources emanating from different legal systems seem to be in the process of merging into a global network, which courts are now ready to make use of, at least in some of the cases they have to decide.

The objective of this paper is to throw light on the practice of combination in European courts, and assess its impact on the development of law. Indeed, the combination of sources can be seen as a response to the emergence of a globalized legal word, where legal systems are no longer isolated by watertight borders, and judges have to look beyond their own system. However, combination without a method raises a series of problems. Free combination may well appear as a mere exercise of arbitrary power, and the critique of a government by judges (*gouvernement des juges*)[4] may find, in the process, another argument.

To examine the phenomenon of normative combination, I will use a series of cases decided by European courts, which concern social fundamental rights, and compare their approaches to the French decision of April 2010.

3. National judges are supposed to be no more than the mouth that pronounces the words of the law.
4. The expression was used by Edouard Lambert in 'Le Gouvernement des juges et la lutte contre la législation sociales aux États-Unis, L'expérience américaine du contrôle judiciaire de la constitutionnalité des lois', Paris, Marcel Giard & Cie., 1921. Lambert criticizes the excess of power exercised the US Supreme Court, which resisted the introduction of statutes to protect the workforce.

The first example concerns the right to take collective action, which was elevated to a fundamental right protected by the European Union (EU), in the *Viking* and *Laval* cases, decided by the ECJ in December 2007.[5] The second example is a decision made by the ECtHR in November 2008, in the case *Demir and Baykara v Turkey*.[6] This case recognized, for the first time, that the right to bargain collectively is an essential element of the right to form and to join trade unions covered by Article 11 of the European Convention for the protection of Human Rights. In all these decisions, the European courts relied on domestic, European and international sources. The French case decided on April 14, 2010[7] also concerns the right of association and the right to collective bargaining: it addresses the conformity with international law of a French statute adopted in 2008, according to which labor unions must obtain at least 10% votes in professional elections at the workplace to participate in collective bargaining with the employer. In that case, just as in the European cases, the Court founded its decision on domestic, European and international sources.

The analysis in this paper focuses on case law developments related to fundamental social rights. This is not neutral, because the rights concerned

5. Cases C-438/05 *International Transport Workers' Federation, Finnish Seamen's Union v Viking Line ABP, OÜ Viking Line Eesti*, 11 Dec. 2007 and C-341/05 *Laval und Partneri Ltd v Svenska Byggnadsarbetareförbundet Svenska Byggnadsarbetareförbundets avdelning 1, Byggettan, Svenska Elektrikerförbundet*, 18 Dec. 2007. Among the numerous articles on these cases, see: A Davies, 'One Step Forward, Two Steps Back? The Viking and Laval Cases in the ECJ', *Industrial Law Journal*, 2008, vol. 37, p. 126; C Barnard, 'Social dumping or dumping socialism?', *Cambridge Law Journal*, 2008, vol. 67, p. 262 and 'Viking and Laval: An Introduction', *Cambridge Yearbook of European Law Studies*, 2007-08, vol. 10, p. 463; T. Novitz, 'Taking collective action', *Competition Law Insight,* 2008, vol. 7(4), p. 10; P Rodière, 'Les arrêts Viking et Laval, le droit de grève et le droit de négociation collective', *Revue Trimestrielle de droit européen,* 2008, p. 47; S Robin-Olivier and E Pataut, 'Europe sociale ou Europe économique?', *Revue de droit du travail*, 2008, p. 80; D Simon, 'Libre circulation des entreprises, conventions collectives et actions syndicales', *Europe,* 2008, *Comm* 18. The recognition of a fundamental right to collective bargaining was confirmed in more recent decisions: ECJ, C-271/08, Commission/Germany, 15 July 2010 and C-45/09, Rosenbladt, 12 Oct. 2010.
6. Demir and Baykara v Turkey, 12 Nov. 2008, App n° 34503/97. On this decision, see namely: K.D. Ewing and J. Hendy, 'The Dramatic Implications of Demir and Baykara', Ind Law J, 2010, vol. 39, p. 2; J.-P. Marguénaud and J Mouly, 'L'avènement d'une Cour européenne des droits sociaux', Recueil Dalloz, 2009, Chron 739; F Sudre, 'L'interprétation constructive de la liberté syndicale, au sens de l'article 11 de la Convention EDH', la Semaine Juridique (J.C.P.), ed. G, 2009, G II 10018 30.
7. Cited above at note 1.

have no precise definition, and lend themselves to various interpretations. Thus, the combination of sources I am describing takes place in a particular context, where judges are left with a wide margin of discretion in the construction of the norm. This is also a field in which they need to buttress their solutions with more references than elsewhere, for the particular reason that the chosen interpretation can more easily be challenged.

The first part of this paper considers the exploitation of various sources of law in the selected cases, a practice which, widespread as these cases indicate, does not seem to rely on any specific method. In the second part, the risks of the development of a practice of the combination of sources without a proper 'method' will be assessed, with particular emphasis on the disruptive impact of this type of courts' self-empowerment on a civil law system, such as French law.

I. The combination of sources: a European practice without a European method

How are sources combined? How do courts select and organize references to sources extracted from national, international and European law? It is quite clear that if a norm (be it domestic, European or international) is binding, there is no serious question about the role played by that norm in the decision. To be sure, when courts have the ability to cite international law, general and undetermined as it is, in order to avoid enforcing domestic law, concerns may arise over the power of courts and the risk of arbitrary decisions. This was well illustrated in France, where a series of cases based on international sources[8] made it clear that superior courts could break free from binding statutory provisions on the basis of very general provisions of international law. However, this attitude prompts fewer questions than the use of sources, which are not supposed to apply in the case. In *Viking*, *Laval*, and *Demir and Baykara*, just as in the French case of April 2010, courts do not only use a combination of sources; they rely on norms they are *not* obliged to enforce. As we will see, as far as European courts are concerned, they appeal to a series of non-binding norms from different systems in order to make a norm come to life or – which is not very different – to give birth to a new interpretation of a norm they have to enforce. Only the ECtHR seems to be aware that this judicial mix of sources (1) requires substantial justification, which, in our opinion, has some connection with the legal tradition, on which the reasoning of the Court is modeled (2). In all cases, including the French deci-

8. See note 2 above.

sion, the combination of sources seems to be guided by a search of convergence, but a comparative method to establish convergence is lacking (3).

1) The judicial mix of sources

Looking at how European courts combine norms having their source in different legal orders, one can identify some common features in judicial approaches.

In the *Viking* and *Laval* cases, the recognition, by the Court of Justice, of a fundamental right to take collective action is derived from references to a series of sources, which the Court makes clear is not comprehensive:

> [T]he right to take collective action, including the right to strike, is recognized both by various international instruments which the Member States have signed or cooperated in, such as the European Social Charter, signed at Turin on 18 October 1961[9] – to which, moreover, express reference is made in Article 136 EC – and Convention n° 87 concerning Freedom of Association and Protection of the Right to Organize, adopted on 9 July 1948 by the International Labor Organization – and by instruments developed by those Member States at Community level or in the context of the European Union, such as the Community Charter of the Fundamental Social Rights of Workers adopted at the meeting of the European Council held in Strasbourg on 9 December 1989,[10] which is also referred to in Ar-

9. Art 6 of the European Social Charter (revised) contains the following provision concerning the right to bargain collectively: 'With a view to ensuring the effective exercise of the right to bargain collectively, the Parties undertake: 1. to promote joint consultation between workers and employers; 2. to promote, where necessary and appropriate, machinery for voluntary negotiations between employers or employers' organisations and workers' organisations, with a view to the regulation of terms and conditions of employment by means of collective agreements; 3. to promote the establishment and use of appropriate machinery for conciliation and voluntary arbitration for the settlement of labour disputes; and recognise: 4. the right of workers and employers to collective action in cases of conflicts of interest, including the right to strike, subject to obligations that might arise out of collective agreements previously entered into.'
10. Paragraph 13 of the Community Charter of Fundamental Social Rights provides that 'the right to resort to collective action in the event of a conflict of interests shall include the right to strike, subject to the obligations arising under national regulations and collective agreements.'

ticle 136 EC, and the Charter of Fundamental Rights of the European Union proclaimed in Nice on 7 December 2000 (OJ 2000 C 364/1).[11]

The fact that the ECJ cites a variety of sources protecting human rights, besides EU law, can be praised as a sign of openness of the EU, since the ECJ is acknowledging the relevance of other instruments and other bodies in the human rights field.[12] To be sure, the Court can be credited, in the *Viking* and *Laval* cases, for its renewed open-mindedness, allowing EU law to be in phase with global changes in the approach to the protection of human rights. However, as we turn to consider the choice of the various sources, some questions arise.

As far as the absence of reference to the European Convention on Human Rights, it can rather easily be explained: at the time the *Viking* and *Laval* cases were decided, it was still unsure whether that Convention protects the right to collective action as an element of the right to form and join trade unions.[13] In addition, this absence of reference to the European Convention does not mean it was totally ignored by the ECJ; the Court does in fact cite the ECtHR case law in one of the last paragraphs of the *Viking* case,[14] when looking at whether the actions were 'appropriate' to reach the aims pursued by trade unions.

It is less easy to understand why the Court remained silent about constitutional traditions of Member States, as the Court itself emphasized in its early case law, that those traditions were to be taken into account in the process of identification of fundamental rights protected at the EU level.[15] To be sure, these 'constitutional traditions common to the Member States'[16] are more difficult to grasp and make use of than international conventions. And the com-

11. See *Viking*, cited above, para 43; *Laval*, cited above, para 90. Except for the ILO conventions, the same instruments are referred to in the recent case, Commission/Germany, C-271/08 (cited above at note 5), concerning the fundamental right to collective bargaining.
12. See Davies, above n 5.
13. On the ECtHR's case law before *Demir and Baykara*, see C. Barnard, EC Employment Law, OUP, 3rd Edition, pp. 747-752, 764, 770-772.
14. *Viking*, above n 1, para 86.
15. See, in the first place, ECJ, 11/70, *Internationale Handelsgesellschaft*, 17 Dec. 1970. On the role of comparative law in the development of EU law, see M. P. Maduro, 'Le rôle de la Cour de justice dans un contexte de pluralisme juridique' Conference at the French Cour de cassation, 17 December 2007, available at: www.network-presidents.eu/spip.php?rubrique89&lang=fr.
16. *Internationale Handelsgesellschaft*, para 4.

parative study of the Member States' constitutional laws is an ever more demanding task in a Union of 27 members. In addition, identifying a 'common' tradition, as required by Article 6 point 3 TEU, requires a definition of what is considered 'common', which is so far lacking in the treaty, and the ECJ has not arrived at one yet. The notion of 'common traditions' is all the more complicated, as it does not always correspond to solutions accepted by all Union members.[17] However difficult the task, Advocate General Mengozzi did not shy away from pointing out, albeit with caution, that 'the constitutional instruments of numerous Member States explicitly protect the right to establish trade unions and the defense of their interests by collective action, the right to strike being, in that connection, the method most regularly referred to'.[18] Was the 'numerous Member States' argument too fragile for the Court to rely on? Should this departure from the Advocate General's reasoning be construed as a sign that the ECJ has now become reluctant to draw any conclusion from a solution which is not followed by all Member States? If so, the potential for the comparison of Member States' laws for the development of EU law and, especially, the promises of Article 6 § 3 of the TEU, according to which the EU abides by the 'constitutional traditions common to the Member States', would be severely limited. It is true, nonetheless, that in its search for common rules, principles or notions, the ECJ's case law has fluctuated between a cautious reference to the laws of all Member States and the identification of a view shared by only a number of them.[19]

In our second example, the *Demir* and *Baykara* case decided by the ECtHR, the Court had to decide whether the right to collective bargaining should be included among the rights protected under Article 11 of the European Convention for the protection of Human Rights, according to which: 'everyone has the right to freedom of peaceful assembly and to freedom of

17. See for instance, Case 222/84 *Johnston*, 15 May 1986, recognising a right to judicial review on the basis of common constitutional traditions, notwithstanding the fact that the law of the Member State concerned did not recognize this right. On this case and, more generally, the debate concerning the method for identifying common traditions, see K. Lenaerts, 'Interlocking Legal Orders or the European Union Variant of E Pluribus Unum' in G. Canivet, M. Andenas and D. Fairgrieve (eds.), *Comparative Law before the Courts*, London, BIICL, 2005, pp. 113-14.
18. *Laval*, para 77.
19. On this complex case law, see M. Fallon, 'L'épreuve comparative devant la Cour de Justice' in S. Robin-Olivier and D. Fasquelle (eds), *Les échanges entre les droits, L'expérience communautaire*, Brussels, Bruylant, 2008, p. 37; and K. Lenaerts, cited above, pp. 99-134.

association with others, including the right to form and to join trade unions for the protection of his interests.'

A series of references to international and domestic law were taken into account in *Demir and Baykara*. Unlike the ECJ, the ECtHR did not limit itself to a consideration of the texts of international conventions. It also relied on their construction by para-judicial organs of international organisations. This innovative development must be emphasized. It is a positive sign that a Court is willing to co-operate with other bodies charged with the protection of human rights. However, it must be kept in mind that an interpretation developed in other contexts may be subject to different constraints and guided by other objectives than those pursued by the ECHR. In that respect, the reference not only to the letter of international conventions but to their construction by committees of experts requires, at least, a cautious approach.

To be very precise, the Court referred to ILO Convention 98, concerning the Right to Organize and to Bargain Collectively, adopted in 1949, and to the interpretation of this convention by the ILO's Committee of Experts. It also mentioned Convention 151 on labor relations in the public service, adopted in 1978.[20]

Among European instruments, the Court uses Article 6(2) of the European Social Charter (which the State concerned, Turkey, has not ratified), according to which all workers and all unions are granted the right to bargain collectively. The Court also finds support in the meaning attributed to this provision by the European Committee of Social Rights (ECSR). Article 28 of the European Union's Charter of Fundamental Rights is also quoted, which indeed, is a less obvious reference for the ECtHR than for the Court of Justice (although, at the time, that Charter had no legal value either in the EU).

Consideration is also given to domestic law. According to the ECtHR, the evolution following constitutional changes in Turkey, since the application was lodged, demonstrates that the country is moving in the direction of a more open conception of the right to organize. Thus the interpretation of the European Convention is also based on developments in domestic law, which show a convergence with international and European standards.

In the French case of April 2010, the Court referred to Article 4 of ILO Convention 98 and Article 5 of ILO Convention 135, Article 11 of the ECHR, articles 5 and 6 of the European Social Charter, Article 28 of the European Charter of Fundamental rights, and provisions of the French labor

20. The Convention provides that the right to take part in the determination of working conditions applies everywhere in the public service, with the exception of the possibilities for states to limit this right for members of the armed forces or the police.

law code. As a matter of fact, the French judicial mix of sources is very close to the European version.

However, it must be pointed out that, in the French case, all the references used by the Court are part of the so-called 'visa', at the very beginning of the decision, which indicates the legal basis of the decision. Thus, the Court is considered to have formally 'applied' the articles of all those instruments and deduced the solution from them. As opposed to European courts, the French superior court is not using persuasive arguments in referring to international and European law: all the provisions quoted are supposed to be the law to be enforced. In addition, the French superior court was pushed in the direction of using the whole series of references both by the lower court, which had referred to them in its decision, and by the author of the appeal, whose argument was that none of these references implied that the French statute was illegal. To be sure, the superior court was not obliged to refer to all of the quoted sources, but could have quashed the former judges' decision for having misinterpreted one or the other provision of European or international law. But that would not have answered completely the question of the conformity of the French statute with European and international law. That would have been, even if formally acceptable, an incomplete answer, on the substance of the law, to the questions raised by the case. It would also have left it open for lower courts to set aside the contested statute, both in the case and in other similar actions, for not abiding by a provision of European or international law not considered by the *Cour de cassation* in its decision.

However, the specificity of the French case is not such that the case cannot suffer any comparison with the European decision. One important reason why the comparison is still appropriate derives from the fact that one of the quoted provisions of European law (Article 28 of the European Charter of Fundamental Rights) is not binding in the situation of the case (the selection of a labor union for collective bargaining purposes), which does not fall under EU law jurisdiction. We will consider that question further in the second part of this paper, but this suffices to show that the practice of mixing references of different sources which are not actually applicable in the case is quite comparable, in spite of specific judicial contexts. The French *Cour de Cassation* is no more concerned than European courts, it seems, with the legal force, in the particular case submitted to it, of the sources it uses. In other words, the legal value of the reference is not the major reason for its mobilization.

Another distinction that could be pointed out, between the French case and the European cases, is due to the fact that the French court is not, as the ECtHR, namely, 'interpreting' a provision of the law it has to apply, taking into account the development of the law in other systems. Rather, it has to decide whether French law violates the quoted sources of international and European law, which are considered superior to French statutes, according to Article 55 of the French Constitution. Yet, French judges are, in fact, in a similar situation as European courts because the existence of a violation of international and European law depends on the interpretation given to that law. *Vice versa*, the exercise of interpretation that the ECtHR and the ECJ are practicing is meant to assess the conformity of the law of a Member State with the ECHR or EU law. This common aim brings the different decisions closer together than one may think, *prima facie*.

The three courts also have in common to adopt the same pattern in citing sources, in spite of their different situations and functions: they quote sources with a larger scale first, and continue with those developed on a smaller scale. The order goes from international, to European, and then domestic sources (when the latter are quoted). The significance, if any, of this ordering of references is difficult to grasp.

To be sure, there is no hierarchy between those sources of law; no supremacy principle applies,[21] even if the method suggests a ranking. Rather, courts may consider exploring the larger context as a prerequisite, before coming back to the European and national options, which, after all, may well reveal specific choices, appropriate to the local environment (legal, social, economic or cultural). When, as in the European cases under scrutiny, the question is about extension of the scope of a provision or identification of the existence of a fundamental right, examining developments in the international treatment of human rights in order to put European and domestic law in perspective is a most defensible approach. Considering international law first is a way to ensure that European law does not lag behind universal solutions. One may fear this may lead to alignment of European norms with universal conceptions, which is neither required, nor always justified. International norms are not an impassable objective for the European protection of human rights, which should remain free to develop a stronger system of protection.[22]

21. Except for the relationship between international and European sources, on one side, and national statutes, on the other, the former being superior to the latter.
22. As an example, see joined cases C-402/05 P and C-415/05 P, Yassin Abdullah Kadi and Al Barakaat International Foundation v Council of the European Union and Commission of the European Communities, 3 Sept. 2008, in which the ECJ considered that a regulation implementing UN resolutions had to be reviewed under the EU-specific conception of fundamental rights.

In the French case, where all sources are supposed to be 'applied', the order of the quoting is even more difficult to explain. In the absence of hierarchy between the international and European norms referred to, the Court could be tempted to look at the most general norm before moving to more specific ones, relying on the principle of interpretation, according to which special rules prevail over general ones. But none of the quoted norms are more general than the others, and such a ranking is thus no more rational than the one based on the origin norms. As a result, the order does not seem to be founded on any rational basis, as if courts were trying to smoothen, or even hide, through ranking sources (from the one with the larger scope to the one with the smallest), a benign sort of formalism, the legal disorder resulting from the globalization of sources.

2) Justifying the combination: the influence of legal traditions?

Although the combination of sources is neither required, nor so usual, in any of the judicial systems considered, the ECtHR is the only court which goes to great lengths, in the *Demir and Baykara* case, to explain why it made use of such a variety of sources to construe the European Convention. This, in our opinion, has something to do with legal traditions having an influence on the reasoning of Courts.

In a civil law system, such as the French, courts are not accustomed to distinguishing the authorities they refer to, binding or persuasive, and justifying the use of the latter.

In systems that have been under the influence of the civil law tradition, such as the EU legal system, it should come as no surprise that such questions are also relatively neglected. It is indeed quite striking that the ECJ does not devote much energy to explaining the choice of references from which it infers the existence of a new social fundamental right. It seems sufficient for the Court to indicate that Member States have 'signed or cooperated in' the various international instruments cited, that some of them were even mentioned in the treaty (Art. 151 TFUE refers to the European Social Charter and the Community Charter of the Fundamental Social Rights of Workers) or that the instruments concerned were 'developed' by those Member States 'at Community level' or 'in the context of the European Union' (the Community Charter of the Fundamental Social Rights of Workers and the Charter of Fundamental Rights of the European Union). All these arguments have one thing in common: they acknowledge that the references are not binding, but at the same time cannot be ignored by Member States, which have cooperated in their creation and, for some of them, decided that they should at least consider them when taking action. The magic here is that this soft system of references has the power to give birth to a new fundamental right and general principle of Community law. Although it is not the first time it operates, the ECJ has never before used such an array of references.[23]

The thorough exercise of justification that the ECtHR has gone through is also linked with the fact that the combination of sources relied on in the interpretation of the European Convention is not so common, but rather consists in a new way of achieving the 'evolutive' interpretation that the Convention deserves, according to the ECtHR. The *Demir and Baykara* case shows that the ECtHR felt compelled to provide a detailed explanation of the technique of interpretation relied on, for that technique was not a 'conventional' one, as the Court indicated.

First, according to the ECtHR, the use of norms of international and domestic origin should be conceived in a very flexible way[24] because sources are chosen by the Court in order to help determine the 'appropriate' interpretation of the Convention. The Court also observes that it has often referred to the 'living' nature of the Convention, which must be interpreted in the light of present-day conditions, and that it has always taken into account the evolving norms of national and international law in its interpretation of Convention provisions.[25] When it considers the object and purpose of the Convention provisions, 'the international law background to the legal question before it' must be examined, the Court contends, because, 'being made up of a set of rules and principles that are accepted by the vast majority of States, the common international or domestic law standards of European States reflect a reality that the Court cannot disregard when it is called upon to clarify the scope of a Convention provision that more conventional means of interpretation have not enabled it to establish with a sufficient degree of certainty.'[26]

This language acknowledges the distinction between, on the one hand, 'conventional means of interpretation', and, on the other, the use of a combination of domestic and international sources. Among the multiple arguments developed by the Court to justify departure from a conventional methodology, reference is made to the rules of interpretation provided for in the Vi-

23. In some rare cases, the ECJ referred to ILO conventions (see, for instance, ECJ, 149/77, Defrenne, 15 June 1978) or the European social charter (ECJ, 24/86, Blaizot, 2 Feb. 1988), but this remains exceptional, as compared to the many cases, in which the Court resorts to the ECHR. The combination of those sources to identify a fundamental right is an innovation.
24. See *Demir and Baykara*, above n 2, para 76: 'it depends on the legal question'.
25. *Ibid*, para 68.
26. *Ibid*, para 76.

enna Convention on the Law of Treaties, according to which recourse may be had to supplementary means of interpretation, either to confirm a meaning determined by other means, or to establish the meaning where it would otherwise be ambiguous, obscure, or manifestly absurd or unreasonable.[27]

Not surprisingly, the Court also insists on the need to interpret and apply the Convention in a manner which renders its rights practical and effective, not theoretical and illusory. This idea has long been a major basis for extending the scope of the rights protected under the European Convention and is, as a matter of fact, particularly persuasive. It is thus quite obvious that, as opposed to the ECJ, and the French *Cour de Cassation*, the ECtHR is struggling to make it clear, for the parties and all readers of the decision, that the choice made is not arbitrary: this can be seen as a remarkable feature of the common law tradition.

3) Identifying convergence: a method of interpretation?

In *Demir and Baykara*, the effect given to international and domestic law standards depends on their convergence: these references, although picked from different systems, gain force from their ability to be classified as 'common' standards. As the Court mentions, 'the consensus emerging from specialized international instruments and from the practice of Contracting States may constitute a relevant consideration for the Court when it interprets the provisions of the Convention in specific cases'.[28]

Although the search for convergence is neither explicit in the *Viking and Laval* cases nor in the French case, the accumulation of references pursues, it seems, the same objective. As far as the Court of Justice is concerned, the recognition of a new fundamental right is justified by the convergence of European and international sources, in favor of such a solution. In other words, the solution is so wide spread, so generally shared by different legal systems that it has to be followed.

In the French case, although the sources quoted are all supposed to be binding, which is the formal reason why they are mentioned, the Court also seems to find comfort in convergence. That all the sources cited tolerate a similar margin of discretion in determining unions' rights to participate to collective bargaining makes the solution more solid and stable. And again, instead of turning down the reference to the Charter of Fundamental Rights, which could have been done as the charter is not applicable to the situation

27. Art 32 of the Vienna Convention.
28. *Ibid.*

concerned, the *Cour de Cassation* chose to add it to the list of converging sources, as if it was a way to buttress its solution.

If the search of convergence can be considered a common objective for European courts trying to justify innovative solutions, such a quest is a hard task, which still lacks a proper method.

The quest of 'a consensus' or 'common ground' requires a difficult exercise of comparison to determine whether there is something in common or not. This difficulty brings us back to the problem of identification of 'common traditions' by the Court of Justice. We must insist once again on the flexibility of the method of identifying a common ground or, at least, a convergence of the laws developed within different legal systems. This flexible method is an argument that can be raised against the use of comparative law in courts, due to the large powers it seems to be vesting in judges.[29]

As in the cases decided by the ECJ, the comparative method used by the ECtHR remains superficial when it comes to identifying the perimeter of the references to other sources that should be considered. To be sure, the search for a common ground among the norms of international law does not depend on whether the instruments have been signed or ratified by the state concerned: it is sufficient, according to the ECtHR, that the relevant international instruments denote a continuous evolution in the norms and principles applied in international law or in the domestic law of the majority of member States of the Council of Europe and show, in a precise area, that there is common ground in modern societies.[30] In *Demir and Baykara* the consideration of such a 'perceptible evolution, in both international law and domestic legal system' proved sufficiently powerful to trigger a departure from previous case law. But there is, as a matter of fact, a gap to be bridged between the power of recognized convergence and the uncertain method through which this convergence is assessed.

29. See, for instance, N. Underhill's remarks on the decision in *A and Others v National Blood Authority (No 1)* [2001] 3 All ER 289 (Court) in G Canivet, M Andenas and D Fairgrieve (eds), *Comparative Law before the Courts* (London, BIICL, 2005) pp. 78-9. See also the position of Justice Scalia in the debate on the Constitutional relevance of foreign courts' decisions, according to which the use of foreign law invites manipulation (transcript of the debate accessible at: www.freerepublic.com/focus/news/1352357/posts).
30. *Demir and Baykara*, above n 2, para 85.

II. The risks of a combination without a method: normative assimilation and normative confusion

To common lawyers, the use of a combination of references may seem rather natural: to buttress their opinion common law judges do not hesitate to summon up a series of authorities, not all of them binding in the case at hand.[31] In a system where the precedent is governed by rules and a long-standing tradition, the subtleties of distinctions between binding and persuasive authorities are, somehow, monitored. Lacking this background, the French and European courts' decisions, especially the decisions of the Court of Justice, face the risk of being criticized for their obscure method, and the excessive power courts have given themselves.

Cases decided by the Court of Justice are, no more than French cases, detailed 'opinions' of judges, who struggle to gather convincing arguments. Rather, the ECJ, strongly influenced by the civil law tradition, decide cases in a rather formal way, primarily deducing solutions from an interpretation of primary or secondary EU law. In our opinion, the 'globalization of sources' and the combination of norms that it fosters is more problematic in such a legal system, where the references used are more important than the argumentation developed, and courts are supposed to play a less significant role in the development of the law.

Although the limitation of the power of courts has not been obvious, neither in EU law, nor in French law, the increased power of courts has not induced explicit adaptations of the method in deciding cases. The style of decisions has progressively changed, indeed. As compared to the first generation of cases, which were usually quite short and mostly based on the interpretation (sometimes creative, to be sure) of written law,[32] more recent cases include extensive citations to previous case law, and pay great attention to facts, in the particular case to be decided. This evolution has pulled ECJ's case law

31. See for instance: A (FC) and others (Appellants) v Secretary of State for the Home Department (Respondent) [2004] UKHL 56 concerning the application of the Anti-terrorism, Crime and Security Act 2001: reference is made (at [39]) to varied sources including the UN Covenant on Civil and Political Rights of 1966, the doctrine of international organisations such as the Parliamentary Assembly of the Council Europe or the UN Human rights Committee, and decisions of the US and Canadian Supreme Courts. On that case, in a comparative law perspective; see S. Robin-Olivier, 'L'européanisation judiciaire du droit britannique: analyse de la décision de la chambre des Lords dans l'affaire Belmarsh', in *Frontières du droit, critique des droits – Billets d'humeur en l'honneur de Danièle Lochak*, LGDJ (ed.), 2007, p. 271.
32. See for instance the landmark case 26/62, van Gend & Loos, 5 Feb. 1963 on direct effect of EC law.

away from decisions of superior courts in civil law systems, such as the French or the Italian, and brought them closer to cases decided by common law courts. But the common law method, the doctrine of *stare decisis,* the distinction between binding and persuasive precedents, for instance, has not been officially adopted. The way the ECJ decides cases is specific and familiar to none of the lawyers trained in one of the different European legal systems. And it is quite distant from the common law tradition. As Lord Bingham pointed out early on (and this remains true, in spite of the evolution of the European legal system, under UK influence), when English courts are faced with a problem of interpretation of EC law, 'they must follow the European pattern', which is not the traditional way for English courts.[33] Those courts, he adds, quoting the words of the European Court in the Costa v. ENEL case,[34] must limit themselves to deducing from 'the wording and the spirit of the treaty the meaning of the Community rules ...'. As a matter of fact, the European method used by the ECJ, based on deduction of solutions from general rules or principles, is closer to the civil law model than to the common law tradition, when considered by an English judge.

Two of the major problems that have been ignored in the process of combining sources by the ECJ and the French *Cour de Cassation* must be underlined: the issue of the legal value of the different sources, for one, and the lack of consideration for the particular scope of application of each norm or system of norms, for the second. Ignoring the legal force (or absence of legal force) of norms and their respective scope of application may be called benign neglect when those norms are soft references, 'persuasive' and not 'binding', under the common law dichotomy. There is no major issue, when those references only contribute to strengthening a solution. But when the combination of sources becomes an instrument to change the law, the basis for a major transformation of the law, the magic of accumulation, is not sufficient.

1) 'Creative' combination: legal force given to soft law norms

The comparative approach followed by the Court of Justice in the *Laval and Viking* cases is neither a comprehensive analysis of all sources available nor a selection based on the particular legal value of the authorities invoked in those cases. Rather, important differences between the various international texts quoted, in terms of their legal force (the ILO convention is binding on

33. Bulmer v Bollinger [1974] 2 All ER 1226.
34. Case 6/64, 15 July 1964.

signatory states, whereas the Community and EU charters were not), are ignored.

As far as the status of the international documents used in the cases is concerned, the problem of the approach followed by the ECJ is that it is listing a series of references, *pêle-mêle*, without expressing the exact role these references play in the identification of a fundamental right for the EU. The combination of sources ignores the respective legal force of each instrument.

Yet, it is difficult to believe that no distinction can or should be drawn between non-binding norms and norms that states have agreed to abide by. In this respect, the example of the Charter of Fundamental Rights of the EU is enlightening. In all cases considered, the fact that it does not yet have legal force seemed to make no difference. But when the question arose in the course of adopting the Treaty of Lisbon, the binding effect of the Charter led to legal contortions, with some Member States requiring exemption from all legal effect, on their territory, of that instrument, or at least, from some of its provisions concerning social rights.[35]

As we already suggested, the most trivial way to look at the issue is to consider that the combination of references only has a persuasive function in the reasoning of European courts. As other courts do, even at a domestic level,[36] European courts accumulate references to ensure legitimacy based on convergence of the developments in the field. Their interpretation would only go so far as to ensure that European law falls in line with the development of the law in other systems.

However, in the *Laval and Viking* cases, the recognition of the right to take collective action, by a series of instruments of international law and non-binding European Union charters of rights, has this improbable consequence: it is strong enough to justify the birth of a new right in the Community legal order. To be sure, one can contend that, in such cases, the accumulation of references is only meant to show that the right is present 'in the law', awaiting its judicial consecration in the legal system of the European Union. How-

35. See the protocol to the Lisbon Treaty: 'On the application of the Charter of Fundamental Rights of the European Union to Poland and to the United Kingdom', Treaty of Lisbon amending the Treaty on European Union and the Treaty establishing the European Community, signed at Lisbon, 13 December 2007, OJ 2007 C306/1.
36. See for instance: in the House of Lords in England, *A (FC) and others (Appellants) v Secretary of State for the Home Department (Respondent)* [2004] UKHL 56 ('the Belmarsh case'); in Canada, *Health Services and Support – Facilities Subsector Bargaining Association v British Columbia* 2007 SCC 27 ('the Health Services and Support case'); in the Cour de Cassation in France, Cass soc 2 octobre 2001, Bull civ V, no 291 ('the Nikon France case').

ever, it cannot be denied that the combination of non-binding norms is the 'method' used to create hard law norms.

In the process, the distinction between soft law and hard law, or, in other words, between persuasive and binding references, becomes fuzzy, giving more power than expected to some of the recent developments of international and European law. As a matter of fact, it seems there is no such thing as a distinction between soft and hard law in the case law of European courts. Case law is built out of soft and hard instruments, provided they converge to show a direction. It must be recalled that the conflated treatment applies, in the cases, to the identification of new fundamental rights or the development of new interpretations of recognized fundamental rights, which is very similar. This, indeed, is good news for international standards, faced with the eternal critique that 'they are toothless'.[37] It is nonetheless quite disrupting: states can no longer be shielded from international or European standards by revoking international conventions or refusing to ratify them. More importantly, one may fear that the development of the law, through this anarchic use of sources, falls totally out of control.

2) A vanishing trick: extension through combination

The globalized legal world, where a network of legal sources tends to develop, is more complex than the decisions considered suggest. As far as international and European law is concerned, the different systems that coexist are more or less general; they do not necessarily cover the same situations; they do not necessarily apply to all cases, in which the rights they protect are violated. Norms developed in each particular system may not have the same field of application.

This difference is particularly obvious, when comparing EU law and the ECHR. The ECHR applies whenever the rights it mentions are violated, on the territory of a state, which is bound by the convention.

Quite differently, the protection of fundamental rights by EU law only applies within the limit of powers granted to the Union by Member States. The protection of fundamental rights is limited by the restricted jurisdiction of EU law. At the moment, this means that the protection of fundamental rights is only available when it is possible to show that the situation concerned lies within the scope of EU law, for another reason than its impact on a fundamental right that the EU is supposed to protect.

37. On this issue, see J. Atleson, L. Compa *et al*, *International Labor Law, Cases and Materials on Workers' rights in the Global Economy* (Eagan MN, Thomson West, 2007) pp. 88-9.

This condition applies, in particular, to the Charter of Fundamental Rights. As expressed in the Charter itself, this instrument does not grant new powers to the EU. Even if Article 53 states that nothing in the Charter shall be interpreted as restricting or adversely affecting human rights and fundamental freedoms as recognized by Union law and international law and by international agreements to which the Union, the Community or all the Member States are party, including the European Convention for the Protection of Human Rights and Fundamental Freedoms, and by the Member States' constitutions, this is only true, according to this article, in the respective fields of application of the different instruments.

This remains unchanged under the Lisbon treaty: in giving legal force to the Charter, the new treaty did not get rid of this strong limitation. In our opinion, this question of the limit of powers of the Union, a typical issue of federalism, will gain more importance than ever in the near future, in relation with the application of the Charter of Fundamental Rights. Unless, of course, courts decide to ignore the crucial issues arising from the restrictive scope of application of EU law, as the French *Cour de Cassation* did in the case decided last April.

This raises serious concerns: French judges seem to ignore the fundamental question of the applicability of legal norms. They also seem to forget the crucial issue of the limitation of powers of the EU. This is the outcome of a combination of sources which lacks the necessary precautions. Because it refers to so many different norms, and focuses on their convergence more than on anything else, the Courts neglects the possible variation of their scope of application. This has become a secondary question, all the more so as it is not the kind of question that European courts had to deal with in the cases from which the French court draws its inspiration.

Conclusion

As the cases decided by the two European courts show, combining sources is an efficient means for courts to ensure the development of law, in such domains as the protection of fundamental rights. The network of sources emanating from different legal systems is not only *available* to courts: to a certain extent, courts can no longer avoid consideration of mixed sources when deciding cases, they have to take them into account, namely because claimants bring them forward in more and more cases. But in doing so, they must ensure that they do not abuse their powers as courts. In the civil law tradition, or in systems such as EU law, on which that tradition continues to have a great influence, the reference by courts to a proper legal basis used to be particularly crucial, as it was hardly compensated by a generous display of persuasive arguments justifying the solution, as in other legal traditions. If the combination of sources is to become a more common practice, the ECJ, and other courts, especially those belonging to the civil law tradition, that are tempted to adopt the same stance must not only oblige themselves to justify the selection of each element of the judicial mix of sources; they have to come up with a genuine comparative method to assess convergence of the selected references. Moreover, the diversity of the sources cited, considering their legal value or particular scope of application, cannot simply be ignored. A European method of combining legal sources is needed, taking into account these different aspects and issues of the combination. Courts may need support to work it out.

Judicial Method of English Courts And Tribunals in EU Law Cases: A Case Study in Employment Law

Tamara Hervey and Natalie Sheldon[*]

1. Introduction

Hervey's collaborative work with Cryer, Sokhi-Bulley and Bohm on research methodologies in EU and international law[1] considered the different methodologies, in the sense of different systems of methods, or theoretical approaches, that are adopted in the study of EU law in the English language literature. That work found a wide range of different approaches, including positivism and natural law; 'modern' approaches, such as liberalism, constitutionalism, cosmopolitanism and 'new governance'; 'critical approaches', such as (neo) Marxism, feminism, queer theory and post-colonialism; and a range of interdisciplinary approaches (such as law and political science, law and economics, law and sociology, law and history, law and geography), all of which are being employed in the English language scholarly literature on EU law.

In the brief for this chapter, we were asked to consider a range of questions, with respect to the interactions between EU law and English law. Some of these questions are about scholarly writing on EU law in the English context. However, given that the above-mentioned project has already explored such questions in depth, for this chapter, we chose to focus on the questions

* We are grateful for the advice of Employment Judge Rostant, Sheffield Employment Tribunal, and for the support of the Sheffield University summer intern research experience scheme 2009-10. We would also like to thank Sevérine Saintier and Mark Taylor of the School of Law, University of Sheffield, and the participants in the conference *European Legal Method*, Copenhagen Business School, 19 November 2010. All errors remain our responsibility.

1. R Cryer, T Hervey, B Sokhi-Bulley, with A Bohm, *Research Methodologies in EU and International Law* (Oxford, Hart, 2011 forthcoming).

that consider judicial method with respect to EU law in the English courts. These questions include:

1. What are the main characteristics of the national legal method (and theory)? Which sources of law are predominant? Are there predominant theories of interpretation?
2. What has characterized the EU legal method (and theory) in the national legal system over time? Have there been any observable changes in national case law?
3. Can you point to anything that suggests the development of a new legal method and/or theory in your legal system that applies to issues of EU law or does the way issues of EU law are dealt with largely follow traditional national methods and/or theories with some special rules that apply solely to EU law? Or in other words: do EU and national legal method (and theory) live in individual universes or are they interlinked?
4. Would you say that the courts that you study apply a teleological method of interpretation?

In terms of the typology of approaches to the study of EU law established in the Cryer, Hervey, Sokhi-Bulley and Bohm study, the questions for this chapter are grounded in what is essentially a positivist and constitutionalist frame or methodology.[2] The questions are based in the assumption that the practice of courts is an interesting and an appropriate topic for legal scholarship. There is an assumption that courts are bound by the will of the legislature, and that national 'theories of interpretation' of such legislature have been developed that constrain courts (as is proper within the separation of powers doctrine in a constitutional democracy). Interpreting these questions in the context of a common law system, as we do in this chapter, implies that judicial reasoning constitutes an important source of law. The questions also posit a separation between the EU legal system and the English legal system, as be-

2. We agree with Dennis Patterson, in this collection, that 'methodology matters', and with Rob van Gestel and Hans Micklitz, in this collection, that it is important for legal scholarship to question the preconceptions upon which our choice of legal research questions is based, to justify choice of topic and research design, hence the explicit discussion here and in the section immediately below.

ing distinct systemic entities, rather than interacting parts of a single multi-level system.[3]

2. Method

To focus our study on the judicial method of interpretation of EU law in English courts and tribunals, and in particular to be able to make meaningful contributions to the questions above, especially questions 2, 4 and 5, we chose to select one substantive area of law for this chapter. As Bengoetxea observes,[4] it is not possible to answer such questions outside of a jurisdictional and substantive context. Indeed, a more complete understanding of the questions that we study in this chapter would require attention to social and political contexts, such as, for instance, the rise of Thatcherism and its effects on labour relationships during the 1980s and beyond. The selection of a substantive area followed a review of English textbooks[5] on EU law, to determine which

3. Neil Walker notes the difficulties of compartmentalizing different legal orders in the context of a proliferation of transnational regulation, see N Walker, 'Beyond boundary disputes and basic grids: Mapping the global disorder of normative orders' (2008) 6(3&4) *I.CON Symposium* 373-396. Examples of literature that explores or problematises the assumption that international law, EU law and national law are separate systems include P Cardwell, D French and N White, '*Yassin Abdullah Kadi and Al Barakaat International Foundation v Council and Commission (C-402/05 and C-415/05)* Case Comment' (2009) 58 *ICLQ* 229-240; N White, 'The Ties That Bind – the EU, the UN and international law' (2006) XXXVII *Netherlands Yearbook of International Law*, 57-108; M Ličková, 'European Exceptionalism in International Law' (2008) 19 *European Journal of International Law* 463-490. See the discussion in Cryer et al, eds., chapter 3.
4. Joxerramon Bengoetxea, 'European Legal Method from a Spanish perspective', paper presented at the conference *European Legal Method*, 19 November 2010, Copenhagen Business School.
5. It was necessary to look at early books as this was where the main principles of direct effect, indirect effect and supremacy emerged. Although the books focus on the key points of what the cases conclude and how this would affect national courts, in researching this chapter, we focused more on which area of law was discussed. J Steiner, *Textbook on EEC Law* (London; Blackstone Press 1988), J Steiner, *Textbook on EC Law* (4th ed. Blackstone Press, London 1994), J Steiner, *Textbook on EC Law* (5th ed. Blackstone Press, London 1996) J Shaw, *European Community Law*, 2nd ed. (Macmillan; London 1996), P Craig and G De Búrca, *EC Law Text Cases and Materials* (Oxford; Clarendon Press 1995), P Craig and G De Búrca, *EC Law Text Cases and Materials* (2nd ed. Oxford; Clarendon Press 1998) T.C. Hartley, *The Foundations of European Community Law*, (Clarendon Press, Oxford 1981); T.C. Hartley,

English cases were referred to as important examples of the ways EU law has been received in English law from the 1970s[6] to the present day. We noted that many of the English cases concerning the most contentious doctrines of EU law – supremacy, direct effect, indirect effect[7] – are in the field of employment law.[8] We therefore focused our study on employment law.

Employment law is also an appropriate case study for this chapter because there is a significant body of national law in the field that pre-dates the UK's membership of the European Union.[9] In this respect, employment law, like consumer law, can be contrasted with an area such as 'commercial agency

The Foundations of European Community Law, (2nd ed. Clarendon Press, Oxford 1988); T.C. Hartley, *The Foundations of European Community Law*, (3rd ed. Clarendon Press, Oxford 1994); T.C. Hartley, *The Foundations of European Community Law*, (4th ed. Oxford University Press, Oxford 1998); S Weatherill, *Cases and Materials on EC Law* (2nd ed. Blackstone Press, London 1994); S Weatherill, *Cases and Materials on EC Law* (3rd ed. Blackstone Press, London 1996).

6. The UK became a Member State of the European Union in 1973.
7. *Duke* v *GEC Reliance Ltd* [1988] AC 618; *Finnegan* v *Clowney Youth Training Programme Ltd* [1990] 2 AC 407; *Felixstowe Dock & Railway Co* v *British Transport Docks Board* [1976] 2 CMLR 655; *Macarthys* v *Smith*[1979] 1 WLR 1189; Case 152/84 *Marshall* v *Southampton and South-West Hampshire Area Health Authority (Teaching)* [1986] ECR 723; Case C-144/04 *Mangold* v *Rüdiger Helm* [2005] ECR I-9981; Case C-555/07 *Kücükdeveci* v *Swedex GmbH & Co* 19 Jan 2010, nyr in ECR[2010] 2 CMLR 33.
8. C Barnard, *EC Employment Law* (3rd ed. Oxford University Press, Oxford, 2006). Directive 75/117/EEC OJ [1975] L45/ 19 on equal pay for men and women workers. Directive 76/ 207/ EEC OJ [1976] L39/40 on equal treatment with regard to access to employment, vocational training, promotion and working conditions. Directive 79/7/EEC OJ [1979] L6/24 on the progressive implementation of equal treatment with regard to statutory social security schemes. Directive 86/378/EEC OK [1986] L225/40 on the implementation of equal treatment in occupational schemes of social security. Directive 86/613/EEC OJ [1997] L359/56 for equal treatment for men and women carrying out a self-employed activity, including agriculture. Directive 92/85/EC OJ [1992] L245/23 improving the health and safety of workers who are pregnant or have recently given birth. Directive 96/34/EC OJ [1996] L145/4 on reconciling family and working life. Directive 79/ 7 OJ [1979] L6/1 on the progressive implementation of the principle of equal treatment for men and women in matters of social security.
9. In this respect, our choice of focus is justifiable in similar ways to Martijn Hesselink's choice of contract law, see his discussion of German private law before and after EU membership, in this collection.

law', which was effectively 'created' in English law by a Directive in 1986.[10] We suspect (though further research would be necessary to verify this) that, in such areas, English courts simply adopt the 'European legal method' without any apparent difficulty, in contrast to the slow road to reaching the current approach to interpretation (the 'EU compliance mischief rule') that we outline here in the case of employment law.

We also note here that the selection of EU employment law during this time frame as a case study limits the analysis and conclusions in this chapter to areas of EU law where the 'classic Community method'[11] is used. Further research would be necessary to determine the extent to which our conclusions apply to the reception in English law of measures of EU law that have been brought into effect through other mechanisms, such as, for instance, the procedure in Article 155 TFEU[12] or the procedure by which the Common Frame of Reference in European contract law[13] is being developed.

Our selection of employment law as an appropriate case study for this chapter is also confirmed in the literature. In a 1998 edited collection of es-

10. Council Directive 86/653/EEC of 18 December 1986 on the coordination of the laws of the Member States relating to self-employed commercial agents OJ 1986 L 382/17. See S Saintier and J Scholes, *Commercial Agents and the Law* (London: LLP, 2005).
11. The procedure according to which EU legislation is adopted, following the procedure now found in Article 294 TFEU, see J Scott and D M Trubek, 'Mind the Gap: Law and New Approaches to Governance in the European Union' 8 ELJ (2002) 1-18.
12. According to which management and labour may conclude agreements at EU level, and these may be implemented by procedures and practices specific to management and labour.
13. C von Bar and E Clive, *Principles, Definitions and Model Rules of European Private Law, Draft Common Frame of Reference* (Oxford: OUP, 2010) (6 vols). The Draft Common Frame of Reference essentially comprises a research project in comparative law, initiated by work of the European Commission in the early 2000s (e.g., European Commission *Communication on European Contract Law* COM(2001) 398; European Commission, *A more coherent European contract law: an action plan*; COM(2003) 68), and drawing on academic research dating back to the 1990s (e.g., O Lando and H Beale, eds, *Principles of European Contract Law Parts I and II* (Deventer: Kluwer Law International, 1999); C von Bar et al, *Principles, Definitions, and Model Rules of European Private Law: Draft Common Frame of Reference Outline Edition* (Munich: Sellier, 2009). See UK House of Lords European Union Committee, 12th Report 2008-09, *European Contract Law: The Draft Common Frame of Reference* (London: HMSO, 2009) http://www.publications.parliament.uk/pa/ld200809/ ldselect/ ldeucom/ 95/95.pdf. This work is now to be taken forward by the 'Expert Group on a Common Frame of Reference in the area of European contract law', see Commission Decision 2010/233/EU of 26 April 2010 setting up the Expert Group on a Common Frame of Reference in the area of European contract law OJ 2010 L 105/109.

says on *European Community Law in the English Courts*, Lord Justice Mummery, the president of the Employment Appeal Tribunal from 1993-1996, observed that:

> 'A significant number of employment cases illustrate ... 'the intricate pervasiveness of the penetration of European Community Law into the national systems'. Indeed, the impact of Community Law on employment cases in English Courts has been greater than on any other kind of case.'[14]

The 'legal concepts, methods and reasoning'[15] of English courts have been affected greatly by EU Law, and the employment law field shows that effect as well as any other area of law, or perhaps in some respects, even more so.

To focus our analysis further, we drew up a list of employment law cases, mainly those cited in English language textbooks, involving points of EU law.[16] The list formed the broad context for our analysis. From the list, we se-

14. Lord Justice Mummery 'The Community Law Impact in Employment Cases' in M Andenas and F Jacobs, *European Community Law in the English Courts* (Oxford Clarendon Press, 1998) 192.
15. Lord Justice Mummery (n 7) 206.
16. *Amies* v *Inner London Education* Authority [1977] 2 All ER 100; *Snoxell* v *Vauxhall Motors Ltd* [1977] IRLR. 123; *Macarthys Ltd* v *Smith*[1978] 1 WLR 849. 746; *Shields* v *E Coomes (Holdings) Ltd* [1978] 1 WLR. 1408; *Roberts* v *Cleveland AHA* [1978] ICR 370; *Worringham* v *Lloyds Bank Ltd (No.1)* [1980] 1 CMLR 293; *O'Brien* v *Sim-Chem Ltd* [1980] ICR 429; *Jenkins* v *Kingsgate (Clothing Productions) Ltd* [1980] 1 CMLR 81; *Burton v British Railways Board*[1981] 3 CMLR 100; *System Floors Ltd v Daniel* [1982] ICR 54; *Perera* v *Civil Service Commission (No 2)* [1983] ICR 428; *Roberts* v *Tate & Lyle Industries* [1983] ICR 521; *Garland v British Rail Engineering* [1983] 2 AC 751; *Showboat Entertainment Centre Ltd* v *Owens* [1984] 1 WLR 384; *Jeetle* v *Elster* [1985] ICR 389; *Marshall* v *Southampton & South West Hampshire Area Authority(no 2)* [1988] 3 CMLR 389; *Duke* v *Reliance Systems* [1988] AC 618; *Pickstone* v *Freemans plc* [1989] AC 66; *Litster* v *Forth Dry Dock & Engineering Co Ltd* [1990] 1 AC 546; *Finnegan* v *Clowney Youth Training Programme Ltd* [1990] 2 AC 407*; Mckechnie v Ubm Building Supplies (Southern) Ltd* [1991] 2 CMLR 668; *Enderby* v *Frenchay HA (No.1)* [1992] IRLR 15; *Wadman* v *Carpenter Farrer Partnership* [1993] 3 CMLR 93; *Setiya* v *East Yorkshire Health Authority*[1995] ICR 799; *Webb* v *EMO Air Cargo (UK) Ltd* [1995] 1 WLR 1454; *Stewart* v *Cleveland Guest (Engineering) Ltd* [1996] ICR 535; *Diocese of Hallam Trustee* v *Connaughton*[1996] 3 CMLR 93; *British Telecommunications* v *Williams* [1997] IRLR 668; *Bossa* v *Nordstress Ltd*[1998] 2 CMLR 175; *Sirdar* v *Army Board and Another* [2000] IRLR 47; *R* v *Sec state for employment* [1995] 1 AC 1; *Barry* v *Midland Bank Plc*[1999] 1 WLR 1465; *Coote* v *Granada Hospitality Limited* [1999] 3 CMLR 334; *Carmichael and another* v *National*

lected some 10 cases for in-depth analysis in the chapter. In order to consider question 2 above, about changes over time in judicial approaches to EU law, we selected 2-3 key cases from each of the decades, 1970s, 80s, 90s and 2000s. Selection was on the basis of considering how the national judges reasoned in the case; what was their approach; and what, if any, difference did the relevant EU law make to the judge's approach? Discussion of a few cases allowed for depth of analysis in terms of the courts' reasoning in their approaches to EU law, as indicated by questions 3, 4 and 5 above. Many of these key cases were appealed, so we were able to include analysis of courts at different levels in the appellate hierarchy.[17]

Before we turn to the analysis of the English employment case law over time, we need to consider question 1. We therefore set out the contextual background here, explaining, to readers from other Member States, the structure of the employment law jurisdiction in England; the constitutional arrangements for reception of EU law into English law; and English law on judicial methods of interpretation of legislation.

3. Contexts

English Courts and Tribunals Hearing Employment Law Cases

English employment law disputes are heard at first instance by Employment Tribunals.[18] These tribunals were originally created by statute in 1964,[19] and

Power[1999] 1 WLR 2042; *Nagarajan* v *London Regional Transport* [2000] 1 AC 501; *Rhys-Harper* v *Relaxion Group Plc* [2003] UKHL 33; *Johnson* v *Unisys* [2003] 1 AC 518; *Rutherford and Bentley* v *Secretary of State for Trade and Industry (no2)* [2004] EWCA Civ 1186; *Percy* v *Church of Scotland Board of National Mission*[2005] UKHL 73; *Alabaster* v *Woolwich Plc* [2005] 2 CMLR 19; *New Southern Railway Ltd* v *Quinn*[2006] ICR 761; *Azmi* v *Kirklees MBC*[2007] ICR 1154; *Paterson* v *Commissioner of Police of the Metropolis* [2007] ICR 1522; *Sharma and others* v *Manchester City Council* [2008] ICR 623; *Eweida* v *British Airways Plc*[2009] ICR 303; *EBR Attridge Law LLP (formerly Attridge Law)* v *Coleman* [2010] 1 CMLR 28; *Grainger plc* v *Nicholson*[2010] 2 All ER 253; *X* v *Mid Sussex Citizens Advice Bureau* [2010] 1 CMLR 27*; British Airways* v *Williams & Others* [2010] UKSC 16. *O'Brien* v *Ministry of Justice (Formerly Department for Constitutional Affairs)* [2010] UKSC 34.

17. It has not proved possible to have access to decisions of the Industrial Tribunals in early cases, although sometimes their reasoning is repeated verbatim in the appellate court's decision.
18. Known as 'Industrial Tribunals' until 1998. Under the Employment Rights (Dispute Resolution Act) 1998, their name was changed to Employment Tribunals from 1st

since 1971 have dealt with a growing number of employer/employee disputes. Their jurisdiction is entirely statute based. It began with unfair dismissal and has expanded to encompass over 70 different types of claim.[20] There was an aspiration to encourage employment-related complaints to be

August 1998. For the sake of clarity, we refer only to 'Employment Tribunals' throughout this chapter.

19. Industrial Training Act 1964. They were originally created to hear appeals against decisions on the training levies imposed on employers and were essentially an administrative, rather than an *inter partes*, tribunal.
20. The official government website http://www.employmenttribunals. gov.uk/Forms Guidance/jurisdiction List.htm (accessed 21 October 2010) lists some 72 descriptors of jurisdiction. The website lists the sources of this jurisdiction as the Colleges of Education (Compensation) Regulations 1975; Control of Major Accident Hazards Regulations 1999; Deregulation and Contracting Out Act 1994; Disability Discrimination Act 1995; Disability Rights Commission Act 1999; Employment Equality (Age) Regulations 2006; Employment Equality (Religion or Belief) Regulations 2003; Employment Equality (Sexual Orientation) Regulations 2003; Equal Pay Act 1970; Employment Agencies Act 1973; Employment Rights Act 1996; Employment Relations Act 1999; Employment (Industrial) Tribunals Act 1996; Equal Pay Act 1970; Fixed Term Employees (Prevention of Less Favourable Treatment) Regulations 2002; Flexible Working (Procedural Requirements) Regulations 2002; Flexible Working (Eligibility, Complaints and Remedies) Regulations 2002; Health and Safety (Consultation with Employees) Regulations 1996; Health and Safety at Work Act 1974; Industrial Training Levy Orders; Maternity and Parental Leave Regulations 1999; Maternity and Parental Leave (Amendment) Regulations 2002; Merchant Shipping (Working Time: Inland Waterways) Regulations 2004; National Minimum Wage Act 1998; Notification of Existing Substances (Enforcement) Regulations 1994; Paternity and Adoption Leave Regulations 2002; Public Interest Disclosure Act 1998; Part Time Worker (Prevention of Less Favourable Treatment) Regulations 2000; Part Time Worker (Prevention of Less Favourable Treatment) Regulations 2000; Pension Schemes Act 1993; Race Relations Act 1976; Road Transport (Working Time) Regulations 2005; Sex Discrimination Act 1975; Safety Representatives and Safety Committees Regulations 1977; Social Security Pensions Act 1975; Sunday Trading Act 194; Tax Credits Act 2002; Trade Union and Labour Relations (Consolidation) Act 1992; Transfer of Undertakings (Protection of Employment) Regulations 1981; Transnational Information and Consultation Regulations 2010; Trade Union Reform and Employment Rights Act 1993; Working Time Regulations 1998. The Equality Act 2010, brings disability, sex, race and other grounds of discrimination within one piece of legislation, has replaced the Equal Pay Act 1970; the Sex Discrimination Act 1975; the Race Relations Act 1976; the Disability Discrimination Act 1995; the Employment Equality (Religion or Belief) Regulations 2003; the Employment Equality (Sexual Orientation) Regulations 2003; the Employment Equality (Age) Regulations 2006 and the Equality Act (Sexual Orientation) Regulations 2007.

brought in a less formal environment than the ordinary courts.[21] Parties may represent themselves before Employment Tribunals – they need not be represented by a legally qualified advocate (although many parties choose to be so). Employment Tribunals are comprised of an Employment Judge sitting with two lay, 'non-legal members' (who nominally represent the views of labour and management). Employment Tribunals give fully reasoned decisions on request from the parties.

Appeal from the Employment Tribunal lies on a point of law[22] to the Employment Appeal Tribunal and from there to the Court of Appeal and Supreme Court.[23] The Employment Appeal Tribunal (EAT) is also a creature of statute.[24] In English law, lower courts are bound (under the English doctrine of precedent) by the reasons for the decisions given (the *rationes decidendi*) or the legal principles developed in decisions of courts above them in the appellate hierarchy. English appellate courts and tribunals are also bound by their own previous decisions.[25] These principles of English law form an important context for the reception of EU law into English law, and the methods of interpretation of EU law employed by English courts.

21. E Smith and G Thomas, *Smith and Wood's Employment Law*, (9th ed. OUP, Oxford 2008).
22. Although, in general, appeals are allowed on points of law, rather than of fact, the Court of Appeal has held in *Grant* v *Bragg* [2009] EWCA Civ 1228 that one can lodge an appeal based on facts if the judge missed or misinterpreted facts to come to a conclusion that was perverse. Lord Neuberger found that, during the trial, several emails had been ignored which were therefore not given weight in the judge's ruling and an appeal was allowed.
23. Formerly the House of Lords. The Supreme Court was established by Part 3 of the Constitutional Reform Act 2005 and started work on 1 October 2009.
24. The Employment Appeal Tribunal was created in 1975 under the Employment Protection Act 1975, s 87 as a successor to the National Industrial Relations Court which had been abolished in 1974. Before the EAT, cases are heard either by a judge sitting alone, or a judge and two lay members. Three judges are permanently appointed to the EAT (at the present time The Honourable Mr Justice Underhill (President); His Honour Judge Peter Clark; His Honour Judge McMullen QC) and judges from the English High Court, or circuit judges, sit in the EAT for a month or so at a time.
25. The decisions of the Supreme Court (formerly House of Lords) bind all lower courts. There has been a long debate as to whether the decisions of the Supreme Court should bind a future Supreme Court. For some 100 years, the Law Lords considered themselves so bound. This was changed by the Practice Statement on Judicial Precedent [1966] 1 W.L.R. 1234 where it was said that though the doctrine of being bound had many commendable points; 'too rigid adherence to precedent may lead to injustice in a particular case and also unduly restrict the proper development of the law'.

English employment law is almost entirely[26] found in statutory form. EU employment law is implemented in England by statute (primary legislation),[27] or by regulations (secondary legislation) that are adopted on the basis of delegated power given to the minister by a statute.[28] The employment law cases that we discuss in this chapter therefore all involve judicial interpretation of legislation. The English judicial methods of statutory interpretation therefore also form an important part of the context for our discussion here.

English law on statutory interpretation

The constitutional context for the English law on statutory interpretation is the doctrine of Parliamentary sovereignty, which traditionally means that Parliament is empowered to do anything save bind itself for the future.[29] This principle of English constitutional law is often discussed more in terms of exceptions to the rule,[30] but nonetheless remains an important guiding principle in terms of the separation of powers, as it plays out in practice in England. Although the will of Parliament is expressed through legislation, the language in such statutes (including those that implement EU law) may be ambiguous. The role of the judiciary is thus to decipher how the words of the statute

26. Despite the increase over the past years in statute law, the common law still has considerable importance in the field of employment law. As in other areas of law, the common law both forms the context for interpretation of statutes and also, in the absence of statute, e.g. in the area of wrongful dismissal, states the law. Furthermore employment draws on a number on other areas of law, for example, the common law of contract and tort.
27. See, for example, Sex Discrimination Act 1975; Equal Pay Act 1970; Disability Discrimination Act 1995; Employment Rights Act 1996.
28. See, for example, Equal Pay (Amendment) Regulations 1983; Employment Protection (Part-time Employees) Regulation 1995; Transfer of Undertaking (Protection of Employment) Regulations (TUPE) 1981.
29. P Craig and G de Búrca, *EU Law; Text Cases and Materials* (4th ed. OUP, Oxford 2007) 365.
30. For instance, the Human Rights Act 1998 is said to have limited Parliamentary Sovereignty in numerous ways, most notably that any future Parliament remains bound by it. Even if it is theoretically possible for Parliament to repeal or amend the Act, it can definitely be said that Parliament cannot escape the pressure put upon it by international and domestic public opinion on human rights. A second example is the Statute of Westminster 1931 which states that an outgoing Parliament does not possess the power to bind a successive Parliament. The other main exception to the rule is, of course, EU law, see, for instance, P Craig, 'United Kingdom Sovereignty after *Factortame*' 11 Yearbook of European Law (1991) 221; P Craig, 'Britain in the European Union' in J Jowell and D Oliver, eds, *The Changing Constitution* (6th ed. OUP, Oxford, 2007), chapter 4.

should be interpreted. The interpretation of a particular phrase or word often has a significant bearing on the final outcome of a case, and, particularly where appellate courts are concerned, future cases in the same area. How does the English judiciary interpret legislation? What types of rules do they follow in this process?

Although English judges rarely, if ever, themselves explicitly volunteer the information that they are now applying a certain rule of interpretation,[31] in the literature discussing cases from the last five centuries of English law, emphasis is placed on four main 'rules'[32] that assist judges in decision making. These 'classical' rules of interpretation or 'canons of construction' are said to be as follows:

The Literal Rule: The court looks to the exact meaning of the words. The correct interpretation is the plain, literal reading of the words that Parliament chose to employ.

The Golden Rule: The court looks at the whole of the statute, placing the word or section in its context, and gives the words their ordinary meaning, *unless* this produces absurdity. If the conclusion seems absurd, then the court must give the words a meaning more in keeping with the context of the whole statute.

The Purposive Rule: The court focuses on what Parliament may have intended by the words. This is done through examining the general purpose of the section and then looking at it in context. Courts may also look at the record of Parliamentary debate.[33]

The Mischief Rule: The court examines previous common law and the history of the statute, to find what legal deficiency or 'mischief' Parliament sought to remedy when it enacted the statute.

31. S Hanson, *Legal Method* (London, Cavendish Publishing Limited, 1999) 99.
32. Michael Zander comments that the words rules is a 'misnomer'. They are not rules in the ordinary sense in that they point to different solutions to the same problem. Further, one does not have to strictly apply one rule in a given situation. In M Zander, *Law- Making Process*, (6th ed. Cambridge, Cambridge University Press, 2004) 183.
33. *Pepper* v *Hart* [1993] AC 593, heard by seven Law Lords, the House of Lords, the Lord Chancellor dissenting, held that judges could consult Hansard, which is the official record of UK Parliamentary proceedings.

Interpretation however is more a question of judicial style than the use of interpretational rules.[34] In this sense, the judiciary does not set out to use a specific rule, yet as they are interpreting statutes, patterns of their judicial reasoning can be discerned through academic literature,[35] as the following discussion demonstrates.

The literal rule is concerned with the linguistics of the text, rather than considering the purpose of the Act. The judges simply apply what is given to them in the legislation. Lord Esher put the proposition succinctly in 1892:

> 'If the words of an Act are clear you must follow them, even though they lead to a manifest absurdity. The court has nothing to do with the question whether the legislature has committed an absurdity.'[36]

The literal rule gives the greatest respect to Parliamentary sovereignty and the separation of powers, and protects the judiciary from allegations that they are inappropriately 'making the law'. As Lord Diplock commented in *Duport Steel* v *Sirs*:

> 'Where the meaning of the words is plain and unambiguous it is not for the judges to invent fancied ambiguities as an excuse for failing to give effect to its plain meaning'.[37]

However the literal rule can be problematic in that this type of interpretation can seem unfair and causes hardship in some cases.[38] Moreover, the literal rule prevents the courts from considering the aim of Parliament in enacting the statute at issue. The literature often cites *R* v *Harris*[39] as an illustration of

34. J Holland and J Webb, *Learning Legal Rules* (6th ed. Oxford, Oxford University Press, 2008) 230.
35. Sir Carleton Allen summarised 'we are driven in the end to the unsatisfying conclusion that the whole matter ultimately turns on the impalpable and indefinable elements of judicial spirit or attitude.' In C.K. Allen, *Law in the Making* (7th ed., Oxford, Clarendon Press, 1964) 526, 529.
36. *R* v *Judge of the City of London Court* [1892] 1 QB 273 at 290. In M Zander, *The Law- Making Process* (6th ed., Cambridge, Cambridge University Press, 2004).
37. [1980] 1 WLR 142; [1980] 1 All ER 529, 541.
38. In A Gillespie, *The English Legal System* (Oxford University Press, Oxford, 2007), citing the case of *R* v *Human Fertilisation and Embryology Authority, ex p Blood* [1997] 2 WLR 807.
39. (1836) 7 C &P 466.

how the literal rule can result in an illogical decision.[40] The statute in question made it an offence to 'stab, cut or wound' another person. Harris had bitten off her friend's nose in a fight. The words in the statute indicated the use of a weapon, meaning Harris was not guilty under the statute. *Fisher* v *Bell*[41] illustrates how the literal rule can lead to not only absurd, but also potentially dangerous results. A shopkeeper displayed flick-knives in his shop window, yet the Restriction of Offensive Weapons Act 1959 made it an offence to offer such a knife for sale. The shopkeeper argued that that 'offer for sale' had a technical meaning and that the customer makes an offer by taking the product to the shopkeeper. The knife being in the window therefore was not an 'offer', merely an 'invitation to treat', and hence the shop keeper had not committed an offence.[42]

The golden (and purposive) rules are mainly described as accessory to the literal rule; they are seen as being used where the literal rule fails to give the 'right' result. Both the golden and the purposive rule suggest that the court should interpret the word or phrase at issue in the context of the statute. A good example of the golden rule in action is *R* v *Allen*.[43] Allen, who was already married, married Harriet. The statute in question provided 'whosoever being married shall marry any other person during the lifetime of his spouse shall commit bigamy'. In this case, Harriet and Allen were closely related and therefore the apparently bigamous marriage was void. Allen argued that bigamy could not be committed if the second marriage was void. In this case, the court took a purposive approach to interpretation, reading the words in the section 'shall marry' as meaning 'shall go through a marriage ceremony with', taking into account (as per the 'golden rule') the absurdity of the position had they not done so.

Similarly in *Re Sigsworth*,[44] a case of murder and inheritance, the literal rule was specifically avoided. Here, the mother had made a will and under

40. See also *R* v *Munks* [1964] 1 QB 304; [1963] 3 All ER 757, *Fisher* v *Bell* [1961] 1 QB 394; [1960] 3 All ER 731. In G Slapper and D Kelly, T*he English Legal System* (10th ed. Routledge- Cavendish, Abingdon 2009) *R* v *Maginnis* [1987] AC 303, *R* v *Goodwin* [2005] EWCA Crim 3184, *Inland Revenue Commissioners* v *Hinchy* [1960] AC 748, *Bromley LBC* v *GLC* [1983] AC 768, *Whiteley* v *Chappell* (1868-9) 4 LRQB 147.
41. [1961] 1 QB 394.
42. As Holland and Webb point out, this would have been different if the statute had used the words 'expose for sale' J Holland and J Webb, *Learning Legal Rules* (6th ed. Oxford, Oxford University Press, 2008) 233.
43. (1872) LR 1 CCR 367.
44. [1935] Ch 89.

section 46 of the Administration of Estates Act 1925 in which the next of kin would inherit the estate. However, in this case the son had murdered his own mother, meaning he would benefit from the crime he had committed. To avoid this absurdity the court held that under s.46 of the Administration of Estates Act 1925, a son who had murdered his mother could not profit from that crime even though there was only one literal meaning to the word 'issue' (i.e. blood offspring) in the Act.

The academic literature includes many other cases that illustrate the golden rule. It emphasizes the idea of absurdity – the rule applies where the literal meaning is nonsense when the rest of the statute is considered.[45] The purposive rule is similar, but there is no need to show absurdity.

Similar to the golden and purposive rule, the mischief rule emphasizes the need to focus on the objective of the statute. Nonetheless, it is considered narrower than the golden or purposive rules, as the mischief rule is located purely in the context of an identifiable common law *status quo* which existed prior to the statute. The courts are said to be looking for what defect the common law involved, and how it was sought to be remedied by Parliament.[46] For instance, *Smith* v *Hughes*[47] concerned interpretation of the Street Offences Act 1959. Section 1 of the Act stated 'It shall be an offence for a common prostitute to loiter or solicit in a street or public place for the purposes of prostitution'. Prostitutes began trying to attract men by signaling them from windows and balconies. The court decided that the mischief of the Act was to clean up the streets. The words of section 1 did not indicate who had to be in the street; and so the court held that an offence had been committed under the section.

45. *Grey* v *Pearson* (1857) 6 HL Cas 61, *Stock v Frank Jones* (Tipton) [1978] ICR 347, *River Wear Commissioners v Adamson* (1876-77) 2 App Cas 743.
46. Holland and Webb (2008) place emphasis on the classic *Heydon's case* (1584) 3 Co Rep 7a, 7b. The rule is also illustrated in *Royal College of Nursing* v *DHSS* [1981] AC 800; [1981] 1 All ER 545. *Gorris* v *Scott* (1874) LR 9 Ex 125.
47. [1960] 1 WLR 830.

4. Which method(s) is/Are SAID To be used by English courts when interpreting and applying English AND EU law?

In general, the literal rule has often been given decisive weight.[48] There is little dispute that for most of the past hundred years or more, the literal rule has been the dominant one. In 1969, Maxwell on *Interpretation of Statutes* (12th ed.) stated the literal rule was the primary rule, and described the golden and the mischief rule as merely 'other main principles of interpretation'.[49]

However, the literal rule came under scrutiny and has been subjected to criticism. In the 1950s, Herbert Hart, the Professor of Jurisprudence at the University of Oxford, argued that a word has a core meaning 'or standard instance in which no doubts are felt about its application' even though at the edges there is a margin of uncertainty.[50] The margin of uncertainty gives judicial flexibility, even if it is notionally the literal rule that is being applied. Further, as Michael Zander comments, not infrequently the courts say that the meaning of the words is 'plain' but then disagree as to their interpretation.[51] As one commentator has written 'The doctrine of literalness can never be applied successfully to general words. For they always include something more than the scope and object of the statute required and so it leads to ridiculous results'.[52]

In the latter part of the twentieth century, the courts increasingly moved away from literal-mindedness, as seen in cases such as *Rowland*[53] or *Whiteley* v *Chappell,*[54] towards what is nowadays called a purposive approach.[55] In re-

48. See Laws LJ in *Oliver Ashworth (Holdings) Ltd* v *Ballard (Kent) Ltd* [1999] 2 All ER 791, 805 'Where there is a potential clash, the conventional English approach has been to give at least very great and often decisive weight to the literal meaning of the enacting words. This is a tradition which I think is weakening ...'
49. M Zander, *The Law- Making Process*, (6th ed. Cambridge, Cambridge University Press, 2004).
50. H L A Hart, 'Positivism and the separation of Law and Morals', 71 *Harvard Law Review*, 1958, p.593 at p. 607. Cited in M Zander, *The Law- Making Process*, (6th ed. Cambridge, Cambridge University Press, 2004).
51. For example *London and N.E. Railway Co* v *Berriman* [1946] AC 278. In *Ellerman Lines* v *Murray* [1931] all the judges agreed that the meaning was 'plain' but there were at least three different views as to what the plain meaning was.
52. J.A. Corry, 'Administrative Law; Interpretation of Statutes', *University of Toronto Law Journal*, 1935, p.286 at pp. 301-03.
53. *Re Rowland* [1963] Ch. I (Court of Appeal).
54. (1868-9) 4 LR QB.
55. However many other cases still showed the judiciary analysed cases using a literal approach. *Shah* v *Barnet London Borough Council* [1983] 1 All ER 226; *Griffith* v

cent years, most academics have taken the view that the purposive method of interpretation is[56] and should be[57] the dominant technique of judicial interpretation. However as Simon Lee and Marie Fox commented in 1994,[58] when English judges do consider evidence of purpose, in determining the purpose of a statute, they almost invariably limit themselves to the words of the statute, antecedent common law or statute law, and little else. English judges apparently still feel strongly (perhaps instinctively) that they should not ignore the words adopted by Parliament in statutes, and so, where possible and applicable, the literal rule will still be used.

Nonetheless, the literature agrees that the English courts are more inclined to adopt a purposive approach than they were, say, 50 years ago. This is partly attributed to effects of EU law on English law. Although the Court of Justice of the European Union (ECJ) does rely on the literal interpretation of the text, it often adopts a different approach to interpretation of the Treaties and EU legislation – known (at least in the English language literature) as the 'teleological approach'.[59] This approach is similar to the English purposive approach, but takes account of the fact that, in certain Articles, the EU Treaties express the objectives of the EU in very general terms.[60] The ECJ has developed its own idea of the aim or 'telos' of EU law (and indeed the EU itself), upon which it relies in interpreting EU legislation, rather than by refer-

Secretary of State for the Environment [1983] 2 WLR 172; *Lees* v *Secretary of State for Social Services* [1985] 2 All ER 203.

56. Holland and Webb, *Learning Legal Rules* (6th ed. Oxford University Press, Oxford 2006) 234.
57. M Partington, *Introduction to the English Legal System* (4th ed. Oxford, Oxford University Press, 2008).
58. S Lee and M Fox, *Learning Legal Skills* (2nd ed. London, Blackstone, 1994).
59. S Lee and M Fox (above) 82. Cases such as Case 6/72 *Continental Can* [1973] ECR 215, 243 and *Stoke-on Trent City Council* v *B & Q plc* [1991] Ch 51.
60. Article 3 TEU ex Article 2; 'The Union's aim is to promote peace, its values and the well-being of its peoples; 2. The Union shall offer its citizens an area of freedom, security and justice without internal frontiers, in which the free movement of persons is ensured in conjunction with appropriate measures with respect to external border controls, asylum, immigration and the prevention of combating crime.' Article 2 TEU, 'The Union is founded on the values of respect for human dignity, freedom, democracy, equality, the rule of law and respect for human rights, including the rights of persons belonging to minorities. These values are common to the Member States in a society in which pluralism, non-discrimination, tolerance, justice, solidarity and equality between women and men prevail'.

ence to the purpose of the specific legislative act alone.[61] Furthermore, the ECJ's idea of the telos of the EU is that of a changing and dynamic system, and interpretation of its primary legal texts (the Treaties) takes account of these changes over time.

EU law is given legal effect within the UK's constitution (including the law of England) through the European Communities Act 1972. Section 2 (1) of the Act provides that 'all rights, powers, liabilities, obligations and restrictions' created or arising in EU law, which are to be given immediate legal effect in national law, 'shall be recognized and available in law, and be enforced, allowed and followed accordingly'. A directly effective provision of EU law (an 'enforceable Community right' in the words of the Act) is thus deemed to be part of the English legal system, and is to be treated accordingly by English courts and tribunals. Section 2 (4) of the Act provides that '... any enactment passed or to be passed ... shall be construed and have effect subject to the foregoing provisions of this section'. English courts are obliged to modify their approaches to interpretation ('construction' in the words of the Act) of legislation, so as to give effect to directly effective provisions of EU law. Questions of interpretation of EU law must be decided in accordance with the principles laid down by any relevant decision of the ECJ. These principles include the teleological approach to interpretation of EU legislation. Therefore, although the EU Treaties and EU legislation have the force of law in England, and thus become 'part of' English law, the English courts are

61. Case 6/72 Continental Can [1973] ECR 215, 243 where the judgment states 'In order to answer this question (whether Art. 6 EEC applies to changes in the structure of an undertaking) one has to go back to the spirit, general scheme and wording of Article 86, as well as to the system and objectives of the Treaty'. 'Article 86 forms part of the chapter devoted to the common rules for the policy of the Community in the sphere of competition. This policy is derived from Article 3 (f) of the Treaty whereby the activity of the Community includes the establishment of a system to protect competition within the Common Market from distortion'. Case 26/ 62 *NV Algemene Transport- en Expeditie Onderneming van Gend en Loos* v *Nederlandse Administratie der Belastingen* [1963] ECR 1, 12. 'To ascertain whether the provisions of an international treaty extend so far in their effects it is necessary to consider the spirit, general scheme and the wording of those provisions'. The court then goes on to say what the objectives of the EEC Treaty are; Case 106/77 *Amministrazione delle Finanze dello Stato* v *Simmenthal SpA* [1978] ECR 629, 17. 'Furthermore, in accordance with the principle of the precedence of Community law, the relationship between provisions of the Treaty and directly applicable measures of the institutions on the one hand and the national law of the Member states on the other is such that those provisions any measures not only by their entry into force render automatically inapplicable any conflicting provision of current national law...'.

obliged, under the European Communities Act 1972, to interpret EU law by the methods of the ECJ, and not simply the methods which they apply to the main body of English law.

The methods used by the ECJ have been said to constitute the 'European way' which Lord Denning in 1974 stated that the courts of England should follow when called upon to interpret EU Law.[62] In *Bulmer* v *Bollinger*[63] Lord Denning declared:

> 'The [EEC] Treaty is quite unlike any of the enactments to which we have become accustomed ... It lays down general principles. It expresses its aim and purposes. All in sentences of moderate length and commendable style. But it lacks precision. It uses words and phrases without defining what they mean. An English lawyer would look for an interpretation clause, but he would look in vain. There is none. All the way through the Treaty there are gaps and lacunae. These have to be filled in by the judges, or by regulations or directives. It is the European way ... Seeing these differences, what are the English courts to do when they are faced with a problem of interpretation? They must follow the European pattern. No longer must they argue about the precise grammatical sense. They must look to the purpose and intent ... They must divine the spirit of the Treaty and gain inspiration from it. If they find a gap, they must fill it as best they can ... These are the principles, as I understand it, on which the European Court acts.'

Although English judges do not generally discuss the method of interpretation being employed, here Lord Denning specifies the teleological approach. The distinctive nature of EU Law, when compared with national laws on the one hand and international law on the other, as well as the manner in which the Treaties are drafted, have led the ECJ to evolve its own style of interpretation, the dominant mode of which is teleological. The English courts have grasped this concept and accept that the interpretation of EU Law will inevitably involve different methods to the interpretation of English law. In 1981, Lord Diplock stated:[64]

62. L Brown & F Jacobs, *The Court of Justice of the European Communities* (3rd ed., London, Sweet & Maxwell, 1989) 289.
63. [1974] Ch 401, 425.
64. *Henn & Darby* v *DDP* [1981] AC 850.

> 'The European Court, in contrast to English courts, applies teleological rather than historical methods to the interpretation of Treaties and other Community legislation. It seeks to give effect to what it conceives to be the spirit rather than the letter of the Treaties: sometimes, indeed, to an English judge, it may seem to the exclusion of the letter. It views the Communities as living and expanding organisms and the interpretation of the provisions of the Treaties as changing to match their growth.'

So some judges in the higher English courts have stated that EU law requires different methods of interpretation by the English judiciary to the ordinary English 'canons of construction'. To what extent are these statements of principle borne out in judicial practice on the ground, including in lower courts and tribunals? Our investigation of the judicial method of English judges in employment courts and tribunals, when interpreting and applying EU law, explores this question. So as to uncover changes over the 37 years of UK membership of the EU, we arrange our analysis in chronological order.

5. 1970s: Dealing with Direct Effect

Literal and Purposive Rules; Deference to the ECJ; Consistent Interpretation versus Disapplication

Our first case example, *Amies* v *Inner London Education Authority*[65] illustrates the early approach of employment tribunals to interpretation of both EU law and the European Communities Act 1972. Mrs Amies was discriminated against on the grounds of her sex at a time before the UK Sex Discrimination Act 1975 had come into force. She had no rights to non-discrimination in national law, but the Employment Appeal Tribunal (EAT) considered whether the Employment Tribunal (ET) should have considered a claim under Article 119 EEC (now Article 157 TFEU). The EAT, following a literal interpretation of the European Communities Act 1972, section 3 (1), interpreted Article 119 EEC by reference to the ruling of the ECJ in *Defrenne No 2*,[66] holding that the Treaty contained a directly effective provision only with respect to equal pay, not the equal treatment that Mrs Amies sought. No 'enforceable obligation' of EU law, in the sense of the European Communities Act 1972, was therefore engaged. The tribunals rejected Mrs Amies' ar-

65. [1977] 2 All ER 100.
66. Case 43/75 *Defrenne* v *Sabena (No 2)* [1976] ECR 455.

gument to the effect that the principle of equal treatment on ground of sex is inherent in the Treaty, and therefore in itself forms a source of enforceable rights in EU law.[67] The EAT agreed with the ET that, as the ET is a creature of statute, it has jurisdiction only to hear claims as per its statutory duties. Even if the general principle of non-discrimination in EU law was an 'enforceable right', as claimed by Mrs Amies, a claim would have to be brought before the ordinary courts.[68] At the relevant time, the Sex Discrimination Act 1975 was not in force, and so the ET had no jurisdiction to hear a complaint of sex discrimination (as opposed to equal pay). This reasoning is consistent with the EU law doctrine of national procedural autonomy.[69] It is probably still good law. The later case of *Biggs*,[70] in which the EAT (and ET) had jurisdiction in an unfair dismissal claim, can be distinguished, as in that case there was an Act giving jurisdiction,[71] which had an exclusion clause in it that, as it was contrary to EU law, had to be dis-applied.[72] It does not, however, appear to be consistent with the ECJ's rulings in *Mangold* and *Kücükdeveci*.[73] A reference to the ECJ under what is now Article 267 TFEU was not considered necessary in *Amies*, although the EAT noted that it did have the power to make such a reference.

In the *Amies* case, the ET and the EAT both complied with EU law to the extent of noting their obligation to give effect to 'enforceable obligations' of EU law – that is, directly effective rights in EU law. As no such directly effective EU law right was engaged, their interpretation of their obligations was that there was no need to apply EU law. The EAT, even at this early stage of UK membership of the EU, followed the ECJ's interpretation of the *scope* of Article 119 EEC (it applies only to equal pay, and does not involve a broader obligation of non-discrimination) – this was not challenging for the English court as in this respect the ECJ's interpretative method in *Defrenne No 2* is literal. There is no suggestion from the English courts that they would be

67. This idea has been confirmed by the ECJ in Case C 144/04 *Mangold* v *Helm* [2005] ECR I-998I and Case C-555/07 *Kücükdeveci* v *Swedex GmbH & Co* 19 Jan 2010, nyr in ECR. *[2010] IRLR 346*. See further below.
68. Reasoning also reflected in *Snoxell and Davies* v *Vauxhall Motors Ltd* [1978] QB 11.
69. Case 33/76 *Rewe Zentralfinanz* v *Landwirtschaftskammer für das Saarland* [1976] ECR 1989.
70. *Biggs* v *Somerset County Council* [1995] ICR 811.
71. The Trade Union and Labour Relations Act 1974 and the Employment Protection (Consolidation) Act 1978.
72. See discussion below.
73. See further below.

able, or obliged, to do anything other than follow the literal approach as per the ECJ in *Defrenne*. The aspect of *Defrenne No 2* that shows the ECJ's teleological approach to Article 119 EEC, that of the *effect* of Article 119 EEC, was not engaged, and so this case does not really challenge the dominant mode of interpretation in English law in this respect. Equally, the words 'enforceable obligation' in the European Communities Act 1972 were interpreted literally by the national tribunals.

In our second case example from the 1970s, *Macarthys Ltd* v *Smith*, the English courts found that a directly effective provision of EU law (again Article 119 EEC) was engaged. Mrs Smith was paid approximately 20% less than the man who had been employed in her job four months earlier. She claimed equal pay. She was successful at the ET and EAT,[74] as they interpreted the Equal Pay Act 1970 to include a comparator who was not contemporaneously employed. This interpretation went beyond the literal interpretation of the Act, and the EAT was at pains to explain the 'absurdity' that permitted such an approach[75] and the 'mischief' that the Act sought to remedy.[76] However, in addition to this reference to the golden and mischief rules, both tribunals referred to their obligations in EU law to depart from a literal interpretation and interpret the Act to be consistent with the *Defrenne No 2* case:

> 'It seems to us that as far as industrial tribunals, and the appeal tribunal, are concerned the correct approach is to give effect to the *Defrenne* case

74. By decision of 27 June 1977, the Industrial Tribunal upheld Mrs Smiths claim. Macarthys Ltd. appealed against this decision to the Employment Appeal Tribunal which dismissed the appeal by decision of 14 December 1977.
75. '[T]he situation is no different from that which would arise in a case where a man left his employment on day 1 and a woman replaced him, doing precisely the same work, on day 2. Supposing that she was paid less than he was, would she have a claim under the Equal Pay Act 1970? The appellant employers say 'No,' and they have in their favour the literal words of some parts of the Act ... The question, then, is whether we are obliged to construe the Act in this sense however strange the results may be, or whether we are justified in the circumstances of the case in construing the Act so as to permit comparisons to be made with an employee who is no longer employed at the relevant date ... There is no doubt that if the employer's contention is right strange results will follow, such as the example instanced above where on day 1 a male employee leaves his employment and on day 2 he is replaced by a female employee at half the salary.' [1978] 1 WLR 849, 851.
76. '[I]n devising a method of equal pay it is possible to propose various schemes, some more, some less, favourable to women than others. And that the Equal Pay Act 1970 had introduced a scheme which took the middle course between the most and the least favourable.' [1978] 1 WLR 849, 851.

by construing and applying the Equal Pay Act 1970 in conformity with Article 119.'

This 'consistent interpretation' approach (interpret national law so as to be consistent with EU law, thereby giving effect to EU law[77]) has the benefit of avoiding the question of which court has jurisdiction to give effect to a claim based on directly effective EU law, that arose in *Amies*. It also preserves the idea of Parliamentary sovereignty, as the national courts' primary point of reference remains national legislation. Because of this, the 'consistent interpretation' approach is a feature of the reasoning of English courts and tribunals right up until the 1990s, when the *Factortame* case[78] confirmed that the 'dis-application approach' (dis-apply national law that is inconsistent with EU law) is both required by the supremacy of EU law and consistent with UK constitutional law.

The majority[79] in the Court of Appeal (CA) disagreed with the EAT,[80] holding that the use of the present tense in the Act meant that comparison for the purposes of equal pay claims under the Act must be between employees employed at the same time. The meaning of the Act was clear and unambiguous, and there was no good reason or need to depart from the literal approach to statutory interpretation.[81] The 'ordinary and natural meaning'[82] of the words of the Act was to be followed, there being no 'manifest inconsistency' with the context of the Act as a whole, nor 'absurdity' or 'injustice' to demonstrate that Parliament cannot have intended such a meaning.[83] Neither was there any need to do so in order to comply with obligations in EU law. Although the national court was not permitted to ignore Article 119 EEC and apply the literal rule to interpreting the English legislation,[84] Article 119 EEC

77. *Garland* v *British Rail Engineering Ltd* [1983] 2 AC 75. *Duke* v *G.E.C Reliance* [1988] AC 618. *Apple and Pear Development Council* v *Commissioners of Custom & Excise* [1987] 2 CMLR 634. *Pickstone and others* v *Freeman plc* [1988] 2 All ER 803.
78. Case C-213/89 *Factortame v Secretary of State for Transport* [1990] ECR I-2433.
79. Lord Denning disagreed with the majority, reasoning that, interpreting the EU law and the UK law together, the proper interpretation of both Article 119 EEC and the Equal Pay Act 1970 was that they applied to Mrs Smith's situation.
80. [1978] 1 WLR 849 (Employment Appeal Tribunal).
81. [1979] 1 WLR 1189; [1979] ICR 785, 793-794 (Lawton).
82. [1979] 1 WLR 1189; [1979] ICR 785, 796-799 (Cumming Bruce).
83. [1979] 1 WLR 1189; [1979] ICR 785, 796-799 (Cumming Bruce).
84. [1979] ICR 785, 793-797 (Lawton). NB Cumming-Bruce took the opposite view, to the effect that, as the UK legislation was unambiguous, reference to EU law would

may be 'perfectly consistent' with such a literal interpretation.[85] However, the CA was not totally sure of this interpretation of EU law, and so referred to the ECJ to give an 'authoritative interpretation' of the question.[86]

The CA referred to the ECJ on the question of whether Article 119 EEC [now Article 157 TFEU] applies only to contemporaneous work. The ECJ, referring to both the economic and the social aims of EU law,[87] held that it does not, pointing out that these aims would be frustrated if a literal approach to interpretation of Article 119 EEC were adopted,[88] and also pointing out that there is nothing explicit in the text that suggests it is confined to contemporaneous employment.[89]

Following a reference to the ECJ, Lord Denning, MR, approached the final decision of the CA,[90] (that the appeal be dismissed, with costs against the employer) by declaring that provisions of EU law 'take priority over' the English Equal Pay Act 1970. He explained that this priority is required under the European Communities Act 1972: 'Community law is now part of our law: and, whenever there is any inconsistency, Community law has priority'. Denning asserts that EU law does not 'supplant' national law, but is 'part of' the national legal system, suggesting that the two systems are not separate, and are not in a hierarchical relationship. But Denning also suggests both separation and hierarchy by stating that 'whenever there is inconsistency' between the two systems, EU law has priority, and over-rides contradictory national law. This paradox pervades the reasoning of English courts and tribunals.

In *Macarthys*, in both the ET and EAT, there is explicit discussion of the literal approach and the need to depart from it in order to comply with EU law. Explicit discussion of what approach is being taken to interpretation is,

not be required. This is, of course, inconsistent with the obligation in Case 14/83 *Von Colson and Kamann* v *Land Nordrhein-Westfalen* [1984] ECR 1891 and Case C-106/89 *Marleasing SA* v *La Comercial Internacional de Alimentacion SA* [1992] ECR I-4135 to the effect that 'in applying national law and in particular a national law specifically introduced to implement [a directive], national courts are obliged to interpret their national law in the light of the wording and purpose of the directive'. Case C-106/89 *Marleasing* [1992] ECR I-4135 [8].

85. [1979] 1 WLR 1189; [1979] ICR 785, 796-799 (Cumming Bruce).
86. [1979] 1 WLR 1189; [1979] ICR 785, 796-799 (Cumming Bruce) and [1979] ICR 785, 793-797 (Lawton).
87. Case 129/79 *Macarthys* v *Smith* [1980] ECR 1275; [1980] 2 CMLR 205, 209.
88. Case 129/79 *Macarthys* v *Smith* [1980] ECR 1275; [1980] 2 CMLR 205, 208.
89. Case 129/79 *Macarthys* v *Smith* [1980] ECR 1275; [1980] 2 CMLR 205, 214.
90. *Macarthys* v *Smith* [1981] QB 180, 200.

as we have seen, unusual in English judgments, and this in itself marks out cases involving EU law from others. In the CA before the reference to the ECJ, there is also explicit discussion of the literal approach, and how it may in fact be consistent with EU law. The majority judges in the CA, in particular Lawton LJ, are extremely deferential to the literal approach: 'it is not permissible to read into the statute words which are not there, nor to look outside the Act ... and to read the words used in a sense other than their ordinary meaning.'[91] However, the reasoning in the ET and EAT, as well as Denning's reasoning, demonstrate that the ordinary English rules of statutory interpretation do go beyond the literal rule, even without taking EU law obligations into account. In spite of this, before the reference, the CA appears reluctant to depart from a literal approach to interpretation and to 'make the law' through a purposive approach. Following the reference, however, there is no hesitation from the CA that it is obliged to depart from the literal text of the UK legislation, to comply with the ruling of the ECJ. Without a reference to the ECJ, however, there is no sense, in the 1970s, that the English courts or tribunals will adopt a 'teleological approach' to the interpretation of EU law. They adopt the 'golden rule', 'mischief rule' or 'purposive approach' in the English sense, but not the 'teleological approach' in the sense of EU law.

The CA explicitly states that there is no obligation in EU law to alter existing approaches to statutory interpretation. The CA eschews the 'consistent interpretation' approach to compliance with EU law obligations. Rather, in the event of an inconsistency between EU law and national law, the 'dis-application' route is preferred, although it is not made explicit that national law is 'dis-applied':

> Secondly, I do not think that it is permissible, as an aid to construction, to look at the terms of the Treaty. If the terms of the Treaty are adjudged in Luxembourg to be inconsistent with the provisions of the Equal Pay Act 1970, European law will prevail over that municipal legislation. But such a judgment in Luxembourg cannot affect the meaning of the English statute.[92]

As noted above, this approach is also reflected in Denning's judgment in the post-ECJ reference CA ruling.

91. [1979] 1 WLR 1189; [1979] ICR 785, 794-795 (Lawton).
92. [1979] 1 WLR 1189; [1979] ICR 785, 798 (Cumming-Bruce).

To summarise, during the 1970s, the English courts continued to prefer the literal rule, and would only adopt the interpretations based on the 'teleological approach' where an ECJ ruling bound them to do so. The preferred method of giving effect to directly effective EU law was through consistent interpretation of relevant national law.[93]

6. 1980s: Moving from Direct Effect to Indirect Effect

The Weak 'EU Compliance Mischief Rule'; Strong Deference to Deemed Parliamentary intention

The 'consistent interpretation' approach to giving effect to directly effective EU law was stretched almost to breaking point in the first of our cases from the 1980s: *Pickstone* v *Freemans*. In a similar case decided just beforehand,[94] the House of Lords (HL, now Supreme Court) had declined to depart from the 'natural and ordinary meaning' of the relevant UK Act. As we shall see, *Pickstone* v *Freemans* represents a capitulation to mounting pressure to ensure UK compliance with EU law on equal pay, through significant development of UK rules of statutory interpretation.

Pickstone v *Freemans*[95] is another claim involving Article 119 EEC, this time concerning equal pay for work of equal value. Pickstone claimed that her work was of equal value to that carried out by a number of male comparators. The employers' defense was that men and women were employed doing the comparators' job. At first instance, the ET agreed with the employer, adopting a literal interpretation of the relevant provision of the Equal Pay Act 1970, which had been amended in 1983 following the ruling of the ECJ in Case 61/81.[96] At the EAT, the claimant argued that any ambiguity in the UK Act should be construed liberally and consistently with EU law. Alternatively, Article 119 EEC would form the basis for a directly effective claim. The employer argued that there was no ambiguity in the Act to 'let in' EU

93. This seems to resonate with the Czech courts' 'tendency to interpret national law in an EU-compatible way', see Kristina Koldinska's chapter in this collection.
94. *Hayward* v *Cammell Laird Shipbuilders Ltd* [1988] AC 894 also see P Scholfield, 'Recent Cases: Equal Pay' ILJ (1988) 17(1) 241.
95. *Pickstone* v *Freemans Plc* [1989] AC 66.
96. Case 61/81 *Commission of the European Communities* v *United Kingdom of Great Britain and Northern Ireland* [1982] ECR 260.

law.[97] Furthermore EU law is only an aid to the proper interpretation of a statute, and 'cannot supply what the statute does not'.[98]

Adopting a literal approach to statutory interpretation, the EAT agreed with the employer. There was no 'ambiguity' in the Act. The EAT declined to look directly to Article 119 EEC as a directly effective source of individual rights. Rather, they took the view that the 1983 amendment to the UK Act had brought UK law in line with EU law, as properly interpreted.

The CA agreed with the EAT on the ambiguity point.[99] However, the CA took the opposite approach to the question of direct effect of Article 119 EEC. Article 119 EEC creates individual rights, enforceable in national courts. On this point, the CA referred to jurisprudence of the ECJ, which adopts a 'teleological' approach to interpretation.[100] Following *Defrenne No* 2, the CA reasoned that Article 119 EEC enshrines the broad general principle of equal pay for equal work (including work of equal value), and must be interpreted accordingly, not rigidly or inflexibly.[101]

Turning to the proper interpretation of the Equal Pay Act 1970, the CA considered a version of the 'mischief rule', explicitly referring to the 'mischief' which the relevant section, as amended, was intended to cure.[102] The amendment to the section was in response to a ruling of the ECJ to the effect that the UK was not compliant with EU law. Indeed the amendment was made by secondary legislation,[103] relying on a power given by the European Communities Act 1972, to enable such legislation to be adopted in order to implement any obligation of the UK in EU law. However, for Nicholls, LJ, even the mischief rule was insufficient to overcome a literal interpretation of unambiguous statutory wording. He noted that, if Article 119 EEC is interpreted consistently with the jurisprudence of the ECJ, and if the employers are correct on the interpretation of the Equal Pay Act, then the amendment to the Equal Pay Act has failed in its aim to remedy the mischief of non-compliance with EU law and the UK would still be in breach of EU law.

97. [1986] IRLR 886 (EAT) [10].
98. [1986] IRLR 886 (EAT) [10].
99. [1989] AC 66 and [1987] 3 W.L.R. 811.
100. 'I conceive that on these points of Community law it is the duty of this court to give effect to those later decisions of the European Court.' [1987] 3 WLR 811, 819 (Nicholls)
101. Nicholls, LJ; Purchas LJ [1987] 3 WLR 811, *817 (*Nicholls).
102. 'Mischief' is expressly stated five times throughout the judgment. Four times by Nicholls [1987] 3 WLR 811, 820 and once by Purchas *823.*
103. A statutory instrument, Equal Pay (Amendment) Regulations 1983 (S.I. 1983 No. 1794).

However, although 'extremely reluctant'[104] to interpret the Equal Pay Act in such as way as to have these consequences, Nicholls, LJ states that he remains convinced that the words of the Act do not have any ambiguity. Nothing in his interpretation of the European Communities Act 1972, section 2 (4) (the source of the obligation of consistent interpretation) changes this view. A claim therefore should be heard before the ET, based on the directly effective Article 119 EEC.

By contrast, Purchas, LJ, was quite content to ask the first instance tribunal to construe the wording of the Act so as to give effect to the directly effective Article 119 EEC, considering that the European Communities Act 1972, section 2 (4) obliges this, even admitting that 'this involves an otherwise unjustifiable qualification of what are in fact clear words'.[105] In this, Purchas LJ draws on Lord Diplock's speech in *Garland* v *BREL*,[106] although in that case, unlike in *Pickstone* v *Freemans*, it was possible to interpret the UK legislation to be consistent with EU law 'without any undue straining of the ordinary meaning of the language used'.

In the House of Lords (HL, now the Supreme Court), however, the literal approach was abandoned, in favour of a more purposive approach, which draws on both the traditional idea of the purposive approach (look at the wording of the section in the context of the Act as a whole, and what it intends to achieve, as well as Parliamentary debates) and on the EU law version of the 'mischief rule'. Questions of ambiguity (or not) did not feature heavily in their Lordships reasoning.

Lord Keith departed from a literal approach to interpretation of the Equal Pay Act, adopting an approach based on the purpose of the Act, and the version of the mischief rule outlined in the CA.[107] He reasoned that Parliament cannot have intended that employers could easily evade equal pay obligations by employing a token man in the group of women paid less than the com-

104. [1987] 3 WLR 811, *821 (Nicholls).*
105. [1987] 3 WLR 811, 834 (Purchas).
106. [1983] 2 AC 751.
107. 'The opposite result would leave a large gap in the equal work provision, enabling an employer to evade it by employing one token man on the same work as a group of potential women claimants who were deliberately paid less than a group of men employed on work of equal value with that of the women. This would mean that the United Kingdom had failed yet again fully to implement its obligations under article 119 of the Treaty and the Equal Pay Directive, and had not given full effect to the decision of the European Court in Commission of the European Communities v. United [1982] ECR 2601. It is plain that Parliament cannot possibly have intended such a failure.' *[1989] AC 66, 111 (Lord Keith).*

parator man doing a job of equal value. Lord Templeman's reasoning is similar.[108] Moreover, Lord Keith goes on to note that Parliament 'cannot possibly have intended' to fail to give full effect to the ruling of the ECJ in Case 61/81, in response to which the Equal Pay Act was amended. Therefore, '[t]he words must be construed purposively in order to give effect to the manifest broad intention of the maker of the Regulations and of Parliament.'[109] Lord Keith's strong language suggests a desire to avoid UK 'failure' to comply with EU law. Again, Lord Tempelman's views echo this approach. Tempelman pays particular attention to the fact that the relevant Act was drafted in order to give effect to EU law, as interpreted by the ECJ. In this respect, he distinguishes *Duke* v *Reliance Systems*, in which the HL had declined to 'distort' the interpretation of a statute which was *not* intended to give effect to a Directive. The other Law Lords were ultimately convinced by this line of reasoning, although Lords Oliver and Jauncey admitted that at the close of oral argument they had formed the view that the CA had correctly interpreted the Act, and that they had only been persuaded differently by their colleagues' reasoning to the contrary.[110] Lord Oliver expressly notes that it involved 'a departure from a number of well-established rules of construction'.[111]

By the end of the 1980s, then, the UK courts had accepted that a different version of the traditional 'mischief rule' would permit (or even require) departure from the literal text of a UK Act, even where unambiguous, if the Act was manifestly intended to implement a directly effective provision of EU law. This 'weak' 'EU compliance mischief rule' applied where the Act was obviously the response to developing EU law (here, a ruling of the ECJ interpreting a directly effective provision of EU law).

In 1984, the ECJ developed the doctrine of indirect effect, holding that, following the duty of sincere cooperation,[112] 'national courts are required to interpret their national law in the light of the wording and purpose of the Di-

108. *[1989] A.C. 66, 113-124 (Lord Templeman).*

109. *[1989] AC 66, 112.*

110. At first Lord Oliver considered that the words in question were unambiguous and for that reason the words in the newly added section of 1(2)(c) Equal Pay Act should be construed normally giving there literal and strict construction. This would not have led to an absurdity as such, but rather it would have led to a breach of treaty obligations.

111. [*1989] AC 66, 126 (Lord Oliver).*

112. Ex Article 5 EEC, Article 10 EC. Now Article 4 (3) TEU.

rective, in order to achieve the result [intended]'.[113] The EU law doctrine of indirect effect poses significant challenges for judicial methods to interpretation of legislation, particularly in a context where there is a preference for literal approaches.

Indirect effect requires national courts to construe national law, as far as possible,[114] so as to give effect to EU law. The doctrine applies whether the measure of EU law is directly effective or not.[115] The second of the two cases we discuss from the 1980s – *Duke* v *GEC Reliance*[116] – shows the UK courts grappling with their obligations in this respect. This case concerns a claim against a private employer, not an 'emanation of the state', and so the Directive at issue was not directly effective.[117] As the EU law on indirect effect has developed, cases such as *Duke* v *Reliance* have come under question, because the ECJ has held that the obligation of consistent interpretation arising under the doctrine of indirect effect applies to *all* national legislation, whether or not it is intended to implement EU law.[118]

Mrs Duke was dismissed from employment at the age of 60, in conformity with the employer's policy on retirement. Under that policy, men were dismissed at the age of 65. The UK Sex Discrimination Act 1975, while prohibiting discrimination on grounds of sex in dismissal, contained an exemption in section 6 (4) to the effect that the Act did not apply to 'provision in relation to death or retirement'.

At the ET and EAT,[119] no points of EU law were raised. However, in the CA, it was argued that section 6 (4) of the Sex Discrimination Act 1975

113. Case 14/83 *Von Colson and Kamann* v *Land Nordhein-Westfalen* [1984] ECR 1891 [26].
114. Case C-106/89 *Marleasing SA* v *La Comerical Internacionale de Alimentacion SA* [1990] ECR I-4135 [8].
115. *Marleasing* (n 100) [8].
116. *Duke* v *G.E.C Reliance Ltd* [1988] AC 618.
117. Case C-271/91 *Marshall* v *Southampton Area Health Authority (No 2)* [1993] ECR I-4367; Case C-188/90 *Foster (A) and others* v *British Gas plc* [1990] ECR I-3313; Case C-91/92 *Dori (Paola Faccini)* v *Recreb* [1994] ECR I-3325.
118. ECJ cases which illustrate indirect effect such as Case C-106/89 *Marleasing SA* v *La Comerical Internacionale de Alimentacion SA* [1990] ECR I-4135; Case C-240-244/98 *Océano* [2000] ECR I-4491 Case C-456/98 *Centrosteel* v *Adipol* [2000] ECR I-6007 Case C-185/97 *Coote* v *Granada* [1998] ECR I-519; Case C-129/96 *Inter-Environment Wallonie* [1997] ECR I-7411.
119. *Duke* v *Reliance Systems Ltd* [1982] ICR 449 (EAT), Previously heard by an Industrial Tribunal sitting in Bedford on 15 June 1981.

should be interpreted to be consistent with Directive 76/207/EEC,[120] as interpreted by the ECJ in *Marshall* v *Southampton Area Health Authority*.[121] Such an interpretation would require that Mrs Duke be treated equally with respect to the age at which she was required to retire. Sir John Donaldson, MR, held that, as the Directive was not directly effective in Mrs Duke's case (it being a 'horizontal' situation), there was 'no independent right of action based upon that directive' in UK law, and hence, implicitly, no obligation in UK law to interpret the Act consistently with the Directive. The CA considered itself bound by its own previous ruling,[122] and hence did not depart from the interpretation of section 6 (4) adopted there (which was unfavourable to Mrs Duke).

The unanimous view of the HL was that Mrs Duke's appeal should be dismissed. Section 6 (4) made discriminatory retirement ages lawful. This conclusion was reached by looking at the 'plain wording' of the section, the section in the context of other, related UK legislation,[123] and the historical background to the Act.[124] Parliament's intention with respect to compliance with EU law (the weak 'EU compliance mischief rule') could not assist here, as the UK government had taken no steps to amend section 6 (4) in order to comply with the Directive.[125] According to Lord Templeman,

> 'If the Government had intended to sweep away the widespread practice of differential retirement ages, the 1974 White Paper would not have given a contrary assurance and if Parliament had intended to outlaw differential retirement ages, section 6 (4) of the Sex Discrimination Act 1975 would have been very differently worded in order to make clear the profound change which Parliament contemplated.'[126]

120. Council Directive 76/207 EEC concerning equal treatment for men and women as regards access to employment, vocational training and promotion and working conditions (OJ 1976 L39/40).
121. Case C-271/91 *Marshall* v *Southampton Area Health Authority (No 2)* [1993] ECR I-4367.
122. *Roberts* v *Cleveland* [1979] 1 WLR 754.
123. *[1988] AC 618, 631 (Lord Templeman).*
124. *[1988] AC 618, 632*. A 1974 White Paper contained an express reference to the need to maintain differential retirement ages. White Paper, 'Equality for Women', Cmnd. 5724, September 1974.
125. *[1988] AC 618, 633.*
126. *[1988] AC 618, 637 (Lord Templeman).*

To depart from a literal interpretation of the Act would be an inappropriate exercise of judicial power. The UK government must have considered EU law in adopting the Act (draft versions of the Directive were available at the time), and would have adopted different wording if they had intended to change the legal position, as the subsequent *Marshall* case undoubtedly did.

The 'indirect effect' route was not available here:

> 'Nevertheless, it is now submitted that the appellant is entitled to damages from the respondent because Community law requires the Equal Pay Act enacted on 29 May 1970 and the Sex Discrimination Act enacted on 12 November 1975 to be construed in a manner which gives effect to the Equal Treatment Directive dated 9 February 1976 as construed by the European Court of Justice in Marshall's case published on 20 February 1986. Of course a British court will always be willing and anxious to conclude that United Kingdom law is consistent with Community law. Where an Act is passed for the purpose of giving effect to an obligation imposed by a directive or other instrument, a British court will seldom encounter difficulty in concluding that the language of the Act is effective for the intended purpose. But the construction of a British Act of Parliament is a matter of judgment to be determined by British courts and to be derived from the language of the legislation considered in the light of the circumstances prevailing at the date of enactment. ... The Acts were not passed to give effect to the Equal Treatment Directive and were intended to preserve discriminatory retirement ages.'[127]

Von Colson, and the doctrine of indirect effect is dismissed:

> 'The E.E.C. Treaty does not interfere and the European Court of Justice in the *von Colson* case did not assert power to interfere with the method or result of the interpretation of national legislation by national courts.'[128]

The approach taken in *Duke* represents something of a 'high water mark' in the UK courts' approach to obligations of compliance with EU law. The case illustrates how difficult indirect effect is to reconcile with the traditional English rules of statutory interpretation, in the context of UK constitutional law on the sovereignty of Parliament, as understood at that time by the majority

127. *[1988]* AC 618, 639.
128. *[1988] AC 618, 641.*

of senior UK judges. The possibility of a reference to the ECJ, to resolve such difficulties, which had proved so effective in *Macarthys*, was not discussed by the HL. Lord Templeman rejected an argument based on Lord Diplock's judgment in an earlier case,[129] to the effect that section 6 (4) both could and should be construed in a manner consistent with Article 119 EEC, and two EU Directives on sex discrimination.[130] That case could be distinguished from *Duke*, because it was based on Article 119 EEC, which is directly effective as between individuals, whereas the Directive is not.

Not surprisingly, the HL judgment in *Duke* was subjected to a barrage of criticism in the academic literature. This pointed out that it was inconsistent with the obligation to make preliminary references to the ECJ on questions of interpretation of EU law, and with EU law on supremacy,[131] and that it is unduly critical of the style of drafting of EU law.[132]

The 1980s show an evolution of the English 'canons of construction', as applied in the context of UK (primary and especially secondary) legislation that is intended to implement directly effective provisions of EU law. The 'mischief rule' is expanded into a weak version of an 'EU compliance mischief rule', whereby courts take account of Parliament's implied intention to comply with directly effective EU law, especially as interpreted by the ECJ. The need for 'absurdity', or even ambiguity, to permit departure from the literal rule, is significantly weakened. This is consistent with the approach of the ECJ, which does not regard ambiguity in a legislative text as a condition precedent to adopting a purposive interpretation. 'A teleological interpretation can replace a literal reading of words even where they are unambiguous'.[133]

However, at the same time, the cases we discuss here show how difficult the UK courts found compliance with the doctrine of indirect effect. Departure from national 'canons of construction', in cases where the Act concerned

129. *Garland* v *BREL* [1983] AC 751.
130. Council Directive 76/207 EEC concerning equal treatment for men and women as regards access to employment, vocational training and promotion and working conditions (OJ 1976 L39/40); Council Directive 79/7/ EEC of 19 December 1978 on the progressive implementation of the principle of equal treatment for men and women in matters of social security (OJ 1979 16/24). *Duke* v *G.E.C. Reliance* [1988] AC 618.
131. G. R. Rubin, 'Case comment' (1989) JBL 71 and C Docksey and B Fitzpatrick, 'The duty of national courts to interpret provisions of national law in Accordance with Community Law' (1991) 20 ILJ 113.
132. T Rensen, 'British Statutory Interpretation in the light of Community and other International obligations' (1993) 14 Statute Law Review 186, 201.
133. T Rensen (n 118) 186, 191.

was not intended to implement the Directive (for instance, it pre-dated the Directive), and where the Directive was not directly effective ('horizontal' cases), was not deemed feasible at this stage. However, this was to change very soon.

7. 1990s: Increasing Assurance with EU Law

Coming to Terms with Indirect Effect; Emerging 'Teleological Approach'; Developing Relations with the ECJ; 'Dis-Application' of National Law

Shortly after the *Duke* ruling, the HL was faced with another employment law case concerning an indirectly effective EU Directive, this time the Transfer of Undertakings Directive.[134] The case emanated from Scotland, so we do not discuss the Scottish ET, EAT or Court of Session judgments here.[135] In *Litster* v *Forth Dry Dock and Engineering Co Ltd*,[136] a business was transferred to new ownership. One hour before transfer of ownership, the employees were dismissed. The employees claimed unfair dismissal against the new owner. Under Regulation 5 of the Transfer of Undertakings (Protection of Employment) Regulations, 1981,[137] it was provided that a transfer does not terminate employment 'immediately before a transfer' took place. On a literal interpretation, protection could not be claimed by employees dismissed before transfer, even if only hours before the transfer.

The House of Lords took the view that the UK Regulations should be seen as intended to implement the Directive.[138] As in the *Pickstone* case, the inten-

134. Acquired Rights Directive 77/187 EEC on the approximation of the laws of the Member states relating to the safeguarding of employees rights in the event of transfers of undertakings, businesses, or parts of businesses OJ 1977 L61/26, implemented in 1981 by the adoption of the Transfer of Undertaking (Protection of Employment) Regulations 1981 (SI 1981/1794).
135. The Supreme Court is the final court of appeal from the Scottish ET, EAT and Court of Session in civil cases.
136. [1990] 1 AC 546.
137. Transfer of Undertakings (Protection of Employment) Regulations 1981 (SI 1981/1794) (a statutory instrument implemented in the UK to give effect to an EU Directive).
138. *Litster and Others Appellants* v *Forth Dry Dock & Engineering Co. Ltd. (In Receivership) and Another Respondents* [1990] 1 AC 546, 549 'The Regulations of 1981 were intended to implement the obligations of the United Kingdom under Council Directive 77/187/E.E.C.'

tion of Parliament to comply with EU law through the Regulations was implied by the use of the power to adopt law through secondary legislation, as laid down in the European Communities Act 1972.[139] However, a number of ECJ cases[140] that post-dated the Regulations (and thus could not have been 'in the mind of' Parliament at the time of the adoption of the Regulations) were referred to as authoritative on the proper interpretation of the Directive, and, crucially, hence the proper interpretation of the national law. The HL therefore abandoned the literal rule, followed the ECJ's teleological approach, as represented in its case law, and read in no less than thirteen additional words[141] to the text of the Regulations. It did so even though the Directive was not directly effective in this case, but following the doctrine of indirect effect. It is therefore 'possible'[142] for the English courts to depart entirely from the traditional rules of interpretation of statutes to interpret a measure of national law that is, in the view of the judges, intended to implement EU law. The ruling in *Duke* must therefore now be confined to the interpretation of legislation pre-dating the adoption of a Directive, or legislation that the UK courts deem not to be intended to implement EU obligations.

This conclusion is illustrated by the approach of the CA in *Webb* v *EMO*, another case involving the relationship between the Equal Treatment Directive and the UK Sex Discrimination Act 1975. The CA reasoned[143] that, as the UK Act was not adopted to implement the Directive, it was not possible to interpret that Act to be consistent with the Directive, as to do so would be a

139. *Litster and Others Appellants* v *Forth Dry Dock & Engineering Co. Ltd. (In Receivership) and Another Respondents* [1990] 1 AC 546, 553.
140. Case 19/83 *Wendelboe* v *L.J. Music ApS* [1985] ECR 457; Case 105/ 84 *Foreningen af Arbejdsledere i Danmark* v *A/S Danmols Inventar* [1985] ECR 2639; Case 24/85 *Spijkers* v *Gebroeders Benedik Abattoir CV [1986]* ECR 1119; Case 287/86 *Landsorganisationen i Danmark* v *Ny Molle Kro* [1987] ECR 5465; Case 324/86 *Foreningen af Arbejdsledere i Danmark* v *Daddy's Dance Hall A/S* [1988] ECR. 739 and Case 101/87 *Bork (P.) International A/S* v *Foreningen af Arbejdsledere i Danmark* [1988] ECR 3057.
141. Employees 'who would have been so employed, if they had not been unfairly dismissed'. *Litster and Others Appellants* v *Forth Dry Dock & Engineering Co. Ltd. (In Receivership) and Another Respondents* [1990] 1 AC 546, 576.
142. In the *Marleasing* sense, see Case C-106/89 *Marleasing SA* v *La Comerical Internacionale de Alimentacion SA* [1990] ECR I-4135.
143. Referring to both *Duke* and *Litster*, and distinguishing them. *Webb* v *Emo Air Cargo (U.K.) Ltd* [1992] 1 CMLR 793; *Litster and Others Appellants* v *Forth Dry Dock & Engineering Co. Ltd. (In Receivership) and Another Respondents* [1990] 1 AC 546 and *Duke* v *G.E.C Reliance Ltd* [1988] AC 618.

'distortion' of the Act.[144] However, on appeal, the HL considered that there was a question of EU law to be referred to the ECJ. Following that reference, the HL (Lord Keith) accepts that discrimination on the ground of pregnancy is direct sex discrimination, notes that the terms on which direct discrimination is defined in the UK Act are more precise than the ECJ's approach, and that therefore it is not easy to fit the two together.[145] However, in common with the pattern we have seen earlier, having asked for an authoritative interpretation of EU law from the ECJ, the HL's reasoning on the substance of the law is relatively minimal.[146] Again, this involves a significant departure from the literal text of the Act, and effectively an adoption of the ECJ's teleological approach.

Nor is this willingness to avail themselves of the preliminary reference procedure limited to the appellate courts. The case of *P* v *S and Cornwall County Council*[147] provides an example of an ET, deciding that no remedy was available in English law for a dismissal on the grounds of gender reassignment, nevertheless referring to the ECJ on the question of whether the Equal Treatment Directive would apply in such a case.[148] Up until the 1990s,[149] there had been no references directly from an ET to the ECJ

144. *Webb* v *Emo Air Cargo (U.K.) Ltd* [1992] 1 CMLR 793, 814.
145. *Webb* v *Emo Air Cargo (U.K.) Ltd. (No. 2)* [1995] 1 WLR 1454, 1459.
146. *Webb* v *Emo Air Cargo (U.K.) Ltd. (No. 2)* [1995] 1 WLR 1454, 1460. 'The ruling of the European Court proceeds on an interpretation of the broad principles dealt with in articles 2(1) and 5(1) of Council Directive (76/207/E.E.C.). Sections 1(1)(a) and 5(3) of the Act of 1975 set out a more precise test of unlawful discrimination, and the problem is how to fit the terms of that test into the ruling. It seems to me that the only way of doing so is to hold that, in a case where a woman is engaged for an indefinite period, the fact that the reason why she will be temporarily unavailable for work at a time when to her knowledge her services will be particularly required is pregnancy is a circumstance relevant to her case, being a circumstance which could not be present in the case of the hypothetical man'. Lord Keith, with whom the others simply agree, provides minimal reasoning.
147. On 13 March 1993, P. brought an action before the Truro Industrial Tribunal, claiming that she had suffered discrimination on grounds of sex. Both S. and the Council claimed, on the contrary, that P. had been dismissed by reason of redundancy. The Industrial Tribunal found that, whilst there was a case for redundancy, the true reason for the dismissal was the objection on the part of S. and the Council to P.'s intention to undergo a gender-reassignment operation. Case C-13/94 *P* v *S and Cornwall County Council* [1996] ECR I-2143.
148. Case C-13/94, [1996] ECR I-2143.
149. In addition to *P* v *S*, references were made from ETs in Case-408/92*Smith* v *Avdel Systems Ltd* [1994] ECR I-4435 and Case C-152/91 *David Neath* v *Hugh Steeper Ltd* [1993] ECR I-6935. We understand that ETs are not encouraged to refer directly

(though ETs had noted that they were theoretically able to refer as early as the 1970s).[150]

The increasing confidence of the English courts and tribunals in dealing with questions of EU law during the 1990s is also illustrated by many cases where the English court simply decided the question of EU law without a reference to the ECJ.[151] We illustrate these cases by *R* v *Secretary of State for Employment ex parte Equal Opportunities Commission*.[152] The case concerned judicial review of national legislation which gave employment rights (protection against unfair dismissal and entitlement to redundancy pay) only to workers who had worked sixteen or more hours a week, for a minimum of five years. The legislation was found to be in breach of EU law – it fell within Article 119 EEC, and was unjustifiably discriminatory against women. The High Court,[153] CA[154] and HL[155] all referred directly to relevant ECJ case law, but did not feel the need to make a reference in order to apply EU law and adopt the ECJ's approach to interpretation of Article 119 EEC. In these cases, the English courts and tribunals considered that the relevant point of EU law was 'acte clair', or 'acte éclairé' by the ECJ. In referring to such case law, the English courts are perforce adopting methods of interpretation consistent with those of the ECJ.

to the ECJ, but rather to leave this to appellate courts, in part because the rulings of ETs are not useful precedents in the way that rulings of appellate courts are in the English legal system.

150. *Amies* v *Inner London Education Authority* [1977] 2 All ER 100.
151. *Amies* v *Inner London Education* Authority [1977] 2 All ER 100 *Snoxell* v *Vauxhall Motors Ltd* [1977] IRLR. 123; *Macarthys Ltd* v *Smith*[1978] 1 WLR 849. 746; *Shields* v *E Coomes (Holdings) Ltd* [1978] 1 WLR. 1408; *Roberts* v *Cleveland AHA* [1978] ICR 370; *Worringham* v *Lloyds Bank Ltd (No.1)* [1980] 1 CMLR 293; *O'Brien* v *Sim-Chem Ltd* [1980] ICR 429; *System Floors Ltd v Daniel* [1982] ICR 54; *Perera* v *Civil Service Commission (No 2)* [1983] ICR 428.
152. Case C-9/91, [1992] ECR I-4297.
153. *R* v *Secretary of State for Employment, Ex parte Equal Opportunities Commission and Another* [1992] 1 All ER 545
154. Dillon LJ referred to the ECJ's own definition of pay for the purposes of Art 119 EC which was quite broad; '... the concept of pay within the meaning of Article 119 of the Treaty comprises any consideration whether in cash or kind, whether immediate o future, provided that the employee receives it, albeit indirectly, in respect of his employment from his employer' ... [1993] ICR 251, 263F-264B. Referring to the case of Case C-360/ 90 *Arbeiterwohlfahrt der Stadt Berlin e.V* v *Botel* [1992] I ECR 3589 [12]. Also see D Nicol 'Disapplying with relish? The Industrial Tribunals and Acts of Parliament' (1996) PL 579, 586.
155. *R* v *Secretary of State for Employment, Ex parte Equal Opportunities Commission and Another* [1992] 1 All ER 545

The broader context for this increased assurance with the requirements of EU law in the 1990s is the HL ruling in *Factortame*,[156] which brought UK constitutional law within the requirements of the doctrine of supremacy of EU law. As noted above, the doctrine of Parliamentary sovereignty presented the UK with constitutional difficulties with respect to compliance with the doctrine of supremacy of EU law. Where the consistent interpretation approach was not feasible, for instance if the courts took the view that Parliament did not intend the relevant legislation to give effect to directly effective obligations in EU law, then the doctrine of Parliamentary sovereignty bound the UK courts to give effect to the will of Parliament as expressed in the text of the national legislation. This could be contrary to the doctrine of supremacy of EU law. The question came to a head for the UK courts in the *Factortame* case, concerning the question of whether interim relief should be available against the Crown, in circumstances where there was no national legislation to interpret so as to achieve that end, but where the ECJ had ruled that absence of such interim relief was a breach of EU law.[157] In the HL, Lord Bridge reasoned that when the UK joined the EU, the doctrine of supremacy was well established as inherent in the nature of the EEC Treaty.[158] Therefore, the European Communities Act 1972 must be interpreted so that 'it was the duty of a UK court, when delivering final judgment, to override any rule of national law found to be in conflict with any directly enforceable rule of Community law'.[159]

As Paul Craig points out,[160] it is possible to interpret the ruling in *Factortame* as a version of national rules of statutory construction. Unless Parliament has explicitly indicated that it intends a contradictory statute to apply, the national court is to apply enforceable EU law, if it cannot interpret national law in such a way as to be consistent with EU law.

156. *Factortame* v *Secretary of State for Transport* [1990] 2 AC 85.
157. C-213/89 *R.* v *Secretary of State for Transport Ex p. Factortame Ltd* [1990] ECR I-2433.
158. Case 106/77, *Amministrazione delle Finance dello Stato* v *Simmenthal Sp A* [1978] ECR 629; Case 6/64 *Flaminio Costa* v *Enel* [1964] ECR 585; Case 26/62 *NV Algemene Transporten Expeditie Onderneming van Gend en Loos* v *Nederlandse Administratie der Belastingen* [1963] ECR 1.
159. *Factortame Ltd. and Others Appellants* v *Secretary of State for Transport Respondent* [1990] 2 AC 85, 151.
160. P Craig, 'Britain in the European Union' in J. Jowell and D. Oliver (eds), *The Changing Constitution* (5th ed, Oxford, Oxford University Press, 2004).

The combination of *Factortame* and *EOC* opened the way for the EAT in *Biggs* v *Somerset County Council*[161] to depart from the literal wording of the statute giving it jurisdiction in claims to unfair dismissal,[162] so as to give entitlement to claims of unfair dismissal to part time workers and not to apply the time limit of three months within which a claim must be brought. The EAT did not expressly refer to *Factortame*, but the principle of 'dis-application' was crucial to its reasoning.[163] It was argued for the County Council that the ET lacked jurisdiction to hear such a claim, given the statutory basis of its jurisdiction and the clear wording of those statutes.[164] The EAT agreed that,

> 'The industrial tribunal has no general (or inherent) jurisdiction, separate and apart from that conferred by domestic statutes, such as the 1978 Act. Community law does not confer any jurisdiction.'[165]

However, that said, under the European Communities Act 1972, section 2 (1), 'An industrial tribunal may, within the scope of its statutory jurisdiction, administer, apply and enforce not only UK domestic law but also Community law.'[166] Thus,

> 'in the exercise of its statutory jurisdiction, the industrial tribunal is bound to apply and enforce relevant Community law, and disapply an offending provision of UK domestic legislation to the extent that it is incompatible

161. *Biggs* v *Somerset County Council* [1995] ICR 811.
162. The Trade Union and Labour Relations Act 1974 and the Employment Protection (Consolidation) Act 1978.
163. 'The primacy of a directly effective right means that, in cases of conflict, the incompatible provision of domestic law is automatically displaced without formal measure (see *Defrenne v Sabena* (*No.2*) 43/75 [1976] ECR 455)' [33] and 'Thus, in the exercise of its statutory jurisdiction, the industrial tribunal is bound to apply and enforce relevant Community law, and disapply an offending provision of UK domestic legislation to the extent that it is incompatible with Community law, in order to give effect to its obligation to safeguard enforceable Community rights.' [65].
164. 'The industrial tribunal had no jurisdiction to act outside the statutory limits which defined its jurisdiction. It had no jurisdiction to entertain a claim brought by someone who did not satisfy the statutory criteria, including the provisions as to time limits. Ms Biggs's complaint was not submitted within the three-month time limit applicable to unfair dismissal claims within the jurisdiction of the industrial tribunal.' [1995] ICR 811, 825.
165. [1995] ICR 811, 828.
166. [1995] ICR 811, 826.

with Community law, in order to give effect to its obligation to safeguard enforceable Community rights.'[167]

This formulation has been relied upon by ETs from the 1990s onwards.[168]

To conclude this section, we can see that, by the end of the 1990s, both first instance and appellate courts have increasing assurance with EU law, evidenced in willingness to refer to the ECJ[169] and willingness to interpret and apply EU law themselves, and to consider points of EU law to be 'acte clair' rather than making a preliminary reference to the ECJ. The HL ruling in *Factortame* recognizes that, in some circumstances, national courts must 'dis-apply' national law in order to give effect to directly effective EU law where the 'consistent interpretation' approach is not feasible. The reasoning for this approach is based on a purposive interpretation of the European Communities Act 1972, combined with the ECJ's teleological approach to interpretation of EU law, which is itself the source of the doctrine of supremacy of EU law. Moreover, the UK courts and tribunals are becoming increasingly confident with the doctrine of 'indirect effect', departing from the literal text of national statutes, although they will do so only where it is 'possible' in the sense that they take that view that Parliament intended to implement or comply with EU law in the relevant statute.

8. 2000s: Consolidation

Strong 'EU Compliance Mischief Rule' for Direct and Indirect Effect; Reaching beyond the Requirements of EU Law; the new Challenge of *Mangold*

The consolidation of approaches to interpretation of national law that give effect to the UK's obligations in EU law continues into the 2000s. A concise summary of the current position is found in the first of our sample cases from

167. [1995] ICR 811, 827.
168. See, e.g., reports of the ET's reasoning found in *Staffordshire County Council* v *Barber* [1996] ICR 379; *Rastall* v *Midlands Electricity plc and others* [1996] ICR 644; *Director of Public Prosecutions* v *Marshall* [1998] ICR 518; *Davidson* v *City Electrical Factors Ltd* [1998] ICR 443 (Scottish EAT); *X* v *Commissioner of the Police of the Metropolis* [2003] ICR 1031; (implicitly) *Carter and others* v *Ahsan* [2004] ICR 938.
169. The importance of the procedure in Article 267 TFEU to the development of 'European legal methods' in national courts is underlined in the chapters by Wulf-Henning Roth, and Ulla Neergaard and Ruth Nielsen, in this collection.

the 2000s: *R (on the application of Amicus and others)* v *Secretary of State for Trade and Industry and Christian Action Research Education and others.*[170] Another judicial review claim, this case concerned the interpretation of Regulations[171] implementing the EU Framework Directive,[172] particularly in the context of non-discrimination on grounds of sexuality and religion. We consider the ruling of the High Court (QBD).

Drawing on *Pickstone* and *Litster*, the court confirmed that, where national legislation is adopted as secondary legislation under the powers given for that purpose in the European Communities Act 1972, the national court is obliged to adopt a 'purposive' interpretation, so as to give effect to the implied legislative intention to implement the EU obligation.[173] The court refers to *Marleasing* as consistent with this approach,[174] which we have called the 'EU compliance mischief rule' in this chapter. The extent to which this is now consolidated in the practice of English courts and tribunals at all levels is evidenced by the fact that one ET has recently described what we call the 'EU compliance mischief rule' as so uncontroversial as to be 'trite law'.[175] When determining the appropriate interpretation of the relevant EU law provision, with which national law must be interpreted consistently, English courts and tribunals refer extensively to previous jurisprudence of the ECJ. Taking this into account, the consistent interpretation approach is required, if it can be achieved 'without distorting the meaning of domestic legislation'.[176] The word 'distorting' is interpreted quite narrowly in this context, and the approach certainly departs far from the literal rule, and from the golden rule, as no 'absurdity' is required to justify departing from the literal text. It is even permissible for courts to add words to (and presumably strike words from) national legislation, so long as it is 'compatible with the underlying thrust of the legislation' and is 'not inconsistent with the scheme of the legislation or its general principles'.[177]

170. [2004] EWHC 860 (Admin).
171. Employment Equality (Sexual Orientation) Regulations 2003 (SI 2003/1660).
172. Council Directive 2000/78 establishing a general framework for equal treatment in employment and occupation (OJ 2003 L303/16).
173. [2007] ICR 1176 [53].
174. [2007] ICR 1176 [54].
175. *Martin and others* v *Professional Game Match Officials Ltd* Case No 2802438/2008, 12-19 March 2010.
176. Per Lord Keith in *Webb* v *EMO Air Cargo*[1993] 1 WLR 49, 59.
177. *Ghaidan* v *Godwin-Mendoza* [2004] AC 557. Although this is a case which deals with the duty in the Human Rights Act 1998, section 3 (1) to interpret domestic legislation in a manner consistent with the European Convention on Human Rights 1950,

This strong version of the 'EU compliance mischief rule' is also found in the second of our sample cases from the 2000s: *Coleman* v *Attridge Law*.[178] The case concerned the interpretation of the Disability Discrimination Act 1995, as amended, and the Framework Directive 2000/78/EC,[179] in particular whether the Directive simply protects disabled employees themselves, or also those associated with disabled persons, for instance, their primary carers. Where an employee is treated less favourably due to being a primary carer of a disabled child, does this amount to direct discrimination in breach of the equal treatment established by the Directive? Following a reference from the ET, the ECJ[180] held that the Directive did include such 'associative discrimination'.

The claim was then returned to the ET. The ET held it was required to decide whether the Disability Discrimination Act could be read consistently with Directive 2000/78/EC, as interpreted by the ECJ in its ruling to the effect that the Directive applies to associative discrimination. A national court is required to interpret national law as far as possible in order to achieve the result pursued by the Directive.[181] The purpose of the Act, as amended in 2003,[182] was fully, correctly and comprehensively to implement the Directive. That was the manifest intention of Parliament at the time of the amendment. Although a literal interpretation of the Disability Discrimination Act 1995 would not achieve this Parliamentary aim, the insertion of the words 'or a person associated with a disabled person' in the Act would allow for the full implementation of the Directive. Therefore, the ET reasoned, by inserting those words, the Disability Discrimination Act is capable of being interpreted consistently with the Directive. The ET's ruling was upheld by the EAT,[183]

'so far as it is possible to do so', it has been successfully argued that it stands as authority for the equivalent *Marleasing* duty in EU law, see *Revenue and Customs Commissioners* v *IDT Card Services Ireland Ltd* [2006] STC 1252 and *Attridge Law* v *Coleman No 2* [2010] IRLR 10. This approach was used in *Shah* v *First West Yorkshire* Case No 1809311/2009, 20 November 2009 and in *Coleman* v *Attridge Law* [2007] 2 CMLR 24.

178. Case 303/06 *Coleman* v *Attridge Law*[2008] ECR I-5603.
179. OJ 2000 L303/16, P 16-22.
180. Case 303/06 *Coleman* v *Attridge*[2008] ECR I-5603.
181. Case C-106/89 *Marleasing SA v. L A Comercial Internationale de Alimentacioinsa* [1990] ECR 1-4135; Case C-456/98 *Centrosteel v Adipol* [2000] ECR I-6007; Joined Cases C-397/01 to C-304/01 *Pfeiffer and others v Deutsches Rotes Kreuz, Kreisverband Waldshut e V* [2004] ECR I-8835.
182. The Disability Discrimination Act 1995 (Amendment) Regulations 2003, which came into force on 1 October 20040 (SI 2003/1673).
183. *EBR Attridge Law LLP (formerly Attridge Law)* v *Coleman* [2010] 1 C.M.L.R. 28.

finding that 'there is nothing 'impossible' about adding words to the provisions of the 1995 Act so as to cover associative discrimination'.[184]

However, although the principles underlying the strong version of the 'EU compliance mischief rule' are regarded by the court and tribunal as settled in the *Amicus* and *Coleman* cases, and others in the 2000s, it is noteworthy that the counter-arguments are still being put before UK courts. For instance, in *Amicus* it was argued that the 'EU compliance mischief rule' does not comply with legal certainty;[185] that the rule in *Pepper* v *Hart* expresses a narrower principle than the 'EU compliance mischief rule';[186] and that additional words should not be read into the literal text. In *Coleman*, it was argued that, by reading words into the Act, the ET 'distorted' and 'rewrote' the Act;[187] that there was evidence of Parliamentary intention to exclude associative discrimination from the Act;[188] and that there was authority for the proposition[189] that it was not 'possible' to read the Act so as to add words to the text.

184. *EBR Attridge Law LLP (formerly Attridge Law)* v *Coleman* [2010] 1 C.M.L.R. 28 [14].
185. [2004] EWHC 860 (Admin) [55] 'it was not open to a Member State to defend inadequate implementation by the argument that the national courts would adopt a purposive interpretation of national law so as to ensure its compatibility with Community obligations. In order to meet the requirement of legal certainty there must be a sufficiently precise and clear implementation in national law and individuals must be made fully aware of their rights'.
186. [2004] EWHC 860 (Admin) [66].
187. *EBR Attridge LLP (formerly Attridge Law) and another* v *Coleman* [2010] I.C.R. 242 [10].
188. '[T]he Report of the Joint Committee which considered the draft Bill which became the Disability Discrimination Act 2005, and the materials associated with it. One of the issues which had been considered before the committee was whether associative discrimination was proscribed as a matter of EU law. The report records, at [102], that the Minister for Disabled People had informed the Disability Rights Commission that he did not believe that associative discrimination was covered by the terms of the Framework Directive. Mr Solomon submitted that that supported the contention that the 1995 Act (as amended by the 2003 Regulations) cannot have been intended to do so either.' *EBR Attridge LLP (formerly Attridge Law) and another* v *Coleman* [2010] ICR 242 [19].
189. The argument referred to the CA decision in *English* v *Thomas Sanderson Blinds Ltd* [2009] ICR 543 and the judgment of Burton J in the *EOC* case. In both cases, the court did not believe that it was possible to read the United Kingdom legislation (the Sex Discrimination Act 1975 and the Employment Equality (Sexual Orientation) Regulations 2003) in conformity with what was (or was argued to be) the effect of EU law. The EAT dismissed this argument by pointing out that the judgments in question are no more than conclusions, right or wrong, on the particular problem in

If the 'EU compliance mischief rule' is 'trite law', it is not universally accepted as such!

Under the strong version of the 'EU compliance mischief rule', it would now appear that consistent interpretation is only 'impossible' where the national legislation *expressly provides* that it is not intended to comply with the relevant EU law.[190] In those circumstances, where a *directly effective* provision of EU law is at issue,[191] then the 'dis-application' obligation of *Factortame* comes into play. There is CA[192] authority implying that the consistent interpretation approach (permissible 'moulding'[193]) should be the first port of call for English courts, before moving to dis-application. Directly effective rights in EU law do not themselves create a separate right of action, but merely allow domestic courts or tribunals to dis-apply incompatible provisions of domestic law within their jurisdiction.[194] Where the provision of EU law at issue is not directly effective, if the consistent interpretation route is not feasible, then the only remedy available is in damages against the state,[195] under *Francovich.*[196]

those cases. *EBR Attridge LLP (formerly Attridge Law) and another* v *Coleman* [2010] ICR 242 [20].

190. See, eg *Coleman* [2007] ICR 654 [23] 'On this critical aspect of the appeal I prefer the submissions of Mr Allen. It seems to me, as it did to the chairman, that the 1995 Act is capable of interpretation, consistent with an interpretation of the Directive favourable to the claimant, so as to include associative discrimination without distorting the words of the statute and consistent with the domestic courts' responsibility to arrive at a construction which ensures that the Directive is fully effective, as Parliament presumably intended when passing the 2003 Regulations'.
191. As the bulk of EU law that individuals may seek to rely on is in the form of directives (especially in the employment law field, but also in other fields, such as consumer protection), the doctrine of direct effect is somewhat limited, as directives are applicable only against an 'emanation of the state'. The concept of 'emanation of the state' has, however, been given a relatively wide interpretation, see Case 188/89 *Foster* v *British Gas* [1990] ECR I-3313.
192. *Redcar and Cleveland BC* v *Bainbridge No 1*[2007] EWCA Civ 929, citing *Autologic Holdings plc and others* v *HM Commissioners of Inland Revenue* [2005] 3 CMLR 2, [16]-[17] (obiter dictum on the point).
193. *Autologic Holdings plc and others* v *HM Commissioners of Inland Revenue* [2005] 3 CMLR 2, [17]; *Redcar and Cleveland BC* v *Bainbridge No 1* [2007] EWCA Civ 929 [25].
194. See *Biggs* v *Somerset County Council* [1996] 2 CMLR 292.
195. As implied by the ET in *Shah* v *First West Yorkshire* Case No 1809311/2009, 20 November 2009.
196. Cases C6& 9/90) *Francovich (Andrea) and Bonifaci (Daniela)* v *Italy* [1991] ECR I-5357.

As Hervey has argued elsewhere,[197] the strong version of the 'EU compliance mischief rule', as seen in cases such as *Coleman*, is disingenuous, both in terms of its application of the canons of statutory interpretation applied by English courts and tribunals and in terms of the position of Directives in EU constitutional law, given important differences between Directives and other measures of EU law. The 'golden rule' of statutory interpretation requires that words be given their ordinary meaning, unless to do so would result in an 'absurdity', an inconsistency with the rest of the statute[198] or a 'repugnant' result.[199] The plain meaning of the Disability Discrimination Act is that it excluded associative disability. There is nothing absurd, inconsistent or repugnant about interpreting the Disability Discrimination Act in that way. In the context of EU law, English courts and tribunals have moved towards a purposive approach to statutory interpretation. The correct interpretation of an Act of Parliament is determined according to its purpose, which in turn is determined through a consideration of matters beyond the words of the Act themselves. But the English tribunals in *Coleman* impute a purpose of the Act and a Parliamentary intention that cannot have been present, even presumptively, at the time of the amendment to the Disability Discrimination Act. Even taking account of the previous case law of the ECJ in other areas,[200] and its jurisprudence on human rights,[201] Parliament cannot possibly have known, or even really have suspected, that the ECJ would subsequently interpret the Directive to include associative disability. Disability discrimination is a new

197. T Hervey, with M Reeves, H Rodgers, B Riding and T Roberts, 'Annotation of Case C-303/06 *Coleman* v *Attridge Law and Steve Law*' 31 *Journal of Social Welfare and Family Law* (2009) 309-19.
198. *Grey* v *Pearson* (1857) 6 HL Cas 61; *River Wear Commissioners* v *Adamson* (1876-77) 2 App Cas 743.
199. *Re Sigsworth* [1935] Ch 89.
200. Case 152/84 *Marshall* v *Southampton and South-West Hampshire Area Health Authority* (Teaching) [1986] ECR 723; Case C-188/89 *Foster and Others* v *British Gas plc [*1990] ECR I-3313; Case C-91/92 *Dori* v *Recreb Srl* [1994] ECR I-3325; Case14/83 *Von Colson and Kamann* v *Land Nordrhein-Westfalen* [1984] ECR 1891; Case C-106/89 *Marleasing SA* v *La Comercial Internacionale de Alimentacion SA* [1990] ECR I-4135; Case C 334/92 *Wagner Miret* v *Fondo de Garantı'a Salarial* [1993] ECR I-6911; Case C-91/92 *Dori* v *Recreb Srl* [1994] ECR I-3325; Case C-192/*94 El Corte Inglés* v *Christina Blázques Rivero* [1996] ECR I-1281; Case C-111/97 *Evobus Austria* v *Niedero¨sterreichischer Verkehrsorgination* [1998] ECR I-5411; Case C-81/98 *Alcatel Austria* v *Bundesministerium für Wissenschaft und Verkehr* [1999] ECR I-7671.
201. Case C-144/04 *Mangold* v *Helm* [2005] ECR I-9981; Case C-13/05 *Chacón Navas* v *Eurest Colectividades SA* [2006] ECR I-6467.

area of law for the EU, with legislation on the subject only being in place since 2000. There is no pre-existing broad approach in the ECJ's case law to disability discrimination.[202] Indeed, had Parliament known that the ECJ would interpret disability discrimination to include associative disability, the wording of the amendment to the Act would have reflected this. The very best that we could say is that Parliament intended to comply with whatever subsequent interpretations of the Directive the ECJ would give.[203]

But even taking this into account, the nature of Directives is such that they do not impose obligations as between private individuals. This is a long-standing, and much tested, principle of EU constitutional law.[204] Moreover, indirect effect must not be used to introduce direct effect of Directives between private parties, 'by the back door'.[205] The approach of the ET in *Coleman*[206] essentially gives Directive 2000/78/EC direct effect, as between private individuals, by the back door (at least as regards disability discrimination). This is not the approach that EU law requires: rather, where the result envisaged by a Directive cannot be achieved through interpretation of national law that is consistent with national canons of interpretation, it is a matter for the legislature to resolve, not the courts or tribunals. Nothing in EU law therefore requires national courts to depart from the ordinary canons of statutory interpretation. And yet, in developing the strong 'EU compliance mischief rule', the English courts have created the opportunity for them to do so.

202. This analysis may also be supported by reference to the Court's much narrower overall approach to the definition of disability discrimination in Case C-13/05 *Chacón Navas* v *Eurest Colectividades SA* [2006] ECR I-6467.
203. This interpretation is borne out by the submission made to the Employment Appeal Tribunal by the Department of Work and Pensions.
204. Case 152/84 *Marshall* v *Southampton and South-West Hampshire Area Health Authority (Teaching)* [1986] ECR 723 [48]: 'With regard to the argument that a directive may not be relied upon against an individual, it must be emphasised that according to article 189 of the E.E.C. Treaty [now Article 249 EC] the binding nature of a directive, which constitutes the basis for the possibility of relying on the directive before a national court, exists only in relation to 'each member state to which it is addressed'. It follows that a directive may not of itself impose obligations on an individual and that a provision of a directive may not be relied upon as such against such a person. It must therefore be examined whether, in this case, the health authority must be regarded as having acted as an individual.'; see also Case C-91/92 *Dori* v *Recreb Srl* [1994] ECR I-3325.
205. Case C-168/95 *Arcaro* [1996] ECR I-4705, Opinion of Advocate General Elmer [39].
206. Although admirable and understandable in terms of the substantive outcome of the case (protection for Ms. Coleman.

The latest challenge for English courts and tribunals, in terms of their judicial approach to EU law, comes from an emerging doctrine of EU law concerning the primacy of 'general principles' of EU law. To date, the doctrine has been enunciated by the ECJ in cases emanating from other Member States, and only in cases involving the 'general principle' of non-discrimination. In *Mangold*,[207] the ECJ held that the general principle of non-discrimination requires national courts to 'provide ... the legal protection which individuals derive from [the EU general principle of non-discrimination] ... setting aside any provisions of national law which may conflict with that law'.[208] The ECJ has confirmed this new version of the primacy of EU law in *Kücükdeveci*,[209] a case in which the relevant directive was not directly effective. However,

> '... the need to ensure the full effectiveness of the principle of non-discrimination on the grounds of age ... means that the national court, faced with a national provision falling within the scope of EU law, which it considers to be incompatible with that principle, and which cannot be interpreted in conformity with that principle, must decline to apply that provision'.[210]

This new approach of the ECJ blurs the boundaries between direct and indirect effect. It may be that the English courts and tribunals extend the strong 'EU compliance mischief rule' to an even stronger version, implying wording that encapsulates any such directly effective general principles of EU law in relevant English legislation. However, where such consistent interpretation is not deemed 'possible' by English courts or tribunals, a revision to the *Factortame* ratio – which currently applies only to directly effective specific measures of EU law, not to inherent principles of EU law – would seem to be necessary for the future.

207. Case C-144/04 *Mangold* v *Helm* [2005] ECR I-998.
208. Case C-144/04 [2005] ECR I-9981 [77].
209. Case C-555/07 *Kücükdeveci* v *Swedex GmbH & Co KG* nyr in ECR, [2010] 2 CMLR 33.
210. Case C-555/07 *Kücükdeveci* v *Swedex GmbH & Co KG* nyr in ECR, [2010] 2 CMLR 33 [53].

9. Conclusions

Our analysis of the approach to EU law of English courts and tribunals in the area of employment law, from the 1970s to the present day, allows us to draw a number of conclusions about English judicial method in the context of interpretation of EU law, and national law which applies within the scope of EU law. These confirm and expand upon the conclusions of Mummery, LJ, in 1998:

> 'The historian of English Law is familiar with a stable system of almost unbroken continuity evolving in slow motion, little influenced by the civil law systems of mainland Europe. He cannot fail to observe the impact of Community Law on the legal results achieved by its application in employment cases and also (more significantly) on legal concepts, methods and reasoning; judicial review of primary legislation on the ground of incompatibility with Community laws of superior legal force; a shift in the relationship between Parliament and the Courts; purposive methods of interpretation and more liberal use of preparatory materials in relation to a very different style of legislative drafting; the novelty of directly effective measures emanating from a source other than Westminster or Whitehall ...'[211]

To the extent that the employment law case study is generalisable to other areas (and we argued above that it is, subject to the limitations of our method outlined on p 4 at notes 7-10), we make the following observations.

The main characteristics of the English judicial method to statutory interpretation on joining the EU were informed by the constitutional doctrine of Parliamentary sovereignty. This implies a strong deference of the courts to the will of Parliament, as expressed in the text of legislative acts. Thus, the literal rule is the predominant starting point for statutory interpretation. Departure from the literal rule applies where the literal text produces an 'absurdity' (golden rule), or where the text, in the context of the pre-existing legal position, as expressed in the text, or in Parliamentary debate, suggests a different purpose for the Act (purposive and mischief rules). Moreover, judges tend not to engage in explicit discussion of the method of interpretation that they use.

211. Lord Justice Mummery, 'The Community Law Impact in Employment Cases' in M Andenas and F Jacobs, *European Community Law in the English Courts* (Oxford, Oxford University Press, 1998) 208.

The English judiciary began to grapple with EU law in the earliest of cases. Their approach to EU law and reasoning has varied over time. At times, certain courts,[212] and certain members of the judiciary,[213] were more open to the novelty of EU law. But, in general, English courts and tribunals respect the doctrines of supremacy, direct and indirect effect of EU law, and give effect to the obligation to comply with these doctrines as best as they can within their understandings of the duties of the courts under the European Communities Act 1972, and in the context of very different styles of drafting of EU and national law. Over the course of the UK's membership of the EU, we have discerned the emergence of a new approach to cases involving EU law. One obvious difference is the explicit attention given to the rules of interpretation that English courts and tribunals are adopting when dealing with EU law.[214] The English courts recognize the 'teleological' approach of the ECJ, although they do not tend to employ it themselves, except where a reference has been made to the ECJ, and the ECJ has employed it.

The *Factortame* ruling of the HL was crucial to the full acceptance of the doctrine of supremacy of EU law in England, as it clarifies the 'disapplication' obligation. Contrast the approach of the ET and EAT in *Amies* (1970s), where the ET's jurisdiction was considered limited by English statute, to that in *Biggs* (1990s), where it was accepted that the ET would have jurisdiction, in spite of the express wording of the English statute, by the 'disapplication' of the offending statutory rule.

Responding to the challenges of supremacy of EU law, direct and indirect effect, the English courts and tribunals have in effect developed a new rule of statutory interpretation: the 'EU compliance mischief rule'.[215] Contrasting the approach of the CA in *Macarthys* (1970s) to that of the ET and EAT in *Coleman* (2000s) illustrates the novelty of the rule. In *Macarthys*, the CA's starting point was the literal rule, and given that the Act was clear and unambiguous, with no 'absurdity' or 'injustice', there was no good reason to depart

212. The EAT, for instance, was more open to EU law than higher courts.
213. Lord Denning stands out as a pioneer for the integration of EU law, and EU methods of reasoning, into English law.
214. J Holland and J Webb, *Learning Legal Rules* (6th ed. Oxford, Oxford University Press 2006) 238. The judiciary do not say when they are going to use a particular rule of interpretation, and in fact it is hard to find a case where a judge has gone on to say 'I am now going to use the literal approach ...'. Yet when EU Law comes into play, this is exactly what the judiciary do.
215. This conclusion resonates with Jane Reichel's suggestion, in this collection, that Swedish courts have adjusted the Swedish legal system and Swedish judicial methods, to EU law.

from the literal approach. The obligation to comply with EU law is noted, but is secondary to the reasoning. In *Coleman*, the starting point was the obligation to comply with EU law, and the implied intention of Parliament to do so. There was no consideration of whether the text of the Act was 'absurd' or 'unjust'. The tribunals adopted a purposive reading of the Act to comply with EU law as interpreted by the ECJ in jurisprudence – involving a highly teleological, and thus not foreseeable, interpretation of the relevant Directive – which was subsequent to the adoption of the Act.

In its strongest version, then, the EU compliance mischief rule requires English courts and tribunals to imply a Parliamentary intention that is not evident on the face of the relevant legislation, or the context in which it is adopted. In its strong version, it applies to both directly and indirectly effective EU law, and assumes that Parliament intended to comply with whatever EU law turns out to require, following its future interpretation by the ECJ, and, further, that courts and tribunals are obliged to give effect to that Parliamentary intention by departing from the text of the legislation, including reading new words into (and presumably striking words from) the legislation. The EU compliance mischief rule thus constitutes a major challenge to legal certainty, and departure from traditional national rules of interpretation, the context of which is the understanding of the relationship between courts and Parliament encapsulated in the English constitutional doctrine of Parliamentary sovereignty.

This novel approach to statutory interpretation applies only where EU law is engaged. It has not, so far as we can discern (further research would be required to verify this point), affected judicial method in cases involving national law alone, where no point of EU law is engaged. EU law is therefore conceived, in the context of the EU compliance mischief rule, as different from and separate from national law, in terms of the obligations it imposes on courts in exercising their duty to give effect to Parliamentary intention when interpreting statutory language. The separate nature of EU law is also inherent in the approach adopted by the English courts on the 'dis-application' route, following the *Factortame* case, although the language that English judges have used to describe the 'dis-application' route (EU law as 'part of' English law) sometimes suggests otherwise. Given this, we can conclude that, although English courts and tribunals have embraced the constitutional challenges of EU law, EU and domestic law continue to be conceptualized by English courts and tribunals as separate systems.

The Authors/Editors

Rob van Gestel, Professor, Constitutional and Administrative Law Department, Tilburg Law School, The Netherlands

Tamara Hervey, Jean Monnet Professor of European Union Law, School of Law, The University of Sheffield, UK

Martijn W. Hesselink, Professor of European Private Law and Director of the Centre for the Study of European Contract Law, University of Amsterdam, The Netherlands

Dr. Kristina Koldinská, Charles University, Prague, The Czech Republic

Hans-Wolfgang Micklitz, Professor of Economic Law, European University Institute, Florence, Italy

Ulla Neergaard, Professor of EU Law, Faculty of Law, University of Copenhagen, Denmark

Ruth Nielsen, Professor of Business Law, Law Department, Copenhagen Business School, Denmark

Dennis Patterson, Professor of Law and Chair in Legal Philosophy and Legal Theory, European University Institute, Florence; Board of Governors Professor of Law and Philosophy, Rutgers University, New Jersey, USA; Professor of Law and Chair in International Trade and Legal Philosophy, Swansea University, Wales, UK

Jane Reichel, Associate Professor in Public Law, jur.dr., Faculty of Law, Uppsala University

Sophie Robin-Olivier, Professor of Law, University of Paris Ouest-Nanterre La Défense, France, Director of the Center for European and Comparative Legal Studies (CEJEC, www.cejec.eu)

Lynn Roseberry, Associate Professor in Business Law and Head of Department, Law Department, Copenhagen Business School, Denmark

Wulf-Henning Roth, Professor of Private International and Comparative Law, Faculty of Law, Bonn University; chair, German, European and International Economic Law, Germany

Natalie Sheldon, SURE Summer Intern, School of Law, University of Sheffield, UK